PROFESSIONAL CORE CASES FOR TEACHER DECISION-MAKING

PROFESSIONAL CORE CASES FOR TEACHER DECISION-MAKING

GORDON E. GREENWOOD
H. THOMPSON FILLMER

University of Florida

Merrill,
an imprint of Prentice Hall
Upper Saddle River, New Jersey   Columbus, Ohio

Library of Congress Cataloging-in-Publication Data
Greenwood, Gordon E.
    Professional core cases for teacher decision making / Gordon E.
  Greenwood, H. Thompson Fillmer.
        p.   cm.
    Includes bibliographical references.
    ISBN 0-13-432840-X
    1. Teachers—United States—Decision making—Case Studies.
2. Classroom management—United States—Case studies.   3. Curriculum
planning—United States—Case studies.   4. Teaching—United States—
Case studies.   I. Fillmer, H. Thompson.   II. Title.
LB1775.2.G74   1997
371.1'02—dc20   95-43065
                                                                          CIP

Editor: Debra A. Stollenwerk
Production Editor: Christine M. Harrington
Design Coordinator: Jill E. Bonar
Cover Designer: Brian Deep
Production Manager: Patricia A. Tonneman

This book was set in Berkeley by The Clarinda Company and was printed and bound by Book Press. The cover was printed by Phoenix Color Corp.

Photo credits: Scott Cunningham/Merrill/Prentice Hall, pp. 87, 159, 217; Barbara Schwartz/Merrill/Prentice Hall, pp. 1, 299; Anne Vega/Merrill/Prentice Hall, p. 21.

Printed in the United States of America

10 9 8 7 6 5 4 3 2 1

ISBN: 0-13-432840-X

Prentice-Hall International (UK) Limited, *London*
Prentice-Hall of Australia Pty, Limited, *Sydney*
Prentice-Hall of Canada, Inc., *Toronto*
Prentice-Hall Hispanoamericana, S. A., *Mexico*
Prentice-Hall of India Private Limited, *New Delhi*
Prentice-Hall of Japan, Inc., *Toyko*
Simon & Schuster Asia Pte. Ltd., *Singapore*
Editora Prentice-Hall do Brasil, Ltda., *Rio de Janeiro*

*We dedicate this book
to our wives, Patti and Dorothy.
Without their love and encouragement,
this book would not have been written.*

PREFACE

Professional Core Cases for Teacher Decision-Making is a product of two movements in the field of education: (1) the development and expanded use of the case method of college teaching, and (2) the implementation of teacher-certification exam programs throughout the United States. While the use of cases or case studies in college teaching has a long history in a number of different disciplines, this approach has begun to enjoy considerable popularity in the field of education.

A number of casebooks have recently appeared on the market and cases have been incorporated into many regular textbooks as supplementary material. Professional conferences have been held to exchange information and encourage the use of the case method. Indeed, the use of the case method of college teaching seems to be on the increase in many fields of higher education.

FORMAT OF CASES

Cases can take many forms. They can be based on actual events objectively reported, or they can be more or less fictional representations of reality. Cases can vary in length. They can focus on the activities of one primary character or on the behavior of an entire group of people, such as a class of students. They can be in the form of one or many settings and situations, and have even been written in series with each installment to the case adding new people, situations, and information to consider. Cases can be written, audiovisual, computerized, oral, or even live (acted out).

The format used in this book is written dialogue, similar to that used in movie scripts or screenplays. We prefer this format for a number of reasons. First, such a format is familiar through the influence of TV, movies, and the like. Second, it represents the kind of reality students experience when they observe in schools or see themselves teaching through videotape (such as is done in techniques like micro-teaching). Third, the dialogue format more naturally lends itself to activities designed to follow case studies, such as role-playing, sociodrama, and the videotaping of students acting out the courses of action that they recommend to the teacher in the case. Fourth, a number of state teacher-certification programs involve the direct observation of teacher behavior using observation instruments during the first year of teaching. The dialogue format more closely portrays the kind of behavior observed. Fifth, the behavior in the dialogue can be used as behavioral evidence by the students to support the interpretations made when they analyze a case. What people say and do is more of a directly observed behavior than a summary of facts or incidents or a paraphrasing of events. Finally, since we see the use of case studies as a middle step between coursework and actual teaching experience, the more closely the case format resembles events actually unfolding in schools, the better. In short, we view them as realistic vehicles for the analysis of behavior and the generation of courses of action in the real world of teaching.

CASE METHODS AND GOALS

Teaching techniques for working with case material varies among college instructors. One of the more popular techniques involves a skilled instructor working with a large group (e.g., entire class). Some of the techniques for drawing students out and getting them to interact are reminiscent of some of the procedures used in encounter groups of the 1970s. Others involve working with students in small groups and even as individuals. Whatever the teaching techniques used, the focus is on getting the participants to examine and interact with a case that represents a slice of reality or a problem situation to be dealt with. Such work by a student, if skillfully done, involves higher-order thinking.

The case method can involve a number of instructional goals. In education it can provide the student with the opportunity to translate theories, principles, and methods into practice. Cases can also be used as vehicles for getting students to think at the upper levels of Bloom's Cognitive Taxonomy. Additionally, cases can serve as facilitators for (but not substitutes for) actual teaching experiences. Hopefully, working through cases may help teachers develop metacognitive strategies for dealing with actual teaching situations.

It should further be added that a considerable body of literature has focused on developing the teacher's skill as a decision-maker and problem-solver. Shavelson (1973), for example, once described decision-making as the "basic teaching skill." Much work has been done on developing programs to enhance the "teacher's reflective thinking" skills (Sparks-Langer & Colton, 1991). Cases can certainly serve as excellent vehicles for helping both pre-service and in-service teachers develop their decision-making and reflective thinking skills.

Broudy (1990) suggests that cases may even be used as a means of establishing a professional knowledge base in teacher education. He argues that if teaching is to become a profession, it must reach a consensus on which problems teacher education should focus, as is done in such professions as law and medicine. These professional core problems could be presented in teacher education in the form of cases.

One way of developing a professional core of cases is to examine the professional core content of teacher certification exams, and generate cases that reflect the content base underlying the exams in use around the nation. Indeed, the cases presented in this book are derived from two major sources: (1) an analysis of the professional knowledge content commonalities of ten teacher certification exams used in 47 of 50 states (Greenwood & Hankins, 1989) and (2) a research review of the problems of beginning teachers (Veenman, 1984). In addition, the cases were selected to represent elementary, middle, and secondary grade levels, and both beginning and experienced teacher problems.

ADAPTING CASES TO VARYING AUDIENCES

All of this may raise the question regarding the audience for whom this book is intended. An attempt has been made to cover all grade levels with roughly one-third of the cases at elementary, middle school, and secondary grade levels. Not only was the book written for pre-service teachers, but also with educational administrators in mind. At least 20 of the 30 cases seem clearly useful to the field of educational administration or leadership (i.e., cases 1–2, 5–6, 8–11, 13–14, 16–18, 20, 24, and 26–30).

It might further be added that cases involving beginning teachers can be useful to experienced teachers in in-service training as well. Since each case is derived from a professional content area covered by teacher certification exams, experienced teachers have to continually deal with the same basic or generic problems as beginning teachers. While experienced teachers develop routines for dealing with such problems (such as those relating to classroom management, motivation, communication, and classroom materials and supplies), old routines may not work when situations change. In such cases the experienced teacher, like the new teacher, has to learn to analyze the problem situation and generate new strategies for dealing with it.

We suggest the following approach to using the cases with experienced teachers. Let them go through the book and determine which case is most similar to the one they are facing, but at the same time have them indicate how it is different. Then have them rewrite the case based on the differences, but using the case in the book as a format model. Next, have them develop their strategies for analyzing and resolving problem situations, by practicing first on the original case in the book. Then have them transfer what they have learned by analyzing and generating courses of action for their own case.

One might also ask the question as to whether elementary teachers, for example, might benefit from working on secondary cases. We think the answer is *yes* since the generic content on which each case rests may manifest itself at any grade level, albeit in different forms. Curriculum development, instructional resources and materials, child abuse, the use of computers, parental influences, and measurement and evaluation issues, to name a few, are problems—in one form or another—at any grade level.

How might a college instructor working with, say, elementary teachers use middle school or secondary cases? We would suggest a procedure similar to that outlined above for working with experienced teachers. First, examine the cases and identify one that is similar to one that concerns the student. For example, the student might be concerned with how to deal with a physically aggressive boy or how to motivate a class of disadvantaged students to learn. Second, specify how the problem might manifest itself differently at the elementary level. Ask what form such a problem takes at the elementary level and rewrite the case. Finally have the students analyze and resolve the rewritten case using the procedures outlined in the book.

Having students rewrite a case can be an excellent learning experience in itself. If they have trouble deciding what form a problem might take at a certain grade level, it might be a good opportunity to have them talk to experienced teachers and go observe in a school to discover the answer for themselves. Such a dose of realism may be particularly helpful to pre-service teachers in helping them become certain of their career choice, including the grade level at which they would like to teach.

USING CASES IN GRADUATE AND UNDERGRADUATE COURSES

The senior author of this book has used cases in both graduate and undergraduate courses very successfully. Differences in the ways graduate students, as compared to undergraduates, approach the analysis and resolution of cases is probably best explained by the differences found in the experts vs. novices problem-solving literature. The experts use more sophisticated, experienced-based strategies based on a big picture view of the situation. Undergraduate students tend to be more theoretical in their analyses. However, both groups enjoy and benefit from the use of cases.

Perhaps one of the most important uses of cases with undergraduates might be in introduction to education courses. Since such courses are often pivotal in determining whether undergraduates enter the teacher profession or not, cases can provide a reality-based exposure to the field of education. An interesting exercise for prospective teachers is to ask them to skim the cases and rank-order the three that concern them the most as they think about becoming teachers. Such an exercise helps bring their fears and expectations into focus and may suggest which course content may be most relevant to the students' needs.

ORGANIZATION OF BOOK

Users of this book should notice the following key features.

- The table of contents contains a brief description of each of the thirty cases to assist in case selection.
- The text opens with an Introduction, which not only provides a rationale for the use of cases in teacher education, but also contains a sample student paper. It also shows which cases are related to 19 professional teacher-education core categories.
- At the end of each of the thirty cases are ten or more starter questions, primarily generated from the educational psychology and curriculum and instruction perspectives of the authors, to assist in getting the discussion and analysis process started.
- Appendix A matches each case to theories, models, and sets of principles in the fields of educational psychology and curriculum and instruction.

- Appendix B provides the instructor with information on a case method that involves working with students in small groups, with the goal of helping them learn one way to translate theory into practice. Its focus is on learning strategies for analyzing and making decisions about the kinds of situations represented in the cases. Instructional and evaluation procedures are included.

ACKNOWLEDGMENTS

A book such as this requires help from a large number of people. First, we thank our editor, Debbie Stollenwerk, for her encouragement and keen insights as the book was developed. Second, we thank Linda Smith and Patti Greenwood for their excellent word processing and proofreading of the manuscript. We also thank the reviewers of this manuscript for their helpful suggestions and comments: Karen J. Agne, State University of New York, Plattsburgh; Jeanine M. Dell'Olio, Hope College; Jean Dennee, Eastern Illinois University; Beatrice S. Fennimore, Indiana University of Pennsylvania; J. Gary Knowles, University of Michigan; and Charles W. Ryan, Wright State University. Finally, our thanks go to the teachers, administrators, and education majors too numerous to name, for their advice, examples, and case material. You know who you are. Your contribution will help future pre-service and in-service teachers and administrators.

CONTENTS

help from the principal, he turns to another teacher for advice as to whether he should change jobs or not.

PART I
INTRODUCTION

T eaching is a complex art, difficult to describe, study, and evaluate. Dembo and Hillman (1976) argue that being a good teacher involves mastering three areas: (1) teaching skills, (2) conceptual and knowledge skills, and (3) decision-making skills. Gage and Berliner (1992) contend that teaching involves five primary tasks:

1. Choosing instructional objectives
2. Understanding student characteristics
3. Understanding and using ideas about student motivation
4. Selecting and using teaching methods
5. Evaluating student learning.

Shulmann (1987) asserts that teachers need knowledge in six areas: (1) subject matter/content, (2) teaching methods and theory, (3) curriculum, (4) learner characteristics, (5) teaching contexts, and (6) educational goals, aims, and objectives.

Whatever the components of teaching and teacher knowledge, Shavelson (1973) describes decision making as the "basic teaching skill." His argument is that, while knowledge of subject matter or teaching skills is important, being able to describe when and how to use them effectively is critical. Schor (1987) makes a similar argument, contending that teachers develop an "appreciation system" regarding values, practices, knowledge, and theories. These influence how the teacher defines and interprets teaching situations, what the teacher notices or ignores, and what the teacher decides about various courses of action. Lampert and Clark (1990) add: "Research can inform us about how complex and uncertain teaching is, but it cannot describe the sorts of decisions teachers should be taught to make in any particular situation." (p. 29).

From what sources do teachers learn their decision-making skills? Waller and Travers (1963) list six sources: (1) traditions of teaching, (2) social learning (e.g., imitating master teachers), (3) philosophical traditions, (4) scientific research on learning and motivation, (5) school and community conditions and pressures, and (6) the teacher's own needs. There are many ways teachers can learn, develop, and practice their decision-making, as well as other skills and knowledge, while still in teacher training. Practicums, tutoring, micro-teaching, classroom volunteering, and internships are important experience-based opportunities to learn and apply teaching and decision-

3

making skills. Another kind of opportunity especially suited to the development of decision-making skills is the case study.

What is a case study? Cases represent the real-life experiences of teachers. They can be the most difficult situations that teachers have faced or the most recurring or typical situations. Cases can be in many formats: written, oral, audio-visual, computerized, or even acted out live. They can vary considerably in length and can focus entirely on one character or on an entire group such as a class. Whatever their form, cases give both beginning and experienced teachers the opportunity to develop their metacognitive decision-making skills while wrestling with realistic teaching situations.

In terms of Bloom's Cognitive Taxonomy (Bloom, Engelhart, Furst, Hill and Krathwohl, 1956), case studies require higher-order cognitive thinking involving the Application, Analysis and Evaluation levels and, sometimes, the Synthesis level. To examine a case, one has to select a framework (or perhaps several) such as a theory, method, or set of principles to help interpret the situation. The fitness of the framework selected has to be tested and defended by giving reasons, citing evidence, etc. Next, courses of action consistent with the way the situation has been analyzed must be selected or generated. Finally, these courses of action have to be evaluated in terms of how well they might work.

Allonache, Bewich, and Ivey (1989), who have conducted workshops based on conflict theory for the improvement of decision-making skills, focus on four steps: (1) clearly defining the nature of the problem, (2) listing alternative solutions to the problem, (3) weighing the positive and negatives of each alternative solution, and (4) implementing the solution that is chosen.

Many experts in using the case method of teaching focus on the following five steps: (1) identifying the educational issues involved, (2) thinking about the case from multiple points of view (for example, teacher's, principal's, parent's, student's), (3) using professional knowledge (for example, learning theory or classroom management models) in discussing the case, (4) projecting what courses of action the teacher described in the case might try, and (5) forecasting what the probable consequences might be for the courses of action generated.

One goal of the case study method is to help preservice and inservice teachers develop metacognitive decision-making strategies they can use in dealing with similar situations in the real world of day-to-day teaching. While teachers develop effective routines for dealing with many situations, they are constantly confronted with problem situations that call for new perspectives and procedures. It is this aspect of teaching that makes it so challenging and exciting on the one hand, and so stressful on the other. Thus, developing strategies for dealing with such situations and recognizing the components of the strategy used can be one of the most important contributions of the case study method in teacher education.

TEACHING AS A PROFESSION

As valuable as the case study method of teaching might be in assisting teachers in the development of metacognitive decision-making strategies, the question arises, What kind of cases should the preservice and inservice teacher be exposed to? Broudy (1990) argues that education has not yet fully developed as a profession. He contends that "a profession professes a body of concepts that structures its field of practice" (p. 450) as is the situation in law and medicine. He further asserts that "teacher education has not developed a set of problems that can legitimately claim to be so general and important that all who are qualified to teach and to teach teachers should be familiar with them and their standard interpretations and solutions. Such cases in the recognized professions constitute the core of the clinical experience" (p. 452). Broudy's position is that the professional core of problems in education should be identified and presented to preservice and inservice teachers in the form of case studies. Further, he has attempted to begin the process of identifying the professional core of problems in his research at the University of Illinois. Ten general categories of problems have been identified:

1. low social and professional status;
2. low student motivation;
3. problems in parent–school relations;
4. problems with administrators and administration;
5. too many noninstructional duties;
6. time management;
7. student discipline;
8. tracking, labeling, and standardized testing;
9. problems with meeting the needs of minority students; and
10. lack of funding for materials, salaries, and programs. (p. 455)

Veenman (1984) focused on the problems of beginning teachers. After an extensive review of the literature, Veenman found 24 problems identified by beginning teachers in numerous surveys. The top eight problems had the greatest amount of agreement:

1. classroom discipline;
2. motivating students;
3. dealing with individual differences;
4. assessing students' work;
5. relations with parents;
6. organization of class work;
7. insufficient materials and supplies; and
8. dealing with problems of individual students. (p. 154)

The work of Broudy and Veenman were taken into consideration in selecting the cases that are presented in this book. However, an even more important influence is the teacher certification exam movement in the United States.

Practically all states have some type of examination procedure to determine whether or not a candidate should be certified as a teacher (Rudner, 1988). What is examined and the types of instruments used vary, however, from state to state. Some examine beginning teachers only, while others examine inservice teachers as well. Some use multiple-choice-type tests, while others use observation schedules. Certain states examine the teacher's knowledge of the field that the teacher teaches (e.g., English) while others examine the teacher's professional knowledge (e.g., teaching methods, motivation, learning). Still other states observe the teacher teaching in the classroom.

Regardless of the variety of examination methods used, Greenwood and Hankins (1989) analyzed the ten major teacher certification exams (including the National Teacher Exam) that focused on the "professional knowledge" of teachers. Their study revealed the following 19 content-area commonalities underlying the ten examination programs:

1. curriculum development
2. instructional planning
3. instructional objectives
4. instructional resources and materials
5. methods of instruction
6. instructional delivery
7. teacher communication skills
8. classroom management
9. motivational techniques
10. student self-concept
11. individual differences and exceptionalities
12. severe emotional stress
13. child abuse
14. drug abuse
15. measurement and evaluation
16. teacher use of computers
17. extra-classroom influences
18. knowledge of profession
19. educational administration.

It is our intention that this book present cases that represent this professional core and that will make a contribution toward the professionalization of the teacher. To illustrate one approach to case studies, a sample case follows, with a sample analysis and decision for that case.

SAMPLE CASE: ANALYSIS AND DECISION

It may be recalled that Allonache, Bewich and Ivey (1989) focus on four steps in making decisions: (1) clearly defining the nature of the problem; (2) listing alternative solutions to the problem; (3) weighing the positives and negatives of each possible solution; and (4) implementing the solution that is chosen.

Step 1 involves: (a) identifying the different educational issues involved; (b) thinking about the case from multiple points of view (e.g., teacher, parent, student, principal, etc.); and (c) using professional knowledge (e.g., a learning theory or classroom management model) to analyze the case. Step 2 includes projecting what courses of action might be tried (for example, by the teacher) to solve the problem. Step 3 involves forecasting the probable consequences for each course of action generated.

Participants in case studies seldom get to see Step 4—the implementation of the courses of action they choose. However, they can increase the likelihood of the course(s) of action working if they examine it in terms of (a) how clearly it is spelled out, (b) how feasible or practical it is in the context of the situation, and (c) how consistent it is with the nature of the problem as it was defined in the first place (Step 1).

While case studies are handled different ways by different instructors, several general principles apply. First, it takes experience to examine a problem from multiple perspectives. Defining the nature of a problem involves a framework (such as a set of beliefs, a theory, a model, or a set of principles) for conducting the examination or analysis. Preservice and beginning teachers often have trouble learning one or two frameworks in enough depth to use them to examine a problem. Shifting back and forth between several frameworks may be difficult at the beginning.

Second, it makes sense for preservice and beginning teachers to first learn to analyze a problem from the standpoint of the teacher before shifting to that of the parent, the principal or even the student. Multiple perspectives and multiple frameworks are the goal, but may not be the best way to begin.

Third, in selecting the framework(s) for examining or analyzing a problem, it makes sense for preservice or beginning teachers to use those frameworks they are studying in their teacher education programs. For example, they might use a learning theory from an educational psychology course or a teaching method or classroom management model from other courses. In this way they can learn to translate theory into practice. If the teaching profession can ever agree on a set of core problems and cases as discussed earlier, perhaps a set of core knowledge can eventually be identified and used in analyzing and resolving cases.

Fourth, as case study participants learn to analyze a case in terms of the framework(s) used, they need to learn to defend their analysis by citing evidence appropriate to the framework(s) being used. For example, if a learning theory such as operant conditioning is used, then they should cite behavioral data (e.g., baseline data) to support their contentions. Different frameworks (e.g., learning theories) involve different data-collection conventions.

Putting the above principles together, one way for preservice and beginning teachers to learn to use case studies is to: (1) analyze the case in terms of only one or two frameworks initially, (2) learn to support their analysis by presenting evidence appropriate to the framework, (3) generate courses of action that a teacher might implement to solve the problem, (4) weigh the consequences of the various courses and select the one(s) that is most consistent with the analysis of the problem and most likely to solve it, and (5) spell out implementation procedures for a teacher to follow so that the courses of action are stated in a specific and operational way and are practical to implement in the context of the situation. The case analysis approach suggested by these five principles will now be followed in analyzing and resolving the case that follows.

This case, developed from a description of a problem situation provided by the teacher that actually faced it, is entitled "The Stay-In Problem." It involves a beginning secondary teacher teaching out-of-field in a sophomore world history class. The case revolves around a group of six boys and probably focuses more on the "classroom management" professional knowledge content area than any other. After the case is presented, it will be analyzed and resolved drawing upon the work on decision-making presented above.

The Stay-In Problem

Steve Rogers is 21 years old and is beginning his first year of teaching English in Grades 7–12. The school in which he teaches is located in the city of Greenville, which has a population of around 5,000 and is situated in the northern portion of one of the southern border states. Coal mining and agriculture are the chief contributors to the local economy, although the town merchants outnumber other economic groups on the school board.

The school system is consolidated and includes about half of the county population. Greenville has had four superintendents in the last ten years. Financial support of the Greenville Public Schools is about average for the size of the population being served. The junior high school comprises Grades 7 and 8 and is in the same building as the four-year high school.

Greenville High School is located in a square-shaped building constructed of brick and wood in the 1930s. Its floors are wooden and the seats are bolted to the floor. The walls of the room are green and the furniture is old and dark brown. Both the building and its equipment are well-maintained. All the desks have been recently sanded and painted to remove carvings on their surfaces.

Steve sits in the office of the principal, John Sawyer, a bald man in his 50s. The first faculty meeting of the year has just ended a few minutes before.

MR. SAWYER   Steve, I have a problem that I'm going to ask you to help me with. *[Steve leans forward in his chair]* As you probably know, we were expecting Mrs. Dixon to teach social studies for us this fall until we found out that she was pregnant. I've been able to get all of her courses covered except for a world history class. *[Leans forward and speaks warmly]* Steve, I know English is your field but I noticed on your credentials that you took some history courses when you were in college. Will you help me out by taking the class for me this year? We probably won't be able to get a replacement for Mrs. Dixon until next year.

STEVE   *[Hesitantly]* I'd be glad to help in any way that I can, Mr. Sawyer, but world history is really out of my field. Those history courses that I took as a sophomore were in United States history. *[Reluctantly]* I'll give it a try if you want me to but I'm afraid that some of the kids will know more about history than I do.

MR. SAWYER   *[Smiling]* I don't think that there's much danger of that, Steve. They are just average sophomores like the students that you'll have in your English 10 sections. In fact, I'd be greatly surprised if that bright group of kids you have in your third-period English 8 section don't challenge you a heck of a lot more than these kids. Most of the students in your history class are C students. *[Stands up]* Well, Steve, since you're doing me a favor, I'm going to fix the schedule so you won't have to take a study hall this year. I know that you'll be able to use the planning time. *[Smiles again, then becomes serious]* If you have any trouble with the history class, talk to Ray Clark, the Chairman of the Social Studies Department. I've asked him to help you out.

STEVE   *[Stands up]* Thanks, Mr. Sawyer. I'll do my best and hope that I can keep at least a page ahead of them.

MR. SAWYER I hope that you know that I really appreciate your helping me out of this spot. Just keep on top of them and you won't have any trouble. Be firm at first and you can loosen up on them later on. Move them along at whatever pace you want to set.

The fourth-period (11:05 A.M.-12:00 P.M.) world history class meets for the first time. Steve's classroom has a picture of Shakespeare on the wall and a set of maps related to English literature. At one side of the classroom sits a stand containing a set of world history maps that Ray Clark has loaned to Steve. The 34 sophomores become silent as Steve begins to talk.

STEVE *[Smiling as he paces]* I guess it's no secret that history isn't exactly my field. But English and history are very closely related to one another. People who make history often write books—and if they don't write them they are very much influenced by them. *[A tall, athletically built boy in the front row holds up his hand]* Yes?

LARRY What are we going to have to do in here?

STEVE What's your name? *[Steve sits down on top of his desk with a serious look on his face]*

LARRY Larry Zuk.

STEVE *[Sternly]* Well, Larry, we're going to read and discuss history. Studying history is like studying anything else—it's hard work. Read each assignment that I make carefully before you come to class. That way the class discussions will be a lot more meaningful to you. *[He concludes firmly]* Yes? *[Steve looks at a girl in the back row who has held up her hand]*

GIRL What kind of tests will we have?

STEVE They will be mostly essay, although we'll probably have some short-answer quizzes once a week. Oh, yes—*[Pauses]* each Friday I want you to bring in newspaper clippings on current events and place them on the bulletin board over there. *[Steve points]* Of course we'll talk about them first.

LARRY *[Without raising his hand]* We had to do that stuff in the eighth grade and my dad got mad at me for cutting up the newspaper. *[Five other students voice their support]*

STEVE *[Loudly]* Quiet down, all of you. Larry, when you have something to say raise your hand like everyone else. *[Larry smirks]* You just tell your parents that the newspaper clippings are part of your schoolwork and you won't have any trouble.

It is one week later. Steve and Ray Clark sit alone in Ray's room after school. Social studies maps, charts, and diagrams are in evidence all around the classroom. A large bulletin board contains several pictures and newspaper clippings. A large picture of John F. Kennedy hangs on the wall above Ray's desk.

RAY Which kids are giving you the most trouble?

STEVE Larry Zuk, George Ramey, Kenneth Stone, Jack Dickinson, Larry Gage, and — uh—Sam—uh . . .

RAY   Sam Agar?

STEVE   Yeah, Sam Agar.

RAY   *[Nodding]* I know that group well. They have been causing trouble since grade school. What have they been doing?

STEVE   Just smarting off, mostly. You know—asking cute questions, speaking out without holding up their hands, and Larry Zuk got up yesterday while I was talking and sharpened his pencil. I was so surprised that I let him get away with it.

RAY   *[Laughs loudly]* That's Larry. *[Becomes serious]* Well, Steve, you're just going to have to handle them the same way their other teachers have handled them—let them know the rules and enforce them. I'll let Ed *[the vice-principal]* know that you'll be sending him his favorite customers. You've just got to knock a few heads! *[Pauses]* You know, sometimes I wonder what any of these kids really learn in high school. I guess if we can get them reading and writing we have done about all we can do.

STEVE   Yes, I learned more in my first college course than I did in all four years of high school. I hope that I can teach a few of them how to study so that they can make it in college. *[Pauses]* Well, thanks for your help, Ray. I think I'll go see Ed myself before I go home.

The next day Steve meets his world history class. He paces back and forth as he asks the class questions.

STEVE   What is the difference between history and prehistory? Susan.

SUSAN   History began when man began writing things down.

STEVE   How long ago was that, Susan?

SUSAN   *[Looks down at her text]* 4241 B.C. is the oldest writing that has ever been found.

STEVE   Right. It was an old Egyptian calendar. Anything before that date is prehistory. *[Steve looks to the back of the room where the six boys sit together as a group. George Ramey holds up his hand]* Yes, George?

GEORGE   Was this building built before or after history?

STEVE   *[Sarcastically]* Very funny, George.

LARRY   Before, you dumb-dumb! We don't have any Egyptian calendars. *[The whole class laughs]*

STEVE   *[Sharply]* That's enough, Larry. I've warned you once about raising your hand. *[The class quiets down]* Jack Dickinson, how long has man been on the earth?

JACK   We aren't going to get on that evolution bit are we, Mr. Rogers? That's against my religion.

STEVE   *[Smirking]* What **is** your religion, Jack?

JACK   I'm an objector.

STEVE   What kind of an objector?

JACK   We object to being asked questions about history. *[The class laughs again]*

STEVE   *[Loudly and with a look of anger on his face]* All right, that's enough! *[Class quiets down gradually; Steve speaks with controlled anger]* If you guys want to play games, it's going to cost you. The next smart remark. . . .

LARRY   *[Quickly]* Anyone for tennis?

Steve   Okay, Larry. Go to Mr. Irish's office. *[Larry gets up smiling and leaves; the class quiets down]* Now, unless someone else objects *[Looks back at the five boys]* let's get back to work. Who can tell me what artifacts are? *[Pauses, looks around, and frowns]* Okay—since nobody seems to know, we'll just put it on the next test. You'd better know it by then!

It is the end of the same school day and Steve goes to Ed Irish's office. As he enters the office, Ed gets up from behind his desk.

ED   Hi, Steve.

STEVE   Hi, Ed. Did Larry Zuk come to your office the fourth period? *[Steve and Ed both sit down]*

ED   Yes, he did. He told me what happened and I took him down to the boiler room and gave him three whacks. Larry and I are old buddies.

STEVE   Do you think it did any good?

ED   I doubt it. Steve, all six of those boys will probably give you serious trouble sooner or later. The only way that I have been able to calm them down is to lay the wood to them. But now that they are 16 that doesn't work any longer. *[Shakes his head]* I have called their parents and expelled the boys until I am blue in the face. *[With emphasis]* Their parents just aren't interested. Sometimes I think that we have a stay-in problem instead of a drop-out problem in the public schools.

STEVE   Those six boys ruin the class for the rest of the kids.

ED   I know that, Steve. I'll tell you what. I don't think it's fair of John to ask you to bail him out and then stick you with those six hoods. It won't do any good to move them into other classes either.

STEVE   Dividing them won't help?

ED   No. That's already been tried. Larry Zuk alone is so mean and tough that I hear that his parents are actually afraid of him. The other five can be just as tough as Larry.

STEVE   *[Smiling in disbelief]* Really!

ED   Yes. I guess Larry beat his father up bad once.

STEVE   If his dad can't handle him, then how can anyone expect us to?

ED   I agree, Steve. I guess I have reached a decision if you agree to go along with me. I will expel the boys again for three days. In the meantime, I'll tell John that the boys have disrupted another class and ask him to ask the superintendent to recommend to the board that they be permanently expelled. The board meets tomorrow night so chances are you won't have to put up with them in class again. Okay?

STEVE   I don't know, Ed. What will become of them when they are expelled? I'm not sure that they did anything bad enough in my class to warrant permanent expulsion. I. . . .

ED   *[Interrupting]* Your class is just the straw that broke the camel's back. They have been disrupting this school for many years now and will probably eventually end up in the reformatory. *[Pause]* Tell me, Steve—do you want to keep them in your class?

ANALYSIS

In order to fully explain the case entitled the "Stay-In Problem," it is necessary to use at least two psychological theories: operant conditioning and social expectancy theory. There is not enough behavioral information given in the case to do a complete operant analysis nor does operant conditioning really deal with the self-fulfilling prophecy that is operating in the lives of the six boys: Larry Zuk, George, Kenneth, Jack, Larry Gage, and Sam. In terms of actual observed behavior reported in the case, information is available only on Larry Zuk, Henry, and Jack. All other information is self-report or second-hand.

From an operant viewpoint, three categories of disruptive behavior are emitted:

1. speaking out without permission—four times by Larry Zuk
2. asking off-task questions—three times, twice by Larry Zuk and once by George.
3. making smart remarks—four times, once by Larry Zuk and three times by Jack.

In addition, Steve, the teacher, self-reports to Ray Clark that "Larry Zuk got up yesterday while I was talking and sharpened his pencil. I was so surprised I let him get away with it."

Since all the disruptive operants were followed by attempts at Punishment I in the form of verbal reprimands by Steve, it must be concluded that attention is serving as a social reinforcer for the three students. The other students in the class also laugh at the behavior of Larry Zuk and George and thereby serve as another source of reinforcement. When Larry Zuk sharpened his pencil without permission while Steve was speaking, Steve self-reports that he "was so surprised that I let him get away with it" (ignored the response).

It might also be added that Ray indicates that a history of attempted punishment exists which has not reduced the disruptive behavior of the six boys. He says, "Well, Steve, you're just going to have to handle them the same way their other teachers have handled them—let them know the rules and enforce them. I'll let Ed (the vice-principal) know that you'll be sending him his favorite customers."

Later, Ed Irish says, regarding Larry Zuk, "I took him down to the boiler room and gave him three whacks. Larry and I are old buddies." When Steve asks him if he thinks "it did any good," Ed says "I doubt it." In short, a pattern seems to exist in which teachers and other school officials have attempted to use Punishment I as a method of decreasing the disruptive behavior of the six boys and it simply adds to the social reinforcement in the form of attention. By this time the boys have a reputation as "tough guys" to uphold and the other students unwittingly reinforce this behavior with their attention. It is not surprising, therefore, that Steve's attempts to use verbal reprimands and eventually sending Larry Zuk to Irish's office are ineffective.

Speaking of the reputations the six boys have acquired leads into social expectancy theory (Rosenthal & Jacobson, 1968) as a means of examining what is happening in the broader school system context beyond the classroom of Steve, who is a beginning teacher. School officials like Ray Clark and Ed Irish have built up a set of expectations about the boys' disruptive behavior in various classrooms and, other Punishment I procedures having failed to decrease the behavior and believing that the boy's parents are unable or unwilling to help, are considering the ultimate form of punishment: exclusion in the form of permanent expulsion.

Evidence of this is when Ed tells Steve that he has reached a decision: "I'll tell John that the boys have disrupted another class and ask him to ask the superintendent to recommend to the board that they be permanently expelled." Ed refers to the boys as "those six hoods" and says that "it won't do any good to move them into other classes." He adds, regarding Larry Zuk, "that his parents are actually afraid of him." Apparently this is self-report data, possibly gossip.

Brophy and Good (1974) have presented a teacher expectations model which can be broadened to fit the larger school context in this case. They say that teacher expectations about a student can become a self-fulfilling prophecy in the following pattern. (1) The teacher, based on some kind of information such as an I.Q. score or the student's gender, comes to expect certain behavior from a student. (2) Because of the expectations, the teacher behaves differently toward the students as compared to other students. (3) The teacher's behavior tells the student what behavior is expected of the student by the teacher. (4) If the teacher is consistent in expectations and behavior over time and the student does not actively resist or change the pattern in some way, the student's behavior will be shaped to the expected pattern.

Various teachers—Ray Clark, Ed Irish, and others—have developed a set of expectations about the disruptive behavior of the six boys. Steve's classroom problems with them merely confirm the pattern and fulfill it. The boys play the expected role of the "six hoods," since this gives them what social reinforcement is available to them in the situation.

One problem is that little information is given in the case about the six boys other than their disruptive reputation, that Larry Zuk's "parents are actually afraid of him," and that "the other five can be just as tough as Larry." We are given no objective information on their home and family life, their abilities and test scores, their vocational interests, their outside-of-school hobbies and interests, or anything that might be helpful in changing the cycle of events that have transpired. Apparently Ed is still open to intervention by Steve when he asks, "Do you want to keep them in your class?" With so little information available to Steve, what can Steve do in his classroom to try and change the pattern?

DECISION

It is difficult for a beginning teacher like Steve to try to change a pattern of expectations and failed attempts at punishment that have been in place for so long. Many beginning teachers would find it difficult *not* go along with such a convenient solution as expelling the six boys. It would be easy to not worry about "what will become of them" as Steve did. Steve even asks if "they did anything bad enough in my class to warrant permanent expulsion." The following courses of action are presented assuming that the situation is to be dealt with from the standpoint of the teacher and that Steve will put them into operation without having to be persuaded to do so.

First, Steve needs to convince the vice-principal not to have the boys permanently expelled but to give Steve another chance to work with them in his world history class. He might say something to Ed like, "Ed, I really would like another chance to work with them. I know that I'm just a beginner at this teaching business but I'd like to try one more time with them. They can always be expelled if what I try doesn't work out. Would you give me and them one more chance?"

It would be very difficult for a beginning teacher to try to convince the administrators and other teachers of a school that expectations regarding the boys' disruptive behavior need to be changed and the boys given a fresh start. Direct statements to that effect, for example to the principal or at a faculty meeting, are likely to result in Steve's being seen as an inexperienced know-it-all. However, if Steve can effectively change what goes on in his classroom, he will, indirectly, present a model of a different way of working with the boys that may influence others. If successful he may even be asked to explain what he has done and be given the chance to become an effective change agent.

In order to change the situation in his classroom, Steve needs to: (1) change his expectations about the six boys' behavior; (2) find out more about the boys' interests and motivational patterns to help him present appropriate incentives and reinforcers in the classroom; (3) change peer responses to the boys' disruptive behavior; (4) cue the boys regarding expected classroom behavior and its consequence, including expulsion by the school board, and enter into contingency contracts with each; (5) contact the boys' parents regarding the contracts and possible consequences and try to involve them in the contract implementation. The operationalization of these procedures follows.

Although it is assumed that Steve will follow the courses of action that are outlined here and will know how to implement them, he should first examine his own expectations as a teacher. Even if he has no difficulties in this area he will be able to explain the self-fulfilling prophecy process if the opportunity arises. Good and Brophy (1995) suggest that teachers ask themselves the following questions:

1. Do I praise and encourage low-achieving students when they ask questions or make comments?
2. Do I continue to work with low achievers in both failure and success situations?
3. Do I fail to call on them?
4. Are they needlessly criticized for incorrect answers or lack of response?
5. Are they treated as individuals rather than as a group?
6. Do low achievers get to pick the topics they study, have a chance to evaluate their work, and make important decisions?

While the emphasis in these questions is on low achievers, they fit just as well with students who are disruptive and interfere with the achievement of other students. The point is that Steve needs to examine his biases toward the six boys and not contribute to the prevailing expectations regarding the boys' disruptive behavior. Only if he is willing to treat them as individuals, in a way different than others have treated them, will his plan have any chance at all of working.

Next, Steve needs to meet with each of the six boys individually in order to: (1) find out more about their motivations, interests, and family life; (2) explain expected classroom behavior and outline the contingency contract; (3) indicate that he will be contacting the boys' parents. Since Larry Zuk seems to be one of the main troublemakers in Steve's class and a sort of leader among the six boys, Steve should meet with him first. The procedures that he uses with Larry are the same that he should use with the other five.

Steve should first try to get Larry to meet him in his classroom after school. He should tell Larry that he needs to talk to him about something very important to Larry's future. If Larry refuses to meet or fails to show up, Steve should ask Ed Irish to set up the meeting in Ed's office if need be. Steve should try to conduct the conference as follows. He'll have to adjust his remarks according to Larry's reactions, of course.

"Larry, I'm afraid that I got upset and overreacted to your joke about tennis the other day in class. I'm not sure I did the right thing in sending you to Mr. Irish's office. However, I do get upset when something happens to keep me from helping the class learn what I'm trying to teach. In any case, after I cooled down I realized that you and I really don't know much about one another and I feel it's important to get to know as much as I can about my students."

At this point, as long as Larry is cooperative and willing to talk, Steve should ask Larry about his family, his hobbies and interests, his vocational plans, etc. He should even ask him if any part of world history or any subject in school interests him and why. If Larry is uncooperative or indicates that he considers this conversation a waste of time, Steve should move to the next phase.

"Larry, I'm afraid that I stirred up a hornet's nest when I sent you to Mr. Irish's office yesterday. He indicated that you and some of your friends have disrupted classes so often that it was the straw that broke the camel's back. He and others want to permanently expel you from school. Personally, I'm not sure that's a good idea. Is that what you want, Larry? What would you do with your time if you were no longer in school?"

Again, Steve will have to tailor his comments to Larry's reactions. He should next make the following points. "Larry, I'll tell you what I think. I think you should stay in school. I know I wouldn't want to be out on the streets at your age. I can give a little if you will, and I think we can work it out so you can stay in school. All you have to do is stop some of the disruptive things that interfere with my trying to teach and other students trying to learn. Things like making wisecracks, speaking out without raising your hand, asking questions that have nothing to do with the subject, and sharpening your pencil without permission. If you're willing to stop these things, I'm willing to do what I can to make the class more interesting and listen to some of your ideas on how I can do that. What do you say?"

If Larry is willing to cooperate, then Steve needs to explain the contingency contract to him, tell him that he needs to explain the situation to Larry's parents, and that they will need to sign it along with Larry, Steve, and Ed Irish. Finally, Steve will need to mention that he knows that the other students in the class are part of the problem, since they laugh and encourage Larry in his behavior.

The contingency contract should specify the inappropriate behavior as well as the consequences. An example might be "Whenever you argue, make wisecracks, speak out without raising your hand, ask questions that are off the subject, or leave your seat without permission, you will be warned once. If the misbehavior occurs again, you will be sent to the counselor's office." Steve should be alert for opportunities to reinforce competing, opposite appropriate behavior through contingent praise and the assignment of classroom responsibilities. For example, Steve might say, "That's a good question, Larry." Larry might be given the job of taking the roll or leading a small group assignment.

Finally, Steve will need to conduct a planning session with his world history class in order to decrease peer reinforcement of the inappropriate behavior and to specify competing, opposite appropriate behavior. He might begin by saying something like the following:

"Class, I want to avoid situations like the one we had the other day when I sent Larry to Mr. Irish's office. The situation that developed was as much my fault as anybody's, because as a class we didn't have a clear idea about what kind of behavior is appropriate or inappropriate. We all got caught up in the drama unprepared. After all, we're here to learn and learning involves learning how to relate to other human beings as well as learning world history.

"What I'd like for you all to help me with is deciding what behavior is appropriate and inappropriate in this class, and what the consequences should be for each. First, let's brainstorm and list examples of each and I'll write them on the blackboard. Then we can collapse them into types or categories of behavior and talk about what the consequences should be for each type of behavior. Let me begin with "making smart remarks" and "moving about the room without permission." After we all contribute, we'll discuss how we feel about each before collapsing them into categories. Now who can give me an appropriate behavior?"

After completing the final list of appropriate and inappropriate behaviors and consequences that the teacher and most of the class agree on, Steve should make a copy on poster paper and display it appropriately in the room. He may also need to review the contingency contracts and see if they need to be revised in terms of the class's agreements. This approach to involving the students in the decision-making and having them focus on and define appropriate behaviors and consequences should bring peer pressure to bear on the six boys' behavior, provided Steve is consistent in implementing agreements and procedures. Steve should later go over how well the class and he feel the agreements are working and what changes, if any, should be made.

Critique of Analysis and Decision

The analysis and decision presented above meet the previously presented criteria rather well. First it should be noted that two theories or frameworks were used rather than one: operant condition and social expectancy theory. This is because neither theory alone would be sufficient to cover all the problems involved. Operant conditioning is limited to directly observable external behavior and therefore doesn't readily lend itself to analyzing the internal beliefs that were creating the self-fulfilling prophecies at work. If one theory doesn't cover the situation, then it is necessary to combine it with a second one to fully explain the nature of the problem.

Second, the evidence given to support the analysis is presented in an objective form appropriate to the theories used. The operant data is of a baseline observational nature, while the expectancy theory support is quoted directly. Further, the support evidence cited is rather complete and covers the major theoretical contentions made.

Moving to the decision, each course of action suggested is consistent with one of the two theories, either dealing with expectations in operation or behavioral management techniques such as the contingency contract. Further, each course of action is spelled out in enough detail to be considered operational and is feasible (practical) in the context of the situation. Enough detail is given that a teacher reading the suggested courses of action could probably figure what to do and how to do it, at least with a little improvisation. Much more detail would make the decision too long and laborious.

It might be argued that more detail could have been given on the contingency contract and that a sample contract should have been presented. Further, a feasibility issue could be raised as to whether the time demands involved in constructing and implementing such a contract are practical for a teacher such as Steve. While these certainly are valid criticisms, their importance depends on content depth requirements and time demands operating in producing the analysis and decision. The analysis and decision presented is typical of a small group of four to six undergraduate students working for eight 50-minute class periods, with the instructor functioning as a consultant to the group.

Other Frameworks and Methods

"The Stay-In Problem" could have been analyzed from the standpoint of any number of theories or models other than the two used. For example, several classroom management models such as Teacher Effectiveness Training (TET) could have been used. A motivational analysis (such as one using Maslow's need hierarchy) or a learning-oriented theory like observational learning would have fit also. An argument could even be made for concentrating on the teaching methods employed and perhaps moving toward something like cooperative learning techniques. The point is that the two frameworks used are certainly not the only possibilities.

It should also be obvious that the written form of the analysis and decision and the criteria needed to critique the product are not the only way to use case studies. They merely represent one approach. Perhaps just engaging a class in a verbal discussion of a case and trying to decide on the best ways to deal with the issues involved would be just as valuable as the written outcome or product method presented. Even if the framework used for examining the case is the personal beliefs of the discussants, clarifying one's beliefs and following them to their logical conclusions may be an important learning experience.

CASE DEVELOPMENT

The cases that follow were developed to represent the 19 professional knowledge core categories upon which teacher certification exams around the country are based. The categories obtained by Veenman (1984) and Broudy (1990) were included as well. The cases cover grade levels K–12 and include the problems of both beginning and experienced teachers. The thirty cases are organized under six headings: (1) classroom management and motivation; (2) curriculum and planning; (3) instruction and evaluation; (5) pupil adjustment; and (6) conditions of work.

Following each case you may find additional material to consider, such as information from a student's cumulative records, a student's responses to a test or form, or a summary of data relative to a group of students such as test scores. At the end of each case you will find "starter questions" that may help start the discussion of the case. Each question is likely to represent a different framework for looking at the case or focus on a part of the case that may have been overlooked.

In Appendix A you will find a theory grid. The purpose of the theory grid is to suggest possible frameworks (theories, models, set of principles) that might be used to analyze each case. The frameworks presented are derived from our own areas of expertise: educational psychology and curriculum and instruction. Your instructor may suggest other frameworks more appropriate to other types of courses and disciplines.

Following are the 19 professional core categories and the numbers of the cases that relate to each. Some cases relate to more than one category.

Curriculum Development, 9

Instructional Planning, 7, 12

Instructional Objectives, 8

Instructional Resources and Materials, 10, 28

Methods of Instruction, 7, 18, 21

Instructional Delivery, 15

Teacher Communication Skills, 16

Classroom Management, 1, 2, 6, 30

Motivational Techniques, 3, 4

Student Self Concept, 22

Individual Differences and Exceptionalities, 7, 18, 19, 20, 21

Severe Student Emotional Stress, 23

Child Abuse, 24

Drug Abuse, 25

Measurement and Evaluation, 13, 14, 21, 29, 30

Teacher Use of Computers, 11

Extra-Classroom Influences, 17, 27, 29

REFERENCES

Allonache, P., Bewich, G. & Ivey, M (1989). Decision workshops for the improvement of decision-making skills confidence. *Journal of Counseling and Development, 67,* 478–81.

Bloom, B.S., Engelhart, M.D., Furst, E.J., Hill, W.H., & Krathwohl, D.R. (1956). Taxonomy of educational objectives. The classification of educational goals: Handbook 1. Cognitive domain. New York: Longmans Green.

Brophy, J. & Good, T. (1974). *Teacher–student relationships: Causes and consequences.* New York: Holt, Rinehart & Winston.

Broudy, H.S. (1990). Case studies—why and how. *Teachers College Record, 91,* 449–459.

Dembo, M. & Hillman, S. (1976). An instructional model approach to educational psychology. *Contemporary Educational Psychology, 1,* 116–123.

Gage, N.L. & Berliner, D.C. (1992). *Educational Psychology,* Boston: Houghton Mifflin.

Good, T. & Brophy, J. (1995). *Contemporary educational psychology.* White Plains, NY: Longman.

Greenwood, G.E. & Hankins, A.D. (1989). An analysis of professional knowledge content base commonalities among ten teacher certification examinations. *Capstone Journal of Education, 9,* 19–36.

Lampert, M. & Clark, C.M. (1990). Expert knowledge and expert thinking in teaching: A response to Floden and Klinzing, *Educational Researcher, 19,* 21–23.

Rosenthal, R. & Jacobson, L. (1968). *Pygmalion in the classroom.* New York: Holt, Rinehart & Winston.

Rudner, L.M. (1988). Teacher testing: An update. *Educational Measurement: Issues and Practice, 7,* 16–19.

Schor, D.A. (1987). *Educating the reflective practitioner.* San Francisco: Jossey-Bass.

Shavelson, R.J. (1973). What is the basic teaching skill? *Journal of Teacher Eduction, 24,* 144–151.

Shulman, L.S. (1987). Knowledge and teaching: Foundations of the New Reform. *Harvard Educational Review, 57,* 31.

Sparks-Langer, G.M. & Colton, A.B. (1991). Synthesis of research on teachers' reflective thinking. *Educational Leadership, 48,* 37–44.

Veenman, S. (1984). Perceived problems of beginning teachers. *Review of Educational Research, 54,* 143–178.

Waller, N.E. & Travers, R.M.W. (1963). Analysis and investigation of teaching methods. In Gage, N.L. (Ed.), *Handbook of research on teaching.* Chicago: Rand McNally.

PART II

CLASSROOM MANAGEMENT AND MOTIVATION CASES

NASTY NICHOLAS

A s Arlene Saunders drives her newly acquired four-year-old automobile, she admires the magnificent countryside that unfolds before her. The road rises and gently curves around the rolling hills that define the landscape. She enjoys the forests, lakes, and green pastures visible in the distance. The brisk air and tinge of scarlet appearing in the leaves of the maple trees suggest the first touch of fall. Arlene reflects on the major events of her life during the past few months and is filled with a satisfied inner glow.

Just three months ago, she graduated from New England State College with a major in elementary education. After reviewing all the announcements of job openings for teachers in the career placement center of her college, Arlene applied for jobs in three communities within a fifty-mile radius of her home town. Her mother and dad invited her to live at home until she had been hired as a teacher. Meanwhile, she was able to obtain summer employment in a small manufacturing plant in her home town, filling in for workers who were on vacation. This job helped her earn enough money to buy her car.

Shortly after she moved home, two of the three schools to which she had applied for a position invited her to come for an interview. She went first to the school that was her first choice. This was an elementary school in the small town of Revere. Arlene was interviewed by the assistant superintendent in charge of personnel, the elementary principal, and the elementary supervisor. While the supervisor showed her around town, the people who had interviewed her conferred. When she returned to the school, the principal offered her a position in the school as a first-grade teacher. Arlene accepted immediately because it was exactly the type of position she had hoped for.

Revere elementary school is located near the center of the town of Revere and has an enrollment of approximately 500 pupils. There are three sections of each grade from K through 6. The population of Revere is approximately 8,000 and is approximately 80 percent white, 10 percent African-American, 5 percent Hispanic, and 5 percent Asian-American. The major industry is farming, ranging from one-man operations to large farm factories. There are also several light industries that employ most of their workers at relatively low wages, but also have quite a few middle and upper management positions at relatively high wages.

Arlene attended a three-day teachers' workshop during the previous week during which she became even more enthusiastic about her new position. While there, she met several teachers she liked and would like to have as friends.

On the morning of the first day of school Arlene opened her eyes at 6 A.M. and was wide awake. She was so excited to meet her first graders and begin working with them that she couldn't sleep any longer. She showered, dressed, and prepared her breakfast. As she ate her breakfast, she reviewed in her mind the activities she had planned for the day. She was so eager to go to school that she was hardly aware of eating her breakfast.

She arrived at school early because she wanted to have ample time to plan for all her activities. Arlene had obtained the names of the pupils who would be in her class and had already memorized their names. It would be easy for her to match their names with their faces. She had already planned the seating arrangement for the room, so the first thing she did was to attach the pupils' name tags to the desks she had assigned them.

As the children enter the room Arlene asks them their names, helps them put on their nametags, and instructs them to find their desks by identifying their nametags on the desks.

ARLENE   You're all doing so well. I see that Nancy and Gerome have found their desks. Good, Michael, that's your desk.

ZAC   Teacher, that boy's in my desk. See, that's my name right there.

NICK   Shut up, Tattletale. Sit in another seat.

ARLENE   Come with me, Nick. I think I see your desk over there.

NICK   I wanna sit here. Let that tattletale sit over there. *[Shoves Zac, who stumbles forward toward another row of seats]*

ARLENE   *[Crossly]* Nick! Don't you ever push or hit anybody in this class again. Pushing and hitting are against the rules! Do you understand?

NICK   Yeah, yeah. Pushing is against the rules.

ARLENE   Here's your seat, Zac. See, here's your name right here. Z-A-C spells Zac. Nick, can you find your name on that desk over there?

NICK   Sure, I saw it when I came in. I could read last year. I just liked Zac's desk better. Zac, Zac, broke his back. *[Loud laughter]* Look at Zac with the broken back sitting over there. *[Sitting at his own desk and laughing]* Poor tattletale Zac. Broke his back. Has to sit at that poopy old desk. My desk's better, after all.

ARLENE   Thanks for sitting at your own desk, Nick. *[To the class]* I think the first thing we'll do today is learn the names of the other pupils in the class. So I'm going to go around the class and stand beside each desk. As I stand beside your desk, I want you to speak your name loudly enough for everyone in the class to hear you. If you don't want to speak your name, I'll speak it for you. Let's all try to learn the names of everybody in the class.
[As Arlene stands by one of the desks, she sees Nick break his new pencil in two. She ignores this behavior. But as she walks toward the front of that row of desks, Nick snatches the pencils from the desks on each side of him and breaks them in two. When Mark tries to stop him, he slaps him on the arm.]

MARK   Ms. Saunders, Nick broke the pencil you gave me.

SARAH   Mine, too.

LAWANDA   Nick, why'd you break Mark and Sarah's pencils?

NICK   They're dumb old pencils. I don't like them.

MARK   I liked my pencil. You're a nasty person! Nasty Nick. That's what we ought to call you!

NICK   Don't you start calling me names, four eyes, or I'll take care of you! We'll call you Mark Four-eyes. Ha, Ha, Ha.

SARAH   You shouldn't 'uv broke our pencils.

ARLENE   Mark and Sarah are right, Nick. If you want to break your pencil, that's OK because its yours. But I gave those other pencils to Mark and Sarah. Those pencils belong to them. It's wrong to break things that belong to other people. I planned to teach you some of the class rules today. That's one of the rules I'm going to teach you. Who can tell me what the rule is? Chan?

CHAN   Don't break somebody else's things.

ARLENE   That's good, Chan. What else could the rule say about other people's things? Sarah?

SARAH   I don't think people should even touch other people's things.

ARLENE   What do you think about that rule, class?

CHRISTIE   I think it's OK to touch somebody else's things if it's OK with that person. *[Several class members voice agreement with Christie's opinion]*

ARLENE   Well, it seems that all of you agree with Christie's idea. So one of our class rules is "Don't touch somebody else's things unless that person says it's OK." Now, I'll teach you that rule. Who'll show us an example of our rule by walking up one aisle and down another one without touching anything that belongs to someone else? Johnny, let's see how well you do it. *[Johnny walks up and down each aisle without touching anything]*

ARLENE   Thanks, Johnny. That's a good example of our rule. Maria, Can you show us an example of the rule? *[Maria walks all around the perimeter of the classroom without touching anything]* Good, Maria. We've just seen two examples of the rule. What would be a nonexample of the rule? A nonexample of a rule means breaking the rule. Freddie, can you show us a nonexample of our rule? *[Freddie walks to the teacher's desk and picked up a pencil. Then he lays it back down and returns to his desk]* Thank you, Freddie. Who can tell us what Freddie did that was a nonexample of our rule?

ANN   He touched the pencil on your desk.

ARLENE   Good, Ann. Why's that a nonexample of the rule?

ANN   He touched your pencil without asking you if it's OK.

ARLENE   That's right. Very good, Ann. Nick, can you now show us another nonexample of our rule?

NICK   I did. I broke those pencils.

ARLENE   That's right. Can you tell us why that's against the rule?

NICK   They were somebody else's pencils. They didn't want me to break them.

LAWANDA   That's very good, Nick. When you touch something that belongs to someone else, you're breaking a class rule. Can you remember not to do that anymore?

NICK   I knew that's a rule. We had it last year.

ARLENE   I don't know what your rules were last year, but I'm teaching you the rules that you'll have in my class this year.

NICK   I don't care about school rules. We don't need 'em
ARLENE   I saw you playing tag before school today, didn't I?
NICK   Yes, I was playing with some second graders.
ARLENE   Are there rules in tag?
NICK   No.
ARLENE   Are you sure? How do you know who's it?
NICK   Well, yeah. I guess that's a rule.
ARLENE   Can you think of any games that don't have rules?
NICK   *[After several seconds of pondering the question]* No.
ARLENE   Interesting. Why's that, Nick?
NICK   I don't know.
ARLENE   Think about it for a minute. *[Waits for several more seconds]*
NICK   I guess rules help people know how to play the game.
ARLENE   Do you think that's true in class, too, Nick?
NICK   Yeah, I guess so.
ARLENE   That's good thinking, Nick.

Arlene continues to teach the classroom rules by asking the pupils to demonstrate examples and nonexamples. The rules cover such procedures as using the bathroom; raising hands before speaking; using an appropriate voice for speaking to your neighbor; speaking in a small group, and speaking to the entire class; entering and leaving the various centers in the classroom; and other routine classroom functions.

At the end of the school day, Arlene is opening her car door in the parking lot when Pam Reynolds, a kindergarten teacher she paired up with during the teachers' workshop, walks by.

ARLENE   Hi, Pam. How was your first day?
PAM   Great! I have a nice group of pupils. How was your day, Arlene?
ARLENE   I had a great day too. However, I do have a boy who concerns me a bit.
PAM   Who's that?
ARLENE   His name is Nicholas Glaros.
PAM   Oh, wow! I sympathize with you. I suffered with him in my class last year. He's really a problem! What'd he do in your class?
ARLENE   Well, nothing really serious, but he seemed quite willing and able to disrupt a class. I gave pencils to each member of the class and he broke his own and those of two other pupils.
PAM   Sounds like Nick. He was physically abusive to some of the other pupils last year.
ARLENE   Really. Well, maybe you can tell me how to handle Nick—one of the pupils called him Nasty Nick. What types of things did he do? Why do you think he did them? How did you discipline him? Do you have any suggestions for me?
PAM   Whoa! Slow down. Yes, I'll help you in any way that I can. Do you have time to talk now? I have a free hour or so, and I'd planned to visit with you soon so that we could get to know each other better. There's a drugstore with a small eating

area about five blocks from here. Do you have time to meet me there and talk for a while?

ARLENE   Yes, I'd like that. During the teachers' workdays, I'd hoped that we could be friends. We're fairly close in age, I think, and I enjoyed our conversations. I don't know anybody in Revere so I'd really like to have a friend. I'll follow you to the drugstore.

PAM   Great, my car's just over there. I'll lead the way.

Pam and Arlene sit at a booth together in the back of the drugstore where they can be alone.

ARLENE   This is a cozy place. It reminds me of a place my friends and I hung out when I was in high school.

PAM   I drove by here three years ago, shortly after I moved to Revere. It looked so inviting that I turned my car around, parked out front, came in and had a cola. Now, whenever I want to think about something, talk with a friend, or just relax, I come here.

Now, you asked me about Nick Glaros. I can give you quite a bit of information. First, he's very bright. He was able to read children's books when he arrived at kindergarten. I was pleased when I discovered this, because I thought maybe he could read in pairs with some of the other children just on the verge of learning to read. Unfortunately, that was a bad idea. Nick took great pleasure in making fun of the pupils who couldn't read yet.

ARLENE   That's too bad. What did he do to make fun of them?

PAM   I guess you've probably already heard his loud laugh?

ARLENE   Yes, I had a couple samples of it today.

PAM   Well, that's the thing about him that probably got to me the most. I came to abhor the sound of his laugh. He seemed to enjoy hitting and shoving other pupils. Every time he abused another pupil in any way, he'd begin that horrible laugh. When some of the poor readers tried to read, Nick would point and laugh that horrible laugh, remarking that Jane, Sam, or Marta "can't even read."

ARLENE   What did you do?

PAM   I tried everything . . . finally called the principal. He took Nick to his office and paddled him. Nick behaved for a while, but soon he began to act out again. Then I'd send him to the principal, and he was good again for a while . . . and so on. I felt guilty sending him to be paddled and began to bargain with him. He behaved a little better toward the end of year, but not much.

ARLENE   Have you talked with his parents?

PAM   Yes, they came to parents' night last year. The father's a manager of a small manufacturing plant and the mother's a bookkeeper who works in an accounting firm. They are very nice, but seem to have a most objective view of Nick— almost as if he belongs to somebody else. I think he's basically been reared by a day-care center.

For example, they say, Yes, they're very sorry that Nick is abusing other children. They wonder why he does that. What have I done about it? Oh really? Did his behavior improve after the principal paddled him? That's wonderful. Maybe his bad behavior is over now. And so on. What are *you* going to do about Nick, Arlene?

ARLENE   In college we studied both external and internal plans for discipline. I'm committed to the internal plans—to have pupils develop an internal self-discipline. External plans, like paddling, can often force pupils into good behavior. But if pupils don't internalize good behavior, they don't really become self-disciplined.

PAM   That makes sense. Nobody really taught us specific procedures for discipline at my college. The professors talked about the need for discipline, but didn't teach any specific methods or procedures we could use for maintaining discipline. I wish they would have.

ARLENE   We learned that the first step to good discipline is to make certain that the pupils learn the classroom rules, and be sure that they understand the reason for the rules. I started on that today. I taught them a few classroom rules. Then we practiced examples and nonexamples of each rule so that the pupils would know exactly how to follow each rule.

PAM   That's a neat idea! Then if you don't want pupils to talk too loudly, you just demonstrate what volume of talking is too loud.

ARLENE   Exactly. In fact, we did that in class today.

PAM   Would you be willing to meet with me sometime soon and teach me a way to organize a complete system of discipline for my class?

ARLENE   Sure, let's check our schedules. We can probably meet later this week.

Six weeks later, Arlene's pupils are all working in the various centers. Six pupils are working together, finger painting a three-foot-by-six-foot poster. There are two pupils along each side, one pupil at the top and one at the bottom. They are each creating an original painting on a designated area of the poster. Nick's working on the top of the poster. Suddenly, he stands up and deliberately sloshes half a jar of yellow tempera paint down the center of the poster.

TED   Why did you do that, Nick? You ruined our poster!

NICK   [Sloshing the remainder of the paint on Ted] Now I am ruining you, ha, ha, ha. You're yellow, Ted.

TED   [Beginning to cry] Look, my brand new shirt is ruined!

ARLENE   Nick, you put that jar down and come over here right now!
        [As Nick walks towards Arlene, he pushes Doris, and she has to step lively to keep from running across the poster]

DORIS   You're an awful person, Nick. Look what you did to our beautiful poster. I hate you!

MARTA   I don't want to work with Nick anymore, Ms. Saunders. He ruins everything.

TYLER   Me either.

ARLENE   Nick, you're in big trouble this time. You sit in this chair right now, and
          don't you even move until I tell you to. *[Nick docilely does as he is instructed.]*
                [To the pupils at the poster] Let's see what we can do about this. We may be
          able to spread the yellow down the center of the poster and blend in with the
          colors around the outside. There. Do you think that part looks OK?
PAINTERS   Yes. It looks better than before. I like the yellow center. It blends right in.
ARLENE   Do you see how I blended it into the other colors with my hand? Why don't
          you each blend it in along your part of the picture?
                Ted, if you'll take off your shirt and give it to me, I think I might be able to
          fix it. The shirt is washable, and the paint should wash right out of it.
TED   Oh, I hope you can. It's my favorite shirt. Today's the first day I wore it.
ARLENE   *[Holding the shirt under the water faucet]* There, see, the yellow's coming
          right out. I'll soak it for a few minutes and be sure we get it all out.
TED   Thank you. That's my favorite shirt.

At 7:30 the following evening, Arlene is at the Glaros's home. She had called the previous night, explained what had happened at school, and asked if she could come to their home and discuss it with them. They reluctantly agreed.

ARLENE   *[Brightly]* Hello. I'm Arlene Saunders. Thank you for agreeing to see me. I
          wanted to talk with you about Nicholas's behavior at school.
MRS. GLAROS   *[Unenthusiastically inviting Arlene to sit down]* We appreciate your interest in Nick. What seems to be the problem?
MR. GLAROS   Yes. We want to help all we can.
ARLENE   Well, there've been several incidents. They began the first day of school. On
          that day, I had given all the pupils in the class a pencil with their names printed
          on them. As soon as I'd given them out, Nick broke his pencil and then snatched
          the pencils away from two other pupils and broke theirs also. Less than five minutes later, he shoved another pupil into a row of seats. Both incidents were unprovoked.
MR. GLAROS   *[Concerned]* I can't understand why he'd do that.
ARLENE   Neither can I. That's why I'm here. But there's more. After that day, there
          have been twelve incidents that I'm aware of when Nick has either physically or
          verbally abused other pupils, seemingly with no provocation at all. Yesterday, he
          deliberately tried to ruin a poster that a group of six pupils, including him, was
          working on. He threw most of a jar of yellow paint right in the middle of the
          poster. Then, he threw the remainder of the jar on another pupil and drenched
          the pupil's new shirt in yellow paint. Afterwards, he pushed another pupil across
          the room. During this time, he was laughing hysterically.
MRS. GLAROS   *[Shocked]* What did you do about it?
ARLENE   I isolated him from the other pupils for the remainder of the day and told
          him that I was going to talk with his parents about his behavior. I'd like to ask
          you the same question you asked me. What're you going to do about it? Do you

want him to continue to destroy other pupils' property and abuse them until he finally injures someone seriously?

    This has been going on with Nick ever since he entered school. Ms. Reynolds had the same problems with him in kindergarten last year and told you about it then. Have you taken any steps to get help for Nick, or to encourage him to change this behavior? After all, you are ultimately responsible for his behavior.

MS. GLAROS   *[After a long embarrassing silence]* Well, we've talked with him about it.

ARLENE   Did you talk with him about it just once, last year?

MS. GLAROS   *[Angrily]* Are you trying to tell us how to raise our child?

ARLENE   *[Seriously]* No, I'm trying to communicate to you that your son has a serious behavior problem that deserves serious attention. And I see no evidence that it's getting any attention at all.

    His behavior's interfering with my ability to perform my job satisfactorily. I'm giving him all the attention I can, but I'm not qualified to treat serious behavior disorders, and I have 25 other pupils to attend to. Working with a pupil who is out of control is the responsibility of the parents as well as the teacher. This is why I'm here. I felt obligated to let you know that your child's out of control at school, which is the purpose of this visit. Now, I'd like to work with you if you're interested in doing anything about it. Are you?

MR. GLAROS   *[Obviously embarrassed]* Well, of course we want to help our son. I guess that we didn't know the situation was so serious. I'm just not sure what to do.

ARLENE   If you haven't done so, it might be useful to have Nick see a counselor.

MS. GLAROS   *[Shocked]* Oh, I hate to do that! Nick isn't crazy.

ARLENE   Of course he's not. But he's obviously disturbed. Well-adjusted people don't go around assaulting other people regularly. A counselor might be able to find out why he's behaving this way, and help him to stop.

MR. GLAROS   *[With resignation]* Obviously, we haven't realized the seriousness of Nick's situation, Ms. Saunders. We need to consider all our alternatives. Then we'll let you know what we've decided. Thank you for making the effort to bring the seriousness of this situation to our attention.

ARLENE   Thank you for seeing me. I'll cooperate in any way I can to help Nick at school. I'd like for us to work together.

MR. GLAROS   We'd like that, too. I'll call you as soon as we decide what to do.

The next day there is a note from the principal asking Arlene to come to his office after school.

ARLENE   I got your note that you wanted to see me, Mr. Wright.

PRINCIPAL   Thank you for coming, Arlene. The reason I asked you to come is that during the weekend, I've had calls from five parents of your pupils complaining about the behavior of Nicholas Glaros in class on Friday. Can you fill me in on what happened?

ARLENE   Yes, I'll be glad to. *[She describes in detail the events surrounding the paint and poster event, including her visit to the Glaros home Friday evening]*

PRINCIPAL   *[Incredulously]* You're telling me that Nick has lost control of himself and abused other pupils at least once a week since school started?

ARLENE   That's right. But I've been using different strategies to help him learn to establish self-control.

PRINCIPAL   Why didn't you let me know that he's been abusing other pupils? This is a serious problem. Last year he was creating problems in Ms. Reynolds's class. She sent him to me a couple a times, and I paddled him. That seemed to stop the problem.

ARLENE   Yes, Pam told me about that. But he's still abusing other pupils this year.

PRINCIPAL   Then why didn't you come to me for help?

ARLENE   Nick's behavior seemed to be improving markedly for several days just before the poster incident.

PRINCIPAL   Well the parents of the pupils involved in the poster incident want to have a conference with me to find out what we are going to do to ensure their children's safety.

ARLENE   I'd like to attend that conference if it's all right with you.

PRINCIPAL   I'd like for you to attend. In fact, I was going to suggest that you be present. Is Wednesday at three o'clock convenient for you?

ARLENE   Yes, that's convenient for me.

PRINCIPAL   Good. And since you've been working to develop a sense of self-discipline in Nick, I would also like you to develop a plan that will protect the other pupils in the class from Nick's losses of control. Then you can share it with the parents of the five pupils he abused. Would it be convenient for you to meet with me Tuesday afternoon at three and share with me what you plan to tell the parents?

ARLENE   Yes sir. That'll be fine.

PRINCIPAL   Great! But tell me, Arlene, although I know you'll need to think this through thoroughly, what do you think might work in this situation?

REVERE ELEMENTARY SCHOOL

Cumulative Record

Name:	Glaros, Nicholas M.	Home Phone: 555-4837
Address:	693 Grand Avenue	
Father:	Glaros, George L.	Occupation: Plant Manager
Mother:	Glaros, Vivien J.	Occupation: Bookkeeper
Siblings:	None	
DOB:	11/2/89	
AGE:	6	
Health:	Excellent	

Test Record

Intelligence Test	CA	MA	I.Q.	Grade
California Test of Mental Maturity 9/3/94				K
Language	6.0	8.0	133	
Non-Language	6.0	7.3	121	

Peabody Picture Vocabulary Test: 9/3/94—Scored in highest range.

ACADEMIC RECORD

Record the year's average as A, B, C, D, or F

Grades:	K	1	2	3	4	5	6
Reading	A						
English							
Writing							
Spelling							
Arithmetic							
Social St.							
Science							
Art	A						
Phys.Ed	A						
Music	A						

K—Nicholas is working well above grade level in all subject areas. He is creative, able to concentrate for long periods of time, and conscientious about completing his projects. He does not seem interested in making friends of his classmates and they respond in kind.

QUESTIONS

1. From an operant conditioning viewpoint, what undesirable behaviors is Nicholas emitting and what reinforcers are maintaining them? Pinpoint desirable competing behaviors that Arlene can reinforce to replace the undesirable behaviors. What reinforcer should Arlene use to shape Nicholas's behavior? What role have Nicholas's peers played in reinforcing his undesirable behavior?

2. What model of classroom management would be most useful in approaching this situation? For example, would Assertive Discipline, Teacher Effectiveness Training, Reality Therapy or Kounins' model be the best one to use? Why?

3. What are the pros and cons of using corporal punishment as a means of changing Nicholas's behavior as the principal did? How effective is any form of punishment when used alone as a means of control? Under what circumstances can punishment be effective?

4. How might Arlene have employed any of the following behavior modification techniques? (1) the contingency contract; (2) the token economy; (3) time out and/or response cost; (4) group social reinforcement procedures.

5. At what level of Maslow's need hierarchy is Nicholas primarily operating? At what levels are other key persons in the case operating, such as Arlene, the principal, and Nicholas's parents? What are boredom and frustration from a motivational standpoint? How might they relate to Nicholas's high I.Q. and aggressive behavior?

6. What is a gifted child? Is Nicholas gifted? Why do gifted children sometimes become bored and frustrated? What can be done in such cases?

7. How effectively did Arlene handle her conference with Nicholas's parents during the home visit? What parent involvement techniques are available to teachers and schools, and which ones might have been most helpful in this situation?

8. What factors in the home environment contribute to Nicholas's behavior at school? How do factors such as parental warmth, expectations for the child's behavior, and modeling of human relations skills influence the child's behavior at school? What can be done to involve the parents as change agents?

9. What administrative leadership style is exhibited by Arlene's principal? Is he mostly a "supporting," "coaching," "delegating," or "directing" type leader? How would you like to work with him? Why? Should Arlene have reported Nicholas' aggressive acts to him?

10. What does Ms. Glaros's remark to the effect that "Nick doesn't need to see a counselor because he is not crazy" tell you about her? Explain.

11. Describe a plan that will be most effective for Arlene to use in dealing with Nicholas. Show how the plan will not only be best for Nicholas and Arlene but will also be best for the other stakeholders in the situation: (1) Nicholas's peers; (2) Nicholas's parents; (3) the principal; (4) Nicholas's future teachers.

KEEPING YOUR EYES OPEN

Michael Groza is a 22-year-old senior at Zane State College and is majoring in elementary education. He is currently serving an internship in an eighth-grade class at Ft. Henry Middle School, a multicultural urban middle school located in Bridgeton, a city on the Ohio River about 20 miles from his college.

Bridgeton is an old city which was settled by the early explorers as a port city. It quickly grew into a thriving community because of its location. It now has a population of approximately 85,000, approximately 50 percent white, 20 percent African-American, 15 percent Hispanic, and 15 percent Asian-American.

As Michael drove to Bridgeton to report for his internship experience, he was awestruck by the rural scenery surrounding his college town. However, as he neared the outskirts of Bridgeton, it seemed as if he were entering another world. The winding road on which he had been driving widened into an access road entering an expressway stretching over what once had been a thriving manufacturing center.

But now the many deserted brick skeletons of what once were active, busy, industrial factories that manufactured electrical apparatus, glassware, batteries, good china, metal parts, and other products gave testimony to the death of the economy of this area. The demise of these factories was also apparent in the boarded-up doors, broken windows, and graffiti exterior of these buildings.

As Mike's route took him closer to the downtown section close to the river, he came upon what had once been an affluent suburban area dotted with beautiful mansions. But these mansions had long ago been converted to apartment houses which were in bad repair, with chipped paint, broken windows, and trash scattered about the bare lawns, with no evidence of plant life with the exception of a few clumps of weeds here and there.

Later, the mansions gave way to decaying tenement apartment complexes, small dilapidated houses, and abandoned brick buildings which had once been successful manufacturing plants, now with broken windows and boarded-up doors. After driving for three or four miles on the expressway, he saw a sign pointing to the exit ramp that led to Fort Henry Middle school. Obviously, some of his students would be residents of the area he had just driven through.

As he entered the parking lot behind the school, he noticed that several sections of the chain link fence were pulled apart and leaning askew. The cement driveway was cracked with chunks of cement uprooted. The back of the large, old building was covered with graffiti, and selected words, evidently obscene, had been painted over with black paint. The paint on the wooden trim was discolored and chipped off.

Mike opens the back door of the school and walks into the hallway. He is gratified to notice that the hallway has been recently painted a light blue, and the composition floors are clean and shiny. He follows the room numbers to the classroom to which he has been assigned, and sees that his supervising teacher is already in the room.

MIKE Ms. Rudner, I'm Michael Groza. I've been assigned to you for my internship.

MS. RUDNER Welcome, Michael. Please call me Roz. I'm delighted that you're here. I requested an intern this semester because I'm introducing a reading and writing workshop into my English curriculum. Our classes have met for two weeks, and the pupils have pretty much gotten into the swing of things.

MIKE It's nice to meet you, Roz. I go by Mike. I'm really glad that you're using reading and writing workshops. We studied those strategies in my reading and language arts methods courses. Based on my limited knowledge of them, I think they are the approaches I'd like to use. Now I'll have an opportunity to actually use them.

ROZ Good. How about you observing all my classes this week? Then if you feel comfortable with the idea, you can take over one of the classes next Monday. It might be a better experience for you to do the writing workshop. It's more open to innovations than the reading workshop. I think both reading and writing workshops are especially appropriate for a school population like ours.

MIKE In what way?

ROZ Well, our classes generally follow the ethnic make-up of Bridgeton. For instance, the writing class you'll be teaching comprises fifteen whites, six African-Americans, five Hispanics and four Asian-Americans. There's a wide range of ability among the pupils. By using the workshop approach, we can allow each of our pupils to work at his or her level in both reading and writing. That allows each of them to have an opportunity to succeed.

MIKE I didn't expect to jump into teaching so quickly, but I'm delighted that I can. The writing workshop's fine with me, because I became really interested in it when we studied about it in our language arts method class. But I haven't ever taught before, so I may goof up a little here and there.

ROZ I'm not worried, Mike. Both of us are going to be operating on a trial-and-error basis for a while. But when you experiment with new teaching strategies, that's the only way you can go. Our school district has an observation instrument we use. I have a copy here in my desk. Yes, here it is. [Instrument shown at end of case] Go over it briefly, and it will give you a clue regarding the things that we'll discuss about your teaching. I'll fill it out as I observe your class Monday.

MIKE That's fine with me. Let's go for it.

Soon, the first-period eighth-grade class comes into the room visiting with each other, pushing, shoving, and generally acting like eighth-grade students. Mike's mind automatically calls up the name of the singing group, "Motley Crew." This class exemplifies a motley crew. There are 31 pupils. Their dress ranges from Ivy League to dire straits. The majority are wearing either boots or basketball shoes. Long unwashed hair seemes to be the norm, along with gold jewelry and tattoos.

ROZ   All right, class. Please take your seats and quiet down. I want to introduce you to Mr. Groza, our intern from Zane State College. *[Uproar from the class, "Zane State College, Rah, Rah, Rah." Jeers from the boys, "A college gentleman. Woowee, a brain! Look at the suit and tie." From the girls, "Whatta hunk. Sexy. Spend some time with me, Mr. Groza."*

ROZ   That's enough! You're being rude and you all know better than that. *[The class quiets down quickly.]* Mr. Groza's your intern for the remainder of this semester and he'll be in charge of your writing class beginning next week.

STUDENTS   "All right! Great! What a writing teacher! I'm gonna like writing!"

MIKE   I'm happy to be here and I'm looking forward to working with you in the writing class.

ROZ   We're happy you're here, too, Mr. Groza. It's always good to have interns from Zane.

It's Monday and Mike arrives at school earlier and more excited than usual. Today he's taking over the writing workshop. He's studied the various components of the workshop and mentally rehearsed the strategies he plans to use throughout the period. By mutual agreement, Roz will to be a silent observer of the class and not interfere in the instruction or classroom management. During this period, Roz will evaluate his performance using the Teaching Observation Form they have already discussed.

After what seems to be an eternity to Mike, the buses arrive and the pupils in his writing class begin to enter the room.

JAMAL   You're the man today, ain't ya', Mr. Groza!

MIKE   Yes, I'm the man, Jamal. Thanks for remembering.
       [Other pupils enter, greet Mike and visit with each other. When the bell rings, Mike starts the class]

MIKE   Let's get right to work now, class. During the mini-lesson this morning I'm going to review for you the three ways that direct quotations are written. In reviewing your writing Friday, I noticed that some of you aren't punctuating direct quotations correctly. I'm going to write some examples on the board, and I want you to copy them in your writing journal. *[Mike writes these examples on the board:*

> *Mary said, "Wait for me."*
> *"Wait for me," said Mary.*
> *"Wait," said Mary, "until I come."*

[As he is completing the third sentence, a rubber eraser hits the chalkboard just to the left of his head. Mike whirls around.]

MIKE   *[Angrily]* Who threw that?

TOD   Cathy threw it.

CATHY   I did not. You know I didn't, Mr. Groza!

JASON   Tod did it!

TOD   Not me.

> *[Several pupils begin to accuse other pupils. Some stand up and point to others]*

MIKE   Stop it! Get back in your seats and be quiet.

> *[After order is restored, angrily]* There will be no more throwing of objects! You know that's against the rules! *[Pause and quiet]*
>
> Now, look at these three sentences. These are basically the only way you can write direct quotations. Notice that in Sentence 1, the direct quotation's at the end of the sentence. In Sentence 2, the direct quotation's at the beginning of the sentence. In Sentence 3, the name of the speaker separates the words of the direct quotation. The end punctuation's inside the punctuation marks and the first word of the direct quotation's capitalized.

MATT   I always put the periods outside the marks. Why's that wrong?

MIKE   Punctuation marks are called conventions. Because true language is the spoken language, punctuation marks were invented by printers after the printing press was invented. Eventually, rules for punctuation were agreed on by all the printers and became the accepted rules. This doesn't mean they're better than other ways, Matt, like your putting the periods outside the punctuation marks, but they're the accepted way. Other ways aren't accepted by writers and printers, which, I guess, does make them wrong. One of the things we'll do in writing workshop is to learn accepted grammar, usage, and mechanics like punctuation.

SID   Why can't we just go ahead and punctuate the way we want to?

MIKE   You can, if you want to have points taken off for doing it incorrectly.

SID   But you just said that the conventional way isn't really more correct than other ways.

MIKE   But it is the only way accepted by literate people, and I'm trying hard to make you all literate. *[Looks at his watch]* I've already exceeded the time set aside for the mini-lesson, so we need to go on to the state of the class conference. As I call your name, if you're writing a first draft, say *one*. For a second draft, say *two*. If you're conferencing, revising, proofing or publishing, just say the word. Ted?

TED   The word.

MIKE   What?

TED   You said if we're conferencing, revising, proofing, or publishing, just say the word. I'm revising, so I said, "The word."

MIKE   Very funny. You're the type of commodian who needs to be flushed. *[Appreciative laughter from the class]*

> Cathy?

LEE   Conference

> *[Mike polls each class member and indicates their activity for the day on the chart he has prepared. He records on the chart as follows:]*

STATE OF CLASS CHART

Names:	M	T	W	Th	F
Ted	RV				
Cathy	2				
Jamal	1				
Lee	C				

MIKE   Okay. Now we have 40 minutes to work on our writing. Let's get to work. Those of you who are conferencing with each other, do it quietly. Those of you who are conferencing with me, come to my desk one at a time. I'll see Lee first. *[Lee comes up and takes the seat next to Mike, and they begin to discuss his writing. Other conferencing pupils take their chairs and sit by their conferees. Mike is so absorbed in his conference with Lee that he fails to notice a paper airplane sailing from one side of the room to the other. [Tod leaves his seat and walks toward the pencil sharpener.]*

JAMAL   Ouch! What in hell wrong wit'chu, man? *[He jumps out of his seat and shoves Tod off balance]*

TOD   Watch it, Jamal.

JAMAL   You watch it, man. You kick me in the leg.

MIKE   *[Jumping up out of his seat]* What's going on back there?

JAMAL   This honkie jes' walk down the aisle and kick me in the leg.

TOD   He jumped out of his seat and shoved me halfway across the room.

JAMAL   You kick me again, man, and I break yo' head, Maybe I do it anyway jes' for sport.

TOD   I don't want no trouble with you, Jamal.

JAMAL   Then you jes' keep you hans and feet to yo'self.

MIKE   Tod, what're you doing out of your seat, anyway? You're supposed to be working on your second draft.

TOD   I needed to sharpen my pencil.

MIKE   You took sort of a long, out-of-the-way route to the pencil sharpener, didn't you? You go back to your seat. If you need to sharpen your pencil from now on, you ask permission first.

TOD   That's not fair! *[Looking at Ms. Rudner]* Ms. Rudner lets us sharpen our pencils without asking. You're treatin' us like babies. *[Ms. Rudner remains silent]*

MIKE   Maybe you don't kick people on your way to the pencil sharpener while Ms. Rudner is teaching. When you stop acting like a baby, I'll stop treating you like a baby—if, indeed, asking you to get permission to sharpen your pencil is treating you like a baby.

TOD   I didn't even kick Jamal. He just made that fuss to get me into trouble.

JAMAL   Yea, man. And pigs fly, too.

CYNTHIA   He did kick Jamal, Mr. Groza. I saw him.

TOD   You lie, Cynthia!

CYNTHIA   You're the liar, Tod!

MIKE   O.K. That's enough, both of you. Tod, go back to your seat and get to work. *[Mike goes back to his conference with Lee. As Mike reads Lee's composition, two more paper airplanes fly across the room. Sid's reading a comic book and Juan has his head down on his desk with his eyes closed]*

KEVIN   *[Bursts into laughter even though he tries to control it]*

MIKE   What's going on, Kevin? You and Jason are supposed to be conferencing.

KEVIN   We are, Mr. Groza.

MIKE   Then what's all that laughter about? That's not part of your conferencing, is it?

KEVIN   It's my fault, Mr. Groza. I told Jason a joke.

MIKE   Then you go back to your seat, Jason, and you boys can work alone. You don't seem to be able to work together quietly. *[He notices Juan's head down on the desk]* Juan, what are you supposed to be doing?

JUAN   I'm writin' the first draft.

MIKE   Then get your head up off the desk and write!

JUAN   I'm tryin' to think of what to write.

MIKE   Then do it sitting up so that I'll know you're not taking a nap. Mike goes back to his desk and continues to work with Lee. *[Almost immediately, he hears talking and follows the sound. Juan and Kevin are talking across the aisle]*

MIKE   Juan! Kevin! You're not working. Bring your writing journals to me. I want to see how much you've done. You're both supposed to be working on a first draft today. Let me see how much you've written.

JUAN   I didn't write nothing yet. I've been thinkin' in my head what to write.

MIKE   And what did your head decide you should write?

JUAN   I'm still thinkin'.

MIKE   Well, you've been thinking now for 20 minutes. You probably need to begin writing some of your thoughts down on paper. How about you, Kevin? Let me see your journal.

KEVIN   I've been thinkin' too.

MIKE   But you don't have anything written yet?

KEVIN   No.

MIKE   Well, then. You probably don't have any time to waste talking to people, do you?

KEVIN   No.

MIKE   Good. I'll expect to see you begin on that first draft soon.

CATHY   Mr. Groza, you've been conferencing with Lee for almost 20 minutes! The conferences are only supposed to last for five minutes. We're worried that we won't get a chance to conference with you today!

MIKE   You're right, Cathy. I've spent too much time with Lee. There've been too many interruptions. I'll finish with Lee quickly and still have time to meet with the rest of you. Sorry I got off track. Thanks for reminding me.

CATHY   Good. Thank you.

MIKE   O.K., Lee. I think the main thing you need to do is make the beginning of your story more interesting. You can ask the reader a question, or make a dramatic statement, or jump right into the high point of the action. You also need to show the reader that you're angry rather than write, "I was angry." Then you can begin to tell about the events that led up to the action. Is there anything else you want to ask about while you're here?

LEE   No, it's the beginning of the paper that's weak. Those're really good ideas, Mr. Groza. I already know what I'm going to do with the beginning of the story, and that'll give me an chance to show the reader that I'm angry. Thanks for your help!

MIKE   Anytime, Lee. That's why I'm here. Cathy, come on over, and we'll see what you need to do next.

[Just as Cathy is walking toward the desk, a marble rolls across the floor]

MIKE   *[Angrily]* I saw that Jason! You come up here!

JASON   Sorry. That dropped out of my hand as I was gettin' up from my desk.

MIKE   Good try, Jason, but I saw what happened! You deliberately rolled that marble across the floor! I think you'll have to lose about five points on your writing grade to pay for the disruption.

JASON   That ain't fair, Mr. Groza! Since class started this morning, a fight happened between Jamal and Tod, Kevin's sailed three paper airplanes that you didn't even notice, Kevin and Juan've been talkin' the whole period, hardly no one's written a word in their writing journal, and nothin's happened to no one. And now, I roll a marble across the floor and get dropped five points for it. That ain't fair!

MIKE   You've no doubt heard about the straw that broke the camel's back. Your rolling of the marble was that straw. I've been working ever since the period started to have the pupils in this class behave themselves and get to work. Finally, just as things seemed to be settling down, you rolled the marble. Maybe that's why you rolled it. If nothing else, your five points off represent a penalty for using bad judgement and having bad timing.

JASON   That still ain't fair! *[Turning around]* Ms. Rudner, that's not fair, is it?

ROZ   Jason, I'm not here today. I promised Mr. Groza that I would observe his class today, but wouldn't say anything or participate in any way. I've said something in response to your question, but I'll say no more.

MIKE   Thank you, Ms. Rudner. Now, we have just five minutes left, which is how much time we schedule for group sharing. Who has something he or she'd like to share with the group?

LEE   *[After a long period of silence]* I'd like to share my story. I changed the opening as you suggested.

MIKE   That's quick work, Lee. I'm anxious to hear how you changed it. The floor's yours.

LEE   This story's called, "My Inconsiderate Sister." *[Reads aloud]*

MY INCONSIDERATE SISTER

As I was eating breakfast yesterday morning, I looked up and saw my sister coming down the stairway. She was wearing my brand new sweater. "Dammit, I thought. Why's she have to wear my clothes without even asking me if it's O.K.? I haven't even worn that sweater myself yet."

This is my main problem with my sister. She's inconsiderate about my things. Otherwise, she's a good big sister. My friends think she's really pretty, and they think she's very nice. She has many friends in her class at school. She also belongs to many groups and is in charge of some of them. So the people she works with must like her.

I have to admit that she's nice to me. When something bad happens to me and I'm sad, she always comes to my room and talks with me about it and helps me realize that I'm still O.K. When I need help with my homework, she's always willing to explain it to me. She also comes to see my team play baseball and cheers for us. Now that I've thought about my sister and all the nice things she does for me, I've decided that maybe I should be glad that she can wear some of my clothes. I should probably tell her that she can wear any of my clothes anytime she wants to. As nice as she is to me, if I get angry because she wears my new sweater, I would be an inconsiderate brother.

JAMAL   *[Applauding]* Great story, my man! You sound like a real writer.

CATHY   Yes, Lee. I liked it a lot! It was clever how you changed your opinion when you began to think what your sister is really like. I liked the beginning, too. It really lets the reader know you are mad.

      [The bell rings]

MIKE   Well, we timed it perfectly. Think about your writing when you're at home this evening. We'll have the same schedule tomorrow. You have time for a five-minute break while the other classes change. When you return to the room, Ms. Rudner'll resume her role as teacher for your reading workshop next period, and I'll be the silent observer. *[The pupils leave the class for their five-minute break]*

ROZ   *[To Mike]* You're welcome to contribute to the reading workshop, Mike, whenever the spirit moves you. What do you think of your first day of teaching?

MIKE   I think I screwed up royally in many different areas. Basically, I'm disappointed in myself. What did you think of my first day of teaching?

ROZ   I thought you did what most first-day teachers would do. You did some things right and some things wrong. And I'm optimistic that over the course of the semester you'll increasingly do more things right and fewer things wrong.

      I've got to get ready for the reading workshop now. Can we talk about your writing workshop after the last period today?

MIKE   Yes, I'd appreciate the advice.

ROZ   Great. See you then.

After the sixth-period class has ended and all the pupils have gone, Roz and Mike are sitting in their classroom.

ROZ   Well, how would you evaluate your performance this morning, Mike?

MIKE   As I mentioned to you, I'm disappointed. I let the class get out of hand several times. It just seemed to me that so many things were happening at once that I couldn't keep track of them all.

ROZ   A lot of things happen in the classroom at once, and it isn't easy to keep track of everything that's going on.

MIKE   Definitely. But today, there were a lot of things that happened that I could've and should've stopped before they got started.

ROZ   Why do you think you let them go without stopping them?

MIKE   I guess it was because they were all happening at once. I wasn't able to attend to all of them.

ROZ   Is there something you can do to help yourself attend to many different events at the same time?

MIKE   *[Long pause]* There must be. You're able to do it.

ROZ   While you were teaching, I filled out the observation form that I gave you this morning. Let's go over it and maybe you'll find some class management strategies that you can use. *[Hands Mike a completed copy of the Teaching Observation Form]*

ROZ   As you can see, Mike, I evaluated you as acceptable or better on all the topics except those under classroom management. I thought your help for individual pupils was relevant to writing, and your obvious interest in all the students was impressive. To me, those are two of the most important factors on the list. I think you have the potential to achieve an excellent rating on all these topics if you can develop effective strategies in classroom management. Do you agree?

MIKE   That's my goal, and I think I can achieve it with your help. Do you have any suggestions that will help me improve my classroom management?

ROZ   The first item under classroom management is awareness of classroom behavior. I gave you the lowest rating on this item. Jason was right. Many examples of unacceptable behavior took place in the class that you didn't even notice.

MIKE   Did you notice them?

ROZ   Yes, I did. But our agreement was that I don't take any part in the class. Besides, you won't learn where you need help if you aren't allowed to get in trouble. Look at all the things you learned about yourself in just 50 minutes of teaching.

MIKE   Yes, I can see that my major problems are awareness of what's happening in the class, being constant and fair in my discipline, and redirecting unacceptable behavior. I guess the awareness part is most important, because I think that was the basic cause of all my other classroom management problems.

ROZ   Yes, definitely. If you don't know what's going on, you can't do much about it. Also, in redirecting behavior, be sure that you don't scold pupils in front of the class. Just tell them to get to work on whatever their assignment is. In that way, you don't offend the pupils, yet you focus their attention on why they are here in school. They know they're supposed to do schoolwork at school.

MIKE   I really appreciate your advice. I see what you're saying. It makes a lot of sense.

ROZ   Good. Now, before you leave, I want you to write down what classroom management strategies you're going to use in your writing workshop tomorrow to become aware of all the things happening in the classroom and how you plan to handle them.

Teaching Observation Form

BRIDGETON MIDDLE SCHOOL

Teacher: <u>Michael Groza</u>   Date: <u>9/12/94</u>   Class: <u>Writing Workshop</u>   Period: <u>1</u>
Observed by: <u>Ms. Rudner</u>
Ratings: 1 - Poor, needs improvement; 2 - Weak; 3 - Acceptable; 4 Very good;
      5 - Excellent

Topic	Rating
A. Teaching Procedures	
1. Presentation of lesson	4
2. Good motivational techniques	3
3. Good questioning techniques	3
4. Provided for individual differences	3
5. Used a variety of activities	3
6. Clarity of objectives	4
7. Relevance of lesson to objectives	5
8. Overall effectiveness of lesson	3
B. Classroom Management	
9. Awareness of misbehavior	1
10. Consistency in handling misbehavior	1
11. Fair and consistent discipline	1
12. Redirects behavior rather than scolding	2
13. Disciplines with dignity	3
14. Maintains good classroom organization	3
15. Demonstrates interest in all pupils	5

QUESTIONS

1. Describe several ways the writing workshop differs from the traditional approach to teaching writing in the middle school. What are the advantages of a writing workshop? the disadvantages?

2. What are the differences between intrinsic and extrinsic views of motivation? Does the writing workshop focus on intrinsic or extrinsic motivation techniques? Explain.

3. In writing workshops pupils may be required to include examples of specific writing genre, but they choose their own writing selections. How can Mike evaluate each pupil's writing proficiency fairly? How can he report his evaluations to the pupils' parents? How can he defend a grade that a pupil or parent protests?

4. What social class, racial, and home environmental differences exist among the pupils in Mike's writing workshop? Identify some examples of how these differences affected both student and teacher behavior in Mike's class. Does Mike deal with these differences acceptably? Explain.

5. Would you like to have Rosalyn Rudner as your supervising teacher? Why? Does she use a "supporting," "coaching," "delegating," or "directing" leadership style with Mike? Do you think this is an appropriate style to use? Explain.

6. What is Kounin's model of classroom management? What is "withitness" and how does it apply to the way Mike related to his class? What should Mike do differently?

7. What other models of classroom management could Mike have used with his class? How effective would (1) behavior modification, (2) teacher effectiveness training, (3) assertive discipline, or (4) reality therapy have been as methods of classroom management? Which would you recommend to Mike and why?

8. What other teaching methods could Mike have used that might have allowed him to be more aware of what the students in the class were doing? How might he have used visual aids to accomplish this purpose?

9. If you were to use a systematic observation schedule (e.g., Flanders Interaction Analysis) to observe Mike's interactions with his students, what conclusions would you draw? For example, what conclusions would you draw about the amount of teacher direct and indirect behavior? How do such interaction patterns relate to student achievement? What are some other systematic observation instruments that could be used to observe teacher–student interactions?

10. What could Mike's supervising teacher, Ms. Rudner, have done to make him aware of the types of behavior she planned to observe to help her evaluate his teaching?

11. How effectively has Mike planned for instruction? How clear are his objectives? How effective are his rule-setting and enforcement procedures? How adequate is the amount of "student-engaged time"? What improvements can Mike make?

12. What are some of the strategies that you think Mike will suggest to help him deal with the discipline problems in his class? How should he handle his writing workshop differently?

CASE **3**

TOKEN LEARNING

aplewood Elementary School is located in the quiet residential community of Midville, a New England community with a population of approximately 25,000. The student body of the school is primarily from middle class backgrounds, with an 80 percent white/20 percent African-American racial mix.

Sharon Davis has just received tenure in the school district by signing her current contract. She is a product of the College of Education at a nearby land-grant state university and is full of energy, enthusiasm, and ideas. Sharon is particularly happy to be teaching at Maplewood, since it is generally considered to be the best, most progressive school in the city. The physical plant is modern, up-to-date, and immaculately maintained.

Sharon is in her room the last day of preplanning talking to her friend, Mary Jean, who teaches second grade in a room down the hall. Although classes begin the following Monday, Sharon has her room and materials well-organized enough that she can stop and chat with Mary Jean.

SHARON I can't wait until Monday to meet my new third graders! I finally finished getting my materials together. At least I think I have.
MARY JEAN How many will you have this year?
SHARON Twenty-four. How about you?
MARY JEAN Nineteen—and I think that's plenty!
SHARON I know what you mean, but I think I can easily handle twenty-four this year. I'm going to use some of the techniques that I learned at State and have always wanted to try. Jessica [the building principal] has always wanted us to be on the same page as a faculty, with only a few experimental things going on that she approves in advance. Well, this year I told her that if I was going to teach twenty-four third graders I would like to use behavior mod procedures, and she said that made sense.
MARY JEAN You mean behavior modification classroom management procedures?
SHARON Yes, but I mean Precision Teaching—both academically and discipline-wise. You know, the token economy approach, using the Premack Principle and all!
MARY JEAN Boy, you sound like you are really into it—using the behavioral lingo! Weren't those behavioral techniques popular back in the seventies and early eighties? I don't know of any other teachers here at Maplewood that are using

behavioral techniques, except maybe for some of the special ed people. I'm sort of surprised that Jessica approved them, since she's always seemed to be kind of a humanist.

SHARON   She agreed with me that token economies have a long history and seemed to work well. I also pointed out that Sherrie and Arica [*two other teachers*] are both using Assertive Discipline, which is very similar to behavior modification. Just more emphasis on punishment. Jessica agreed with me that behavior modification is a more humanistic approach with its emphasis on positive reinforcement.

MARY JEAN   [*With a puzzled look*] Yes, I guess so, but—well, I always felt like it was a bit contrived. You know, like you're looking for techniques to manipulate the kids with. Like the praise and the tokens were just bribes to get the kids to do what you want them to. [*Pause*] I guess what I'm trying to say is that I want Stacey [*Mary Jean's daughter*] to clean her room because she wants to, not because there's some external reward for doing it.

SHARON   That's fine, but what if Stacey never finds it self-rewarding to clean her room?

MARY JEAN   I see what you mean. Well, I guess she and I would have to talk about it.

SHARON   And you'd shape her behavior by cuing her as to what behavior you wanted, then by giving her social reinforcement in the form of attention, affection, and approval for doing it. Then after she's learned to do it on her own you'd phase out those reinforcers and let Stacey receive her reinforcement from her pride in living in a clean room.

MARY JEAN   Wow! You sure have thought this through!

SHARON   [*Smiling*] I have. A lot of what we teach kids are things they don't find self-rewarding. You have to use behavior modification procedures to get them working, and, once they find the learning activities to be interesting, gradually fade out the original reinforcers.

MARY JEAN   That sure sounds easy when you say it, Sharon, but I wonder—how will you begin?

SHARON   As I told Jessica, the whole program will flow out of a social studies project I will plan with the kids. We are going to create Kidville. Get it?

MARY JEAN   Yes, that's cute! Rhymes with Midville. But how?

SHARON   The whole idea grew out of how I was going to teach a unit on learning about money, so it wouldn't be boring. We are going to create a token economy with play money, a ban, city government, and any other kind of capitalist enterprise the kids can think up.

MARY JEAN   Boy, that will take a lot of work, Sharon!

SHARON   Yes, I know that but I want to do it! I'm really excited about it! Cherie will be my aide again this year and I think she has a good grasp of what I'm going to try to do and how she will fit in. I'm also going to try to involve at least two parent volunteers. That'll be a six-to-one ratio of kids to adults, and should work out well in terms of collecting behavioral data, handing out reinforcement, and giving the children individual attention.

MARY JEAN   Sharon, I am really impressed! I had no idea you were going to do anything this ambitious this year!

It is late afternoon of the same day. Sharon sits around a table in the classroom with her teacher aide, Cherie Sawyer, and her two parent volunteers, Marie Reynolds and Mitzi Clark. Sharon looks at the two parents with a smile as she speaks.

SHARON   Marie and Mitzi, I can't tell you how much we appreciate your helping us out this year. It would be difficult for Cherie and I to do what we plan to do without your help.

MARIE   Thanks, Mrs. Davis, I just hope. . .

SHARON   [Interrupting] Marie, please call me Sharon. I consider us a team—equals. I'm just the team leader. I think you'll find that the children will be calling all of us "teacher" before long.

MARIE   Thanks, Sharon. That certainly makes me feel welcome and at home. But what do you want us to do?

SHARON   We are going to use a system called behavior modification, which was developed by a psychologist named Skinner many years ago.

MITZI   Oh, I think I remember reading about this in a magazine once. Isn't it based on the idea of rewarding good behavior and punishing bad behavior? Like if a child gets a good grade on a paper or behaves well, you should be sure to praise him.

SHARON   That's partly correct. Skinner believed that rewarding, or reinforcing behavior as he called it, is better than punishment. He calls for us to be clear and specific about what behavior we think is important and then to positively reinforce small steps in the right direction. However, he said to try to ignore undesirable behavior and look for opportunities to reinforce desirable behavior that is opposite of the undesirable behavior.

MITZI   [With a confused look] What do you mean "positively reinforce small steps?"

MARIE   That confuses me, too. How do you decide whether a behavior is desirable or undesirable, and how do you reinforce?

SHARON   [Looking at Cherie and smiling] We've got a lot to go over and a lot of this will have to develop as we go along. We will have to plan with the children as well as we go along.

MARIE   [With surprise] With the children? But they're only third-graders. Are they really old enough to make decisions?

SHARON   [Smiling] We adults will have the final decision but, as I think you'll see, we can learn a lot from the children about what motivates them and how they think. [Looking at Mitzi] Mitzi, you're frowning and look confused. What's the matter?

MITZI   I'm not sure how to put it, but it's this business of reinforcing children for their good behavior and work. Aren't we really trying to bribe them for their good behavior? I was just thinking that I want my three children to behave well in the classroom and make good grades because they want to. Not because they'll get a reward for doing it.

SHARON   [Sighing and looking at Cherie] We do have a lot to go over and I guess there is no time like the present to begin. [Pause] Let's start with Skinner's basic assumptions and then go to the steps involved in modifying behavior.

It is the third day of classes. The students are seated on the floor listening to Sharon as she sits in a chair talking to them. Cherie sits in another chair a short distance to Sharon's left. The two parent volunteers are seated on the floor behind the children.

SHARON   Now, children, I want to ask you a question and I want you to think hard before you hold up your hand to speak. The question is, why do people work? Think about people you know, like your parents, and ask yourself why they work.

     [All the children's hands go up and some wave their arms back and forth to indicate their eagerness to answer. Others raise themselves up higher so they can be seen by the teacher.]

SHARON   Okay, children, one at a time. I know you all have something you want to say. Toni Sue, let's start with you.

TONI SUE   My daddy goes to work so he can make money. He says he does it for all of us so we can have things like clothes and toys.

SHARON   That's very good, Toni Sue. That's why a lot of us work. Jerry?

JERRY   My mom says she works because she loves it. She says she'd do it even if they didn't pay her. Just because it's fun.

MIKE   *[Without raising his hand]* Yeah, I'll bet! She wouldn't do it very long if they didn't pay her!

JERRY   *[Frowning]* She would too, stupid!

SHARON   That's enough boys. Remember our rule about raising your hand before talking, Mike. Jerry, I really appreciated how you and Toni Sue raised your hands before you spoke. *[Pause]* But tell me about children. Why don't they get paid for the work they do? Billy?

BILLY   Because we're not big enough. They ought to pay us for going to school!

MIKE   Yeah! We have to give up TV to go to school! *[The children laugh and voice their agreement with Mike.]*

SHARON   But to get paid for going to school you have to produce something or provide a service. Linda?

LINDA   Teacher, what's a service?

SHARON   Have you ever gone to a doctor or a dentist? Have you ever seen a policeman or fireman do their jobs? They don't make anything like a car or a toaster but they provide services that other people want. Terri Ann?

TERRI ANN   A repairman came to our house and fixed our TV yesterday.

SHARON   Very good, Terri Ann. That's a very important service, isn't it? *[The children agree very loudly.]*

SHARON   Billy?

BILLY   *[Enthusiastically]* That's very important! I'd miss my cartoons and that wouldn't be cool at all! *[All the children smile, laugh, and agree in unison with Billy.]*

It is one week later and again the class is arranged in a semi-circle on the floor while Sharon leads the discussion during social studies. Mitzi and Marie sit in the back of the room on chairs with Cherie. All three are intently observing a different child and making tallies in cells on a baseline data chart.

SHARON   Now, children, we've been talking for a week about why people work and you all feel that it would be fun to have jobs like your parents do and make money. Billy?

BILLY   You forgot that we want to spend the money and buy things the way they do too.

SHARON   *[Laughing]* I knew you'd say that, Billy!

BILLY   Yeah! Cool!

SHARON   Well why don't we develop our own town? We can all have jobs in the town and make money. *[The children agree enthusiastically.]*

SHARON   Billy?

BILLY   Do you mean real money?

SHARON   No, we can make our own. But we can use it to buy things in class, just like real money. Toni Sue?

TONI SUE   What kinds of things?

SHARON   Each one of you can have a different job just like adults and bring different things in to sell. One of you could be the banker, for example, and be in charge of lending out the money. *[Billy interrupts by yelling "Me" as he holds up his hand.]* We can decide that later, Billy. Just let me finish. *[Pause]* Some of you might want to open your own business like selling candy. Terrie Ann?

TERRIE ANN   Where would we get the money to buy the candy?

SHARON   From the bank. Each of you would get $20 per week to spend, save, or purchase things for your business. As you earn money from your business, you would have to decide what to do with it. You could buy something with it or perhaps open up another business. Mike?

MIKE   Or even loan it to someone else?

SHARON   Yes, you certainly could and earn interest. Toni Sue?

TONI SUE   What's interest?

SHARON   We'll go into all that. Right now let's talk about what kinds of good and services each of you might like to provide. Mike?

MIKE   Could I be a policeman?

SHARON   Yes, that's a important service. With all that money around we'll certainly need police.

It is Friday afternoon and all the children have boarded buses to go home. Sharon, Cheri, Mitzi, and Marie sit around a table engaged in their weekly planning session.

SHARON   How do you feel about the way Kidville is coming, Marie? Particularly how the children are participating in the planning?

MARIE   I would never have believed it! They act like little adults! *[All four women laugh.]*

SHARON   I've taken the ideas from this morning's discussion, you know, about what they are going to spend money for, and come up with three categories: privileges, penalties, and services. Privileges will be things like being line leader for lunch, carrying messages, and working in the library. Penalties will be "response cost" for things like handing in a sloppy paper, teasing or pushing other children, or inappropriate talking. Services will be things like washing the blackboard, straightening the art area, or being the door holder. I'll have to make a complete list under each of these three categories and then attach a money value to each. Of course, the students will buy the privileges, get paid for the services, and get fined for the penalties.

CHERIE   *[Enthusiastically]* I think it's all going great. Just this week they have learned the meaning of *deposit, withdrawal, balance,* and *interest.* They seem to learn the terms without any real effort.

MARIE   Yes, who would believe that these kids would be capable of creating a town like Kidville, and create jobs that they willingly do such as mail delivery, garbage collection, and street cleaning.

MITZI   Can you believe Toni Sue?! She's quite the capitalist with her candy store. She hoards every penny!

SHARON   Okay, enough of the good things. Problems?

CHERIE   Yes, some of the kids aren't really participating. Mike, for example, just hoards his money and then quits working until he runs out. Also, Toni Sue swears that someone stole money from her candy store when she wasn't looking.

SHARON   Just like real life. I guess we'll just have to get our Kidville police department to investigate.

CHERIE   How are they going to get paid for their services, Sharon?

SHARON   Just wait! I'm going to introduce the concept of taxes tomorrow! *[All four women laugh.]*

SHARON   All in all, I think Kidville is coming along very nicely. I've never seen a group of more motivated third-graders, and I think we're all doing a great job of integrating practically everything we teach into the Kidville program. *[Cherie, Mitzi, and Marie all voice their agreement and congratulate one another.]*

It is the afternoon of the last day of classes before Christmas vacation. The children have left for the day and Sharon sits in the office of Jessica Mason, the school principal. Jessica closes her office door.

JESSICA   Sharon, how's the Kidville project coming along? I've been so busy that I've only been able to slip into your room a couple of times so far this year. The children certainly seemed busy and motivated by what they were doing.

SHARON   Cherie, Marie, Mitzi, and I all enjoy it more than anything we've tried before. Well, that is, Cherie and I—this is the first time for Mitzi and Marie. Most important though, the kids are learning a lot.

JESSICA   Things about the world of business and careers?

SHARON   No, we've found ways of tying in practically everything we teach, from math, to science, to geography.

JESSICA   Any problems?

SHARON   Not that I know of. Do you know of anything?

JESSICA   That's why I asked you to come see me, Sharon. There have been a couple of things.

SHARON   *[Frowning]* Oh?

JESSICA   Well, to begin with, I had a visit from Mitzi last week. She thinks that charting baseline data is a waste of time and thinks that her time would be better spent working with the children.

SHARON   Why didn't she tell me this?

JESSICA   She likes you and didn't want to upset you. She thinks you can only see the strengths of the program. Also, I've had at least three parents come and talk to me about their concerns.

SHARON   *[With surprise]* Really! Who?

JESSICA   Toni Sue Sanders's mother for one.

SHARON   Toni Sue! That's really unbelievable! That child seems to be getting more out of Kidville than anyone! Why you ought to see how serious and involved she is in running her candy store and the way she saves her profits.

JESSICA   That's what's bothering Mrs. Sanders. That's all Toni Sue is interested in. She feels that a child as young as Toni Sue should be exploring more than the world of business. I think Mrs. Sanders and her husband want her exposed more to the arts—music, dancing, painting, and the like. They feel she is becoming too one-dimensional. *[Pause]* Understand, Sharon, that many of the parents like what you're doing, but there *is* a vocal opposition and perhaps you should consider what they're saying.

SHARON   What are they really saying, Jessica?

JESSICA   Well, to put it in my own words, I guess what they're saying is that they want their children to develop their own ambitions and explore their own potentials—not have their behavior shaped by a teacher and her team who decide for them. *[Pause]* I think they are also saying that their children are motivated to do what they are doing, running a candy store for example, for the wrong reason.

SHARON   *[Angrily]* And what's that?

JESSICA   For rewards external to the activity instead of doing things for their own self-reward. *[Pause]* I guess that reminds me of my brother-in-law who has just retired to Florida with my sister. He spent over thirty years working at a post office job that he hated. The pay and fringe benefits were excellent he always said. But can you imagine doing something you dislike for that long because of the external rewards?

SHARON   No, I can't. I love teaching and really wouldn't want to do anything else at this time in my life. *[Pause]* However, Jessica, I must admit that at this point I am a very confused teacher. What do you think about all this? What do you think I should do?

JESSICA   Sharon, you know I think you are an excellent, dedicated, creative teacher and I'm not going to tell you to change what you are doing. I'm just giving you some feedback and I know you'll give it serious consideration.

SHARON   I appreciate you saying that, Jessica. However, let me ask the question in another way. What would you do if you were in my place?

JESSICA   That's a hard question to answer, since I think we have different teaching philosophies. I believe that our job as teachers is to help each child become strong enough so they can become independent people—learn to think for themselves and solve their own problems. I think that children need to have the opportunity to explore as many things as possible and discover for themselves what excites and motivates them. Then they ought to have the opportunity to develop themselves fully in those areas that excite and motivate them.

SHARON   But, Jessica, some children would never explore anything if you don't give them some guidance. They don't know what they want until you give them some direction. And what about all those things they often don't like but that society thinks they need to know to be effective citizens—like reading, writing, and arithmetic? You can sugar-coat many of the things they need to learn but aren't terribly enthusiastic about.

JESSICA   While I agree with you that you have to sugar-coat things that kids aren't interested in, I feel that if you really get to know the child—what the child is interested in, what he watches on TV and does after school—you can use those interests to design what you are teaching.

SHARON   But, Jessica, don't you see? That's what I've been doing in Kidville! I've tried to learn what kinds of things the kids *are* interested in and use them as reinforcers for what they *aren't* interested in.

JESSICA   Look at it this way, Sharon: maybe you are trying to shape the child to your curriculum, instead of shaping the curriculum to what you know about the child.

SHARON   [Nonplussed] I don't know. I guess I thought I was doing both.

JESSICA   Let me ask you to think about two things, Sharon, and then let's get together next week and discuss what you want to do. One, what are the weaknesses as well as the strengths of Kidville? Two, what changes, if any, do you want to make in your program?

Reinforcement Menu

MRS. DAVIS'S THIRD-GRADE CLASS

Privileges

Teacher Assistant	$ .20
Line Leader	.50
Secretary	.50
Special Art Attendance	2.00
Extra Activity Period	2.00
Library Work	1.50
Missing Special Activities	4.00
Messenger	.20
Morning Leader	.10

Penalties

Inappropriate Talking	$ .50
Sloppy Paper	.40
Teasing Others	2.00
Cafeteria/Recess Problems	4.00
Not Singing	.50
Hurting Others	1.00
Leaving Name Off Paper	.30
Messy Desk	.20
Not Listening	.30
Running In Hall	.50
Not Following Directions	.30
Fooling Around	.50

Services

Door Holder	$ .20
Board Washer	1.00
Sink Cleaner	1.20
Desk Checker	.50
Mail Person	.60
Reading Center Organizer	.50
Paper Shelves Organizer	.10
Art Area Organizer	.80
Math Center Organizer	.50
Teacher's Desk Organizer	.50

QUESTIONS

1. Is human motivation environmentally determined, as Skinner contends, or is it a reciprocal process between the individual and the environment, as Bandura argues? Or is the cause of human motivation a function of the way each individual perceives the world, as Rogers proposes?

2. Can one person motivate another, as the "carrot and stick" theory contends? Or does motivation emanate entirely from within the individual? Can a teacher do more to motivate a student than just find out what the student is interested in and use that so that student will choose to be motivated and participate?

3. What is the difference between the intrinsic and extrinsic models of motivation? How do they differ in terms of the cause and nature of human motivation, the kind of data that are appropriate for measuring motivation, and techniques for fostering motivational change? How do these differences apply to the ways that Sharon and Jessica look at human motivation?

4. What is operant conditioning? What assumptions does it make about the cause of behavior, the nature of learning, the kind of data that it is appropriate to collect on children, and how behavior is changed?

5. What is behavior modification? How is it similar to precision teaching, applied behavior analysis, contingency management, and programmed instruction? How is behavior modification used with groups as well as individuals?

6. What is a token economy? What is the Premack Principle? How effective are token economies in working with students of varying ability and age levels? What relationships exist between intrinsic and extrinsic reinforcers? Can extrinsic reinforcers reduce the intrinsically reinforcing quality of an activity?

7. What is meant in operant conditioning by "fading out" one reinforcer and "fading in" another? How could Sharon take advantage of this technique?

8. How do you account for differences in the way human beings respond to attempts by teachers, parents, or employers to motivate them? Why are some people very difficult to "shape" with external reinforcers and others very easy? Why do some people primarily engage in activities that are self-reinforcing? Why would some people, like Jessica's brother-in-law, allow themselves to be "shaped" into performing a job that they dislike their entire work lives? How do belief systems like "internal-external attributions" or "internal-external locus of control" help explain such differences?

9. What is an "attribution training program?" How would such a program be similar to or different from Kidville?

10. How would humanistic psychologists like Maslow and Rogers view Kidville? To what extent would a program like Kidville foster the goal of self-actualization in children?

11. How effective has Sharon been in communicating with and involving the parents of her students? What parent involvement techniques can teachers use? What would you recommend to Sharon?

12. How effective is Sharon as a team leader? How well does she work with Cherie, Mitzi, and Marie?

13. How significantly would the curriculum and instruction be affected by the "teachers" spending so much time recording data and distributing tokens?

CASE 4

WHAT PRICE GLORY?

Howard Middle School is located in the southern city of Spartanville which has a population of approximately 125,000. Its student body is 71 percent white, 25 percent African-American, 3 percent Hispanic, and 1 percent Asian-American. The school's physical plant is only three years old and is well equipped.

Frank Duncan is in his second year of teaching social studies at Howard. It is early in a new school year and Frank is introducing a new unit to his second-period World History class of 30 sixth-grade students.

FRANK   We're starting a new unit today that you'll notice is entitled "The Glory that was Greece" in your text. The ancient Greeks lived long ago, before the time of Christ, and developed a civilization that is very important to us today. Much of our heritage in art, theater, philosophy, science, and even the idea of democracy itself comes from ancient Greece. *[Smiling]* Maybe one of the most important things the Greeks gave us was the Olympic Games. How many of you knew that the Olympics began in Greece? *[Many hands go up]*. Good. The unit exam and the Friday quizzes will be objective, just like before. In other words, they will be multiple-choice, matching, and fill-in-the-blank. No true or false since they didn't work well on the last test. *[Pause]* Now remember, it isn't enough to just read the material—you need to underline important names, dates, battles, and key terms in your text, since that's what you'll be tested on. Yes, Ann?

ANN   Is it OK if I make an outline instead of underlining?

FRANK   That's fine, if the items in your outline are specific enough. But be sure you review the outline just before each quiz. *[Picks up papers from his desk and begins to hand them out row by row]* Please take a copy of this outline map of ancient Greece. Begin to put city–states, major battles, and important sites on it as we talk about them. Be sure to put an X on the map to indicate the location of each important item. Put your name in the upper right hand corner now, please, so you won't forget. Your map is due on the day we take the unit exam, so be careful not to lose it. *[A few students groan]* Now open your notebooks and take some notes as I give a little introduction on how the Greek civilization began. Most of this information is not in your text. *[Students open their notebooks; some try to borrow papers, and others search for pencils. Two students, Bart and Bobby Joe, whisper to one another as Bart borrows a piece of paper from Bobby Joe.]*

BART *[Whispering]* You coming over tonight?

BOBBY JOE I think my mother will let me. Around six?

BART Yeah. Then you can eat lasagna with us.

BOBBY JOE Cool!

BART Yeah and I got into that bulletin board on my old man's computer. He's away so I'll tell Mom we want to play some computer games and I'll show you some of the pictures. You can't believe it!

BOBBY JOE You mean the sex pictures? Really?!

BART You better believe it!

BOBBY JOE What kind of . . .

FRANK Bart and Bobby Joe, I'd appreciate it very much if you two would stop talking so I can begin! *[Pause]* Now, to really understand where the Greeks originally came from, we need to go back to the year 1500 B.C. and the Island of Crete. Let's all get our outline maps out now and find the Island of Crete.

It is one week later and Frank is conducting a discussion of the Persian invasion of Greece.

FRANK The Great King of Persia, Darius, was succeeded by his son Xerxes. Like his father, Xerxes tried to invade Greece. *[Puts a map of ancient Greece on the overhead projector]* Now follow what I am showing you on your own outline map. *[Points to map]* This was the route that Xerxes decided to follow in bringing his army and navy down into Greece. *[Pointing]* Now right here was a narrow mountain pass called Thermopylae. Find it on your map and mark it with an X because a very important and famous battle was fought here. Yes, Ann?

ANN *[Pointing to her map]* Is it here or here, Mr. Duncan?

FRANK *[Walking to Ann's desk and pointing out the spot on her map]* Here. Have all the rest of you found it? *[Pause]* Now back to the story because it's an exciting one. Even though the Greeks heard that the Persians were coming to invade, you remember that I said that the city–states were rivals and didn't get along with one another. Well, they just kept arguing with one another and couldn't put their armies together to try to stop Xerxes. This was a real problem, since even if they united they were still outnumbered two or three to one by the Persians. So what do you think they did? Bart?

BART Well, it says in the book that the Spartans sent one of their two kings to stop them. Two kings doesn't make any sense though, Mr. Duncan. That's crazy! *[Several students laugh]*

FRANK Maybe so, by the way we look at things today, Bart, but Sparta had two kings and it seemed to work rather well. Remember, the Spartans were soldiers and seemed to be at war all of the time. While one king led the soldiers in battle, the other stayed at home to rule the people.

BART Cool! But what did they do when they weren't at war and both kings were home?

FRANK *[With controlled anger]* It worked out fine, Bart. Because of their traditions, the two kings had a clear division of labor and didn't usually fight with one another. Yes, Bobby Joe?

BOBBY JOE But isn't that like a lot of families where the mom and dad both want to wear the pants? The other day I heard my dad say . . .

FRANK *[Interrupting]* Bobby Joe, can't we get back to the Battle of Thermopylae?! The two kings of Sparta got along just fine with one another! Take my word for it! *[Pause]* Now, back to where we were. One of the kings of Sparta took his personal bodyguard of 300 soldiers to the Pass of Thermopylae. Greeks from other city–states joined them on the way, so he had maybe a thousand men at most to hold off over a hundred thousand Persians when he got there. Bart?

BART He must have been crazy. Sounds like Custer being outnumbered by the Sioux and the Cheyenne at Little Big Horn. I saw that on a movie on TV the other day and . . .

FRANK *[Interrupting angrily]* Bart, let's stick to the subject or we'll never get the Battle of Thermopylae fought.

BART *[Smirking]* Does that mean there won't be a quiz on Friday?

FRANK No it doesn't mean that, Bart, as you know perfectly well! Now back to the battle and I'd appreciate it if you raised your hand, Bart, before you speak out again! *[Pause]* So even though they were outnumbered, the Spartans held the Persians off for three days. How did they do that? Billy Bob?

BILLY BOB The pass was narrow. Only a few soldiers could get into it at a time to fight.

FRANK Right! Jerry?

JERRY Also, the Spartans trained all the time and were tougher soldiers than the Persians.

FRANK That's right! What else, Ann?

ANN The Spartans had bigger shields and longer spears.

FRANK Very good, Ann! So by choosing to hold a narrow mountain pass, Leonidas took advantage of his small army's strengths and didn't let the Persians use their advantage in terms of size. *[Pause]* So what happened? Bobby Joe, what do you think happened and why?

BOBBY JOE *[Frowning and looking down]* Oh, I don't know. I suppose the Spartans won.

FRANK Didn't you read the assignment?

BOBBY JOE *[Sullenly]* No.

FRANK *[With a slight edge]* May I ask why not?

BOBBY JOE I hate to read this stuff! It's a real pain!

FRANK *[With surprise]* What do you mean, Bobby Joe? Don't you enjoy learning about the heroism of soldiers who are vastly outnumbered but fight to the death for their cause?

BOBBY JOE I guess that's OK, it's just history—any kind! Who cares what a bunch of solders who carried shields like Captain America did two thousand years ago! *[Smirking]* Can you imagine how long the Spartans would hold that pass today against a division of Marines carrying machine guns? *[Several students laugh and voice their agreement]*

FRANK *[Angrily]* That's not funny, Bobby Joe! I didn't ask for any cute remarks! *[Pause]* Bobby Joe, do you mean you don't see any connection at all between what has happened in the past and what is happening today?

BOBBY JOE   *[Testily]* No! Not that means anything. *[Several hands go up]*

FRANK   Yes, Ann?

ANN   *[Hesitantly]* I sort of agree, Mr. Duncan. My mother is always telling me what things were like when she was my age and, well, things are just different today.

FRANK   *[Somewhat shaken]* Thanks, Ann. I guess I'm a bit surprised at what you're saying. Let me ask you all a question. How many of you see any value in studying history? *[About one-third of the class, including Ann, raise their hands. Others hesitate as though deciding.]* This is such an important issue that I think we need to spend the next class meeting discussing it. I'm going to come prepared with good reasons for studying history. All of you should come prepared with your arguments and we'll see what we can learn from one another.

It is the next class meeting, and Frank leads a discussion on the value of history as the second period begins.

FRANK   I'd like to proceed this way. I'll make arguments in favor of learning history one at a time. Your job is to either agree with the argument or give your reasons as to why you oppose it. At the end of class we'll take a show of hands and see where people stand. Ann?

ANN   Should we take notes?

FRANK   No, it's more important that you get into the discussion and think about what we're discussing. *[Pause]* My first argument in favor of history is based on a famous quote from, I believe, George Santayana who wrote "a nation that does not know history is fated to repeat it." Someone else, I don't remember who, said that we need to study history so we won't get traveling so fast that we fail to look back and make sure we're traveling forward. In other words, history repeats itself and, as a nation, we need to profit from past mistakes so we won't repeat them again. Now, who would like to argue for or against this argument? Bart?

BART   No offense, Mr. Duncan, but I don't agree. Things are never the same way twice. You said history repeats itself but look at the Japanese and the Germans. My dad said that we hated the Japanese and Germans during World War II. All those old black and white World War II movies make them out to be evil monsters that murdered women and children. Now look. Today we are friends with them and trade with them and all. See? Past history has nothing to do with what's happening now.

FRANK   But don't you see a lesson there? Enemies become friends. Yes, Bobby Joe.

BOBBY JOE   The Japanese still aren't our friends. They still won't trade with us. And besides, we won't even get to World War II. Our textbook doesn't go up to the present. It's just old stuff!

FRANK   It's true that our book only goes up to the Renaissance, but a lot of books start with the present and go backwards. The one our school district uses just doesn't do that for this grade. *[Pause]* Doesn't anybody see any reason for studying history? Yes, Marsha?

MARSHA   Well, I think our leaders had better know history or we just might blow ourselves up with atomic bombs and all. Our leaders had better know what mistakes have been made in the past or we'll all end up paying for it!

BART   *[With slight sarcasm]* No offense, Mr. Duncan, but no matter what argument anyone gives about how good it is to learn history, there is one fact they can't argue with: it's just plan boring. There's too many important things happening right now to stop and worry about what happened back in the days before TV, computers, and machine guns.

FRANK   *[Shocked]* Billy?

BILLY   I'm afraid I agree with Bart, Mr. Duncan. When you compare studying history to doing other things it's just plain boring.

FRANK   Like what kind of other things?

BILLY   Oh, things like playing a new video game, watching a new superhero on TV, or reading a new comic that's just come out. Now those things are interesting!

BART   *[Smirking]* And I can name a few more, Mr. Duncan! *[Most of class laughs]*

FRANK   Yes, I'll bet you can, Bart, like watching rock videos.

BART   Yeah! *[Class laughs]*

FRANK   OK, it's almost time for the bell. How many of you see any value in studying history? *[One third of class raises hands]*

It is two weeks later and Frank is returning the unit exam on Greece to the second-period class. Out of 30 students, there were no A's, three B's, eight C's, eleven D's, and eight F's using a grading scale of 90–100 = A, 80–89 = B, 70–79 = C, and 60–69 = D on a 100-item objective exam.

FRANK   Needless to say, I was disappointed that we had no A's and so many D's and F's. I don't know whether that means you people are not studying or that you don't know how to study. Remember I told you that you have to underline when you read and go over the material again just before the exam. Yes, Bart?

BART   Mr. Duncan, how can I keep going over some of this stuff again and again?! Like the Delian League and ostracism and guys like Aeschylus. I just can't remember all this junk!

FRANK   No but I'll bet you can tell me what the new line-up of TV shows is for the fall. And I'll bet you can name all the new Marvel Comics that have come out in the last year. And I'm sure you can give me the names of the three best computer games that have come out on the market in the last month.

BART   Well, of course I can! But that's not the same thing. All that stuff is fun—interesting! It's what I like to do after school.

FRANK   It's too bad, Bart, that you don't find history to be fun too the way I do. But I think you'll find in life that some of the things that aren't fun at first become interesting when you really get into them. It's true that you have to work a little at first when you're first learning something.

BART   But I never had to learn how to enjoy reading comic books or playing computer games. They were never hard work.

FRANK   *[Forcefully]* Well, the bottom line, Bart, is that this is world history, not a
course in comic books or computer games. Unless you and some other people
in here find a way to get interested, I'm afraid you are going to end up receiv-
ing grades that neither you nor your parents are going to be proud of. Do I
make myself clear?! *[Quiet]* Now. I'll be glad to work with any of you who
need help. If you don't have anyone to study with before an exam, I'll be glad
to schedule a study session with you. *[Smiling]* And, by the way, I enjoy watching television too. I even have a computer at home with a 200-megabyte hard
disk and 16 RAM. It even has a 28,800-baud modem. *[Students voice surprise]*
There. Enough on that. Now it's time to begin a new unit. We did the "Glory
That Was Greece" and now it's time to move on to "The Grandeur That Was
Rome." *[Several students groan, including Bart and Bobby Joe.]* The contributions
of the Greeks to civilization were many, but they might have been lost forever
if what started out as a small city-state in what is now Italy hadn't conquered
the then–known world and preserved it. And, if you think the Spartans were
tough, you should have seen the Roman legions. *[Students begin to take notes.]*

It is two weeks later and Frank is leading a discussion on the rise of the Roman
Empire.

FRANK   Our topic today is the change of the Roman government from a republic to an
empire. What is the difference between these two forms of government? *[Only
one hand goes up]* Ann?
ANN   I think a republic is like a democracy and an empire is like, well, where they
have a king.
FRANK   That's a good start, Ann. Can anyone add to Ann's definitions? *[No hands go
up.]* No one? How about you, Bart?
BART   I don't know. All I know is they used to have a lot of wild parties! *[The class
laughs.]*
FRANK   *[Discouraged]* That may or may not be historical fact, Bart. But it doesn't have
anything to do with the question. *[Pause]* Well, if none of you know the difference between a republic and an empire, you'd better find what it is before the
quiz on Friday. I'll guarantee you I'll be asking that question. *[Several students
groan.]* Now, who can tell me who the first real Roman emperor was? *[Only Ann
raises her hand]* Ann?
ANN   Julius Caesar?
FRANK   No, he wasn't the first real emperor, although he might have been if he hadn't
been assassinated first. Anyone else? *[No response.]* Well, I guess you'd better
use the rest of the period to read the assignment. Get busy and I'll walk around
to see how you're doing.

It is after school on Thursday of the next week. Frank sits in the office of Ray Sta-
pleton, the social studies curriculum director, in the school district administration
building downtown.

FRANK   I really appreciate your seeing me, Ray. I know how busy you are.

RAY   Not at all, Frank. That's the fun part of my job, working with teachers! How can I help you?

FRANK   *[Hesitantly]* Ray, it's my second-period world history class. It started out with the students not seeing any value studying history—well, most of them. We tried to discuss the importance of history and I thought they understood, Ray. But now they just seem bored. No serious behavior problems, but they just don't seem interested in learning.

RAY   How many students do you have in that class, Frank?

FRANK   Thirty sixth-graders.

RAY   So if I understand you correctly, Frank, you have a motivation problem on your hands?

FRANK   Yes, I hadn't thought to label it that way but, yes, I'd say that's the essence of the problem. They just don't seem interested in the subject and their low test scores just seem to depress them further instead of encouraging them to work harder.

RAY   What kinds of tests do you give, Frank?

FRANK   Objective—multiple-choice, matching and fill-in-the-blank mostly. I give a quiz every Friday as well as a unit exam. I try to tie what they are studying in with current events by having them cut out newspaper articles for our bulletin board. On Friday after the quiz we discuss the relationship between the newspaper articles and what we're studying. *[Pause]* I'm at my wit's end, Ray. I just don't know what to do to get them interested!

RAY   *[Looking into a desk drawer]* I may have something here that might help, Frank. Yes, here's what I want. *[Hands Frank a sheet of paper]* I picked this up at a workshop I attended on motivation. Basically, it's a list of eleven motivational techniques recommended by various experts. I was thinking that they might give you some ideas. They are a mixture of intrinsic and extrinsic techniques.

FRANK   What do you mean, Ray?

RAY   Well, I'm sure that you've heard of behavior modification techniques; sometimes they're called precision teaching.

FRANK   Yes, of course, although I've never used them.

RAY   Well, they are generally called extrinsic motivational techniques since they focus on the idea that motivation is outside the child in the form of a reward or punishment. They reward kids for every small step they make in the right direction. The idea is realistic in the sense that a lot of things we do, such as working at jobs we don't really like, we do for a reward external to the job like money.

FRANK   I understand, but that won't work for me. In my class the rewards are grades and the students seem to have given up on raising their grades. What do you mean by intrinsic?

RAY   Well, as I understand it, those are things that motivate us from within. The idea here is to find out what the pupil sees as motivating or fun and then adjust your teaching to take advantage of that. The extrinsic view is to use rewards to motivate the pupil to learn the material. On the other hand, the intrinsic view is to change the curriculum to take into consideration the interests of the students.

FRANK   [Looking at handout] Oh, I see! That's what Technique 7 means by "Capitalize on student interests." Also, Technique 9 is interesting when it says, "Change the routine and do what the students don't expect from time to time." I can see how both of them make good sense, but I just don't see how to use them with my class.

RAY   For example?

FRANK   Well, OK, take Number 7. My kids are interested in TV, comics, superheroes, and video games. At least that's true of most of the boys. Now how on earth do I apply that to the way I teach world history to a group of bored sixth graders?

ELEVEN MOTIVATIONAL TECHNIQUES

1. Introduce learning tasks in ways that will motivate students. Explain why it is worth the students' while to learn the task.

2. Make clear what it is you want the students to do as evidence that they have learned the task. Give clear directions about what you expect from them.

3. Have the students break down the learning task into steps or short-term activities that lead to accomplishing the long-term task.

4. Give the students contingent praise, both in oral and written form, to reinforce their learning.

5. Minimize both competition among students and punishment for failure.

6. Use evaluation procedures that maximize motivation. Make grades become incentives and reinforcers, not the main reason for learning.

7. Capitalize on student interests. Find out what they are and incorporate them into what is being taught.

8. Arouse the students' curiosity by sometimes introducing stimuli that are novel, complex, ambiguous, surprising, contradictory, or baffling.

9. Change the routine and do what the students don't expect from time to time. Introduce variety and surprise.

10. When giving explanations, use examples that are familiar to the students.

11. Have students apply what they have learned previously.

A Sample of Items from Frank Duncan's Unit Exam on Ancient Greece

I. Matching Match the names of the people listed in the right-hand column with the important roles they played in ancient Greece. Write the letter identifying the person's name in the blank to the left of the role that he played. Some of the people's names will not be used.

_____ 1. The commander of the 300 Spartans at Thermopylae.

_____ 2. Macedonian king who conquered Asia Minor, Persia, the Fertile Crescent, Egypt, and parts of India.

_____ 3. Alexandrian scientist who claimed that the earth rotated and revolved around the sun.

_____ 4. The Father of History, who wrote the history of the Persian War.

_____ 5. The leader of Athens from 460 to 429 B.C. during its Golden Age.

A. Solon
B. Aristarchus
C. Pericles
D. Hippocrates
E. Aeschylus
F. Philip of Macedon
G. Alexander the Great
H. Herodotus
I. Leonidas
J. Plato

II. Multiple Choice For each question select the one best answer and write the letter preceding your choice in the blank to the left of the question.

_____ 1. In what year did the Spartans end the Peloponnesian War by forcing Athens to surrender?
  A. 490 B.C.   B. 480 B.C.   C. 431 B.C.   D. 404 B.C.

_____ 2. Geographically Greece is about the size of which American state?
  A. Florida   B. Maine   C. Texas   D. Delaware

_____ 3. At what battle did the Greeks finally defeat the Persians on land in 479 B.C. and end the Persian invasion?
  A. Plataea   B. Salamis   C. Marathon   D. Thermopylae

_____ 4. In which Greek city–state did democracy first develop?
  A. Corinth   B. Thebes   C. Sparta   D. Athens

_____ 5. Which of the following types of columns found on Greek buildings is the most elaborate in design?
  A. Doric   B. Ionic   C. Corinthian   D. Delian

III. Completion Fill in the blank by writing in the correct term or name as required.

1. The 300-year period after Alexander the Great is called the _____Age.

2. The lowest class of citizens in Sparta who acted as slaves were called the

   _____.

3. The famous temple dedicated to Athena that was located atop the Acropolis was called the _____.

4. In the seventh century B.C., Athens was governed by a council of nobles called _____, who were elected annually from among the nobles.

5. Prior to 338 B.C. the Greeks, who had the same language and religion although they lived in different city–states, called their land _____. Today we call it Greece.

QUESTIONS

1. What are the differences between the intrinsic and extrinsic views of motivation? How do they differ in terms of underlying assumptions, research methods, and applications? How many of the eleven motivational techniques would you classify as intrinsic?

2. What is behavior modification and how well do Frank and Ray understand the procedures associated with it? What behavior modification procedures would work best in Frank's class? How effective would techniques—such as those relating to the token economy, the contingency contract, or the Premack Principle—be in Frank's class?

3. In terms of Maslow's need hierarchy, what different needs are operating among Frank and his students? Particularly compare Frank, Ann, Bart, and Bobby Joe. To what extent do immediate needs like TV, video games, and comics take precedence over long-term needs like profiting from the lessons of history?

4. What are Frank's course objectives, both cognitive and affective? What levels of the Cognitive and Affective Taxonomies is he aiming for?

5. How do the sample test items at the end of the case reflect Frank's cognitive objectives? How could a test be written to measure higher-order cognitive objectives? What are the advantages and disadvantages of objective tests as compared to essay tests? What other means of evaluation and learning activities might Frank have used besides objective tests?

6. From the perspective of cognitive psychology (particularly information processing theory), Ausubel's meaningful verbal learning theory, or Bruner's discovery learning theory, how might Frank have organized and presented the material so that a student like Bart wouldn't have to "keep going over some of this stuff again and again?"

7. From the standpoint of observational learning, to what extent does Bart serve as a model to the other students in his valuing of history? What are inhibition and disinhibition and how do they apply to Bart and Frank's reactions to his comments? What could Frank do to take advantage of the principles of observational learning to change his students' behavior?

8. How do the students' home environments influence their interests and learning in the classroom? Are there any ways that Frank can involve the home and parents of the students to increase student motivation and learning?

9. What does it mean to say that a teacher should shape the curriculum to the child rather than the child to the curriculum? How might a teacher do this?

10. How much sense does it make, from a curriculum standpoint, to organize a sixth-grade world history course chronologically from prehistory to the Renaissance? Would student interest increase if the course began with the present and moved backwards chronologically? What would be the most effective way to use current events in such a course? What else could be done to make the course more interesting to the students?

11. Which of the eleven motivational techniques could Frank use in his class? Are there others he should consider? What changes should Frank make in the way that he teaches his class?

12. How might Frank use educational technology such as movies, film strips, computers, etc., to increase motivation in his classroom? Which of the eleven motivational principles would be involved in using educational technology?

Taking Charge

Central High School is located in the downtown section of a large midwestern city. Its architecture is characteristic of school buildings constructed shortly after World War II. While the physical plant is fairly well maintained, the houses, buildings, and factories surrounding the school reflect the decline and decay so common to inner-city areas after middle and upper class citizens move out into the suburbs. The school's attendance area is roughly 50 percent African-American, 30 percent White, and 20 percent Hispanic.

Troy Scott received his degree in education from a large land grant university in an adjoining state. He is twenty-two years old, single, and ready to begin his first year of teaching social studies. He sits in the office of the building principal, Charles Dobson, three days before classes are scheduled to begin.

MR. DOBSON   Well, Troy, what is your impression of our teacher preplanning activities so far?

TROY   I guess I'm a bit over-awed and apprehensive, Mr. Dobson.

MR. DOBSON   What's the source of the apprehension, Troy?

TROY   Well, take the teachers' meeting yesterday in the auditorium. All that discussion about guns and drugs on campus, disrespect, students fighting with teachers and with one another, and lockers being broken into. . . I guess I'm just a small-town boy who believes that school should be about teaching and learning, and that students and teachers should respect one another. I'm not sure what I'm getting into.

MR. DOBSON   *[Smiling]* Don't overreact to what was discussed in that meeting, Troy. Don't think that those are everyday occurrences here. They do happen, and for that reason have to be discussed and dealt with just as any problem does. But they are the exception, not the rule. Things may not be as quiet here as they were in the small town that you grew up in but we do run a pretty tight ship. The students here aren't going to run you out of the classroom. There is an old saying among teachers that it's best to be a strict disciplinarian at first and then loosen up later on when you have things under control. I think that's good advice for you to follow here at Central. Another maxim I'd add would be that you should never make a threat that you don't intend to carry out. If you do, the kids will figure you as a "softie" and eat you alive. You can't have learning in your classroom, Troy, until you have good discipline. Remember that and you'll do all right here.

TROY   Thanks for the advice, Mr. Dobson. I'll try to remember that.

MR. DOBSON   Good. I'm sure you will do just fine. Now let's talk about your load. Mary Kincaid, the chair of your department, has been sick all week so I'm sort of doing her job here. We've assigned you to three world history classes, a U.S. history class, and a psychology class.

TROY   A psychology class?! I get to teach seniors?

MR. DOBSON   [Smiling] Yes, that's the least we could do, giving you three preparations your first year of teaching and all. Mary usually reserves psychology and sociology for herself, but she thought that with your strong background in the subject you might as well have a crack at it this year. And I might add that since it is an elective, a sizeable number of the students in that class are college-bound, unlike the history classes, for example.

TROY   This is wonderful, Mr. Dobson! It will be a real pleasure working with that class!

MR. DOBSON   Well, Mary has already ordered the textbooks so you'll have to use the one that she chose, but I understand that it's the most commonly used one around the state.

TROY   Yes, I know the one you mean. That'll work out just fine.

MR. DOBSON   Mary told me on the phone today that she'll definitely be in to meet her classes on Monday when school begins. So, if you have any questions you can catch her then, I'm sure. Otherwise, you might talk to Al Stafford. He's been in the department a long time and can probably handle any questions you have.

TROY   [Standing up] Thanks, Mr. Dobson. I'm sure things will work out just fine.

It is second period, and Troy meets with 33 seniors in his psychology class for the first time.

TROY   That was the bell, folks! Now will everybody find a seat and quiet down please. [All quiet down but two students who continue to talk. Troy walks over to them.] What is your name?

STUDENT   Angel. Angel Garcia.

TROY   [Looking at other student] And you?

STUDENT   Hosea. Hosea Sanchez.

TROY   [Smiling] Angel and Hosea, would you two please stop talking and listen to what I have to say?

ANGEL   [Smiling] Sure, man. Sorry.

TROY   How many of you are seniors? [All hands go up.] I thought so, but I wanted to be sure. [Pause] I don't mind telling you that psychology is one of my favorite subjects and I'm really looking forward to teaching this class. How many of you think you'll be going on to college when you graduate? [Twenty-one hands go up] That's great! I want to teach this class so it will help you make the transition to college. For those of you who don't think you'll be going to college, my goal is to

help you see how psychology applies to your lives and will help you become
more effective, better adjusted human beings, capable of solving the human relations problems that constantly confront us. Yes, Maria, isn't it?

MARIA   Yes, sir. How will we be graded in here?

TROY   I was coming to that, Maria. Please bear with me. First, let me say that as seniors, especially those of you who are going to college, you've got to start thinking as adults rather than as adolescents. All of us in the room have to start thinking of one another as adults and equals. College is for adult learners.
Adolescents don't last too long there. Yes, Angel?

ANGEL   Does that mean I can call you by your first name, man?

TROY   No, it doesn't, Angel. I think that you'll find that college professors aren't usually called by their first names by their students. *[Clears his throat]* However, to
get back to Maria's question about grades, I plan on giving two combination objective and essay-type exams in here each grading period. Think of them as a
mid-term and a final. I want you to do a lot of independent work and read
broadly in this class. We'll be doing a lot of projects in small groups of four to
six people, so it's important for us to get to know one another. Now I want us to
begin today by asking what psychology is as a science. I realize that you haven't
had a chance to read the first chapter but I'd like to get your ideas before you
start studying the field. Jerome, how about you? What is psychology?

JEROME   *[Looks down at floor]* Don't know. Jus' the study of crazy people, I suppose.

TROY   That's certainly part of it. Abnormal psychology certainly focuses on that.

TYRONE   You mean psychology's abnormal?

TROY   No, Tyrone. The study of abnormal behavior is one branch or field of psychology. But the study of normal, well-adjusted behavior is also important, as well as
topics like how people learn.

JEROME   Some people never learn, like Angel. He's too dumb.

ANGEL   You wouldn't know dumb if you saw it, Jerome, because you're dumber than
dumb! I'll bet your I.Q. isn't over 60! *[Jerome stands up]*

TROY   *[Angrily]* Angel and Jerome! Shut up! Jerome sit down! Here we are trying to
have a simple discussion on the nature of psychology and all you guys can do is
pick a fight with one another!

HOSEA   *[Smiling]* Throw them out, Mr. Scott, so us decent students can talk psychology.

ANGEL   *[Looking at Hosea]* You jerk! I thought you were my friend, man!

JEROME   He's too ugly to have any friends! *[Points his finger at Angel]* Get out, man!
You're asking for it!

TROY   *[With controlled anger]* Stop! Not another word! The next one who says anything goes to the Dean's Office.

JEROME   Anything.

TROY   Very cute, Jerome. For Pete's sake, guys! Can't we have a simple discussion
without your getting into a fight? Now please calm down and stop yelling at one
another *[Pause]* Now, back to the topic. What else do psychologists study besides abnormal behavior?

It is Friday of the same week. Troy sits in a chair talking to Mary Kincaid, the Social Studies Department Chair, in her classroom after school.

MARY   What kind of trouble, Troy? It's only the first week of school! Psychology is an elective course and the kids that take it are usually well behaved.

TROY   I know, Mary, but they're constantly arguing and bickering with one another! We can't carry on a simple class discussion without their getting at one another's throats!

MARY   Like who? Do I know any of these kids?

TROY   Well, it's boys more than girls, although the girls chime in after the trouble starts. I guess Angel Garcia, Hosea Sanchez, Jerome Jonson, and Tyrone King are the worse. They seem to be the agitators and start things.

MARY   Yes, I had Tyrone in world history when he was a sophomore and I've heard of the others from other teachers. They can be a bit noisy but not what I'd call troublemakers. Do they use cuss words or hit one another?

TROY   No, they just mouth off and disrupt what I'm trying to do all the time. We can't carry on a decent discussion about anything.

MARY   Well, Troy, it seems to me that there are some racial and ethnic overtones operating here and you've simply got to let them know that you're not going to put up with it!

TROY   What do you suggest, Mary?

MARY   I generally find that it's best to make the limits clear and to have a progressively severe set of punishments to use when they step out of line. Make the rules and the consequences clear and, above all, be consistent. They get the picture pretty quickly.

TROY   What kind of consequences do you use, Mary?

MARY   Well, I usually begin by reprimanding them in front of the class. Then I'll often change their seating. After that I begin to cut their grades. The next step usually involves communicating with their parents—well, at least trying to, since some parents don't care at all. All this time I am meeting with them one-on-one and trying to communicate with them. [Smiling] And, of course, the fact that they don't like to stay after school and talk to me also helps discourage their behavior.

TROY   What if none of that works?

MARY   Well, as a last resort I send them down to Roy Haskins [Dean of Boys]. But I don't do that until I've tried everything else.

TROY   What does Roy do?

MARY   Oh, he threatens them, makes them stay in his office all day, punishes them by making them clean up the grounds, and sometimes is able to get their parents involved.

TROY   Does he paddle them?

MARY   Oh, he has in a few cases, of course, but it doesn't do much good the way the School Board has corporal punishment set up.

TROY   What do you mean?

MARY You have to inform or try to inform the parents, you have to have witnesses present, and they just give them a few licks with the paddle anyhow. Doesn't do much good, considering the amount of time it takes and the little physical punishment that is involved.

TROY Can Roy expel a student?

MARY Only the School Board can expel a student. Roy can start the process by recommending it, but it can take some time preparing the case and getting on the School Board agenda. All that does, of course, is dump the problem child out on the streets where he gets in worse trouble.

TROY What about in-school suspension?

MARY We have it, of course, but that means that the child is out of the classroom where he can be learning. Also, some poor teacher has to run it and it's a thankless job!

TROY I see what you mean. Thanks, Mary. I'm going to crack down a bit, establish a clear set of rules, and systematically enforce them. I'm not going to put up with this disruption all year!

MARY *[Smiling]* Good for you, Troy! Take charge!

It is Monday of the next week and Troy meets his second-period psychology class.

TROY Class, before we begin our work on what it means to call psychology a science and to contrast it with various pseudo-sciences such as astrology and numerology—a discussion that I think you'll find fascinating and that I really look forward to—I want to bring up another matter: our behavior in the classroom. Certainly, the way we treat and relate to one another is a topic related to psychology, I would say. *[Pause]* I've noticed that when we've had discussions in this class, they keep deteriorating into shouting matches and threats of physical violence. Let me read you this list of rules that I put together this weekend. *[Reads]* First, raise your hand and get recognized before you speak. Second, treat your fellow classmates with courtesy: don't yell at them or try to put them down. Remember what Thumper said in the movie *Bambi*: If you can't say something nice about someone, don't say anything at all. Third, don't touch other people's persons or property. Don't knock peoples' books on the floor on the way to the pencil sharpener, for example. *[Laughs]* And finally, ask permission before you move around the room. Don't get up and sharpen you pencil without asking first, for instance. Yes, Hosea?

HOSEA This really upsets me, man. I mean, that's making this place like a prison. *[Chorus of agreement]* I mean, this is a psychology class and we're suppose to learn how to get along with other people and all.

TROY *[Emphatically]* But Hosea, what we've been doing in here isn't working. You people *aren't* getting along with one another. Angel?

ANGEL What's going to happen when people don't follow those rules?

TROY I've given that a lot of thought, Angel, and basically I feel that we need to go slow at first until people learn different ways of relating to one another. I'll start with a clear warning, then on the second offense I'll either ask the person to change seats and move to the back of the room or I'll make a grade deduction depending on what the offense is. In the case of a third offense, I'll ask the person to go to the Dean's Office. Yes, Jerome?

JEROME   That's not fair, man. Takes all the fun out of this class.

TROY   That's another thing. Jerome, Angel, and Hosea, I'd appreciate if you'd stop calling me *man*. My name is Mr. Scott. And what's not fair is the way people keep disrupting this class and treating one another. (Loud and with emphasis) It has to stop, people! *[Pause]* Jerome, I was watching a boxing match on TV the other night and one of the fighters kept hitting the other with low blows below the belt. The referee warned him twice and the third time he deducted a point and the fighter lost the round. That's sort of what I'm trying to do in here. Let's stop the fighting! *[Moans, groans, and boos follow.]*

It is second period, almost two and one-half weeks later. During that time Troy has consistently given five to seven reprimands per day and has moved Hosea and Jerome to opposite corner seats at the back of the room. Tyrone and Angel have consistently received more reprimands and grade point deductions than anyone in the room except for Hosea and Jerome. Troy has just returned the mid-grading-period exam, which was a combination of fifty objective and two essay items covering the nature of psychology as a science and the distinction between it and various pseudo-sciences.

TROY   Since the fifty objective items count a point each and the two essays are worth 20 points each, you could have made a total possible score of 90 points. The highest score in the class was 72 and the average score was 46.5. Needless to say, I'm more than a little disappointed.

HOSEA   *[Looking at the paper of the girl who sits in front of him]* Yes and I know who messed us up.

TROY   *[Angrily]* Hosea, what are you talking about? You didn't raise your hand again.

HOSEA   Maria! *[Mockingly]* She's always such a good student and tries to make us look bad! All she does is study! She wouldn't know what to do on a date!

TROY   That's it, Hosea! I'm deducting points from your test score! Now if I were you I'd apologize to her!

HOSEA   *[Standing up]* I will not! She's a bitch and is always causing trouble!

TROY   Hosea, sit down!

HOSEA   I will not! I've had enough of you too!

TROY   Hosea, leave this room right now and go to Mr. Haskins' office!

HOSEA   That's better than being in here, man! *[Leaves room with a menacing look.]*

It is 20 minutes later, still second period, and Hosea returns to class with a smirk on his face and hands Troy a note from Roy Haskins, the dean of boys. The note says, "I discussed Hosea's inappropriate behavior with him and he assured me that it won't happen again. Let's discuss this matter at your leisure." Troy reads the note with disbelief.

TROY   Take that chair over there, Hosea. I'll talk to Mr. Haskins later.

It is after school on the same day and Troy walks over to Roy Haskins office and takes an outside chair until Roy opens his office door, lets a student out, and walks toward Troy.

ROY   Hello, Mr. Scott. Come on in. *[Shuts office door behind them and motions to Troy to have a seat.]*
TROY   Roy, did Hosea tell you what he did in my class?
ROY   From what I gather he got frustrated over a test and blew up. You threw him out of class. Is that right?
TROY   Essentially, yes. But in the process he called the student that made the top score a bitch and told me that he didn't care whether I liked it or not!
ROY   *[Smiling]* Look, Troy. Today I've had to deal with kids beating one another up, several others caught stealing from lockers, three kids so high on crack they were totally strung out, and five girls who said they were molested physically by male students. Hosea's misbehavior simply pales in comparison. Troy, you've got to learn to handle these situations yourself.
TROY   *[Angrily]* Roy, are you telling me I have to put up with that kind of disrespect from students?
ROY   Absolutely not. I'm sure you know Kathy Andrews. She's a short, thin, wiry sort of a woman and she doesn't put up with a thing. She tells football players twice her size what they're going to do and they sure don't argue with her. It's an attitude, Troy. The students know when you mean business and simply aren't going to put up with any monkey business. You've got to learn to take charge, Troy, or you'll never be a good teacher.

Troy sits in the office of Charles Dobson, the building principal, the next afternoon after school.

MR. DOBSON   How can I help you, Troy?
TROY   Mr. Dobson, I'm in a real quandary about a discipline problem that has developed in my second-period psychology class.
MR. DOBSON   *[Frowning]* I'm really very busy this morning, Troy. Could you explain the problem in as few words as possible?
TROY   Yes, well, the class is very disruptive and is constantly yelling at one another and interrupting what I'm trying to do. Three or four boys are usually the initiators, and after talking to Mary Kincaid I tried to follow her advice and crack down. I told them that they needed to get permission before they speak and so forth. I was very systematic in enforcing the rules and although all this began to take a lot of class time and I was giving out a lot of reprimands and grade reductions, I felt like I was making progress until I returned a test and one of the students, Hosea Sanchez, blew up. He not only verbally attacked the student that

made the top grade, but began shouting at me, so I sent him to the Dean's office. Now, here's what really bothered me. Twenty minutes later he's right back in my classroom with a note from Roy Haskins basically saying he's talked to Hosea and was sure that Hosea won't do it again! Hosea sits there with a smirk on his face like he's gotten away with something. *[Pause]* So, anyhow, I went down and talked to Roy and, in a nut shell, he told me that he has bigger problems than mine and that I needed to handle discipline problems in my classroom and not send them to him. What am I supposed to do, Mr. Dobson?

MR. DOBSON   *[Smiling]* Troy, I seem to remember our talking about this earlier. Now think about it. Suppose every teacher in this school sent his or her discipline problems down to Roy. How would he ever have time to handle the really serious ones? Troy, you simply have to learn to handle problems such as this one yourself. Part of being a good teacher is learning how to take charge of the discipline problems in your classroom yourself. Roy Haskins simply can't do it for you.

TROY   *[Confused]* Well, I guess I thought that I was taking charge, Mr. Dobson. But what are you supposed to do when a student like Hosea stands up and challenges you to your face?

Data on Students in Troy Scott's Second Period Psychology Class

Name	Eligible for School Lunch	I.Q.*	Exam I	No. of Reprimands	No. Times Grade Reduced	Seat Moved
1. Anderson, Willie	Yes	87	17 (F)	2	2	No
2. Bond, Julius	No	98	37 (C)	2	2	No
3. Cross, Harriet	No	110	68 (A)	0	0	No
4. Dixon, Shirley	No	123	65 (A)	0	0	No
5. Fidalgo, Carlos	Yes	90	21 (D)	2	2	No
6. Garcia, Angel	Yes	121	35 (C−)	12	9	No
7. Garrett, Marvin	No	105	49 (C)	1	0	No
8. Gonzalez, Maria	No	133	72 (A)	0	0	No
9. Hall, Greg	No	114	61 (B)	0	0	No
10. Johnson, Jerome	Yes	98	39 (C)	13	13	Yes
11. Kerr, James	No	109	47 (C)	1	0	No
12. King, Tyrone	Yes	97	30 (D)	11	5	No
13. Lawrence, Fred	No	118	59 (B)	0	0	No
14. Learner, Tami	No	128	54 (C)	0	0	No
15. Lewis, Tekha	Yes	101	48 (C)	3	2	No
16. Martin, Germaine	Yes	105	38 (C)	2	1	No
17. Miller, Jamal	Yes	97	24 (D)	3	2	No
18. Mitchell, Waka	Yes	103	44 (C)	2	1	No
19. Murdock, Beth	No	121	57 (B)	0	0	No
20. O'Sullivan, Terry	No	110	50 (C)	0	0	No
21. Platt, Heidi	No	128	52 (C)	0	0	No
22. Posada, Alyssa	Yes	113	47 (C)	1	1	No
23. Ramos, Victor	Yes	86	28 (D)	4	3	No
24. Robinson, James	No	112	42 (C)	2	0	No
25. Sanchez, Hosea	Yes	111	31 (D)	15	13	Yes
26. Scott, Danette	No	115	45 (C)	1	0	No
27. Shaw, Robert	No	123	50 (C)	1	0	No
28. Taylor, Mia	Yes	118	46 (C)	2	0	No
29. Thomas, Renae	Yes	105	46 (C)	2	0	No
30. Walker, Laverna	Yes	107	46 (C)	3	1	No
31. Washington, Cassandra	Yes	98	48 (C)	3	1	No
32. Waters, Vernell	Yes	94	45 (C)	3	2	No
33. Weary, Derreck	No	101	45 (C)	3	2	No

*Total I.Q. on Otis–Lennon Mental Ability Test, Level 4, given in tenth grade.

QUESTIONS

1. What models of classroom management would be useful in approaching this situation? For example, would Assertive Discipline, Teacher Effectiveness Training, Reality Therapy, or Kounin's model be the best one to use? Why?

2. What are the pros and cons of corporal punishment? How effective is any form of punishment when used alone as a means of control? Under what circumstances can punishment be effective?

3. How might Troy have used any of the following behavior modification techniques: (1) the contingency contract; (2) the token economy; (3) time out and response cost; (4) group social reinforcement procedures?

4. At what level of Maslow's need hierarchy are the following persons primarily operating: (1) Troy (2) Mr. Dobson (3) Roy Haskins (4) Hosea?

5. What parent involvement techniques are available to teachers and schools? Which ones might be most helpful in this situation? How helpful would home visits or parent volunteers be in this situation?

6. What is the difference between intrinsic and extrinsic models of motivation? What intrinsic techniques might work best in this situation? For example, how might Troy have gone about determining student interests and taken advantage of them in his teaching?

7. What racial/ethnic and/or social class differences seem to be operating in Troy's class? How could Troy have taken these differences into consideration?

8. How effectively has Troy planned for instruction? How clear are his objectives? How effective are his rule-setting and enforcement procedures? What should Troy have done differently?

9. Which of the following styles of administrative leadership is exhibited by Mr. Dobson: (1) supporting; (2) coaching; (3) delegating; (4) directing? Which style do Roy Haskins and Mary Kincaid exhibit?

10. What type of school climate will be created by the administrative procedures followed by Mr. Dobson and Roy Haskins? How will the major stakeholders (administrators, teachers, students, parents) be affected?

11. What should Troy try next when he teaches his class? How can he handle situations like the scene with Hosea within the classroom? What should he do if a student physically attacks him or another student in the classroom? Are there ways that other teachers can help Troy?

CASE 6

GETTING TO KNOW YOU

Brittany Boyd is a bright, attractive, twenty-one-year-old, beginning mathematics teacher who recently graduated with a B.S. degree in mathematics education from a prestigious private university in the northeast. Prior to her graduation she applied for an opening in the mathematics department in Whitman High School, the first high school built in the city. Whitman now serves the low, low-middle, SES pupils living in the inner city. The student body of Whitman is approximately 50 percent white, 35 percent African-American, 10 percent Hispanic, and 5 percent Asian-American.

Brittany was quickly invited to the school for an interview and was hired on the spot. Her teaching assignment is to teach three ninth-grade Pre-Algebra and two eleventh-grade Algebra One classes.

It is a beautiful, sunny September day as Brittany prepares for her first class as a math teacher. She puts a paper with a pupil's name on top of a math textbook on each desk in the room. No sooner has she finished than a bell rings, and pupils begin streaming into the building. As the 30 ninth-grade pupils enrolled in her first-period Pre-Algebra class enter the room, she instructs them to find their seats, pull the card from the jacket inside the cover of their book, sign the card, and pass it up the aisle to the front seat.

BRITTANY   Good morning class. My name's Brittany Boyd. I'm your Pre-Algebra teacher and I'm looking forward to working with you. I enjoy math more than any other subject because it's logical, consistent, useful, and fascinating. And I want to help you learn to understand and enjoy math as much as I do.

I also enjoyed high school more than other time in my life. So I'm going to try to make your experience in my class as pleasant as I can. I believe that pupils learn better when they're in a friendly, supportive environment. I believe that pupils should enjoy high school, participate in many activities, and learn to get along with each other. I'll encourage you to take charge of your own learning. In this class I want you all to work at your own speed. Think of me as a helper, rather than a teacher. We're all learners working together—a society of learners. That makes us equal. And since I want us all to feel equal, I'd like you to call me Britt and I'll call you by your first names.

ANNIE   That sounds really neat, Britt. But what do you mean "take charge of our own learning." I'm not sure I can teach myself math. It's not my best subject *[laughs]*.

BRITT No matter how a teacher works with pupils, if the pupils learn anything, they actually teach it to themselves. The teacher just makes information available to them. And I intend to do that. My way is just a little different.

MARIO But, what's your way?

BRITT My way recognizes individual differences. We all work at different speeds. Those of you who work faster will be able to learn more math. If you have trouble with math, you'll learn more slowly, but you'll learn effectively. I'll make it possible for all of you to move at your own rate.

HORACE How'll you do that?

BRITT Each of you will work through the book at your own speed—completing all the exercises. As you finish each unit and do the exercises in that unit, you'll come to me and I'll give you a test on that unit. If you pass the test, you'll go on to the next unit. If you don't pass the test, you'll repeat the unit.

CONSUELA *[Concerned]* But what if I can't understand the textbook? Math's hard for me.

BRITT You come to me and I'll explain what you don't understand. Then you'll be able to complete the unit on your own.

HORACE Sounds neat to me, Britt. I'm always behind the rest of the class. Now, I won't have to hurry.

Approximately three weeks later, Brittany is checking her pupils' progress in their math exercises. She is disappointed that none of them has progressed as much as she thinks they should have.

BRITTANY *[Approaching a pupil's desk]* Annie, weren't you working on Unit 3 all last week?

ANNIE *[Pausing]* I guess so.

BRITT What's taking you so long to finish it? I thought I saw you writing cards or something Monday.

ANNIE I'm a pledge in the Delta Club. We've got to plan a party for the active members, and my job's to send out all the invitations.

BRITT *[Angrily]* Math class isn't the place for writing invitations. No wonder you're not making any progress in math! Half the grade period's over and you haven't learned enough math to make a passing grade.

ANNIE *[Shocked]* But you told us that high school was a place that we should do things that help us develop socially and emotionally. That's what the club's supposed to do, isn't it, Britt? Why're you angry with me for doing what you said to do? *[Worried]* You can't fail me in math! You told us to work at our own speed. That's what I did. Now you're telling me that I'm not passing the course.

BRITT I'm angry with you because in math class you're supposed to do math! Delta Club is important. But you'll notice that girls must have a C average to join it. You'd better have at least six units of math passed in three weeks or you won't need to worry about the sorority at all!

ANNIE   *[Angrily]* But that's not fair! You're going back on your word! You're not in-terested in us developing socially at all! All you're interested in is what we do in math! You lied to us! *[Loud laughter erupts from across the room]*

BRITT   *[Shouting]* Horace! Mario! What's going on over there?

MARIO   Sorry, Britt. Horace just told me a funny joke.

BRITT   What math unit are you working on, Mario?

MARIO   I'm on Unit 3.

BRITT   How about you, Horace?

HORACE   Unit 2.

BRITT   What in the world are you boys doing in class? It's the third week of school and you've done only two or three units. You should be able to finish three units a week as the bare minimum.

HORACE   But you told us to work at our own pace, Britt.

BRITT   *[With emphasis]* Yes, but the key word there is work, Horace! You both have just been goofing off!

HORACE   *[Confused]* But what about the social part of bein' in high school stuff you talked about at first? Ain't that important now? You said it was then. I done two units of math. Math's hard for me. I think doin' two units already's good.

BRITT   I think it's ridiculous. *[With emphasis]* It's not even a passing grade!

The next day after classes are over, Britt meets with her friend Nora, a science teacher whose classroom is just down the hall from Britt's room. Nora's in her fifth year of teaching and is quite popular with the students although she has a reputation of being a very strict teacher.

BRITT   Hi, Nora. Thanks for taking time to talk with me.

NORA   Thanks for asking me. I enjoy visiting with you. How're things in Pre-Algebra?

BRITT   Not Good. I think I've unwittingly created a monster.

NORA   How'd you do that?

BRITT   Well, I've loved mathematics since I first learned about numbers. And I've wanted to be a teacher for as long as I can remember. When I finally earned a degree in both mathematics and teaching and obtained a job and my own stu-dents, I guess I started off on the wrong foot.

NORA   How so?

BRITT   I'm such a humanist that I thought if I allowed pupils to work at their own speed, they'd get excited about math and truly learn the basic principles. So I told them how great it is to be an adolescent and experience all the social and emotional experiences that adolescents have—experiences that I had as an ado-lescent. I wanted them to feel that I understood them and their problems and that we were one, big, happy family. I even went to the extreme of asking them to call me Britt.

NORA   *[Disapproving]* A definite no-no. But you already know that. Tell me what's happened.

BRITT   Well, I've also allowed them do club activities and other kinds of personal work in class, and visit with each other while I expected them to be working. I told them they could be responsible for their own learning and work independently through the math text. I gave them an appropriate test as they completed each unit. Yesterday, I was in a state of panic because I realized that the first grading period is almost over and there isn't a pupil in the class I could pass with a clear conscience. They've just been visiting, playing around, and doing work that's not related to mathematics. But, there's no way I can fail an entire math class! I came to the stark realization that I've got to do something different, and do it quickly.

NORA   *[Impressed]* Very well put! Obviously, you've truly created a monster. But it's just as obvious that you know what to do to correct it. And that's the important thing. Right?

BRITT   Right! *[Pause]*

NORA   But you want me to tell you what to do. Right?

BRITT   No. That's not really necessary. I know what needs to be done. First, I've got to make specific assignments, ensure that the pupils complete them, and test their knowledge. Then I need to establish some clear rules, make pupils aware of them, establish appropriate penalties for violations of the rules, and enforce them.

NORA   *[Enthusiastically]* Bravo! Bravo!

BRITT   *[Angrily]* But I just hate it! I feel like a policeman!

NORA   Nobody likes to enforce the rules, Britt. But you'll have to do it if you're going to succeed as a teacher. Reasonable rules and reasonable enforcement empower pupils to develop self-discipline. And that's exactly what you have to do. I know it and you know it. In fact, you knew it before you even came here to talk with me, didn't you?

BRITT   Yes, I did. I just didn't want to face up to it.

NORA   And are you ready to do it now?

BRITT   Yes. I have to.

NORA   Now, I'm going to hold your feet to the fire. When do you plan to begin?

BRITT   I'm going to draw up the rules tonight, and I'll begin to enforce them tomorrow. Since I have three weeks until grades are due, I think I can help the pupils do enough work to give them reasonable grades.

NORA   *[Enthusiastically]* That's great! The longer you put it off, the harder it'll be. I'll be anxious to hear how it works out.

BRITT   *[Sincerely]* You'll be the first to know. Thanks for the moral support.

NORA   Good luck!

The following morning, Britt decides to inform her class of the new rules at the beginning of the period.

BRITT   Good morning, class. Before we begin today's assignment, there are some things I need to tell you. For some time now, I've been unhappy with the way

I've been managing the class. I take full responsibility for this, because I think I'm doing a poor job of teaching you. I was wrong. I thought you'd learn on your own, but that's not true. It's not true of any pupils your age. So we have to change our approach to the class. One of the first changes I've made is that from now on, you'll address me as Ms. Boyd.

ANNIE   Why do we have to do that? What's wrong with *Britt*?

BRITT   Do you call any of your other teachers by their first names?

ANNIE   Well . . . *[Long pause]* No, I guess not.

BRITT   You guess not?

ANNIE   No, I know that we don't.

BRITT   That's what I thought. You see, pupils, or young people in general, shouldn't address authority figures or adults by their first names. But the fact that you do this with me is my fault. I invited you to do it. And that means that I'm to blame.

HEATHER   But that's no big deal, Bri—Ms. Boyd. We'll just call you Ms. Boyd from now on.

CLASS   *[All agree]*

BRITT   That's fine. And I'll insist that you do that. But there are many other inappropriate behaviors that I've allowed. In fact, I spent last evening making a list of them. I'll distribute them to you now. Since the first grading period is just three weeks away, the rules will go into effect today. *[Distributes list]*

EVERETT   *[Shocked]* Wow! These are really bad. We won't even be able to move!

BRITT   That's not true, Everett. Unless, of course, you move out of your seat and move around the room without permission. And, Everett, please notice that there's a five-point penalty for speaking aloud without permission.

ANDREA   Why're you being so strict, Ms. Boyd? Nobody in this class's done nothin' really bad.

BRITT   That's five penalty points for you, Andrea.

ANDREA   *[Angrily]* That's not fair.

BRITT   That should be another five penalty points, Andrea. But since this is the first day, I'll overlook it. But that's the way it is from now on. Now, in response to your statement—I know that nobody's done anything really bad. But I've been allowing you to do things that just aren't appropriate for pupils to do in school. For instance, don't all your other teachers pretty much have the same list of rules? *[No one volunteers an answer]* Well, I think your silence indicates that they do. But the most serious result of my lack of structure is that none of you is learning Pre-Algebra.

O.K. Let's get on with today's lesson. We're going to begin with Unit 4. I'm going to explain the operations to you, and then you're going to do the exercise and finish it this period.

ANDREA   *[Raising her hand and obtaining Britt's permission to speak]* But I've already done Unit 4. *[Others raise their hands to indicate that they've done it, too]*

BRITT   That's fine. Then it'll be a good review for you. *[Moans and groans]*

It's the middle of the second week of the new rules. The class is doing an exercise which reviews the addition, subtraction, multiplication, and division of decimals. Britt's at her desk grading homework. She hears voices in the back of the room. Rodney and Bud are whispering. Brett walks to the board and writes both their names on the board. They stop talking. Erin raises her hand.

BRITT   Erin?

ERIN   May I sharpen my pencil, please?

BRITT   Yes, you may.

> *[Erin leaves her seat and walks toward the pencil sharpener. Horace sticks out his foot and trips her]*

ERIN   Horace, you just about made me fall! It's dangerous to do things like that!

HORACE   I didn't do nothin' to you!

BRITT   *[Rising from her chair and walking to Horace's desk]* Did you trip Erin, Horace?

HORACE   No, she just said that so I'd get in trouble.

> *[Heather raises her hand]*

BRITT   Heather?

HEATHER   Horace did trip her. I saw him. Just as she was passing his chair, he stuck out his foot and tripped her.

HORACE   You're a liar Heather. Erin told a lie and you swore to it.

PATRICK   You're the liar, Horace. I saw what happened, too. It was just what Erin said.

HORACE   You wimp, Patrick. Wait 'till I get hold of you after school!

PATRICK   Oh dear, I'm scared to death! The only people I've ever seen you pick on are girls, Horace. It'll be fun to see how you handle a boy! You'll probably wet your pants!

BRITT   *[Loudly]* All right! All of you, calm down! Horace, I'm giving you ten penalty points. It seems that all the witnesses support Erin's view of the incident, not yours.

HORACE   That ain't fair! It's just their word against mine.

BRITT   Now you're talking without permission, Horace. That means five more points taken off. Now all of you, get back to work. Erin go ahead and sharpen your pencil. *[She turns and walks toward her desk]*

> *[As Britt turns away from Horace, he shoots a bird at her back. Bud sees him and bursts into laughter]*

BRITT   What are you laughing at, Bud?

BUD   Nothin'.

HEATHER   Horace gave you the finger when you were walking toward your desk, Ms. Boyd.

BRITT   Is that true, Horace?

HORACE   No.

BRITT   It that true, Bud?

BUD   *[After a long pause]* Yes, he did it.

HORACE   *[Angrily]* I'll get you after school, man!

PATRICK   You won't even be able to see straight after I'm done with you, jerk!

BRITT *[With concern]* Some of you seem to be totally out of control today. I don't
    know what's the matter. But let's all just calm down and work on the review that
    you've been assigned to do. *[She returns to her desk and observes the members of*
    the class as they settle down to work. After about ten minutes, Annie raises her
    hand.] Annie?

ANNIE Ms. Boyd, I don't mean to be rude, but I just don't like this class anymore. It's
    no fun.

BRITT What do you mean, Annie?

ANNIE Well, at the beginning of the semester, this was my favorite class. I liked
    the way you were friends with us, and I looked forward to coming here.
    Now, it's a real drag. Everyone's fighting with one another! You're making
    us work too hard, giving us penalty points, and not being fun like you used
    to be. This isn't a fun class anymore. *[With emphasis]* You went back on
    your word!

ELAINE I agree. I don't even like math, but I used to really like to come here. But I
    hate it now!

DONNA I feel the same way.

RODNEY Me, too.

HORACE I'm just about afraid to say somethin' more. But I agree with Annie.

BRITT *[Appalled]* I'm shocked! I really don't know what to say! Are you saying this is
    all my fault?

HORACE I think it's got somethin' to do with the rules you made.

BRITT What do you mean by "something to do with?"

ANNIE I think I know what he means. The rules seem fair enough, but it seems like
    the way you enforce them's too strict or something.

MARIO I don't mean this the way it sounds, but it's almost like you're the queen and
    we're your subjects. It didn't used to be like that. *[The bell rings and pupils gather*
    up their supplies and plan to leave the room.]

BRITT *[Disheartened]* We won't have time to continue this discussion today, but I
    promise that we'll continue it tomorrow.

During lunch period that day, Jack McFarland, the building principal, stops at Britt's
table and asks if she could stop in his office briefly after her last class. She assures him
that she can and they agree to meet at 3:45. At the appointed time, Brittany enters his
office.

JACK Thanks for coming, Brittany. A matter's come up about one of your classes that
    I thought we should discuss as soon as possible.

BRITT What matter are you referring to, Jack?

JACK Late yesterday afternoon, Ms. Bailey, Annie's mother, called me and expressed a
    concern about Annie's attitude toward your Pre-Algebra class.

BRITT *[Taken aback]* What a coincidence! That entire class and I had a discussion
    about their attitudes toward my Pre-Algebra class, just today.

JACK   Ms. Bailey said that some of the other pupils' mothers had talked with her about this matter, also.

BRITT   That may be. I suspect that most of the pupils have talked with their parents about the class.

JACK   It seems to me that this's a pretty serious matter. Would you mind sharing with me exactly what's going on with that class?

BRITT   I'm afraid that it's a rather long and involved story.

JACK   I'll take whatever time's necessary to listen to it, especially in view of the fact that there seems to be quite a large group of parents who're concerned about your handling of the class.

BRITT   O.K. I need to begin at the beginning of class. I was so delighted to have a position in a good school like this, teaching a subject that I love to pupils who were interested in and capable of learning the subject, that I was too lenient in my discipline.

JACK   How were you too lenient?

BRITT   The first mistake was caused by the fact that I'm close in age to the pupils. We developed a relationship that was more like peer friendships than pupil–teacher relationships.

JACK   What do you mean by that? Did you socialize after school, go places together?

BRITT   No. I'm not quite that foolish. The friendships didn't go to that extreme. Basically, I allowed the pupils to call me *Britt* and told them how much fun they should have in high school and how important social and emotional experiences are at their age. I thought I was taking individual differences into consideration. But I soon realized that was a mistake and stopped it immediately.

JACK   How else were you too lenient?

BRITT   In an effort to take into consideration their individual differences, I told them they could complete each unit at their own rate. I gave the unit tests whenever they had completed a unit. Unfortunately, they took advantage of this privilege and did about everything else but mathematics in my class.

JACK   *[With disgust]* I assume that you also stopped this practice.

BRITT   Yes, I did. But in correcting these situations I believe that I was guilty of overkill.

JACK   How so?

BRITT   *[Handing Jack a copy of the Standards of Behavior for Ms. Boyd's Class.]* About two weeks ago, I distributed this document to the class and immediately began to enforce the standards. In so doing, I went from a classroom management system that was too lenient to one that was too strict in the span of one day.

JACK   How did the pupils react?

BRITT   I suspect that Annie's mother may have provided you with some of this information. When I begin enforcing the rules strictly, the pupils followed them well for a couple of weeks. Then they began to treat me and each other unkindly, which they'd never done before.

JACK   Explain what you mean. What kinds of things did they do?

BRITT   Oh, little annoying things that kids this age do—tripping people on their way to the pencil sharpener, knocking other pupils' books off their desk, yelling insults at each other. I even had the beginnings of a fight in class today. I think their behavior today concerned them enough for them to bring it to my attention.

JACK   How did they do that?

BRITT   Well, it was Annie Bailey, in fact, who's one of my favorite and brightest pupils. She said that she's really upset about what's happening to her in our class. She said that class had been her favorite at the beginning of the year, and that I'd been her favorite teacher. And she thought this was true of some of the other pupils also. But now the pupils aren't nice to each other, and I'm too strict in enforcing the rules, and the class just isn't fun anymore. Mario Caderia contributed to the discussion by saying that it's almost like I'm a queen and they're my subjects.

JACK   So, what was the outcome of this group therapy session?

BRITT   Unfortunately, Annie didn't make her comments about the class until the period was almost over. The bell rang before I had a chance to respond.

JACK   Didn't you say anything to them about their concerns?

BRITT   Of course. I assured them that we'd continue the discussion tomorrow. And we will.

JACK   I'm sorry this situation occurred. I hate it when parents call me and complain about my school.

BRITT   Jack, they weren't really complaining about the school. They were complaining about me. How many of them complained?

JACK   Well, Ms. Bailey called me, but she said that several other parents were concerned.

BRITT   Then, basically, you had only one parent complain.

JACK   Britt, as principal of this school, I don't want even one parent to complain. And, furthermore, you can't afford to have parents complain about you, either. You're not on tenure. Are you aware of the fact that the Board of Education can fire you without cause? They can merely send you a letter thanking you for your year of service and notifying you that you will not be employed by the school system next year. And you'll be gone.

BRITT   I'm aware of that. And I don't want parents to complain, either. I acknowledge that because of my lack of experience I'm responsible for the pupils' concerns. But I'm certain that I can straighten out the matter tomorrow in class. What do you want me to do? I'll be glad to talk with Ms. Bailey. I'll invite her to my class, visit her at home, or meet with the parents with whom she's spoken. You tell me what to do, and I'll do it.

Standards of Behavior for Ms. Boyd's Classes

STANDARDS

1. Refer to your teacher as Ms. Boyd.

2. Be in your seat ready to begin class when the bell rings.

3. Remain in your seat until given permission to leave it.

4. Remain silent unless given permission to speak.

5. Raise your hand to obtain permission to speak or leave your seat.

6. Turn in class assignments when due.

7. Bring appropriate classroom tools—paper, pencils, text, ruler—to class every day.

8. Treat each other and the teacher with respect.

9. Keep your hands and feet to yourselves.

10. Refrain from throwing objects in the classroom.

Penalty Points

- Five penalty points will be given for violations of Standards 1, 2, 4, 5, and 7.

- Ten penalty points will be given for violations of Standards 3, 6, 8, 9, and 10.

QUESTIONS

1. What decisions did Britt make during the first week of class that allowed behavior problems to develop? How could Britt have avoided this situation? How would this situation have changed if Britt would have allowed the pupils to contract for grades?

2. On what philosophy of education was Britt's first strategy for classroom management based? her second strategy? Which of these strategies do you prefer? Why?

3. Nora told Britt that it is important for teachers to establish rules and enforce them. How does rule setting and enforcement relate to student learning?

4. What are some limitations of the "Standards of Behavior" Britt developed? How can they be improved?

5. What psychological principles would explain the unruly, rebellious behavior on the part of her pupils that resulted when the "Standards of Behavior" were implemented? How would the reaction have been different if pupils had been involved in setting the standards?

6. Which of the following models of classroom management would work best in this classroom: (1) Behavior Modification; (2) Assertive Discipline; (3) Reality Therapy; (4) Teacher Effectiveness Training; (5) Kounin's Model?

7. From the perspective of Maslow's need hierarchy, at what need levels are Britt, Annie, Nora, and Jack primarily operating? How does this explain their behavior?

8. Britt refers to herself as a humanist. What is a humanistic teacher, and how would such a teacher handle classroom management? What is Invitational Learning?

9. What administrative leadership style is exhibited by Jack McFarland? Is he more of a "supporting," "coaching," "delegating," or "directing" type leader? How would you like to work with him? Why? Should Britt have reported her management problems to Jack when they first occurred instead of to Nora? Why?

10. How much social distance should exist between a teacher and her students? How can the teacher know when the line has been crossed?

11. An old teacher adage is that a teacher should be strict at first and ease up later. Do you agree?

12. If you were Jack, what advice would you give Britt about what to do next? Should she get rid of her "Standards of Behavior?"

PART III

CURRICULUM AND PLANNING

INDIVIDUALIZING INSTRUCTION

The bell signaled the end of his third-period seventh-grade geography class, and Steve breathed a sigh of relief as he dismissed the pupils for lunch. He experienced a heavy sense of concern as he sat at his desk and watched the 30 energetic seventh-graders leave the room and head toward the cafeteria.

Steven Jackson is an African-American who has just taught his first three classes as a full-fledged teacher at Lafayette Middle School. LMS is a relatively new school, located in a suburban area of a southern city with a population of approximately 100,000. This city is also the home of the state university from which Steve graduated last spring. The student population of LMS is approximately 45 percent white, 40 percent African-American, 10 percent Hispanic, and 5 percent Asian-American.

The previous week, Steve attended a three-day orientation for LMS teachers. He learned much about the philosophy, policies, facilities, and teachers of his new school. But, as he reflected back over those days, he concluded that although he had learned much about Lafayette Middle School policies, he had not learned much to help him cope with the situations that occurred in his first three periods of seventh-grade geography, especially the third period class.

This class is not like the classes he envisioned when he was learning to be a teacher. He was at a loss to know how to cope with some of the problems that he identified. Therefore, he is not enthusiastic about meeting two more seventh-grade geography classes during the sixth and seventh periods. At least he has a respite from classes during the fourth period, which is his lunch break, and the fifth period, which is his planning period. After the pupils have had time to enter the cafeteria, Steve leaves the room and heads for the cafeteria himself.

The fried chicken, mashed potatoes and gravy, creamed peas, home-made rolls and apple pie on his plate temporarily distract him from his feelings of discouragement about the third-period class. As Steve enjoys his lunch, Fred Taylor, an eighth-grade math teacher with ten years of teaching experience, approaches his table.

FRED   *[Setting his tray on the table next to Steve]* Well, Steve, do you think you know enough about world geography and map-reading skills to keep your pupils occupied for a year?

STEVE   [*Delighted to see Fred*] Hello, Fred. I'm pleased to see that we have the same lunch period.

FRED   Me, too. And the next period's my planning period, so I have two free periods back-to-back!

STEVE   [*Excited*] That's great! Fifth period's my planning period, too.

FRED   Good. It's nice to have a friend to work with during free periods even if you're working on different things. [*Pause*] So, you didn't answer my geography and map-reading question.

STEVE   [*Exaggerated*] Listen, man! I've got enough knowledge on those two topics to keep my pupils occupied for five years. [*Seriously*] But I think I have real problems in my third-period class.

FRED   [*Concerned*] What are they?

STEVE   My class has such a diverse pupil population that I think each of the 30 pupils needs an individualized program.

FRED   [*Sympathetically*] Oh, one of those classes, eh? What seems to be the major problem?

STEVE   [*After a long pause*] I think the major problem is my lack of knowledge of teaching strategies. I'm not sure how to establish a classroom procedure for a class like that. If it's really true that a little knowledge is a dangerous thing, I'm quite dangerous. During the three classes I taught this morning I thought of all the things I'd like to know about teaching and don't. I had a sinking feeling in the pit of my stomach: I think it was fear.

FRED   [*Teasing*] Oh, come on, I'll bet you've learned all kinds of new and exciting teaching strategies at State University that hadn't even been developed when I was in college.

STEVE   [*Seriously*] I've learned the names and descriptions of what were described to us as new and exciting teaching strategies, but we were never taught how to implement them.

FRED   Didn't your professors explain these strategies in class?

STEVE   [*Unenthusiastically*] Yes, they described some of them. But they didn't provide us with any opportunities to use them.

FRED   How about the school in which you did your internship?

STEVE   No help there, either. My experience was successful, and I received an A for my grade. But I didn't do much planning or experiment with different teaching strategies. I just took over the program that the supervising teacher had already established and continued with it.

FRED   What are some of the strategies you are talking about?

STEVE   Some of them are strategies that I'd like to use in my class. My pupils are widely diverse in race, ethnicity, socio-economic background, and intellectual ability. There are also pupils who are physically and emotionally challenged. I know that all of these pupils can be educated through appropriate teaching strategies that enable each pupil to learn effectively and be interested in what he or she is learning. I also know that all the pupils in that class have special needs and that I should be able to individualize instruction for them. But I'm not sure how to individualize instruction to meet all those needs.

FRED   Well, you're certainly on the right track if you want to meet the needs of all the pupils. What else are you frustrated about? We might as will discuss all your concerns while we're at it.

STEVE   We also discussed various philosophies of teaching, such as essentialism, behaviorism, and progressivism. We talked about pupil-centered learning and subject-centered learning in relationship to the philosophies of teaching. I can define these things, but I don't know how to implement them. That's another area in which I feel unprepared.

FRED   Many of the teaching methods and strategies you mentioned, Steve, must be applied in a particular context. It's difficult to deal with individual differences in general, but within a specific class, you *can* determine individual needs. Let's talk specifically about your third-period class. What is your major concern right now?

STEVE   [Contemplating] I guess the most immediate concern's the wide range of abilities. Obviously, LMS doesn't group students by ability.

FRED   No, we don't. Ten years ago, when the school opened, I was one of the faculty members. And at that time, we did group by ability. The brightest pupils were grouped together, as were the average and the below average. We referred to the classes in which they were grouped as accelerated, general, and basic classes.

STEVE   What made the school decide to change the grouping? Didn't it help the teachers meet the particular needs of each of these groups?

FRED   Yes, it did help, and there were other advantages academically. But the social stigma of the pupils in the basic class was devastating to their self-concepts. In fact, even the teachers of the basic classes felt stigmatized. At the other end of the scale, many of the accelerated pupils became priggish snobs—an insufferable group. Those problems—combined with the issues of democracy, students rights, inclusion, and universal education—generated quite a bit of pressure from many different sources to group heterogeneously. And so, three years after the school opened, we changed to that form of grouping. Well, enough about that. What other problems are you having with your third-period class?

STEVE   Well, in addition to the wide range of ability, there are several pupils who can't read the text. It's a seventh-grade geography book, but it's really too hard for them to read. Then, there are two pupils from special education who told me that they're going to be in that geography class every day. They were really ballistic all morning!

FRED   Do you mean that they're real trouble-makers?

STEVE   No. They seem to be pretty nice. But they're hyperactive and I hadn't prepared any special assignment for them because I didn't know they would be there. They can't read the text or understand the concepts we were discussing. I don't know anything about special education. But I do know LMS has a special education teacher because I met her at the orientation. Why isn't she teaching the special education kids?

FRED   This's one of the new practices related to this recent concept of inclusion. Many folks think that pupils are really more alike than they are different. So it's better for everybody to include as many types of pupils as possible in the regular classroom, including the physically, emotionally, and intellectually challenged. This is the first year we've included these pupils in regular classes.

STEVE   Well, I noticed a problem related to this idea of inclusion. The members of groups that say they want to mix with other groups all hung around with their own group. The African-Americans sat together, the whites sat together, the Hispanics sat together, the Asian-Americans sat together, and the special education pupils sat together. They don't show much evidence of wanting to associate with members of other cultures.

FRED   [Smiling] I'm sure it's hard for members of one group to break the ice and mingle with people from other groups. It takes courage to meet new friends. That's why it's important to provide opportunities for the various groups to interact.

STEVE   Yes, I agree. I know that's true. But I tend to be impatient about progress. [Emotionally] I'm just really frustrated!

FRED   Calm down, Steve! Things aren't as bad as they seem. The solution to your problem lies in finding the right strategy for each situation. And what you need to do right now is to get more information about your pupils.

STEVE   What kind of information?

FRED   Well, you said that there's a wide range of ability in the class. Do you know how wide a range it actually is?

STEVE   No, not exactly.

FRED   If you have time to stop in the office after school, the secretary, Diane, will give you the cumulative records of your pupils. Then you'll have specific information to work with.

STEVE   [Enthusiastically] That's a good idea! I can do that!

FRED   Good. Next, you should talk with Gail Perez, the special education teacher. She might have some information about the special education pupils in your class.

STEVE   I remember her from the orientation. Maybe I can stop in her office before the fifth period begins.

FRED   Good! I think those are the most important things that need to be done immediately. After we have that information, we can make some specific plans. Go ahead now and see if you can find Gail. Tomorrow, we'll make great plans.

STEVE   Thanks a lot, Fred. I don't know what I'd do without you. I'll see you at lunch tomorrow.

Fred is already at the table eating when Steve arrives after his third-period class.

FRED   Hi, Steve. How were your classes this morning?

STEVE   [Brightly] They were about the same as they were yesterday. But I have a much more positive attitude today than I did yesterday.

FRED   I'm glad to hear that. [Teasing] You were quite a drag yesterday. To what can we attribute your change in attitude?

STEVE   Mainly to your positive attitude. At this time yesterday, I felt that I was a failure as a teacher. But you convinced me that I can, indeed, learn to apply appropriate strategies to any class that I teach. Now I'm trying to discover which are the best strategies to use for my third-period class.

FRED   *[Encouragingly]* 'Attaboy! That's the kind of attitude I like to hear! Tell me what you discovered about your third-period pupils.

STEVE   I'll let you see for yourself (Hands Fred a sheet showing last year's achievement scores of the third-period pupils) Notice that there was an eight-year range of achievement among those pupils on last year's reading and social studies achievement scores.

FRED   That's a pretty wide range. But the information on the individual pupils will help you to make some significant decisions, won't it?

STEVE   Yes, it will. I've already grouped the pupils according to their reading ability.

FRED   Well, what are some of your options for using this information? I'm interested in hearing them. Maybe you'll end up helping me to become a better teacher.

STEVE   *[Lightly]* You flatter me. But I love it. *[Seriously]* You said yesterday that the solution to my problem lies in finding the right strategy for each situation. The test information will help me to do this.

FRED   What strategies are you going to use?

STEVE   I don't know yet. There are several different ones that I could use to present the geographic and map-reading concepts.

FRED   What options are you considering?

STEVE   When I was in middle school, my teachers mostly taught by using basic texts plus workbooks that accompany the texts. All classroom activity revolved around the text. Sometimes the teacher read it to us or lectured about it. Then we were asked to respond orally or in writing above the information that had been presented. Our learning was evaluated through a common test, usually objective. But I've already decided to use that strategy only in a limited way, if at all.

FRED   Yes, that's quite a common method of teaching. I guess that's the lecture method. What are some of your other options?

STEVE   My thinking's been entirely too crazy. I've been considering planning individual assignments for all 30 pupils. Then I came to my senses and realized that I'm not ready to do that yet. But that would obviously be the ideal way to teach—a way that would allow me to meet the needs of every pupil. Eventually, I may be able to carry through with that type of organization.

FRED   Yes, that type of program requires a lot of organizational ability plus tutoring skills. But I'm sure you'll be able to operate a program like that before long. You're a hard worker.

STEVE   *[Pleased]* Thanks for the vote of confidence. But I have some ideas about an organizational plan that I'd like to share with you.

FRED   *[Smiling]* I somehow thought you would. Let's have it.

STEVE   As you already know, I'm determined to use variety in my teaching so that the pupils will stay interested in their classroom assignments. So I've planned to select a basic core of knowledge that all pupils should know. It'll be a subject-centered assignment, since both the pupils and I have had most experience with this approach. However, I won't use the lecture method. I've decided to use the unit method of teaching as the basic organization for this part of the class.

FRED   I suspected that you would. *[Lightly]* And I remind you that this is another one of the teaching strategies you said you didn't understand enough to use in your class.

STEVE   I know. I know. You're right when you say that it's easier to understand a teaching strategy when you're relating it to a particular subject and group of pupils.

FRED   Tell me more about the unit you're planning to teach. How will pupils learn the content if you're not using the lecture method?

STEVE   Since this will be my first attempt at teaching a unit, I'll use the text as the basic source. But we won't go through it chapter by chapter. I do plan to require that all pupils learn some specific information that's in the book. This is selected information that I believe all pupils should know.

FRED   And have you decided what information this is?

STEVE   Yes, I have. There are three major units in our text: Map and Globe Skills, Human Use of the Earth, and North American Culture. All pupils will have occasion to use information and skills from all these areas.

FRED   Yes, this seems to be really basic information for them to know. How will they study these units?

STEVE   The plans are in the developmental stages right now, but I definitely plan to integrate the basic map and globe skills into the other two units. This will help pupils see the relevance of map and globe skills by applying them to real situations.

FRED   Good idea. Will the pupils be given a common reading assignment to complete?

STEVE   I told you earlier that I've identified all my pupils by reading level. Assigning pupils at approximately the same reading level to a common group will help me to individualize instruction. I can now give each of these groups a reading list that they will be able to read. Accompanying the reading list will be a series of questions to be answered from specific reading selections. I guess these questions are called reading guides.

FRED   How will these reading guides differ from group to group?

STEVE   I hope to use them to individualize instruction. But I'll differentiate between groups rather than individuals. Is this called *groupilizing* instruction?

FRED   *[Laughing]* What a punster! Upun my word!

STEVE   *[Groans]* Oh, that's bad. But on a serious note, I plan to ask the best readers the most complicated and difficult questions and the poorest readers the least complicated and difficult questions, with the other groups ranging along a continuum in between the extremes. I hope to think of a way that the groups can share information with each other. This would basically replace my lecturing to them about the information. I'm not sure how to do this yet. I'd like to be creative and ask pupils to use posters, models, sketches, oral and written reports, and other types of presentations. As I've mentioned before, I'd like to provide some variety. Most of these pupils have a very short attention span.

FRED   Speaking of individualizing instruction, were you able to see Gail Perez yesterday?

STEVE   *[Enthusiastically]* Yes! Good news from Gail! She assured me that even though her two pupils will be in my class, she'll prepare appropriate lessons for them to do, based on what my class is doing. By making assignments on the basis of reading ability, the way I described to you, I can help Gail's pupils blend right in with the rest of the class. She'll evaluate their work based on their ability, assign their grades, and generally be responsible for them.

FRED   Great! That sounds like a good program for those pupils.

[Teasing] I noticed that you're now talking about individualized instruction. Yesterday, you told me that you didn't know enough to individualize instruction in any of your classes.

STEVE   Well, I learned a lot since I saw you yesterday.

FRED   Or maybe you really do know enough about the strategies to implement them in specific classes for specific pupils. Sometimes it's very difficult to discuss concepts in general, but not so difficult to apply them specifically.

STEVE   Fred, you're a Twentieth-Century Socrates.

FRED   I've been called a lot of things. But this is the first time I've been compared to Socrates.

STEVE   I'm being serious. In an educational philosophy class we learned about the Socratic Method of teaching. It basically involved Socrates questioning his disciples until they came up with answers to his questions. That's exactly what you've been doing with me. I think you'll make a good teacher out of me despite all my shortcomings. Thanks for all your help.

FRED   *[Sternly]* We're not finished yet! You've been pussy-footing around all the hard questions I've asked you today. When we eat lunch tomorrow, I want you to tell me how you're going to organize your class the remainder of the year. Then you can tell me how you plan to manage and evaluate all these papers, projects, and reports. And by tomorrow, I'll probably have additional questions for you.

STEVE   *[Smiling]* You've got a deal. See you tomorrow.

The next day Steve enters the cafeteria, goes through the line, makes selections to put on his tray, and proceeds to his regular table. As he is unloading his tray, he sees Fred going through the cafeteria line. Steve's quite pleased with his planning and is eager to share it with Fred. Fred joins him at the table.

FRED   You must be hungry today. You even beat me to the table. How was your third-period class?

STEVE   It was really busy. I introduced them to the three subject-centered units I told you about yesterday,

FRED   And?

STEVE   And I was generally pleased with the results. The pupils seemed to like the idea of accepting more responsibility for their own learning. They also liked the idea of individual assignments.

I also gave them an overview of what we would be doing during the last half of the course. I thought maybe they could be thinking about things they would like to do.

FRED   You've been holding out on me. You haven't told me yet what you've been planning.

STEVE   Well, as you already know, I'm determined to include a lot of variety in my teaching so that the pupils will stay interested in their classroom assignments. And since our first units are subject-centered and are basically assigned by me, I decided that the remainder of the units will be pupil-centered, individualized, and selected by the pupils from a pool of topics.

FRED   Will the topics be related to each other or entirely different?

STEVE   Since we have such a wide range of cultural diversity in this class, I devised a plan that would allow the different ethnic groups to study the geography of their native lands and the culture of their own people. For instance, there's quite a large section in the text on the African culture region. Perhaps the African-American pupils would want to select some topics from this section. They could work individually, or plan to relate their projects to those of their coworkers. I'd also encourage them to seek information about the geographic area from which their family came, relatives who still reside in that area, and how they happened to locate in this city. They might even locate other friends or relatives whose roots are in the same location. When they complete their unit, we could sponsor an African Culture Week during which they could present appropriate pro-grams—exhibits of native costumes, art, and other memorabilia, speakers, special foods, literature by African-American writers, music, and dancing.

By using map and globe skills they learned in the subject-centered unit, they could display the geographic location of the area: longitude and latitude, climate, geographic features, how the climate and geography influence the dress, occupations, cultural activities, homes, foods, etc.

Hispanic pupils could use the section of the book on Southern American culture, as a basis for their presentations during our Hispanic Culture Week.

Asian-Americans could select the appropriate region from the section on Asian culture regions for their presentations.

In such assignments, the only limitation on the type and variety of projects is the imagination of the pupil. And I would encourage them to learn everything they always wanted to know about the country of their origin.

FRED   It all sounds very interesting and creative to me. But the thought of keeping track of and evaluating all these projects boggles my mind. How will you ever do it?

STEVE   Basically, I plan to give common tests on the subject-centered units. On the pupil-centered projects, I plan to evaluate pupils according to quality, quantity, creativity, and accuracy.

FRED   [Chuckling] Whatever that means.

STEVE   Those are pretty general criteria, aren't they?

FRED   Yes, they are. And the reason I'm pushing you is that if you're really going to have all these individual projects, you're going to need some rather specific criteria for evaluating them. Otherwise, both you and the pupils will be most unhappy at the end of the grading period. As you know, pupils will want to know exactly how you graded this project or that project. You need to spell out your grading procedure very specifically—even if it means considering mechanical aspects, such as number of pages, form, neatness, following a specific outline, and material covered, to name a few. And you may need to provide criteria for posters and maps as well.

Another option might be to approve each project individually and tell what the specific requirements will be for an A, B, etc.

STEVE   You're right, Fred. Grading units will be a very complicated task. I just didn't think it through when I was considering how I could individualize instruction.

FRED   Have you given any thought to the teaching methods you're going to use?

STEVE   *[Emotionally]* You've really touched a raw nerve with that question! And the answer is yes! That's about all I have been thinking about.

FRED   *[Concerned]* You've been uneasy about teaching strategies since school started. You seem to be using a variety of methods in your planning. What kinds of concerns do you have about teaching methods?

STEVE   I don't feel confident that I know enough to match the appropriate method with the different assignments or the goals of the assignment. I've seen so many pupils bored out of their minds because the teacher is using a boring, uninteresting teaching method. I don't want to do that to my pupils.

FRED   But from what you've told me so far, I think your teaching methods are appropriate. You've varied them. They seem to be appropriate for the assignments. And they seem to be methods that the pupils can handle.

STEVE   I appreciate your confidence, but what I really need to know is, How can I know which teaching method to use for each assignment? And how many different methods do I have to use to keep my pupils from being bored? And what are the most effective methods? Man, this teaching business is rough, Fred! I'm still really confused!

Sixth-Grade Records of Steven Jackson's Seventh-Grade Class

Name	Race[1]	Vocab.[2]	Comp.[2]	Social St.[2]
1. Boca, Joseph	H	7.1	7.2	7.4
2. Barnard, Ella	B	3.9	4.1	4.0
3. Bradley, Curtis	B	6.8	6.9	7.0
4. Cardone, Len	W	6.0	5.8	5.9
5. Chang, Won	A	7.9	7.8	7.8
6. Desher, Karen	W	6.7	6.8	6.7
7. Fambro, Tom	W	6.0	6.0	6.1
8. Fay, Mary	B	4.1	4.3	4.1
9. Hawke, Ellen	W	7.5	7.4	7.5
10. Hiam, Sami	A	8.9	8.5	8.7
11. Irwan, Teresa	W	7.8	7.0	6.9
12. Jackson, Rufus	B	7.0	7.1	7.0
13. Johnson, Jess	B	7.3	7.2	7.2
14. Jones, Alex	W	5.1	5.1	5.2
15. Kiley, Mark	W	6.4	6.5	6.4
16. Kincaid, Garth	B	8.4	8.6	8.6
17. Lane, Rose	B	7.1	7.0	7.0
18. Lindsey, Leo	W	4.1	4.3	4.1
19. Lopez, Juan	H	6.8	6.5	6.6
20. McCoy, Ann	W	6.2	6.4	6.3
21. Perez, Jose	H	5.0	5.2	5.1
22. Puzo, Rita	H	6.9	6.7	7.0
23. Ragan, Peter*	W	2.9	2.3	2.3
24. Rodriguez, Aida	H	9.8	9.7	9.8
25. Scott, Irene	B	6.8	6.7	6.8
26. Selleck, Jay	B	6.2	6.0	6.0
27. Taylor, Charles	W	3.1	3.2	3.2
28. Valdez, Raul	H	6.6	6.8	6.7
29. Williams, Eli	B	7.7	7.8	7.9
30. Wylie, Martha*	W	2.5	2.2	2.2

[1]Race: A - Asian; B - African-American; H - Hispanic; W - White

[2]Subtests from Iowa Tests of Basic Skills: Vocabulary, Composition, and Social Studies. Scores represent grade level performance.

*Special Education Pupils

QUESTIONS

1. What are Steve's instructional objectives for his third-period geography class? Which objectives are most relative: the cognitive domain or affective domain?

2. What could Steve's supervising teacher have done during his internship to better prepare him to be a teacher?

3. What does individualizing instruction mean? What advice did Fred give to Steve on how to meet the individual needs of his pupils? What other strategies might Steve use?

4. What are some of the advantages of grouping pupils in classes on the basis of ability? disadvantages? What are some of the advantages of heterogeneous grouping? disadvantages?

5. What are some strategies Steve can use to help the pupils of varying abilities, socio-economic levels, and ethnic backgrounds learn to know and feel comfortable with each other?

6. In what ways do subject-centered and pupil-centered classes differ? What are the advantages and disadvantages of each?

7. Describe unit teaching. What are the advantages and disadvantages of this approach to teaching?

8. How effective would the following approaches to instruction be for Steve to use with his third-period class: individualized instruction, cooperative learning, peer tutoring, learning centers, and in-class grouping?

9. What does it mean to say that "a good teacher shapes the curriculum to the pupil rather than the pupil to the curriculum?" Does Steve plan to do this? How?

10. What strategies can Steve use to help the pupils in his class who cannot read in order to acquire information about geography and map-reading skills? Examine the situation from an information-processing theory perspective.

11. Suggest some responses that you think Steve might have for Fred's questions regarding grouping, keeping pupils on task, evaluating pupil projects, and classroom management.

12. At what need level does Steve seem to be primarily operating from the standpoint of Maslow's need hierarchy? What would a self-actualizing teacher be like?

13. What is the most effective way for Steve to evaluate? What criteria should he use?

14. How can Steve plan for variety in his teaching?

15. What advice should Fred give Steve regarding what he should do next? What should he tell him about choosing different teaching methods and keeping the pupils from getting bored?

OBJECTING TO OBJECTIVES

Brad Grimes is beginning his seventh year of teaching at Rogers Elementary, located in a western state. The physical plant is eleven years old and is located in an attendance area that is predominately white (10 percent African-American). In all, there are eleven elementary schools in Kinston County, which has a population of approximately 50,000 people. Ranching, farming, and mining are the primary industries in the region.

Mary Combs, the building principal, motions to Brad to take a chair in her office. Brad sits down and the two begin to talk.

MARY   How are things going so far, Brad?

BRAD   *[Smiling]* So far, so good, Mary. This group of kids seem a lot like the ones I had last year.

MARY   *[Laughing]* Yes, and the year before that, I'll bet.

BRAD   *[Begins to laugh]* You've got that right, Mary!

MARY   Well, things don't change real fast around here, Brad. But there are certainly worse places to teach. *[Pause]* Brad, I've asked you here to see if you're willing to represent us on the County Curriculum Committee this year. Dr. Rogers *[superintendent of schools]* asked me to recommend somebody for language arts in Grades 4–6 and, well, I think you're the best person for the job. The committee plans to meet every Friday afternoon until it's finished with its work. Naturally, I'm willing to get a regular sub to cover your class on Friday afternoons if you're willing to serve. It would likely be Ms. Burcham—you remember her, and you could coordinate things with her so your class won't miss a beat. What do you think?

BRAD   *[With surprise]* I appreciate your thinking of me, Mary. Of course I'd be glad to do it. It should be an interesting experience. Language arts you say?

MARY   Yes, and I understand that an old professor of yours, Dr. Will England, will be working with that committee as a consultant. I saw his name on your college course transcript.

BRAD   Oh, yes. It'll be good to see him again! I learned a lot from his curriculum and instruction courses.

MARY   Yes, I've heard others say the same thing. *[Pause]* Well, good, that takes care of language arts. Now I've got to see if some of our other teachers will serve.

BRAD   I thought the Curriculum Committee was a sort of standing committee consisting of the same group of experienced teachers each year. That's why I was a
bit surprised when you asked me.

MARY   They've decided to change things this year. I guess they've decided to add
some new blood and shake things up a bit. You'll mostly be working with new
people.

BRAD   Great! This should be interesting!

It is Friday afternoon two weeks later. Brad and nine other teachers sit around a
large oval-shaped table in a conference room in the county administration building. Dr.
England stands and addresses the teachers. As he does so he writes from time to time on
a large pad of paper that folds back over an easel.

DR. ENGLAND   Let's see, so ten of the eleven schools are represented?

SARAH   That's right, Dr. England. There's no one from Tydings Elementary. Deanna
Rhea was going to do it but had to back out at the last minute and they couldn't
get anyone to replace her.

DR. ENGLAND   I'm sorry to hear that. Nothing serious I hope.

SARAH   [Smiling] Only if you consider a radical mastectomy serious! [Murmurs of sur-
prise]

DR. ENGLAND   [Smiling] I'd say that's pretty serious! I hope all goes well for her!

SARAH   [Frowning] As they say, as well as can be expected.

DR. ENGLAND   Well, let's wish her the best. However, the ten of you will have to do
the job and I'm sure you'll do it well! [Pause] As you know, it's our job to revise
the language arts curriculum for Grades 4–6. It's been a while since that area has
had any work so we'll need to start from scratch. We'll be focusing on instructional objectives between now and the first of the year. [Passing out handouts]
We'll need to begin by making a number of decisions. For example, we'll need to
decide which convention for writing instructional objectives we want to use: the
Mager, the Gronlund, or the Eisner. We'll also need to decide whether we want
to use only the Cognitive Taxonomy or whether the Affective Taxonomy also
makes sense for us. [Pause] Realizing that such decisions are usually based on
one's teaching philosophy, I ask you to begin by looking at the Teaching Philosophy handout. You can see that it has ten items on it, and you are asked whether
you primarily agree or disagree with them. Please take a few minutes and mark
your choices so we can discuss them. [All ten teachers mark choices.]

All right! Let's share a little bit and see if it can help us decide which instructional objectives convention we want to use. Now, how many of you
marked that you agree with the first item about the curriculum being organized
along subject-matter lines and being carefully sequenced. [Six hands go up.] OK.
Now the second item is about trusting students to determine their own goals
and to make choices about what they learn. [Four hands go up.] OK. I think I see
a pattern here already. [Continues with remaining eight questions.] Well, does
anyone see the pattern? Yes, Brad?

BRAD   I think we have a split here between the humanists and the behaviorists.

DR. ENGLAND   That's it, Brad. Yes, Sarah?

SARAH   Dr. England, isn't it true that most states require the behavioral objective?

DR. ENGLAND   That's true.

SARAH   Then why don't we go along with the majority?

DR. ENGLAND   We can if we choose to, but almost half of us don't favor the behavioral objective. Yes, Sally?

SALLY   I happen to be one of those. As I see it, behavioral objectives just focus on the outcomes, or products, of education and not on the process. Also, they're very limited in what you can apply them to. They work best with learning the lower levels of Bloom's Taxonomy, not the upper levels.

SARAH   I disagree. I think the only real problem is understanding how to write them. If you know what you're doing, you can use behavioral objectives at any level of Bloom's Taxonomy.

SALLY   [Angrily] For your information, Sarah, I have written behavioral objectives before and made an A in Dr. England's course!

SARAH   Now, Sally, I didn't mean. . .

DR. ENGLAND   [Interrupting] Now, folks, let's agree to disagree pleasantly!

SALLY   [Animatedly] I guess what I'm saying is that the behavioral objective tends to become the tail that wags the dog. I know what educational experiences I want my students to have, but I'm a creative kind of person who likes to let the outcomes flow from the situation, not be structured in advance. For example, I can specify in advance that I want to take my kids to the zoo and visit certain animals. But why do I have to decide in advance of their having the experience what I want them to do when they get back to the classroom? Even if I do, I might change my mind if something happens to excite the children's curiosity that I didn't anticipate.

SARAH   [Gently] All you're really doing is changing your outcomes when you get back. There's no rule that you can't change your objectives. It's just that you'll never know what they're really learning unless you make some attempt to assess outcomes.

SALLY   [Angrily] You still don't get it, do you, Sarah? You're forcing an instructional objective structure on me that doesn't fit the way I teach! That's the problem with education. People have reduced things to routines and crushed creativity.

DR. ENGLAND   The positions that you two are taking are familiar ones in education and, I think, probably relate to different teacher personality types.

SARAH   What do you mean?

DR. ENGLAND   Well, the theory is that some teachers prefer structure and routine, perhaps due to some kind of security needs. They prefer to reduce things to steps and systems. Others are more open and flexible, and flow with change better. It might be said that they abhor systems. They prefer spontaneity in human relations. For example, some of us can't take a vacation without planning every hotel, every meal, what we're going to see, and so forth. Others can just jump into a camper and take off.

Sarah   In other words, the structured personality types prefer behavioral objectives and the spontaneous types like process objectives.

Sally   And don't forget, folks, we're not just deciding for ourselves but also for the teachers that come after us and use the curriculum materials we develop. We should make them as flexible as possible. *[Pause]* But that only gets at part of the problem.

Dr. England   What are you referring to, Sally?

Sally   I'm referring to whether or not we see ourselves as teaching children or subject matter.

Sarah   *[Angrily]* You're not going to bring up that old saw, are you, Sally?! That went out with the sixties and seventies. People today are concerned about accountability, declining SAT scores, and teaching problem-solving skills. The era of worrying about kids' self-concepts and human relations skills at the expense of their learning subject matter is gone! And for good, I hope!

Dr. England   *[Smiling]* Please . . .

Sally   *[Interrupting]* Please, Dr. England! I've got to say this! *[Pause]* We're all upper elementary teachers sitting around this table. Our students are human beings, and one day, some of them will be in the position to straighten out some of the environmental, political, and economic messes that our generation has handed them. If you think that knowing just subject matter is going to prepare them for this task, I think you're mistaken. They have to learn to care for other people and they have to value those things that will help this planet and the people on it to survive.

Sarah   In other words, Sally, you think we ought to use the Affective Taxonomy in writing our objectives. It's so hard to use! We'll never get beyond writing objectives!

Dr. England   *[Interrupting]* OK, let me jump in here. [Pause] Now, having heard this delightful disagreement between Sally and Sarah *[Laughter]*, let's see where we stand. How many prefer the Mager convention? *[Six hands go up]* How many the Eisner? *[Four hands are raised]* OK. How many feel we should confine ourselves to the Cognitive Taxonomy? *[Six hands]* How many feel the Affective Taxonomy should also be considered? *[Four hands]* Well, I guess we all know how the members of a hung jury must feel. *[Everyone laughs]* Let's adjourn for today and think this over until next Friday. Consider the matter carefully, because Sally is right in saying that what we do will affect what future teachers do in this county for some time.

It is three weeks later and Brad is attending a teachers' meeting in the school library. Mary Combs has just finished her agenda.

Mary   There's just one more item. As you may know, I've asked Brad Grimes to serve as our school's representative on the County Language Arts Curriculum Committee! He asked me for a few minutes at the end of this meeting to ask your advice. *[Smiling]* Brad, the floor is yours.

BRAD   *[Standing]* Thanks, Mary. Ms. Combs is right in saying I need your input. The
        Language Arts Curriculum Committee for Grades 4–6 has been meeting for a
        month now and we've gotten hung up on instructional objectives. I want to be
        sure that I represent our school's position on that committee. Let me ask you to
        raise your hands to tell me how you feel about a couple of issues we can't seem
        to get beyond. Here goes. First, how many of you prefer the behavioral objec-
        tives format as the best way to write objectives? *[All hands go up, except for three]*
        Thank you. I guess there's a clear majority on that. Now, how many of you feel
        that the Affective Taxonomy should be used as well as the Cognitive Taxonomy
        in writing objectives? *[Three hands go up.]* Thanks a lot. That's all I needed. *[Sits
        back down]*

MARY   Well, Brad, you didn't vote yourself. How do you feel about those two issues?

BRAD   *[Smiling]* After hearing the committee argue over them for a month, I guess
        I've finally come around to what the Committee is calling the humanist position.
        I guess I'm in a clear minority, though, and I have no problem representing the
        school's position.

MARY   *[Smiling]* Well, don't forget to be your own person, Brad. You don't have to
        feel you're a slave to the majority view of this school. *[General chorus of agree-
        ment.]*

It is the next regularly scheduled Friday meeting of the Curriculum Committee.
All ten teachers are present, and Dr. England is presiding.

DR. ENGLAND   I gather, then, that by a majority vote, however slim it might be, we
        have decided to use the behavioral objective format in combination with Bloom's
        Cognitive Taxonomy. We have discussed Eisner's "Expressive Objective" and
        Gronlund's "General and Specific Objectives" format, as well as using the Affec-
        tive Taxonomy in addition to the Cognitive Taxonomy. As I understand it, no-
        body has really changed his mind.

SALLY   Dr. England, I'd like to know where you stand on this.

BRAD   Me too.

DR. ENGLAND   My role as a consultant is to help you teachers decide what you want
        to do, not to try to convince you to follow my views. I'm an objective, outside fa-
        cilitator.

BRAD   Does that role prevent you from telling us what you believe as a professional?
        After all, several of us have taken your courses, and while you've explained all
        these instructional objectives conventions to us as well as all three taxonomies,
        we still don't know where you stand.

DR. ENGLAND   *[Smiling]* Well then, I guess I've been fairly objective in my teaching
        and didn't let my biases show.

SALLY   Then you admit that you have biases on these issues. Are you willing to tell us
        what they are?

DR. ENGLAND   I guess you have me there, Sally. First, I'm going to consider your 6–4
        split final and proceed accordingly. However, I have to admit that I personally

lean toward Gronlund's approach, since, in my judgement it combines the best of the other two. Also, I feel that going with the Cognitive Taxonomy alone is a bit narrow. Both the Affective and Psychomotor Taxonomies are important as well. However, I realize that this is a conservative era and I understand why cognition might be deemed so important by parents, teachers, administrators, and politicians. I remember how important the Affective Taxonomy was back in the seventies, perhaps even at the expense of the Cognitive Taxonomy. Things change, and education seems to follow the general liberal or conservative mood of the nation. *[Pause]* Now, can we finally get down to business?

BRAD   I guess so. *[Others agree]*

DR. ENGLAND   Now, let's begin by remembering language arts in Grades 4–6 encompasses four areas: reading, writing, speaking, and listening. We need to cover all four in our work. *[Hands out sample curriculum materials.]* Some of these curriculum materials are from other states and some are from here. I've mixed them together so you'll treat them without prejudice and be more inclined to develop new material. *[Pause]* Second, since we're going to use the behavioral objective convention, we need to review the three characteristics or criteria of good behavioral objectives: that they specify the desired terminal behavior; that they specify the conditions surrounding the performance; and that they state the criteria or levels of acceptable performance.

SALLY   Oh, brother!

BRAD   I agree, Sally.

DR. ENGLAND   *[Smiling]* We've been over all that now, people. Let's let bygones be bygones. *[Pause]* We'll need to practice writing a few behavioral objectives to make sure we understand the three criteria, then we need to review all six levels of Bloom's Cognitive Taxonomy in a similar manner. Let's review with a simple example. Let's say that we want to write a behavioral objective about getting our students to be able to recognize run-on sentences. How would we begin? Sarah?

SARAH   I'd start with the conditions, like "Given a list of twenty sentences, ten of which are run-on sentences, the student will be able to identify at least nine of ten."

DR. ENGLAND   Great! But what did Sarah leave out? Midge?

MIDGE   The conditions of the performance. Identify how? orally? circle the run-on sentences? What?

DR. ENGLAND   Very good. And which of Bloom's levels would such an objective represent? Sarah? *[As Sarah answers, Brad and Sally look at one another with frowns on their faces and shake their heads in exasperation.]*

It is more than a month later. Dr. England has had to cancel several scheduled meetings of the committee for a variety of reasons, ranging from illness to conflicting meeting times. Finally, he calls a Friday afternoon meeting, even though he knows that all committee members will not be able to attend.

DR. ENGLAND   You may recall that we started out with ten instead of eleven teachers, and now I'm afraid Sarah and Joy are going to have to leave the committee due to illness, and Midge is being moved to another job at the district level. *[A chorus of disbelief]* That leaves us with only seven committee members. I've talked to the administration and they feel that we're too far along to bring in new members. Yes, Sally?

SALLY   *[Smiling at Brad]* Dr. England, don't you want to give us your Teaching Philosophy test again?

DR. ENGLAND   *[With a puzzled expression]* Give the test again? Why?

SALLY   If you look at the composition of the committee now, I think you'll notice that the humanists now outnumber the behaviorists.

DR. ENGLAND   *[Frowning]* You mean you want to change the rules now? How many of you want to change? *[Four hands go up, including Brad's.]* Oh, my! You mean you want to bring in the Affective Taxonomy and move to the Expressive Objective format? Aren't we too far along for that?

SALLY   Not really. We've agreed on a list of language arts skills for Grades 4–6, and our assignment for this meeting was to write them up in the form of behavioral objectives tied to Bloom's Taxonomy—I guess we've all done that. *[All nod their heads yes.]* But we haven't finalized our work by any means.

TANYA   Well, I've finalized my work. I'm not going to go back and redo the skills in the form of Expressive Objectives! *[Two other teachers agree].*

DR. ENGLAND   Now let's not all get excited. Let's calm down and think this through. When you consider the big picture—that is what's best for the school system and not just your own beliefs—and also the fact that other teachers who have now left us did considerable work on this, how many of you really think we should change our work plan? *[Three hands go up.]* How many of you think we should proceed the way we were going? *[Three other hands are raised.]* Brad, you didn't vote.

BRAD   Well, I'd like to change, but when you put it that way, I'm not real sure what I think is right. Teachers are going to have to live with what we do for some time, and I know that my beliefs are minority beliefs in my school. Do I have the right to impose my views on them?

SALLY   You're on the committee doing the work, Brad, not them! Vote the honesty of your convictions!

DR. ENGLAND   Well, Brad, I'm afraid it's up to you! We've got to move off center and get these language arts skills converted to objectives. *[Holds up list of skills.]* It's your call! What's the verdict?

Sample of Language Arts Skills, Grades 4–6, Kinston County School District

READING

1. Read and recite poetry.

2. Distinguish between fact and fantasy.

3. Describe the feelings of characters in stories about other times and places.

4. Follow written instructions to complete a task.

5. Use maps, atlases, and globes.

WRITING

1. Write ideas in complete sentences.

2. Distinguish complete sentences from sentence fragments and run-on sentences.

3. Recognize four types of sentences: declarative, interrogative, exclamatory, and imperative.

4. Identify the parts of speech in sentences.

5. Write sentences in which the subject and verb agree in tense, number and gender.

SPEAKING

1. Give oral directions completely and clearly.

2. Ask questions to clarify points presented by the teacher or others.

3. Maintain eye contact with the audience while speaking.

4. Tell the cause/effect relationship of stated events.

5. Speak from notes or an outline.

LISTENING

1. Summarize the main ideas of an oral presentation or group discussion.

2. Retell a story using the correct sequence of events.

3. Identify who, what, where, when, why, and how from spoken information.

4. Be courteous when participating in group discussions.

5. Answer questions and make statements in complete sentences.

QUESTIONS

1. What is the purpose of instructional objectives in education? How do they differ from educational goals and aims? How do long-, intermediate-, and short-range objectives differ?

2. What are the cognitive, affective, and psychomotor domains, and how are they used in writing instructional objectives? Writing examinations and asking classroom questions? What are the criticisms of each of the three taxonomies?

3. What differences exist between the Mager, Gronlund, and Eisner conventions in writing instructional objectives? On what set of theoretical assumptions does each rest? What are the advantages and disadvantages of each? Which is the most widely used and why?

4. What administrative leadership style is used by Dr. England in leading the committee: supporting, coaching, delegating, or directing? How effective a leader do you feel Dr. England is?

5. What is the difference between the behavioristic and humanistic philosophies of teaching? How do these positions relate to the development and selection of instructional objectives and curriculum materials? How do they relate to instructional practices and evaluation procedures? Which is the most effective in impacting on student learning?

6. What is the difference between processes and products in education? How is each measured, and what difference does it make which the teacher focuses on?

7. How do evaluation procedures relate to the instructional objectives convention used? What evaluation procedures work best with the behavioral objective, for example? The expressive objective?

8. Examine the sample of language arts skills for Grades 4–6 presented at the end of the case. How well does each skill fit under the reading, writing, speaking, and listening domains? Which instructional objectives convention would work best with these skills?

9. What human relations techniques might Dr. England have used with the committee so the members could have communicated more clearly and worked together more cooperatively? What were Dr. England's goals in working with the committee?

10. From the standpoint of Maslow's need hierarchy, at what need levels do Brad, Sarah, Sally, and Dr. England seem to primarily be operating? How could these differences be taken into consideration in helping the committee work together more effectively?

11. Is Dr. England correct when he says that "Things change, and education seems to follow the general liberal or conservative mood of the nation"? If so, what can a teacher do when his/her educational philosophy and practices are in the minority and don't fit in with those espoused by the school system, other teachers, parents, and politicians?

12. What decision should Brad make about which convention and taxonomy(ies) the committee should use? What are the likely consequences if he votes to change the procedure? What will they be if he sticks to the current plan?

C A S E **9**

DENEQUA'S DILEMMA

Denequa Johnson is a bright, attractive African-American who graduated with a B.S.Ed with a major in English from Dred Scott College, a private midwestern school with a long and distinguished history of providing African-American students with a quality education. Denequa's ambition is to be an English teacher in a high school with a range of cultural diversity.

Shortly after her graduation Denequa applied for a teaching position in English in a suburban high school located in a large urban city in the Southwest. The school, James A. Garfield High School, is located in a lower-middle-class neighborhood and has a student population that is 60 percent white, 25 percent African-American, 10 percent Hispanic, and 5 percent Asian-American. When she was invited to come to the school for an interview, she accepted the invitation. After her interview, Denequa was offered a position in the English Department teaching two sections of American literature and three sections of world literature. She accepted the position immediately.

The Friday before the last week in August, Garfield High School sponsored an all-day workshop for the school faculty and administrative staff. The final session of the workshop was a meeting of the various departments. The English Department met, appropriately, in the school library. When Denequa entered the library, two men in their fifties were seated in comfortable chairs in the center of the reading room. One of the men smiled and virtually jumped up out of his seat.

HARRY   I do believe that you must be Ms. Johnson, our new English teacher. I'm Harry Phillips. Please call me Harry. I teach English and world literature. I'm glad that you're here. This is Brad Gessner, who teaches American literature and grammar. *[As Harry speaks, two women in their thirties and a man in his forties enter the room.]* And here come the other members of the English Department. The beautiful woman in the red dress is Arlene Vacca, English literature and grammar, and the other beautiful woman is Consuela Perez, English and world literature. The handsome man is Mike Sayers, American literature and grammar. *[As they are introduced, the three teachers smile and shake Denequa's hand]*

DENEQUA   I'm really pleased to meet you. My first name is Denequa; most people call me Denny. I'd appreciate it if you would, too. I've been so excited for school to start that I could hardly wait. *[Natalie Valdez, the principal, enters the room]*

HARRY   *[Jumping up immediately from his chair] [Dramatically]* As I live and breathe, we are twice honored, first by a wonderful new teacher, and now a visit from our principal. To what do we owe this honor, Nat?

NAT   *[Smiling]* I just wanted an excuse to see you, Harry. *[Enthusiastically]* And besides that, I have great news for your department! The finance office has appropriated money for new materials for the English classes in all the district high schools!

ARLENE   *[Excited]* New materials! Does this mean literature anthologies?

NAT   I interpreted the information from the superintendent for instruction to mean that we can purchase any materials that we want to use for our English classes—literature anthologies, novels, paperbacks, grammar texts, workbooks, etc.

CONSUELA   *[Teasing]* That's right up your alley, Harry. You can buy several sets of *The Great Books of the Western World.*

HARRY   *[Smiling]* You must be a mind reader, Consuela. Those were my thoughts exactly.

NAT   *[Appreciating the banter]* I knew that there would be some really interesting suggestions about how we should spend the money. That's the main reason I showed up for the meeting. This group has to make some hard decisions so that we can order whatever materials we choose early next semester. We want to order them soon, so that we'll be ready to use them by this time next year. Since Evelyn Rosser, who chaired this department for years, retired at the end of last semester, your department doesn't have a chair.

HARRY   Well, I think that fate has provided us with a perfect chair in the form of a newly-graduated English teacher from an institution of higher learning. We need some new ideas to keep us old war horses in line. I move that we elect Denny Johnson as our new chair.

MIKE   *[Enthusiastically]* A capital idea! Denny seems like she'd be an open-minded chairperson. I second the motion!

DENNY   *[Shocked]* Whoa! I'm the new kid on the block! I haven't yet taught my first high school English class. I'm not qualified to be chair of the department. I don't know the procedures of the school yet. In fact, I haven't even finished my course syllabi yet.

CONSUELA   *[Obviously taken aback by the nomination]* It would really be a time-consuming job, Denny. But we'll all help you as much as we can. If you don't accept the position, Harry will probably campaign for it. Then he'll want us to become a Latin Grammar School. I don't know your position yet, but it would have to be more reasonable than Harry's.

HARRY   Thanks for the compliment, Consuela. It sounds as if we're all in favor of Denny for chair because she'll protect us from each other, or maybe protect you from me. I move for a vote. All in favor of having Denny Johnson as chair of the English Department say "aye" *[Members unanimously respond "aye"]*

NAT   It sounds as if we have a new department chair. Congratulations, Denny! I know that you'll be up to the task. Are you willing to accept the position?

DENNY   *[Dumbfounded]* Are you sure this wasn't a put-up job? I can't believe it all happened so fast!

BRAD   I hope you'll accept the position, Denny. The fact that you don't know all our biases and prejudices will be an advantage to us all. You can be a neutral chair. We'll all cooperate with you. Will you agree to do it?

DENNY   Well, I'm flattered, but I'm also scared to death. Will the rest of you share Brad's commitment to cooperate with me? I'm sure I'm the least-qualified person here to hold the position. *[Members of the group all commit their support]*

NAT   *[Bantering]* This is quite a weird group, Denny, but I can assure you that they'll be good department members. None of them will probably agree with anyone else in the department, but they'll attend the meetings and participate.

DENNY   OK, then. I'll do it. Thank you for having confidence in me—I think.

HARRY   *[Rising and shaking her hand]* Congratulations, Denny. I'm sure you'll do a great job as chair. Now, since we've taken care of the business at hand, you can perform your first official duty by adjourning the meeting.

DENNY   *[Looks at Nat, who nods]* *[Solemnly]* I declare this first meeting of the English Department adjourned. *[Pounds her fist on the table]* *[The faculty members leave; Denny and Natalie stay]*

NAT   Do you have a minute, Denny?

DENNY   Sure.

After the other teachers leave, Nat and Denny sit down at one of the library tables.

NAT   The thought never occurred to me that those five strong-willed people would relinquish any control of the department to a newcomer. But, as Consuela and Brad said, you come in with a clean slate. None of them has any reason to oppose your being the chair.

The reason I wanted to talk with you is to tell you that I realize this task will be a burden to you, since this is your first year of teaching. And, in addition, the superintendent has appointed me a member of an accreditation team that's scheduled to evaluate at least five high schools this year. So I'll be out of town for several weeks at a time, and you'll be on your own.

I am, however, prepared to offer you an incentive. To compensate you for the time you'll devote to the selection of materials, I'll release you from teaching one course all next year. So instead of teaching five courses, I'll see to it that you are scheduled to teach only four.

DENNY   *[Obviously pleased]* That's very generous, Nat. I was planning to do the work without any rewards.

NAT   I know you were, but I'll feel better about asking you if I can provide a bit of a reward. I'm really putting the responsibility of determining what materials to buy next year squarely on your shoulders, and I want you to have some reward for all this responsibility.

DENNY   Well, I hope I'm up to the task. Several of the members seem to feel strongly about the curriculum and it seems as if the majority are pretty conservative.

NAT   Yes you're right. There is a wide range of opinion, strongly felt, among our English faculty. From our interview this summer, I got the idea that you're in favor of more cultural diversity in our literature program, and I'm hoping that you can bring about some changes in that direction.

DENNY   Yes, I feel strongly that literature of all the cultures should be studied in high school. I have the idea that Consuela, Arlene, and Mike are my only allies in the department. Harry is definitely the most conservative of the group, with Brad supporting him on most issues.

NAT   You called it exactly right. So you can see that you have your work cut out for you. Your job is to see that the English materials are selected as soon as possible. You probably will not achieve a consensus from the department, but you must find a way to convince all the members to approve the order of the new materials. This must be done by the end of this semester.

Two weeks later, the six members of the English department gather in the library to have their first official meeting to consider the selection of new materials for their English classes. After the teachers have all arrived, taken their seats, and visited a while, Denny calls the meeting to order.

DENNY   Thank you all for coming. As members of the English Department, our charge is to recommend to the county the type of books, anthologies, and other materials we want to use in our classes beginning next year. *[At this point she pauses]*

CONSUELA   It seems to me that before we can select teaching materials, we should agree on what we want our pupils to learn in the various courses, so that we'll have some idea of the materials we want to use.

HARRY   I agree that we need to have some course objectives. Since you've all been giving me a bad time about the Great Books, I'd like to acknowledge formally my desire to use the Great Books as the basis for my world literature class.

CONSUELA   *[Good naturedly]* What a surprise!

HARRY   I jumped in to mention this now only because the Great Books, by definition, include the most profound literature written by the greatest writers and scholars of Western civilization.

CONSUELA   *[Seriously]* But isn't that a terribly elitist posture? The literature of Western culture is a Johnny-come-lately contributor to world literature. Civilization began in the Middle East, where Asia and Africa meet. Do you plan to totally ignore the vast reservoir of Asian and African literature?

HARRY   *[On the defensive]* I'm aware of all the other bodies of classical literature. But *we* are a part of Western civilization, and there is a limit to the amount of literature that can be included in one literature class.

CONSUELA   *[Smiling]* You've done it! You just made a statement that I agree with. *[Pause]* But if the amount of literature we can study is limited, why not include a random sampling of world literature instead of just Western literature? After all, the course we are discussing is called "World Literature."

DENNY   *[Excited]* Even better, why not allow the pupils to select literature that's related to a topic they are studying or are interested in for some other reason?

HARRY   *[Disgusted]* John Dewey, himself, couldn't have stated it better.

ARLENE   *[Rationally]* I think we've heard the extreme positions. I have trouble with
             your position, Harry, because many of our pupils are neither interested in, nor
             capable of dealing with, the great ideas of Western civilization.

HARRY   *[Strongly]* I don't agree!

ARLENE   Obviously. But last year in my English literature class, I asked the pupils,
             "Who is James A. Garfield, after whom our school is named?" *[Emphatically]*
             Not a single pupil in that class of 35 knew! Can you imagine these pupils be-
             coming excited about Charlemagne's battles?

             [Turning to Denny] And, Denny, I'm a strong advocate of pupil-centered
             learning, but I can't imagine these pupils being able to select appropriate literary
             selections and studying them on their own. I think we need to present them
             with appropriate choices, not just send them out to find literature to read.

DENNY   You make good points in both examples, Arlene. What's your suggestion?

ARLENE   I use an anthology initially to help pupils find selections that they can use in
             related assignments. Then I let them decide where to go from there. I use the
             suggested activities, additional reading selections, and the teachers' guide in the
             anthology.

MIKE   *[Interrupting]* A cookbook approach?

ARLENE   *[Sharply]* I prefer to think of it as a resource guide. What's your approach to
             teaching American lit, Mike?

MIKE   *[After a long pause]* I think I've been most successful overall when I spend a
             good share of time on novels in my American literature class. I have each pupil
             first select a problem confronting our society today that he or she would like to
             study: crime, poverty, greed, disease, hunger, etc. I've identified many novels
             over the years which deal with one or more of these issues. We spend class time
             discussing the novels and proposing various courses of action that they could
             take to solve the problem. After all, these pupils will soon be the citizens society
             must depend upon to solve these problems

BRAD   *[In mock despair]* The saints preserve us!

DENNY   Brad, we haven't heard from you. What type of materials do you prefer?

BRAD   I'm a compromiser, I guess. I basically support the subject-centered cur-
             riculum, and spend most of the semester assigning specific readings from an
             anthology to introduce the pupils to a wide range of American writers. After
             they've read many authors from the anthology, I allow them to choose one or
             two authors they especially like and read sufficient writings by those authors
             to become familiar with their style. So I end the class with a pupil-centered
             approach, but have subject-centered requirements for the vast majority of the
             course.

DENNY   Interesting. We seem to have a representative in our department from most
             of the different philosophies of curriculum: the child-centered, subject-centered,
             perennialist, and reconstructionist. The pupil centered advocates seem to out-
             number the subject-centered advocates four to two in various degrees of inten-
             sity.

ARLENE   We pretty much knew this already. The question now seems to be, What do
             we do about it? What materials do we buy for our different literature and gram-
             mar courses?

DENNY   According to Natalie, Dr. Rogers, the assistant superintendent for instruction, told her that we have virtually unlimited freedom in the types of materials we adopt, as long as their content is related to American, English and world literature plus grammar and composition. So if we decide we would like to use different approaches to these areas, now is the time to make the change. Then we could purchase the appropriate materials immediately.

CONSUELA   *[Excited]* Are we really authorized to do this?

DENNY   Natalie said that the district is willing to purchase whatever the English Departments of the various high schools in the district request, as long as it doesn't exceed the amount of money allotted to each school.

HARRY   Well, so far we've verified what we already knew about our colleagues' philosophy of curriculum. But it doesn't seem as if we've made much progress towards selecting the types of materials we want to use.

MIKE   Maybe we have made some progress, Harry. We learned that we can revise our entire English program if we choose. We could eliminate the grammar course and integrate specific grammatical concepts into literature units if we choose. We could even build our literature units around thematic units. For instance, some possible units for American literature could be the American Novel, African-American Literature, Victorian Poetry, and War Literature. There are unlimited possibilities.

DENNY   That's true. We could do the same thing with English and World literature if we chose. *[Enthusiastically]* In fact, we could change the names of our classes to something different from American, English and World Literature.

CONSUELA   Do you have any special changes in mind, Denny?

DENNY   No, not really. Remember, I haven't even taught a full semester in this school. But I do think that now's the time to make any changes we want to make.

ARLENE   I think we should ask all the school publishing companies to send us all their most recent materials. I've seen some that are really impressive.

DENNY   Great idea, Arlene! If I give you a list of all the appropriate publishing companies, will you call them and make your request? You can call from the office telephone.

ARLENE   Sure, I'll do that.

DENNY   That's great, Arlene. Thanks.

BRAD   I don't want to muddy the water, but ever since our state mandated School Advisory Committees a few years ago, parents have been involved in decisions affecting their children. Should we seek any input from parents on our curriculum study?

DENNY   It's interesting that you should ask that question, Brad. Natalie came to my room after class Monday and told me that Ms. Riley, the president of the Garfield School Advisory Committee called her last week. She'd heard that we're planning to order new materials for the English classes and asked if the members of SAC could have some input.

MIKE   I'm not excited at all about involving parents in educational decision-making! I think teachers are the only professionals who go to their clients and ask them how to provide services! I think that policy contributes to the growing attitudes in some quarters that teachers are incompetent.

DENNY   How do you respond to the idea of my asking the president of SAC to attend our meetings to represent the members of that group?

MIKE   That sounds like the best arrangement we could hope for. I'd be willing to have one representative share the opinion of the parents, although I don't know how she'd be able to arrive at a common opinion.

CONSUELA   Yes. That's a pretty modest request. I think we should invite her to meet with us as the SAC representative. Do you know her philosophy of curriculum?

DENNY   No, Consuela. I don't. Is this something we should find out before we invite her?

MIKE   It probably isn't necessary. She has only one vote and maybe wouldn't even want to use it.

DENNY   What do the rest of you think? Do you want me to go ahead and invite Peg, or do you think we should find out more about how she plans to participate? *[All suggest that Denny should invite her to be a member of the committee]* O.K. I'll invite her tomorrow to become the seventh member of our committee. *[Looks at her watch]* We've been here almost an hour. I don't believe in meetings that go on forever, but I think some important points have been brought out. I'd like to review them quickly.

First, we all have different philosophies of curriculum. Any curriculum guides we devise or textbooks we adopt will have to involve some compromise.

Second, the sky's the limit. We can organize the English curriculum in any way that we agree is acceptable.

Third, we agreed to invite Peg Riley, president of the SAC, to serve as a member of our committee and share parents' views with us.

Are you all in agreement with these points? *[All answer affirmatively]* Good. Let's plan to meet here at the same time four weeks from today. I'd like each of you to bring to the meeting one or more descriptions of a course of study for the classes you teach. Are you willing to do this? *[All answer affirmatively]* Great! Thank you for a productive meeting.

When Denny arrives in the library for the next meeting of the committee, all members of the committee are there, and it's obvious that they've all met Peg. All are involved in animated conversation.

HARRY   *[Seeing her enter the room]* Ah, here is our esteemed leader now. *[Looking at Peg]* Have you met Denequa, Peg?

PEG   *[Smiling]* Yes. She was kind enough to meet with me and invite me to become a member of this committee.

DENNY   Hi, everybody. Thank you for arriving so promptly. *[Looking at Peg]* Welcome to our committee, Peg. *[Peg smiles and nods]*

At the close of our last meeting you all agreed to bring one or more suggested courses of study for the classes you teach. Let's begin the meeting by talking about your suggestions.

ARLENE   You've all seen the new materials in English, American, and World literature that school publishing companies have sent to us and I've forwarded to you. I'm using an anthology of English literature now, but some of the new materials are so much improved that I definitely want to make a change! Literature, grammar, and composition are integral parts of the units. I could easily incorporate our present grammar and writing course into the English literature course with any of several of these new materials.

CONSUELA   If you go this route, you won't be able to take pupils' needs and interests into consideration at all.

BRAD   *[Impatiently]* Why can't pupils make choices among the literary selections included in the anthologies? Generally, high school pupils don't have sufficient background in literature to select literature that they will enjoy or that will meet their needs and interests. That's why we have teachers to teach literature courses.

PEG   *[Raising her hand]* May I say something?

DENNY   Sure, you're a member of our committee.

PEG   Well, my daughter's majoring in elementary education at State University. So, after I became a member of the committee, I read a curriculum book from a course she took last semester. It told about some of the curriculum philosophies, like pupil-centered and subject-centered curriculum. But I also found a really interesting questionnaire designed to help you discover what theory of curriculum you believe. Here are copies for you to see. *[Distributes a copy to each committee member]*

MIKE   Well, the philosophies of our faculty are represented on it. What do you want us to do with this? *[Holds up the questionnaire]*

PEG   I mainly wanted to tell you what I did with it.

DENNY   *[Uncertainly]* Please do. I'm sure we'll all be interested.

PEG   *[Directing her remarks to Denny]* During the week that you invited me to serve on this committee, the Garfield SAC group had our regular meeting. We typically have between 40 and 50 members, which is pretty good as SAC meetings go. During that meeting I asked each of the members to complete the questionnaire. Then I gave each of them as many questionnaires as they wanted to distribute to other parents who did not attend the meeting. Between then and now, I've received 150 completed questionnaires. *[Distributes a questionnaire with the numbers written in]* Here are the numbers for all the responses. *[Committee members spend several minutes studying the responses]*

PEG   I found that 109 parents are subject-centered: 63 checked the subject-centered curriculum and 46 checked the perennialist, which is also subject-centered. Of the 41 remaining, 23 checked student-centered and 18 checked reconstructionist, which is also student-centered. So the parents of your pupils favor the subject-centered curriculum two–to–one.

HARRY   That's assuming that they really understand the differences between the various curriculum theories.

PEG   Why wouldn't they?

MIKE   *[Jumping in]* People who work as teachers spend four to six years studying curriculum theory and practice along with many related subjects.

PEG   Well, everybody doesn't have to go to college to learn about subjects taught in college.

CONSUELA   That's true. But how does one identify those who take the time to learn and those who don't when distributing questionnaires?

BRAD   Peg, did you follow scientific procedures in making this questionnaire available?

PEG   I don't know what you mean. The parents all answered the questions and I tabulated their answers. We can all see what their opinions are.

BRAD   That may not be the case, Peg. When researchers develop tests or questionnaires, they administer them to carefully drawn random samples of people. Then they use statistical techniques to determine whether the responses are biased or are an accurate representation of the views of the people being surveyed. I'm sure you've seen how they do this on TV to predict that a candidate has won an election.

PEG   I don't know how you can just disregard the opinion of 150 parents.

HARRY   We certainly wouldn't disregard it if we knew that their views were really representative of the parents in this school district.

PEG   [Angrily] I think you're all just picking the questionnaire apart because most of you prefer the pupil-centered approach and you don't want to know that most of the parents prefer the subject-centered approach!

MIKE   Can you guarantee that 50 or 60 questionnaires weren't filled out by one person, or five, or ten people who like the student-centered approach and wanted to stack the deck, so to speak?

PEG   [Outraged] That's a horrible thing to say!

HARRY   Assessing public opinion is a very complicated science. Opinion surveys can be extremely accurate, as Brad has pointed out regarding political elections. But we also see how carefully the instruments are developed, samples are chosen and questions are formed. Unfortunately, I don't think this questionnaire can tell us much at all and don't believe it should be a serious factor in our decision-making.

PEG   Well, I think this is insulting to the SAC. I intend to call a special meeting and report to them how I've been treated here today. [Stands up and starts walking toward the door]

DENNY   Please, Peg. Wait a minute. We still want you to be a member of our committee and to help us decide how to revise our curriculum.

HARRY   [Conciliatory] Yes. We'd like your input. You can react specifically to the various types of materials we consider. As you know, I'm a strong supporter of the subject-centered curriculum. I really wish we could use the questionnaire, but it's not done carefully enough. And before you go to the SAC and complain about our not using the questionnaire, you should check with someone who uses questionnaires professionally. You'll find that everything we said here is true. Besides, the questionnaire doesn't really relate to the decisions we have to make. [Pleading] Please stay. We'd really like to have you on the committee.

PEG   I really am interested in the English curriculum. And I'm sorry I got so upset, but you've got to realize that I try to represent the parents I talk to in SAC. As long as you're willing to genuinely listen to the viewpoint of the parents, whether its scientifically gathered or not, I'll stay on the committee.

DENNY   I think we'd all agree to that, Peg. *[All teachers nod affirmatively].*

Now, at the end of the last meeting you all agreed to bring to this meeting one or more descriptions of an English course of study for the classes you teach. Who will share their course of study with us?

MIKE   I pretty much expanded the thoughts I shared with you at our first meeting. I listed some major world problems that are also problems in the United States and our own community, such as crime, poverty, greed, disease, hunger, and unemployment. Included with each problem is a list of American novels which deal with these problems. Pupils will read these novels for the purpose of becoming familiar with these problems and possible solutions for them.

CONSUELA   That's an interesting approach, Mike, but I think it's awfully narrow. The novel is only one aspect of American literature. We need to include the short story, essay, and poetry, at the very minimum.

HARRY   I agree! And you all know what I would do for world literature—*The Great Books of the Western World.* And I already have my course outlined.

CONSUELA   That's just as narrow a treatment of world literature as Mike's approach is to American literature.

ARLENE   I agree. Both of these approaches are novel, but not appealing at all to me. I'd much rather select any of the wonderful anthologies I distributed to you for each of our three literature courses than select some narrow, special-interest type of course such as those recommended by Mike and Harry.

CONSUELA   Since I believe that pupils have a right to select literature that meets their interests and needs, I don't think we should rely on one anthology. Instead, I believe that we should order several different anthologies each for the three literature courses with their accompanying grammar and writing materials. Then we'd be prepared to encourage pupils to tailor specific programs for themselves based upon their needs and interests.

BRAD   I haven't taught a pupil yet here at Garfield who has enough background in American literature to be able to plan a reasonable program of study without any help from the teacher. My idea is to assign specific writers for my pupils to read. After they become familiar with many works by those authors, they may make their own reading selections. So I would prefer to have paperback collections of books by specific writers than to use anthologies with just a sample or two from a zillion different authors.

DENNY   As I've stated earlier, I pretty much share Consuela's views, but I'd be happy to have just one anthology for each literature course we teach. Peg, have you had a chance to think about a program you think would appeal to the parents in SAC?

PEG   I must admit that I'm not really very well versed in the various theories and applications involved in teaching English. But based on what I do know, I think that the parents want anthologies used and they want teachers to make the assignments to the pupils. But I don't think they'd like American literature to be just the study of novels. And I don't think they'd like world literature to be just the Great Books. So it seems that we have two faculty that want to impose narrow limits on reading selections, two faculty that want pupils to determine their own literature program, and two that want a combined program of teacher assignment and pupil choice. My vote would not provide anyone with a clear majority, even if I *were* sufficiently prepared or sufficiently foolish to cast a deciding vote. *[Laughter from everyone]*

DENNY   Well, it's time to adjourn and we haven't made a decision. I'm beginning to think that we never will, regardless of how many more times we meet.

HARRY   Since I got you into this situation, Denny, I'd like to help you get out of it. I'd like to move that we as a department authorize Denny and Natalie to meet and make the final decision on the materials our school should select for our English, American and world literature plus grammar and writing. *[Smiling]* Understood in the motion is that we will accept their decision without accusations, bitterness, or rancor. I believe Denny understands the teaching philosophy of each of us well enough that she will be able to advise Natalie on available programs that each of us will be able to adapt so that we can use at least part of the material and supplement what we can't use with our own choices. All in favor of the motion vote "Aye."

ALL COMMITTEE MEMBERS   Aye.

HARRY   Motion carried. Thank you madame chair, for an excellent job of leading our committee.

DENNY   Thank you, Harry, I think! Thank you, members of the committee. This isn't a task I relish, but I'll consult with Natalie and make the decision. I'll inform you all in writing as soon as it's made. Let's meet again in four weeks and we can begin making plans for using the new materials, whatever they are.

After classes the following day, Denny meets with Natalie to talk about the outcome of yesterday's meeting of the English curriculum committee. She has just finished explaining the discussion related to the questionnaire, the deadlock of the committee members, and the unexpected motion by Harry.

NAT   Well, I think the situation was resolved quite well under the circumstances. Sometimes disagreements among members of a department can become nasty. It sounds as if your colleagues really have confidence in you and trust you. And, basically, even though they disagree philosophically about how to teach literature, they seem to respect each other and get along well. I'm really pleased about that!

DENNY   The factor that disturbs me most about the entire situation is that we seem to be so caught up in the child-centered, subject centered aspect of the curriculum that we don't seem to be able to move beyond that.

And I need your advice on another aspect related to the selection of classroom materials that bothers me. Since this is the first year I've been here, I'm not really aware of the general curriculum philosophy of the faculty and administration. I don't want our faculty to select materials that are philosophically out of step with those of the rest of the school.

NAT   I think we're about the same as most high schools. When a school has math, science, English, and social studies departments, one must consider it to be subject-centered. Otherwise, groups of teachers would work with one group of students on broad thematic units.

DENNY   But teachers in those departments can organize their classes around thematic units.

NAT   Sure, and many of them do.

DENNY   Well, I've come to the conclusion that our department's faculty are letting personal beliefs get in the way of selecting quality materials. Have you examined the materials carefully?

NAT   I'm not sure that I've done it carefully. I have read all the tables of contents and paged through the books.

DENNY   Well, I've shared with you the discussions that have taken place in all our meetings. You know the other schools in the district. And you know my colleagues much better than I do. And you know what materials are available. So, I'd like you to help me out by making a recommendation on the materials I should select. I'll accept full responsibility for the selection, but I need your advice. What is the best choice, or should I say compromise, that can be made, that which will allow the greatest number of teachers to do their own thing, and not get angry with me? Or should I just choose the approach that I favor and believe is most justified and let the chips fall where they may?

Indicate the degree to which you agree or disagree with the following statements about the high school English curriculum. On the line before the number of each statement, write 5 if you strongly agree, 4 if you somewhat agree, 3 if you are neutral, 2 if you somewhat disagree and 1 if you strongly disagree.

_____ 1. Literature read in high school English classes should be classic literature written by the masters.

_____ 2. English teachers should be facilitators who help each pupil select reading material and written projects to meet his/her needs.

_____ 3. Pupils should read great literature that is related to the humanities.

_____ 4. The study of literature should lead pupils to relate to and extend their own experiences.

_____ 5. Schools should reinstate the teaching of formal grammar in English classes.

_____ 6. Literature read in English classes should encourage project-oriented issues, such as strategies for reducing the spread of AIDS.

_____ 7. The study of literature must focus on the development of rational beings and the cultivation of intellect.

_____ 8. Literature should help pupils learn to deal with the significant crises that confront the world, such as poverty, hunger, and terrorism.

_____ 9. Schools should encourage discipline, competence, and accomplishment.

_____ 10. Pupils' interests should be the key factor in selecting selections for them to read in English class.

_____ 11. Literature anthologies should be made up of the great works of the Western culture that have come down through the ages.

_____ 12. Pupils should be encouraged to select literature that will be meaningful to them in their current stage of development.

_____ 13. The ultimate aim of education is to develop rational and intellectually competent people.

_____ 14. Literary selections to be read should emerge from the needs and interests of each pupil.

_____ 15. Literature should be chosen for study on the basis of its ability to help readers develop their power to reason.

_____ 16. Schools should encourage pupils to read _avant-garde_ literature that recommends radical social change.

_____ 17. Pupils should study literature that indoctrinates them with traditional values.

_____ 18. The study of literature should encourage reflective thinking directed towards problem-solving activities.

_____ 19. English teachers should promote the permanency of classical literature.

_____ 20. Traditional literature tends to promote social ills, such as oppression of the poor and minorities, camouflaged as social values.

_____ 21. Literature that transmits a common core of knowledge and values should be studied in English classes.

_____ 22. Literature should be chosen to help pupils meet current needs, not prepare for future events.

_____ 23. Great literature that has prevailed through the ages should be chosen for study by pupils in English classes.

_____ 24. Authors who suggest procedures that lead toward social betterment should be studied in schools.

Philosophy for Teaching English Literature Score Sheet

Below are brief descriptions of the various philosophies that affect the selection literature chosen for high school English classes.Below each statement are the numbers of each item on the inventory that reflect the philosophy of that statement. On the line above the number of the statement write the number you assigned to that statement. Total all the numbers following each philosophy. The philosophy with the highest total is your first choice.

SUBJECT-CENTERED CURRICULUM

There are at least three different curriculum theorists that may generally consider themselves to be advocates of the subject-centered curriculum: essentialists, basic skills advocates, and perennialists. Members of these groups believe that subjects should make up the core of the curriculum, teachers should be trained as subject-matter specialists, and textbooks and materials should be organized by subjects.

____ + ____ + ____ + ____ + ____ + ____ = ____
  1   5   9   13   17   21   Total

STUDENT-CENTERED CURRICULUM

Just as the academic disciplines are the center of the basic skills curriculum, the pupil is the center of the student-centered curriculum. Advocates of this approach believe that when the curriculum is based on the interests and needs of the students, intrinsic motivation results, and the students learn more efficiently and effectively.

____ + ____ + ____ + ____ + ____ + ____ = ____
  2   6   10   14   18   22   Total

PERENNIALIST CURRICULUM

This is a form of subject-centered curriculum, but it differs fundamentally in that it stresses the development of the intellect and suggests that the only types of studies that have the power to do this are the three R's, Latin, logic, and the classics.

____ + ____ + ____ + ____ + ____ + ____ = ____
  3   7   11   14   19   23   Total

RECONSTRUCTIONIST CURRICULUM

Reconstructionists believe that schools should take the lead to reconstruct society. Pupils should identify major areas of controversy, conflict, and social inconsistency and explore how these situations can be resolved.

____ + ____ + ____ + ____ + ____ + ____ = ____
  3   8   12   15   20   24   Total

QUESTIONS

1. Why do you think the more experienced teachers selected Denequa to be chair of the department? Why would this be a difficult position for a beginning teacher to fill? What actions did Denny take which indicated that she was equal to the task? Which of the following administrative styles did she use: supporting, coaching, delegating, or directing? What style did Nat use?

2. What are the different types of subject-centered curriculum theories? Of student-centered curriculum theories? List at least three basic differences between these curricula.

3. Briefly define each of the following curriculum theories: Perennialism, Progressivism, Essentialism, Existentialism, Behaviorism, and Reconstructionism. How do these differ from the subject-centered and student-centered curriculum theories? Which of these curriculum theories most closely resembles your own?

4. What are school advisory committees? What are their functions? Was it appropriate for Denny to invite Peg to serve on the materials selection committee as the representative of the GHS SAC? Why? What are the advantages and disadvantages of parent involvement in the school's decision-making process?

5. Were the members of the department justified when they questioned the use of the questionnaire distributed by the SAC? Why? What is meant when a questionnaire or test is reported to be reliable? valid? How do test and questionnaire makers establish reliability and validity? If the questionnaire were reliable and valid, should the committee have used the results in selecting the English materials? Why?

6. What is random selection of subjects? What process would Peg have used if she wished to randomly survey parent opinion regarding curriculum and textbook selection? What other stakeholders might have been surveyed other than parents?

7. To what extent should the state and/or school system participate in the development and selection of curriculum guides and textbooks? How much freedom should a school or department have in making such selections? Should students have been included on the committee? What about a district-level curriculum supervisor? English teachers from other schools?

8. What types of democratic procedures should a person chairing a committee, like Denny, use? What are *Robert's Rules of Order* and do they help or hinder the democratic process?

9. At what level of Maslow's need hierarchy are the following persons primarily operating: Denny, Nat, Harry, Consuela, and Peg? How would this knowledge be helpful in working with these persons?

10. Write a brief description of the curriculum guides and types of textbooks you think Denny will recommend for adoption for the three English classes. Do you agree or disagree with this choice? Why?

TEACHING IN POVERTY

huck Rogers, a 45-year-old science teacher with 23 years of high-school teaching experience, recently resigned from his long-held position in a prestigious high school in a large midwestern city. He has accepted a position at Chavez High School, which is located in a low-income area of a medium-sized border town in the Southwest.

On the Friday before classes were to begin in August, Chavez High School had a one-day preservice workshop for the school administration and faculty. Chuck had been disappointed when he first drove to the school to look it over. The cornerstone on the building placed the year of its construction as 1950. The brick building was the worse for wear. Bricks were broken off, the building was spattered with old paint that had been thrown by vandals, and broken basement windows had been boarded over rather than replaced. In general, the building was in poor condition.

As he walked through the hall leading to the auditorium, Chuck was equally disappointed with the interior of the building. Walls were dirty, stained, and, in some places covered with graffiti. Both varnish and stain had worn away from the hardwood floors. The bare spots were dirty and worn.

The classrooms had fared no better over the years. They were sparsely furnished. Desks were old and in disrepair. Large chunks of plaster had chipped off the walls and the paint was old and faded.

At the preservice workshop, Chuck sat beside an African-American male in a row near the front.

CHUCK   *[Extending his right hand]* Good morning. I'm Chuck Rogers, the new science teacher.

ALONZO   Hi, Chuck. I'm Alonzo Johnson, physical education teacher and football coach. Welcome aboard.
    [At this point the principal, Juan Correa walks to the microphone and begins to speak.]

JUAN   It's always a pleasure for me to welcome our teachers back to Chavez High School for another year. I'm convinced that we have the most difficult teaching situation and the best teaching staff in the entire city. Maybe the state.

Each year I see all of you working with pupils who are potential drop-outs, maybe even potential criminals, and turning these pupils around so that they become good members of society. I know all of you share my views that there is no job more valuable or more satisfying than being a teacher. I'm sure you're rewarded every day as you change the directions of pupils' lives.

ALONZO   *[Nudges Chuck on the arm and whispers]* We have to be rewarded by our pupils' progress. We certainly aren't rewarded with material things, like money. *[The principal continues his welcoming address by describing the undesirable environment in which the student body lives, the great contribution the teachers make in lifting the pupils above this environment, and the many contributions that Chavez High School makes to the pupils, their parents, and the community. Finally, he brings the address to a close and announces that lunch will be served in the cafeteria].*

Alonzo invites Chuck to eat with him, and they walk through the cafeteria line and sit together at a long cafeteria table.

ALONZO   So, Chuck. How did you manage to end up at Snake Pit High School?

CHUCK   Snake Pit High School? Is that what the students call it?

ALONZO   That's what just about everybody calls it. You must be new in town or you would have known that.

CHUCK   Yes. I just arrived a couple of weeks ago. I taught at Lakeview High School in Cleveland for the past 23 years.

ALONZO   Wow! That's a long time. I don't mean to be nosy, but there must be a special reason why you left there and came here. I won't be offended if it's something you don't want to share. But, on the other hand, if it's something I can help you with, I'd really like to help.

CHUCK   Thanks! That's really nice of you. But, at this point, I'm not sure what anybody can do to help. My daughter, her husband, and her three children have lived here for about fifteen years. This past March, her husband was killed in an automobile accident. Kathy's OK financially, but she really needs help with the kids. Kenny's in day-care, Kari's in nursery school, and Kelly's in kindergarten. Kathy owns a large house, so I offered to move in with her and help with the kids. She was delighted at my offer. Said she wanted to ask me to come, but didn't think she should. So—here I am.

ALONZO   Chuck, you're really a nice man. That's quite a sacrifice for you to make.

CHUCK   Well, I've always been especially close with Kathy, Ken, and their children. Ken's death was so sudden and this was something that I can do to help. And it seems to be working out very nicely. The kids like Grandpa. And our schedules are great. Kathy can deliver Kenny to day-care and Kari to nursery school on her way to work, and I can deliver Kelly on my way. I pick them all up on my way home from school and entertain them until Kathy arrives home from work.

ALONZO   Sounds like a good situation for all of you. It might have worked out better for you, though, if you'd been able to find a job at a better school. This is probably the worst high school in the entire area. Who am I kidding? It might be the worst in the nation. There are so many different cultures represented by the students that it's like a United Nations. Different student groups have trouble getting along. On top of that, most of the teachers are disaffected. They can't relate to the kids and don't really try. They just go through the motions of teaching and try to get through the day as best they can.

CHUCK   Surely you jest. And if that's the case, why are you here?

ALONZO   I'm just a sucker. I'm a good football coach *[laughs]* along with being immodest. But most important of all, I like the kids here. I feel sorry for them. Most of them come from single-parent families, live in poverty, and don't have a nice grandpa like you to help look after them. They don't have anything to do after school except get into trouble. So I intimidate them into going out for football.

CHUCK   You're a good man, Alonzo.

ALONZO   I'm a conniving man also, Chuck. I really work these kids hard, get them in top physical condition, teach them the fundamentals of the sport, and insist on complete discipline, which is the quality they lack most, as a result of their backgrounds. My reward is that we win the district championship almost every year and everybody thinks I'm a great coach.

CHUCK   That's impressive! And I'm sure you *are* a great coach! Isn't it interesting how kids like this respond so well to sports?

ALONZO   Yes, I've been trying to convince educators of this for years. We need more city recreation programs in the low SES sections of cities. We need people who aren't afraid to teach discipline to these kids. That's the best way to get them up and out of the ghetto.

CHUCK   I'm glad we met. That's my philosophy of teaching science, too. I know that the outcome isn't nearly as dramatic as the outcome that can be achieved by sports. But there are many kids who just aren't able to compete in sports.

ALONZO   You're right. And I'm glad you're here. If you can reach some of the pupils I can't reach, we can be an awesome team.

CHUCK   Even though we work in the snake pit?

ALONZO   *[Smiling]* Definitely! Even though we teach in the snake pit.

After the workshop ends, Chuck approaches the principal and extends his hand.

CHUCK   Remember me? I'm the new science teacher, Chuck Rogers.

JUAN   Of course! I'm delighted to have you as a teacher, Chuck! How are your daughter and her children?

CHUCK   Much better now than when I came down for the interview. We're pretty well settled into a routine, and I think our arrangement will work out very well. Thanks for asking.

JUAN   Your daughter's lucky to have such a caring father. *[Begins walking down the hall]* If you'll come to the office with me, I'll give you your schedule. Have you met any of our teachers, yet?

CHUCK   Yes, I sat with Alonzo, the coach, at lunch, and we had a nice visit. I think he and I will become good friends. After the workshop, he introduced me to several other teachers, but I didn't have much of an opportunity to visit with them.

JUAN   I think you'll like our teachers. They are a dedicated group and we all pull together here at Chavez. Here we are at the office; come in and sit down. I'll give
you your schedule.

CHUCK   You've already told me that I'll be teaching three general science courses and
two chemistry courses.

JUAN   [Hesitantly] Er, I had to make a change on your schedule, but I'm not sure
what it was. Let me check. [Pulls a paper out of the filing cabinet] Ah, here we are.
[Hands the paper to Chuck]

CHUCK   Whoa. [Obviously upset] I see that I'm scheduled for three different preparations instead of two, and a study hall that you didn't mention when I interviewed for the job. I understood that I was to teach three sections of general science, and two sections of chemistry. Nothing was mentioned about supervising a
study hall or teaching biology. Isn't it illegal to offer a verbal contract and then
change it when the teacher arrives?

JUAN   [Solicitously] I'm sorry that you're unhappy, Chuck. All our teachers teach five
classes, have a homeroom period, and supervise a study hall. Finances are so
tight in our district that we can't afford the number of teachers necessary to allow us to have a free period. I assumed that you knew that all our teachers have
a study hall along with their teaching assignment. It didn't occur to me to mention it.

CHUCK   [Emphatically] I wish it had occurred to you! Under these circumstances, I
probably would have applied for a position in a neighboring district!

JUAN   [Subdued] I really apologize. The biology assignment was unavoidable. Only
enough pupils signed up for chemistry to fill one class. The remainder signed up
for biology. I'm sorry you're disappointed. But I know that you'll have such opportunities to make a difference in the lives of our pupils that you'll soon be glad
you came here. I'll support you in every way that I can. But we are a very poor
district, and all our teachers have heavy teaching loads.

We all work hard here. This is a large high school, but I don't even have an
assistant. We have only one janitor for the whole building. But we do a good job
with what we have. We make good productive citizens out of high-risk pupils.
You'll love it here after a few weeks of classes. I promise you.

CHUCK   Well, it's too late to get another job now. I can put up with anything for a
year, I guess. Will you show me where my textbooks are stored?

JUAN   [Elated] Yes! Yes! I'll take you there now! By the end of the year, you'll
love teaching at Chavez! You won't want to leave! [They walk down the
hall and stop beside a door. Juan opens the door and reveals a large, cluttered
storeroom.]

Ah! Here we are. Let's look. Yes! Here are chemistry books. Over there are
biology. And back there are general science. [All the books are old and battered.
Some have loose pages sticking out of them.]

CHUCK   [Picking up a general science text and opening it] [Incredulously] This book was
printed in 1955. It's forty years out of date! And all of them are falling apart.
Let's see. How many of them are there? Only forty? I have forty books for over a
hundred general science students? This situation gets worse and worse! I can't
believe it! These biology and chemistry books are falling apart.

JUAN   *[Resigned]* This is just another result of our poor funding. The powers that be seem to think that schools in richer neighborhoods should be given most of the money appropriated for schools. Oh, well. The basic principles of science are timeless. I'm confident that you can update whenever it's appropriate. And there are no more than 38 pupils in any general science class. So you can use that set of books for all three classes. And look! There are many extra biology and chemistry books.

    [Confidently] See. Everything will work out fine. You'll teach the pupils well. I know it!

    The following Friday Kathy made arrangements for the children to go home with a friend after school. Since Chuck has some free time after school, he goes over to the football field and watches the team practice. After a while, the assistant coaches take over the drills and Alonzo walks over to talk with Chuck.

ALONZO   Hi, Chuck. Thanks for coming to practice. How are things going in the science department?

CHUCK   Well, other than the fact that our texts are forty years out of date and we have no science equipment, I guess we're doing pretty well. Your football players look pretty deadly. I don't believe I've ever seen high-school players who block and tackle as enthusiastically and as effectively as yours. How do you get them to do that?

ALONZO   Well, most of these kids don't have many material things at home. And some of them have trouble with academic learning. But if they apply themselves here and do what I tell them to do, they can compete with any other high school kid who steps onto the football field. They all know this, and they love it. They're especially hard on teams they refer to as the "rich guys."

    I've heard some really complimentary and unsolicited comments about your science classes. So you must be doing something right. The boys were particularly impressed with the crushing of a can. You must have some equipment.

CHUCK   *[Laughing]* That demonstration gets them every time. We've been studying air pressure. I brought a clean five-gallon kerosene can and a camping stove from home. I really don't have a single piece of science apparatus—no bunsen burner, no test tubes, no beakers, no hoses, no magnets. Nothing!

    Anyway, I put a small amount of water in the can, set it on the stove and allow the water to boil for a while. This heats the air and allows many air molecules to escape out with the steam. Then I take the can off the stove, put the cap on, and allow the air to cool. Since much of the air escaped as steam, there's less air pressure inside than outside the can. So the outside air rushes in to fill the void and crushes the sides of the can as dramatically as if someone were pounding it with a sledge hammer. The can rolls all over the table with its sides crushing in toward the center of the can. Very dramatic. It illustrates that air pressure tends to remain equal inside and outside of objects and what happens when it doesn't. If the pressure becomes greater inside the can, the sides blow out.

ALONZO   That's a great demonstration. No wonder the boys liked it. Sort of violent. You seem to be making the most of your lack of equipment.

CHUCK   I've read several articles explaining how science can be taught with equipment and supplies found in most kitchens. I think that pupils are more impressed when you demonstrate science with common items that they know about than they are when you use unfamiliar science apparatus.

It would be nice, however, if the school would pay for the materials that I use. I'll spend a lot of money just for things like vinegar, baking soda, magnets, rubber bands, nails and other small items. Even if the school paid for it all, they'd still be getting a tremendous bargain.

ALONZO   Ain't it the truth? I spend a small personal fortune buying Gatorade on hot days!

CHUCK   I guess that just comes with the job when you teach at Chavez High School.

ALONZO   Right on. I've got to get back to the field. Thanks for coming over.

CHUCK   I enjoyed it. I'm bringing my family to the games.

ALONZO   Great! I hope we win 'em all.

CHUCK   Somehow I think you will

After Thanksgiving break, Chuck is in the cafeteria eating lunch. Juan approaches with his tray and sits beside him.

CHUCK   Hi, Juan. I didn't know you ate in the cafeteria. I haven't seen you here before.

JUAN   I don't eat here very often. Usually only when I want to talk with someone.

CHUCK   Then you must want to talk with someone today. How's that for being perceptive?

JUAN   *[Laughs]* Very perceptive. And you are the person I want to talk with.

CHUCK   That's fine. Fire away.

JUAN   First I want to tell you that I'm hearing good things about your classes from the pupils.

CHUCK   That's great. I'm glad you're not hearing the bad things. *[Smiles]*

JUAN   *[After an awkward silence]* I wanted to work into this topic smoothly and cleverly, but I can't quite figure out how to do it. Since you've been here, it seems as if we have many more pupils interested in science than ever before.

CHUCK   I don't have any way to know about past interest in science, but several pupils are doing experiments for extra credit just because they have special interests.

Why do I have the feeling that this visit is going to involve me in additional work, expense, and/or time? You know, I hope, that it's costing me out of my own pocket to generate this additional interest in science and these extra experiments?

JUAN   I suspected as much. And I really appreciate it. But more important, the pupils appreciate it and are responding positively by becoming good students in science.

If there was any way I could do it, Chuck, I'd give you a whopping raise in salary and provide you with a large budget for science equipment and books. I know that with additional supplies, you could build a tremendous program in science. But, unfortunately, there's no way that I can obtain any additional money for any program. You understand that, don't you?

CHUCK   Yes, I understand it, Juan. But that doesn't make life any easier for me. But I know that you didn't come here to apologize for not giving me a higher salary or more science materials.

JUAN   One of the many things I like about you is that you are so direct. I'm never at a loss to know what you're thinking. So I will respond in kind and tell you why I'm here. I want you to be the sponsor of our science club.

CHUCK   That's a surprise. I didn't even know that we have a science club.

JUAN   Well, that's the other part. You'll need to start it first before you can be the sponsor.

CHUCK   *[Strongly]* No way! You're already exploiting me to the hilt—six classes counting study hall, three preparations, old books, no equipment. And now you're wanting me to start and sponsor a science club. You're out of your mind!

JUAN   *[Pleading]* Please, Chuck. You know how important it is to interest these kids in academics. You've got them interested in science. Now we have to provide additional incentives to keep them interested.

CHUCK   Did I hear a *we* in there somewhere? What's your role in all this?

JUAN   It's my idea and I'm encouraging you. I'll support whatever you want to do. Think about how important this is, Chuck. Alonzo has the kids interested in football. I'm sure we'll win the district championship this year. Don't you think it's equally important for our students to be competitive in academics? If you started the science club by the beginning of next semester, we'd have pupils ready to compete in the spring science fair.

CHUCK   You have this all figured out already, don't you, Juan? And you're just taking it for granted that I'll say yes, aren't you?

JUAN   *[Emotionally]* Yes, I am. Because you're one of the best teachers we have, and you could make the science club a success. You *like* the kids in this school and want them to have some of the same opportunities that kids from wealthier school districts have. *[Pause]*

I want these things for our kids, too. I'm not going to apologize for asking you to help them. And I think you'll at least consider this science club seriously. And I think you'll come to my office on Monday morning and tell me that you're going to do it. Then I'll offer you all the help I can, which probably isn't much. But you know I'd give you anything you wanted if I could.

CHUCK   That's a big help, Juan. Now let's talk about something else.

After dinner that evening, Chuck is sitting in the living room staring into space. Kathy and the children are also in the room, but he seems not to be aware of them.

KATHY   A penny for your thoughts, Dad.

CHUCK   Oh, I'm just thinking about my conversation with Juan during lunch hour today. He asked me to start a science club at school and be the sponsor.

KATHY   Oh, that man! He must be trying to work you to death.

CHUCK   *[Smiling]* He's really a mess. The whole school's a mess. It operates on a shoestring. In many ways it really makes a difference in the lives of the pupils. But some of the faculty have to spend so much time, effort, and money to accomplish this difference. *[A long pause]* It just doesn't seem right.

KATHY   What doesn't seem right, Dad?

CHUCK   This school. At Lakeview High School, the pupil population was primarily middle and upper-middle class. The pupils' families provided them with private lessons in music, art, athletics—whatever they wanted to do. Yet the school also sponsored all these activities.

　　　　　But here at Chavez High School the kids are poor. They have very little at home. But the school's poor, too. It can't furnish the services that Lakeview furnished the well-to-do kids. It seems that schools serving well-to-do kids don't really need to offer these services and schools serving poor kids should offer them all. But that's not the case.

KATHY   If you're any example, the teachers in Chavez are exploited. You have the heaviest teaching loads in the district. It's not fair. I worry about you. You're worn out all the time. You're already doing more than any teacher should be asked to do, and now Juan's asking you to do another big job, and you won't get anything for it.

CHUCK   I know. But he's caught in the middle, too. He really cares for those kids.

KATHY   *[Pleading]* But Dad, you can't change their lives that much. A science club isn't going to raise them out of poverty. Neither is a football championship. Football season ends. They graduate. Then they are gone.

　　　　　[Long pause] I know what you could do. Why don't you spend some time during Christmas break interviewing at high schools that have good facilities, supplies, and equipment. You could have a lighter teaching load, more promising students, a nicer environment, and the means to be a more effective teacher.

CHUCK   That's a thought. The Caldwell District just north of here is really a wealthy district because of all the oil wells located there. I've heard that they have everything it's possible to have there.

KATHY   Why don't you write and say you want to make a change at the end of the year? You're on a yearly contract, aren't you?

CHUCK   Yes, I am. And two of the high schools in that district are actually closer to our house than Chavez.

　　　　　[Enthusiastically] I'm going to do it, Kathy! Thanks for the suggestion.

　　　　Near the end of the spring semester, Chuck is driving home after school. Since Kathy had made arrangements to take the children to the playground after work, he and Alonzo had time to go to the local drugstore for coffee and conversation.

They discussed what a good year it's been for Chavez High School. The football team won the district championship and advanced to the statewide quarter finals before losing a game—the highest they had ever advanced.

Four of Chuck's science students won blue ribbons in the state science fair—a first for the school. Of course, Chuck had to provide transportation for them and buy them their meals out of his own pocket. But, nevertheless, it was a gratifying year.

As Chuck parks his car in front of the house, Kathy comes out the front door waving a letter.

KATHY   Dad! Dad! You got a letter from Caldwell School District. Hurry and read it to see if they're offering you a job!

CHUCK   OK. OK. Calm down. Let's take it into the house and read it. *[He sits on the couch, removes the letter from the envelope, and reads it.]*

[Smiling] They did offer me a job, Kathy! And it's a terrific offer! The salary is $3,000 more than I'm making now! They want me to be the advisor to the science club and teach three sections of general science and two sections of physics. I've really missed teaching physics. Plus, I'd have a free period instead of being required to monitor a study hall, as I do here. And they have two fully equipped science laboratories. Wow!

KATHY   You're going to take it, aren't you?

CHUCK   I'm not sure.

KATHY   *[Astounded]* Dad! I can't believe what you just said. Why in the world would you even have the slightest reservation about accepting that position? It offers you everything you've been saying that you want!

CHUCK   I know it does. I couldn't ask for anything more.

KATHY   Then why don't you just call now and accept the job? You won't have ol' cheapskate Juan asking you to spend your own money for supplies, do additional jobs for no pay, work overtime for no pay. He really exploits you and the other teachers.

CHUCK   I know. But his motives are honorable.

KATHY   But wouldn't you like to work with those smart students and use all that modern laboratory equipment, and have time to prepare your lessons at Caldwell?

CHUCK   Yes, that would be wonderful. But I also know that I will miss the students here. They work under so many disadvantages. And, yet, many of them become successful. I think I've contributed to the success of many of them. That's even more important than money.

KATHY   Don't tell me that you're going to return to Chavez and work yourself into exhaustion for another year when you could have this really prestigious position at Caldwell.

CHUCK   I just have to think about it long and hard, Kathy. I need to decide why I teach and what I really want to accomplish.

CHAVEZ HIGH SCHOOL

Schedule of Classes for Chuck Rogers

Period	Time	Subject	Grade	Enrollment
HR	8:05–8:30	Homeroom	9	38
1	8:35–9:30	General Science	9	34
2	9:35–10:30	Chemistry	11	30
3	10:35–11:30	Biology	9	30
4	11:30–12:30	Study Hall	——	130
5	12:35–1:30	Lunch	——	——
6	1:35–2:30	Chemistry	11	33
7	2:35–3:30	General Science	10	34

CALDWELL HIGH SCHOOL

Proposed Schedule of Classes for Chuck Rogers

Period	Time	Subject	Grade	Enrollment
HR	8:05–8:30	Homeroom	9	32
1	8:35–9:30	General Science	9	29
2	9:35–10:30	Physics	11	24
3	10:35–11:30	Planning Period	——	——
4	11:35–12:30	Lunch	——	——
5	12:35–1:30	General Science	9	30
6	1:35–2:30	Physics	11	27
7	2:35–3:30	General Science	9	32

QUESTIONS

1. On what level of Maslow's hierarchy do Alonzo and Chuck function? Does Juan function on the same level? Explain.

2. How does Alonzo explain his success as a football coach to Chuck? What psychological principles of motivation might better explain Alonzo's success in helping the pupils at Chavez become successful football players?

3. What impact does the surrounding environment have on the school climate at Chavez High School? What effect does poverty have on learning? What steps have Alonzo and Chuck taken to minimize the negative effects that poverty sometimes has on schooling?

4. What effect, if any, do you think the multicultural nature of CHS has on the students? the teachers? What are some of the special concerns of teachers in multicultural settings? What are the characteristics of teachers who can effectively work with students from subcultures other than their own?

5. What teacher characteristics have made Chuck successful in dealing with the pupils at Chavez High School? What effect might Chuck's "kitchen science" have had on his students? Why?

6. What is teacher burnout, and how does it relate to stress? What are the sources of stress in Chuck's situation? What can teachers do to cope with stress?

7. In what ways will Chuck's teaching methodology be different if he accepts the position at Caldwell High School? Give specific examples and the rationale behind them.

8. What administrative leadership style is exhibited by Juan Correa? Is he more of a "supporting," "coaching," "delegating," or "directing" type leader? How would you like to work with him? Why?

9. How might CHS involve its parents in the school's program? Do such parent involvement techniques as home visits, classroom volunteering, parent participation in advisory committees, and parent attendance at school events relate to school achievement?

10. What is social class and how does it differ from socioeconomic status? What is Chuck's SES? How effective are middle-class, white teachers in working with multicultural students? What teaching effectiveness variables are involved?

11. What are some strategies that Juan Correa, the building principal, can use to get the school board and upper administration to more adequately fund the school and its program? What formulas are used to determine the amount and extent of a school's funding? Given such funding formulas, how can some schools obtain more adequate funding than others in the same school district?

12. Do you think that Chuck should go to Caldwell High School or stay at Chavez High School? Explain why.

CASE 11

COMPUTER CONFUSION

The town of Oakmont is a middle-class suburban community near the large city of Spartica in the southeastern United States. The population is approximately 50 percent white, 25 percent Hispanic, 15 percent African-American, and 10 percent Asian-American. Many of the residents work and shop in nearby Spartica.

On the first weekend in August, Marc Santoya and Sam Altman have just finished playing their weekly tennis game. When they were in college, Marc majored in business education and Sam majored in computer science and graduated two years ago. Marc graduated in May and has been hired by Oakmont Middle School as a business education teacher. Sam is the regional manager of his computer company. The two of them have just completed their game.

SAM   Great game, Marc. You really played over your head.

MARC   Really? I didn't think I was as sharp as usual.

SAM   You wish. My game was off today because I was thinking about a business proposition I want to run by you.

MARC   That sounds serious. Is it related to your business or mine?

SAM   Well, actually, it's related to both our businesses. My company donates money each year to certain schools who agree to use our computers and computer programs in their business classes. In the past we worked with high schools, but we believe now that computer-assisted instruction, or CAI, is more appropriate and more effective if it's introduced in the middle school.

MARC   Why's that?

SAM   Because computers have become more available, children are becoming users at a much younger age. They seem to learn just as efficiently as older kids. Since you teach general business classes to sixth graders, you're in a perfect position to receive one of our grants. It's really a win–win situation. My company gets a tax write-off, good advertising, and increases sales. Your students will get effective computer experiences that make them more employable.

MARC   You're scaring me to death, Sam. I know little about computers and have never used CAI in my classes.

SAM   *[Smiling]* Even though you seem to be a slow learner on the tennis court, I think you'd be a whiz-bang CAI instructor. And by teaching your pupils how to use computers, you help them become more employable than they would be otherwise. That's worth a little extra effort on your part, isn't it?

MARC   You always did have a way of putting questions to get the answers you want, Sam.

SAM   Seriously, the timing's perfect, Marc. If you apply for the grant now, you'll know whether you're funded in time to move the computers into your room before school starts. The software will arrive in time for me to give you some instruction on loading the programs in the computers and helping pupils use the function keys before classes begin in the fall.

MARC   You've convinced me, Sam. But I should talk this over with my principal, Margaret Darst, before we send in the application. I'll call her Monday and see what she thinks about it. She's pretty conservative, generally, and hasn't ever mentioned CAI since I've known her. But maybe she's figured that our budget is too small to even consider CAI. Well, I'll find out soon. I'll call you Monday evening at home and let you know what happens.

SAM   That sounds good, Marc. But before we can apply for the grant, I'll need to ask you some questions about your business courses.

MARC   Fire away.

SAM   O.K., I'll ask them all at once. Do all sixth graders enroll in business education? How many business classes are there? What's the average enrollment of each class? What topics are taught in business education?

MARC   I'll answer them all at once. Yes—six—30—keyboard, office practices, and careers.

SAM   Good. We have a great keyboard program. Once pupils learn the keyboard, they can go right on to word processing. We have the best-selling software programs in office practices and interest inventories, and several programs on careers, including choosing careers, writing applications, and interviewing that pupils can use as soon as they learn word processing. If you're awarded the grant, you can really improve the quality of your business education program.

MARC   You've got me now! I'm sure that computers will give us more flexibility in our courses, because we can individualize instruction and be sure that the pupils are learning what they ought to learn. I really appreciate the time and effort you're devoting to our school, Sam. You're a good friend.

SAM   Well, let's wait and see how things turn out before you smother me with gratitude, Marc. If you beat me as badly in tennis next Saturday as you did today, I may withdraw my offer. [Laughs] Meanwhile, I'll look forward to hearing from you Monday evening.

On Monday afternoon, Marc is in the office of his principal. He has just finished explaining to Margaret Darst, his principal, the offer that Sam's computer company has made and what the benefits are for the school and the pupils.

MARGARET   That's wonderful, Marc! I don't see how we could justify not applying for the grant. Although I haven't been a strong advocate of CAI, I do subscribe to a professional journal on computer-assisted instruction and read each issue carefully. One statistic I see regularly is that about 70 percent of CAI involves drill and practice. It's probably fair to say that CAI is like an electronic workbook. *[Pause]*

However, let me point out that on the few occasions I've visited schools with computers, I've found that the computers are available to pupils mainly during lunch hour and study halls. The most popular programs used during those times are arcade-type games that are entertaining, but not especially educational. And I've seen research articles in the journal to back this up.

I'm also concerned about research reports in the journal which found that girls are generally uninterested in CAI. They suggest that girls don't appreciate the aggressiveness and violence that provides motivation for playing some of the computer games. When you combine that with lack of interest and/or ability in mechanics that is typical of many girls, well, they just don't get excited about the computer.

MARC   *[Smiling]* Wow! It's reassuring to know that I never need to be in doubt of your position on an issue! *[Pause]* I've some misgivings about using computers too, mainly because I don't feel very well qualified to direct computer-assisted instruction. And I'm also not convinced that computer-based instruction will solve all our problems.

MARGARET   Even though I'm a bit concerned about the use of computerized instruction, Marc, I wouldn't want to be responsible for denying an opportunity for our students to become computer literate. And I agree that business people are definitely looking for computer-literate employees.

MARC   Sam agreed to help me learn what I need to know to work with the computers if we get the grant, so I may well be qualified to direct CAI by the time school starts.

MARGARET   Fair enough. Let's go for it, then, Marc. I appreciate your willingness to assume this extra responsibility in behalf of the school and pupils. Please don't hesitate to come to me if I can be of assistance.

MARC   Thanks, Margaret. I'll talk with Sam this evening and tell him to go ahead with the plans. I'll keep you informed of our progress.

Three weeks after his meeting with Ms. Darst, Marc receives a phone call from Sam.

SAM   Hold onto your hat, Marc. The grant recipient has just been announced and you're the lucky winner! Congratulations!

MARC   Wow! I hardly know what to say. 'Thank you' seems to be most appropriate. What do I do now, Sam?

SAM   I have a contract that you, your principal, and the district superintendent must sign to indicate that you accept the grant and agree to its terms. The terms generally are that you'll use our hardware and software in your business classes.

Why don't I drop a contract in the mail for each of you? I'll include a stamped, return address envelope. Then you can sign and return it to my office.

MARC   Sounds good to me. I'll call Margaret and ask her to alert the superintendent to look for the contract. Is our tennis game for 10 o'clock Saturday still on?

SAM   You bet! I'm going to beat you this time!

On Monday, the first day of school, Marc feels comfortable with the idea that his classes will work with computers all year. He has learned to load the free-standing computers and worked through all the programs the pupils will use in the business classes this year. He also devised a record-keeping system that enables him to individualize instruction and keep track of each pupil's progress.

Marc greets the 16 boys and 14 girls in his first-period business class as they enter the room. The 15 computers are in place and ready to go. Marc asks the pupils to select a partner and then select a computer. He notices that the boys pair off with boys and the girls pair off with girls.

Marc then calls the roll, has pupils introduce themselves, and explains how the school received a grant that made the computers available, and that they're the only students in the school district who are using CAI. He gives a general introduction on the use of the computers and announces that the first unit of study in the class will be learning the computer (typewriter) keyboard.

MARC   Now I want you to take the disk on the stand in front of your box and slide it into the slot in the middle of the box. Good. Now turn on your screen by pushing in the white button below your screen on the right. Good. Now turn on the computer by pushing up the white lever on the right of your box. At this point, you should hear your computer booting up.

TOM   Mr. Santoya, something's wrong with our computer.

JANE   Ours too. It isn't doing anything.

ANN   We're having trouble, too.

JOANNE   Our box is making a horrible sound.

MARC   *[Walking toward Tom and Ann's desks]* OK, I'll come around and look at all the computers with problems as soon as I can. I'll work on Tom and Jack's first. Let me push this button and release your disk.

NOLAN   I can help, Mr. Santoya, I have a computer like these at home and can probably tell what's wrong.

MARC   Please do, Nolan. Thanks. That'll be a big help.

FRED   I'll help. I have a computer, too.

WILL   Me, too.

   [Marc, Nolan, Fred, and Will manage to get all the computers loaded correctly. By the end of the hour, most of the pupils have begun to work on Lesson 1 of the keyboard program.]

On Tuesday before class, Marc meets with Fred, Nolan, and Will.

MARC   Some of the pupils in class have never worked on a computer before. Yesterday, some of them couldn't get their disk loaded right, or they pressed various function keys by mistake and didn't know how to correct the problem that it caused. As you know, we spent the entire hour yesterday correcting those problems. I couldn't have given the help they needed by myself.

Since you three are familiar with computers, you can get some valuable business experience in this class working as supervisors and tutors. And I'm willing to give you double credit. Since you already know the keyboard, I'll give you class credit for that. In addition, I'll give you credit for supervising and tutoring the other pupils in the class on using the computers. Basically, your job will be to help your classmates become familiar with the keyboard and keep a record of their progress through the programs. If you agree to do this, it'll mean that each of you will work with one individual pupil and four teams of two pupils.

NOLAN   Why can't we go on to the office practices program instead of working with the beginning pupils?

WILL   C'mon, man. Don't you know a good deal when you see one?

FRED   Yea, Nolan. I like the idea of having supervisory experience. It might make the difference in getting us a job.

NOLAN   OK. That's cool.

MARC   Great! I think you've made the right choice. Can you decide among yourselves which individuals and teams you want to work with?

BOYS   Yes, we can divvy them up.

MARC   OK. Have at it.

Several days later, the pupils in Marc's first-period class are working on their computers. Mark walks to a computer at which two girls are working. On the screen he sees several lines as follows:

ffffjjjjffffjjjjffffjjjjffffjjjjffffjjjjffffjjjjffffjjjjffffjjjjffffjjjjffffjjjjffffjjjjffffjjjj

MARC   Susan, Ruth. What's that you're doing on your computer?

SUSAN   My sister was in your business class two years ago. She gave me the typing book she used in that class and we're using that.

MARC   Why would you use an old-fashioned typing drill manual when you can use a streamlined computer program that moves you along as fast as you're able to move?

RUTH   We don't like to work on the computer, Mr. Santoya. We're trying to work up the nerve to ask you if we could use a typewriter instead.

MARC   I don't understand. Why don't you like the computer?

SUSAN   It just seems so complicated. I don't understand how it works. It's almost scary the way it moves through the program. It seems to be controlling us instead of us controlling it. Some of the other girls don't like it either.

MARC   How many lessons have you done on the computer?

SUSAN AND RUTH   Just one.

MARC   You're already behind the rest of the class. If you work from that old typing book, you'll get even farther behind. And you won't learn nearly as much as you will from the CAI program. Besides, this is only the first week of classes. Do you think that you've given the computer a fair chance?

SUSAN   I guess we've just decided that we don't like it.

MARC   Well, for now, I'd like you to work with the computer at least until you become familiar with it. Then I think you'll like it. Will you be willing to at least try?

SUSAN AND RUTH   [Sighing] OK.

The following Monday morning pupils in the first-period class are beginning to work on their programs.

JANE   Mr. Santoya, there's something wrong with my computer. The wrong letters are coming up on the screen!

LIONEL   Mine, too. This is really weird.

GERARDO   [Laughing] The computers have all gone crazy! Mine is typing everything wrong. I know I'm pressing the right keys.

WILL   I know what's happened Mr. Santoya. Somebody's pried off some of the letter caps and mixed them up.

MARC   Thanks, Will. Let's identify the caps that are on the wrong keys and put them back where they belong. We'll record the machines that have been tampered with and then find out who did the tampering.

That afternoon, after his sixth-period class begins working on their computers, Marc selects several pupils and invites them into his office.

MARC   Do you know why you're here? [No response] Then I'll give you a clue. Four computers were vandalized during this period last Friday. The keycaps were pried off their stems and switched around. Fortunately, I remembered that the computers that were tampered with were those at which you were working.

BLAKE   I was at one of the computers, but I didn't have nothing to do with the tampering. I told Sam not to do it.

MARC   Is that right, Sam?

SAM   Yes, Blake wouldn't go along with us. He was chicken!

MARC   Maybe Blake's the only one of the five of you who uses good judgment. These computers cost more than $2,000 each. Vandalizing school property is a criminal offense. You could be arrested for what you did.

TONY   [Frightened] We were just messin' around, Mr. Santoya. We didn't really hurt nothing! We just wanted to play a joke on the next class.

MARC   I'm sure that's true. But sometimes jokes like that are more harmful than funny. This joke, for instance, caused my first-period class to miss almost a full period of instruction while we were trying to get the computers working again.

CHARLIE   What're you going to do to us?

MARC   Well, I could report this incident to the police, who would treat it as vandalism. *[Boys groan audibly]* Or I could ask Ms. Darst to suspend you from school. *[More groans]* Or I could ask your parents to come into the school and tell them what you've done. *[Groans]*. But I've decided not to do any of those things. *[Sighs of relief]*

I think I know you all well enough to believe that you meant this to be a harmless joke, even though it could be considered by the police as a criminal offense.

Ms. Darst knows about this incident and has given me responsibility for deciding your punishment. So I've decided that I'm going to penalize those of you who were involved in this activity for using bad judgment. You'll all receive an *F* for the first week's work in this class.

Several days later, Nolan appears at Marc's office after school and asks if they can talk for a few minutes. Marc invites him in.

NOLAN   I've come to ask why the three of us who already know how to type can't begin working on the office practices program. It seems like a waste of time for us to help other guys learn a keyboard program that we already know how to do.

MARC   It seemed to me that when we discussed this earlier, Fred and Will were very much in favor of it. Have they changed their minds?

NOLAN   Well, no. I guess I'm speaking just for myself.

MARC   As I mentioned when we discussed this before, two of the most important roles in business are inservice training and supervision. Assistant managers for companies and retail stores spend most of their time supervising employees and conducting inservice training. This is an opportunity that few sixth-grade students have. When your classmates become more familiar with the computer, we'll all move along at our own speed and complete as many programs as we can this year.

NOLAN   But a lot of us have experience working with computers, and we can work on our own without bothering you at all. And we'll be learning materials that we don't know.

MARC   Remember, you are the only one interested in changing the assignment. But I'm sure you can work on your own, Nolan, and you'll do exactly that in a few weeks. I think you'll have a much more valuable learning experience as a supervisor for the beginning pupils than you could get by moving ahead right now. And as far as I know, Fred and Will are pleased with the assignment. So I want all of you to do that for the time being.

The following Monday, the pupils sit down at their desks and turn on their computers. Marc is seated at his desk reviewing the progress records of the previous week, which were given to him by the three supervisors. He hears giggling from one side of the room and follows the sound to Nolan and Will, who are sitting together at a computer. Mark walks to them and sees that they are playing a computer game. Two of the pupils they are supposed to be supervising are sitting together at another computer.

MARC   Why are you boys sitting here and not working with the keyboard students assigned to you? *[Neither boy answers]* What program is that on your screen?
NOLAN   It's a computer game. I brought it from home.
MARC   And was it also your idea to put the two keyboard students assigned to you and Will together so that you would have a computer to play on?
NOLAN   Yes, It's really boring supervising those pupils when we could be working on something new.
MARC   *[Angrily]* I explained to you last week why you are working with partners! What you are doing now makes the two of you guilty of breaking several agreements! First of all, you're not helping your assigned pupils learn to use the keyboard. Second, you're wasting your own time. And third, you're violating your assigned role in this class. Nolan, you and I discussed this last week! You're both in a supervisory role which requires you to help the students assigned to you learn as efficiently as possible. Much of your grade for the first few weeks of this class is based on your behavior as supervisors. This morning's behavior has seriously affected your performance in this role. Nolan, this entire matter seems to have been planned by you. You deliberately involved Will in it. Not only did you waste your own time, but you also kept another supervisor from doing his work. Such behavior is completely unacceptable. Your grade as a supervisor as of today is *F*. You'll be able to make it up if you are a perfect supervisor for the remainder of the six-week grade period.

Will, even though this situation was planned and carried out by Nolan, you're just as guilty as he because you participated in it. You're guilty by association. Because you weren't in on the planning, I have lowered your grade in the class to a *D*. You, too, can bring up the grade with good work. I don't plan to report this incident to your parents. But if either of you is guilty of any other violations of the rules, I'll schedule a conference with your parents and report both incidents. Do you both understand this?
NOLAN AND WILL   *[Contritely]* Yes sir.
MARC   Good, Now get back to your computers and supervise your partners.

Oakmont Middle School has parent conferences during the twelfth and twenty-fourth weeks of classes. Parents come to school from 7 to 9:30 P.M. They go to each of their children's six classes for approximately 20 minutes, with five minutes allotted for changing classes.

By 7:05, several parents from Marc's first period class are seated in his classroom. He expresses delight that so many parents have come. He opens the meeting by explaining briefly how Oakmont happened to receive the $50,000 grant that provided the computers and related hardware and software. Then he asks for questions and/or discussion.

MR. LOPEZ   My son says he isn't getting to work on a computer like the other kids and doesn't seem to study much in his business subjects at all. He says that he and some other students are tutoring other pupils and keeping records on them. I don't understand what he's doing, and why he isn't involved in learning regular business topics. It seems to me that you're getting the students to teach your class for you.

MARC   *[Frowning]* Your son, Nolan, is very much involved in general business education, Mr. Lopez. The first topic we studied this year was keyboard. Nolan and two other pupils already know the keyboard. It would be a waste of their time to require them to work for several weeks on material that they have already mastered. When I proposed that they work as supervisors and tutors, they all three agreed to do so for class credit. So I taught them how to supervise and provide in-service education for the other pupils. Business employers prefer to hire personnel who have had supervisory experience for their executive training programs.

MR. LOPEZ   *[Angrily]* Call it what you will, I believe that supervising students and recording progress of students is the job of the teacher. Asking students to do your work is exploitation, and I don't want Nolan to do be held back like that.

MARC   *[Controlled and deliberate]* Supervising students and recording their progress are legitimate assignments for business students. They're included in the school district's business education curriculum.

MR. LOPEZ   Are you refusing to release Nolan from this assignment?

MARC   *[Definitely]* Not at all. I intend to release all three of them from the supervision assignment and have informed them of this. I'm waiting for the appropriate time to do so. Mr. DeRusso, you had a question.

MR. DERUSSO   If the school received $50,000 of computer equipment, why are you wasting it on teaching typing and office practices? These procedures can be done just as well with typewriters, which the school already has. I think that is a flagrant misuse of school facilities. Why not use the computers for social studies or composition?

MARC   To be eligible to receive the grant, Oakmont Middle School was required to sign an agreement that we would use the computers and software to teach business classes.

MR. DERUSSO   Why, then, couldn't the computers be used to teach economics, marketing, insurance, or something more creative than office practices and careers? It seems to me that the computers will be wasted for at least half a year.

MARC   The school district's business curriculum specialists don't feel that the courses are a waste of time. They require that typing and word processing be taught the first semester and office practices and careers be taught the second. Aside from that, I've learned that computer programs do not exist for the topics you mentioned. They tend to focus more on subjects that can be learned through drill, such as those we are using.

MS. FEINER   I've two questions on an entirely different topic. My daughter and several other girls in your class really dislike working on the computer. My friend who owns a computer store says that this is generally true of the girls she knows. Why are you forcing them to use the computer when they have such a mental block against it?

MARC   It's true that many girls do not like computers. But employers favor job applicants who are computer literate. I've already talked with Susan and her friend Ruth about this. They agreed to give the computer a chance. I hope you and the other parents will emphasize to your daughters the importance of mastering the computer. If they are truly considering a career in business, failure to become computer literate may be quite costly to them later on. *[Bell rings]*

   The ringing bell means that it's time for you to go on to your child's second-period class. Thanks for coming. If you have any additional questions, I'll be glad to meet with you individually whenever it's mutually convenient.

   After the program is over and the parents have gone, Margaret Darst stops by Marc's room.

MARC   Hi, Margaret. A lot of parents showed up, didn't they?

MARGARET   They certainly did! Some were quite vocal, too.

MARC   Yes I had some that weren't happy with various aspects of CAI. Some of their questions were hard to deal with.

MARGARET   Yes, and I'm afraid you're going to have to deal with some of them in more depth than you did this evening.

MARC   Really? Which questions in particular?

MARGARET   Several parents weren't satisfied with your responses to their questions. I can give you a brief summary since I just finished taking with them. Mr. Lopez thinks you are exploiting some of the pupils and is considering complaining to the superintendent; Mr. DeRusso believes that the computer programs you are using are not much more than glorified workbooks; Ms. Feiner is upset because Susan and several of her girlfriends are unhappy using computers. She agrees with you that they should become computer literate, but she's concerned that they are so upset and fearful.

   Let's think about these problems, Marc, and decide how to handle them. I want you to have individual conferences with each of these parents soon. But first, I want to meet with you in my office, starting tomorrow, and have you explain what you think each parent is saying and how you're going to answer their concerns. OK?

Individualized Student Progress Record

MR. SANTOYA'S FIRST-PERIOD GENERAL BUSINESS CLASS

Name:	**Keyboard** 1 2 3 4 5 6 7 8 9 10 11 12	**Word Processing** 1 2 3 4 5 6 7 8 9 10 11 12
Alou, V.	x x x x x x x x	
Ancell, J.	x x x x x x x x	
Barlis, C.	x x x x x x x x x x	
Beall, R.	x x x	
Busby, B.	x x x x x	
Cadiz, M.	x x x x x	
Chuani, S.	x x x x x x x	
Comas, H.	x x x x x x x x	
D'Amato, P.	x x x x x x x x x	
DeRusso, B.	x x x x x	
Feiner, N.	x x x x x x x x x	
Fouts, W.*		
Ghani, Z.	x x x x x x x x x x x x	
Han, L.	x x x x x x x x x x x x	
Howell, T.	x x x x x x	
Jackson, W.	x x x x	
Letz, V.	x x x x x x x x x x x	
Lopez, N.*		
Masuda, Y.	x x x x x x x x	
Pitts, E.	x x x x x x	
Ponce, D.	x x x x x x x x x x x x	
Powers, R.	x x x	
Ryan, N.	x x x x x x	
Schell, S.	x x x x x	
Smith, F.*		
Snipes, K.	x x x x x	
Sommers, L.	x x x x x x x x x x x	
Tillman, C.	x x x x x x x x x x x x x	
Urban, D.	x x x x x	
Winston, P.	x x x x x x x	

* = Student supervisor of other students
X = Lesson successfully completed

QUESTIONS

1. How effectively did Marc plan in his effort to integrate CAI in his general business course? What do his instructional objectives seem to be? How could he have organized things differently?

2. Did the software that was available to Marc seem appropriate for his course objectives? Is it true that most computer software is geared to drill and practice and is not appropriate for more academic courses, such as social studies and English?

3. What administrative leadership style is exhibited by Ms. Darst? Is she more of a "supporting," "coaching," "delegating," or "directing" type leader? Why do you think so?

4. How intrinsically motivating are computer games for students like Nolan? How can a teacher like Marc take advantage of the intrinsically motivating qualities of such software?

5. Are there gender differences in how boys and girls respond to computers? If so, why do such differences exist? Did Marc handle this problem well?

6. How effectively did Marc handle the vandalism problem involving Sam and Blake? What model of classroom management does Marc seem to use? How might the organization of the entire CAI program and the problems that stemmed from it have been handled from a behavior modification or observational learning standpoint?

7. Was it good pedagogy for Marc to allow Nolan, Will, and Fred to serve as student supervisors? How else could Marc have handled the fact that these students were ahead of the rest of the class? Is there anything that Marc could have done to prevent the dissatisfaction that arose, especially in the case of Nolan and his father?

8. How well did Marc relate to the parents at the parent conference? From a teacher effectiveness training standpoint, who "owned" the problem? What roadblocks to communication existed? How effectively did Marc use I-messages and active listening techniques?

9. Should all preservice and inservice teachers be required to take CAI courses? Why or why not?

10. What are the components of an effective teacher–parent conference? How should Marc prepare himself for his individual conferences with the parents?

ALICE IN WONDERLAND

lice Perez is a 22-year-old graduate of a state liberal arts college, located in a far western state. Although all the students in State College are required to major in one of the liberal arts, the college has made provisions for students who want to obtain teacher certification. Such students can obtain either elementary or secondary teaching certification by attending three summer sessions during which they enroll in the required education courses and serve an internship in a public school. Alice majored in English and attended the summer sessions to complete all the requirements to make her eligible for state certification as an elementary teacher.

During the summer after her graduation, Alice applied for teaching positions in three school districts located in or near the large metropolitan area which is the shopping center for residents of the small town in which she grew up.

Almost immediately, Alice received an invitation to come to the administration building of the Highlands School District to interview for a first-grade teaching position in Balboa Elementary School, which is located in a lower-middle-class suburb of the metropolitan area in which Alice wanted to teach. After meeting with the assistant superintendent for personnel of the district, the district elementary supervisor, and the principal of Balboa Elementary School, the principal thanked her for coming and assured her that she would hear from him soon.

On her way home, Alice drove into the suburb in which Balboa Elementary School is located. She passed several small shopping centers that had been well maintained—landscaped with recently mowed lawns, buildings recently painted, parking lot surfaces in good condition. When she arrived at the school grounds, she found a similar well-maintained appearance. The lawns were attractive and the playground displayed a variety of different types of equipment that were relatively new and in good repair.

Alice had learned during her interview that the school population of Balboa is approximately 60 percent white, 20 percent African-American, 10 percent Hispanic, and 10 percent Asian-American. Since she is Hispanic, Alice was interested in teaching in a school that is culturally diverse. She was pleased with her interviews, the community in which the school is located, and the cultural diversity of the area. She decided that if the position were offered to her, she would accept it.

The week following her interview, Alice received a letter from Hector Ruiz, the principal of Balboa Elementary School. Contained in the envelope was a letter offering her the first-grade teaching position, a contract spelling out the details of the employ-ment conditions, and a stamped envelope addressed to the principal. Alice signed the contract, put it in the envelope, and mailed it back immediately. She at once began to envision herself teaching a class of bright, smiling, culturally diverse pupils who loved her and eagerly devoured the knowledge she imparted to them.

The Friday before classes are scheduled to begin, an all-day pre-school workshop is held at the school auditorium for all the teachers in the school. Alice arrives early and is pleased to notice that there are snacks and coffee available in the cafeteria. As she walks through the line, an older woman in front of her turns to face her.

MARGO   Good morning. You must be our new first-grade teacher. I'm Margo Matza, a
         third-grade teacher.
ALICE   Hi, Margo. I'm Alice Perez, and I am the new first-grade teacher. It's nice to
         meet you. This is my first year of teaching, and I'll probably need some help
         from some of you experienced teachers.
MARGO   Well, I'm probably what you call an old-timer. This will be my seventh year
         of teaching here. It seems as if I've always taught here. If I can ever help you
         with anything, please don't hesitate to ask me. Maybe between the two of us, we
         can solve most problems that come up.
ALICE   Thanks, Margo. It's nice to have someone I can talk with.
         [They make their selections of coffee and fruit from the cafeteria trays and
         start toward the tables]
MARGO   Let's sit here with LaShonda and Alma. This is LaShonda Johnson. We call
         her Shon. And this is Alma Russo. Shon and Alma are beginning their sixth year
         of teaching here, so they are old-timers, too.
SHON   Hi, Alice, welcome aboard!
ALMA   We're glad you're here, Alice. We hope you'll enjoy the school and the faculty.
         One nice thing about Balboa is that the faculty all get along well together.
ALICE   That's great. Everyone I've met so far seems really nice. So far I've met you
         three. [Everybody laughs]
SHON   [Looking at her watch] OK, ladies, we had better get a move on or we'll be late
         for the workshop. [They walk together to the auditorium where they find seats near
         the front.]

In the preservice workshop, a professor of education, Dr. Lori Erdman, is dis-cussing strategies for individualizing instruction.

DR. ERDMAN   So one of the most recent ideas to be introduced into the lower elemen-
              tary grades is to acknowledge that even very young pupils are able to acquire
              language best by actually using language in real situations.
SHON   Could you give us some examples of this, Dr. Erdman?
DR. ERDMAN   Sure, I'll be glad to. Probably when you were in school, you spent many
              hours in kindergarten and grades 1 and 2 doing phonics exercises in a work-
              book. And maybe some of you have used or are still using phonics workbooks.

Am I right? [*Most of the teachers nod in agreement*] Well, I'm about to talk with you about a new way of teaching language skills to pupils.

Research evidence now suggests that children learn the sounds of English much more efficiently by using the language in social situations—dictating stories for the teacher to write on the board or writing letters to each other or to family members. I know several kindergarten teachers who bring a medium-sized carton to class and have the pupils decorate it. Then they cut a slot in the top, attach it to the wall, and use it for a mailbox. They encourage pupils to write letters to them and to each other and put them in the box. The teachers write a letter to five or six pupils each day also. Every day there is a letter-reading time set aside.

ALICE   But surely there are pupils in the lower grades who can't read and write.

DR. ERDMAN   Of course. But this is the beauty of this strategy. If pupils don't know all the letters, they just invent a mark that represents that letter. In fact, this type of writing is referred to as "invented spelling." After the message is written, its writers are asked to read it. They can do this, because they know what it's supposed to say. So basically, they have experiences in both reading and writing.

ALICE   But doesn't this teach them incorrect information?

DR. ERDMAN   Good question. And the answer is that it doesn't. Basically, it helps them become interested and confident in reading and writing. And researchers have found that pupils who are encouraged to use this strategy go through the same developmental stages of spelling. The only difference is that some pupils go through faster than others. And pupils who are allowed to write and then read their own writing learn at least as well and often better than those who are drilled on writing and phonics. But there is evidence that they read and write more than the pupils who are not encouraged to read and write at an early age.

Dr. Erdman's presentation of early reading and writing generates many questions and much discussion among the teachers, which continues until it is time to break for lunch. As the teachers leave the auditorium and begin to walk toward the cafeteria for lunch, Margo spots Alice and runs to catch up with her.

MARGO   Alice, have you made plans to eat with anybody?

ALICE   [*Obviously pleased*] No, I haven't.

MARGO   [*Enthusiastically*] Great! Why don't we eat together?

ALICE   I'd really like that. Right now, I'm in a state of panic!

MARGO   Really? Well, we can't have that, can we? Why are you in a state of panic? What can I do to help?

ALICE   I was really interested in Dr. Erdman's talk this morning. But it also terrified me!

MARGO   Why's that?

ALICE   I feel so inadequate! I don't know anything about the ideas she talked about! In fact, I'm beginning to think that I don't know enough about schools or pupils even to be a teacher! And Monday I'm going to have my own class for an entire day, and all day Tuesday, and Wednesday and every day for an entire year! *[Her voice begins to quiver]* And I don't have any idea what to do with them on Monday!

MARGO   Alice, I'd be willing to bet great sums of money that every teacher in the workshop this morning had that exact same feeling their first day of teaching.

ALICE   Did you?

MARGO   Absolutely! I can still remember the butterflies in my stomach for several days before school started. And I'll tell you something reassuring. By lunchtime on the first day of class, the butterflies had all disappeared.

ALICE   While Dr. Erdman was talking, I was thinking about Monday morning. I imagined all the pupils sitting in their chairs talking to each other or looking at me. Then I thought, "I need to give these pupils something to do." *[Tears well up in her eyes]* And then my mind went completely blank! I couldn't think of anything to do or say!

MARGO   Alice, you are a certificated teacher, aren't you?

ALICE   Yes. I majored in English at a liberal arts college, but in addition to my liberal arts degree, I completed all the education courses I needed to become certificated as an elementary teacher. And I did an internship in an elementary school during my senior year.

MARGO   Then you have had experience in working with children.

ALICE   In a manner of speaking, I did. But I had this experience during the spring quarter and I was in a fourth-grade class with an older teacher, Ms. Pruitt, who had taught for years. By spring, she had everything so well organized that I was like her understudy in a play. One day I just took her place and followed the script that was already in place. I made no decisions at all. The lessons were planned for the entire year, the tests were already made up, the pupils were already familiar with the class procedures, and there were no discipline problems. I didn't learn anything about planning lessons, organizing a class, grading pupils, meeting individual differences, or other problems common to every classroom. Ms. Pruitt had already implemented all these procedures.

MARGO   Would you like for your class to be as highly planned as Ms. Pruitt's class seemed to be?

ALICE   *[Thoughtfully]* At the time I didn't think I would want my own class as highly organized as that. But now I wish Ms. Pruitt would come in on Monday and work with them for a week or so to get them organized.

MARGO   What didn't you like about Ms. Pruitt's class while you were there?

ALICE   I guess I was upset because it seemed so controlled. I remember that at the time I thought the pupils acted like little robots, performing their tasks without any emotion, enjoyment, or interest.

MARGO   Then you really wouldn't want her to set up your class, would you?

ALICE   *[Definitely]* No, not really. I want my classes to be fun and interesting and productive!

MARGO   *[Clapping her hands]* Good for you! So what you need to do between now and Monday is to plan how you can begin to get your class started in that direction.

ALICE   [With uncertainty] That's what I'm worried about. I don't know where to begin.

MARGO   [Enthusiastically] Well, let's begin by starting with what you know. How was Ms. Pruitt's class organized?

ALICE   I'm not sure what you mean by organized.

MARGO   Well, let's begin with the organization of subject matter. Did she have a separate period for language arts, a separate period for arithmetic, and so on?

ALICE   Yes, she did. She taught English the first period, arithmetic the second and so on. Is that what you mean?

MARGO   Yes. That's the subject-centered curriculum, which is probably still the most common type of organization. Is that the way you want your class to be organized?

ALICE   [After a long pause] Well, I'm not sure. What are some other options? That's the only organization I know. My elementary school classes were organized that way and so were Ms. Pruitt's.

MARGO   [Looking at her watch] My, how time flies! We're going to have to leave right now if we want to get to the next session of the workshop on time. It may be of real interest to you because Dr. Erdman is going to talk about the integrated curriculum. That will give you at least one other option for organizing your curriculum.

   [They both clear their trays, set them in a container, and hurry off to the auditorium for the second session of the workshop.]

After the workshop Margo and Alice walk down the hall together on their way back to their respective classrooms.

MARGO   Well, Alice, what do you think of the integrated curriculum now that you've heard Dr. Erdman's ideas about it?

ALICE   It's quite clear that she believes the integrated curriculum is the way to go. And, she pretty much convinced me, too. I think I would feel more comfortable with that type of organization than the one that Ms. Pruitt used.

MARGO   Then you've answered one of the major questions you had at lunch. Why don't you take some time over the weekend and make lesson plans for the first two or three weeks of classes. That will give you a bit of breathing space before you write your plan for the remainder of the school year.

ALICE   That's a good idea. How do I go about doing that? What do I write?

MARGO   Just make a plan similar to the one Dr. Erdman showed us. Select a topic that's appropriate for first graders. Then plan ways to integrate numbers, music, poetry, stories, science, social studies—whatever you want to include in your curriculum.

ALICE   [With determination] OK. I'll do it!

MARGO   Great! Let's have lunch together on Monday and we'll talk about it.

As the lunch period begins on Monday, Alice hurries to the cafeteria and looks to see if Margo has arrived yet. She locates her sitting alone at a table near the back, so she goes through the cafeteria line and joins Margo.

MARGO   Good morning. How was your class this morning?

ALICE   Pretty good. We spent the morning locating our assigned seats, learning to recognize our names and the names of some of the other pupils, and learning the routine for using the bathroom.

MARGO   *[Smiling]* Well, those sound to me like pretty important activities for first graders. Tell me about your class. How many pupils do you have, what are they like, and how did they respond to their new teacher?

ALICE   There are 25 pupils in the class, and they are really a culturally diverse group, which is what I hoped for. There are 13 whites, five African-Americans, four Hispanics, and three Asian-Americans. They seemed to respond to me OK. In fact, we had a pretty good time this morning.

MARGO   Good, I'm glad! Did you make any decisions regarding your class organization?

ALICE   Yes, I've decided to use an integrated curriculum. Dr. Erdman's presentation Friday convinced me that I'd feel more comfortable using that organization than I would using the subject-centered approach.

MARGO   What will be the central theme for your unit?

ALICE   I've begun to organize two different themes that I think will last for two to four weeks. I don't have much of an idea yet about how long it takes first graders to complete a task. And I'm sure that I have a vast range of ability levels in my class.

MARGO   That's a good way to begin. You'll soon begin to gauge how much time certain types of activities require in your class. What are the themes you have chosen?

ALICE   The first unit will be "My Home and Family." As you know I'm really dedicated to the idea of establishing a multicultural curriculum for my class. Literature about families from the various ethnic groups will be the central focus of the unit. But pupils will also have opportunities to tell about the national origin of their families and share aspects of their cultural heritage—holidays, foods, activities, etc. We will have related art and music, locate countries on maps, and play games that are favorites of the various groups.

MARGO   *[Impressed]* That sounds like a unit designed by an experienced teacher! I like it! Tell me about the other unit.

ALICE   Its theme is "Shapes," and it's basically an arithmetic unit. But it will also include stories, baking (cookies in various shapes), colors, traffic signs, songs, etc. The possibilities are unlimited.

MARGO   I can tell that you've given the curriculum much thought over the weekend. And I like the idea of educating for diversity. That's an especially important objective in this particular school. Have you considered how you will organize your room for instruction?

ALICE   What do you mean, organize the room?

MARGO   I mean how are you going to arrange your chairs and tables? Are your pupils going to work in groups? Will you set up special areas, such as an art area, book area, math area, science area?

ALICE   I haven't even thought of the room arrangement. How would you arrange the room to teach these units?

MARGO   I can't answer that question. The arrangement of the classroom will depend on the types of activities you plan to have the pupils do. With such a diverse class, you'll probably need to do some type of grouping. *[Looking at her watch]* Where does the time go? The fifth-period class starts in five minutes. We need to be on our way.

ALICE   *[With disappointment]* Darn! I didn't realize it was so late. I really want to talk with you more about the arrangement of the class.

MARGO   *[Standing and picking up her tray]* Why don't we meet in the faculty lounge as soon as the pupils leave? We can have a Coke and talk for a half hour or so.

ALICE   Thanks, Margo. I'll be there. You've really been a big help to me.

After the last pupil has left the room, Alice starts toward the faculty lounge. As she turns into the hallway on which the lounge is located, she sees Margo approaching from the other direction. They both arrive at the lounge at the same time.

MARGO   Great timing!

ALICE   I was just about to say that to you. *[Reaching into her purse for change]* How about something to drink?

MARGO   Yes. But I want mine to be a diet drink.

ALICE   *[Drops change into the vending machine and pushes the appropriate buttons, retrieves two cans and hands one to Margo]* One diet drink coming up.

MARGO   Thank you, ma'am. How was your class today?

ALICE   It went well. We're still getting acquainted with each other and practicing classroom procedures, like using the bathroom, raising our hands to talk, walking instead of running, and those types of things. But I'm really in a quandary about the classroom organization you asked about at lunch today.

MARGO   What, specifically, is causing you problems?

ALICE   Well, basically, I've organized the classroom into five interest centers. When we get ready to go to these centers, I explain to the whole class what they will do in each of these centers. Then, each group goes to one of the centers and works there. After 20–30 minutes, depending on how well they are working, I have them shift centers. While they are working in the centers, I spend time with each group. When time for recess comes, they all go to recess together. After recess, they go to the next center.

When we begin the family unit, I plan to have the same interest center idea, except the various groups will work on their own project in their own centers. I can continue to move to the various centers whenever a group or individual pupil seems to need help.

But I've decided that the randomly-assigned groups that I'm working with now will not work when we begin the family unit.

MARGO   Why is that?

ALICE   Well, there's such a wide range of ability, cultural diversity, and of SES background that I decided the grouping must be done by design rather than at random.

MARGO   And what type of design do you have in mind?

ALICE   I'm not sure. That's why I wanted to talk with you. I know the pupils range in ability from very low to very high. I think this is good and I'm pleased about it. But I don't want to group them by ability. I don't want the smartest pupils all in one group and the slowest pupils all in another group. I don't think this type of grouping is good for either the highest or the lowest groups.

MARGO   I agree. So what other options do you have for grouping?

ALICE   I'm interested in the type of grouping in which each group contains a fairly representative distribution of the class population. The problem is how to set up that type of grouping. Well, I saw Mr. Ruiz in the hall when we were coming back in from recess, and I asked him if he had some tests I could use to test my pupils' abilities. He said all the kindergarten pupils were given reading readiness tests last spring. He also told me that I can pick up the scores in his office this afternoon. I just have to get there before he leaves at 4:30.

MARGO   That's a really good idea. The readiness tests should be accurate enough to help you discover how large the range of ability of the pupils in your classes really is. It may also help you to match your groups by ability. That was a good idea, Margo, to ask about test results. I hadn't even thought of that possibility. But if you're planning to pick them up before 4:30, you'd better get a move on, because it's 4:25 now.

ALICE   You're right! *[Stands up and slides out of her seat]* Here I go! Thanks a lot, Margo. You're really a big help to me. *[She rushes off down the hallway]*

Alice hurries to the lunchroom immediately after the third period. She's carrying a file folder containing several sheets of paper. She hurries through the serving line and goes to the table at which she and Margo ate yesterday.

She doesn't have long to wait. Soon Margo comes across the cafeteria carrying her tray and sits down across from Alice.

MARGO   You beat me here today! You must have rushed to arrive here so quickly.

ALICE   *[Excitedly]* I did! I have some really interesting information for you. Mr. Ruiz let me take home the scores for the reading readiness test the kindergarten teacher gave to my class last year. The results are really interesting. *[She hands Margo a copy of the information]* The test is the Lee–Clark Readiness Test and it's designed to provide an estimate of pupils' skills in the areas of letter symbols, concepts, and word symbols. The total score of these three areas allows the pupils to be rated from low to high in the development of the three areas.

MARGO   These scores indicate that you do have quite a wide range among the pupils in your class, at least in the skills measured by this test. And I think your decision to group the pupils heterogeneously rather than homogeneously is a good decision. What strategy do you plan to use to ensure that your groups are arranged heterogeneously according to ability?

ALICE   [*After a long pause*] Well, to tell the truth, I haven't really gotten down to specifics. I know that it can be done, and I intend to do it. But I just haven't thought through exactly how I will do it.

MARGO   You're right that there are many ways that it can be done. But you need to group them carefully and then be able to explain specifically how you did it. Now, tell me what other characteristics you plan to factor into your grouping plan.

ALICE   As you probably also noticed from the last names of my pupils, there is also quite a wide range of ethic backgrounds among my pupils.

MARGO   Yes, I did notice that. And I agree with you that it would be worthwhile to use the ethnic backgrounds of your pupils to teach about cultural diversity. How could you possibly make it any more interesting and relevant than by relating it to their own family background? But this is an area that must be handled quite carefully. Have you thought of any specific projects you could assign to your groups that would be challenging and yet provide all the representatives of various cultures with assignments that would help to high-light some significant aspects of their culture for the other members of the group?

ALICE   Well, the unit on families could provide opportunities to learn about the different religious and historical events the different ethnic groups celebrate; family activities, such as games and leisure time activities; differences in family rules for children, etc.

MARGO   That's true. Have you decided the mechanics of such assignments, such as how they should be organized, how the pupils will share them, what forms the presentations could take, how much time you will allow for planning and presentations, and the various strategies pupils may use in their presentations? And will you have each group make the same types of presentations?

ALICE   No, I haven't progressed that far in my planning yet.

MARGO   If you plan to have heterogeneous groups, you must consider how you will plan assignments so that they will challenge the most advanced members of the group and yet not be unfair to the least advantaged members. And how will you assign grades so that you are not unfair to the less able or catering to the most able pupils? On what kinds of assessments will you base pupils' grades? Will these assessments be spelled out clearly so that they will be acceptable to all your pupils? to all the parents of your pupils?

ALICE   [*Emotionally*] Wow! You really ask hard questions. I was all excited when I came in this morning because I thought I had made great progress by finding these readiness scores. You really took the wind out of my sails.

MARGO   [*Embarrassed*] Oh, I'm sorry Alice! I have been inconsiderate. You certainly have made wonderful progress in your planning over the past several days, and I've been very impressed. I guess since you've moved along so fast, I just moved along fast, too. I'm really excited about what you're doing and want to hear every detail about the plan.

ALICE   Oh, that's OK. You've really been a great help. I couldn't have done all this planning without your encouragement and suggestions. At this point I'm wanting to get all the loose ends tied up, too. Do you have some suggestions about the organization, mechanics, and strategies of the unit assignments and how I can evaluate the various projects and activities?

MARGO   I don't right now, because I don't know who will be in the five groups you plan to form or what your overall objectives for the family unit will be. How will you organize the school day? Why don't you suggest how you will form your pupils into groups using their ethnic background, ability, and what other factors you think you should consider, such as which pupils are already friends, which ones don't seem to get along, and other aspects of the class interaction?

Next, you need to plan your overall assignment regarding families. Then you should break that down into specific assignments for each group and possible assignments based on ability level and talents for each individual in each group.

ALICE   [Overwhelmed] Wow! That's really a heavy assignment.

MARGO   [Calmly] I don't think it's as overwhelming as you might think. After you assign pupils to groups, the hardest part is done. Remember that the assignments for each group will be basically the same. They'll just relate to different ethnic groups. Select some more difficult and detailed assignments for the really able pupils and then ease off the assignments for the average pupils, and ease off even a little more for the below-average pupils.

With first graders, there will be virtually no independent research, because none of them can read or write well enough. You might have the highest pupils interview parents and give reports to the class, other pupils copy maps and show where the various ethnic groups came from originally, and others pupils sing ethnic songs or listen to stories translated from various ethnic groups.

ALICE   That's true. Some pupils might be able to bring ethnic foods, wear ethnic costumes, or describe various customs.

MARGO   Good! It sounds like you're on the right track. When do you think you can have your unit ready to assign to the pupils?

ALICE   I've decided that I will explain the unit and assign pupils to the five groups tomorrow. The groups will then know their general assignment. By Friday, I hope to have all the assignments made to every pupil and have them working on them. Right now, I envision this as a two-week project, but I'm not going to announce any time period to the pupils. If they work more slowly than I anticipate, I can allow them all the time they need.

MARGO   Great idea! Let's have lunch tomorrow and you can show me your groups, the overall theme of the unit, and the assignments for the various group members. Then we can discuss your criteria for evaluating the assignments.

ALICE   [Enthusiastically] It's a deal! I'll be here with the goods tomorrow!

Lee–Clark Reading Readiness Test, K–1 Results

Student's Name	Letter Symbols	Concepts	Word Symbols	Total
1. Ahrano, Juan	7	4	6	17
2. Blair, Louise	16	15	14	45
3. Canard, Robert	23	19	20	62
4. Cheng, Zyung	20	14	15	49
5. Dace, Dana	16	13	14	43
6. Davis, Lamar	14	15	16	45
7. Gouge, Brigette	5	3	6	14
8. Ha, Nhi	20	18	19	57
9. Hafner, Lawrence	21	20	19	60
10. Insalaca, Renato	19	17	17	53
11. Johnson, Merlakia	14	13	12	39
12. Ivory, Hattie	15	17	18	50
13. Jarvis, Jack	8	4	7	19
14. Jump, Ruth	14	12	11	37
15. Kearns, Julie	10	11	9	30
16. Latsko, Leah	18	19	18	55
17. Lewis, Roselyn	18	17	18	55
18. Li, Mei	24	19	20	63
19. Lopez, Sergio	16	15	15	46
20. Martinez, Carmen	22	29	18	60
21. Nelson, DeLisha	17	15	16	48
22. Peeples, Matthew	12	9	11	32
23. Roberts, Takilya	6	3	5	14
24. Skaggs, Larry	12	16	17	45
25. Wagner, Christopher	20	18	17	55

QUESTIONS

1. What rationale does Dr. Erdman use for recommending meaningful reading and writing to replace the formal study of phonics in the early grades? Do you agree with her? Why?

2. The teaching strategy that Dr. Erdman explained during her morning workshop is called the "whole language" or "top-down" approach. The approach Alice learned in college is called the "skills" or "bottom-up" approach. Briefly describe the theoretical foundations on which each of these approaches is based. What are the advantages and disadvantages of each?

3. Why did Alice feel that her internship experience had not been successful? How could her supervising teacher, Ms. Pruitt, have made the internship more valuable?

4. How did Alice first organize her class into small groups? Why did she decide that this organization was not satisfactory? How did she organize groups for studying the family unit? Why? How does this type of organization help to take student differences into consideration? How else might she have grouped her pupils?

5. In the afternoon session of her workshop, Dr. Erdman taught the participants how to use thematic units, cooperative learning, portfolio assessment, and dialogue journals. Which of these strategies is Alice planning to use in implementing her unit? Which of these strategies would be least appropriate for a first-grade class? Why? Which would be the most effective strategy?

6. How has Alice organized her school day? How does this organization differ from the organization used by her supervising teacher, Ms. Pruitt? What are the advantages and disadvantages of each of these types of organization?

7. Using the information presented in this case, explain Alice's strengths and weaknesses as a teacher. How can teacher education programs better prepare teachers like Alice?

8. Evaluate Margo's effectiveness as a mentor to Alice. What were Margo's strong points? her weak points?

9. Margo described the subject-centered curriculum and the integrated curriculum. What other types of curriculum models exist? What are their advantages and disadvantages?

10. What role do instructional objectives play in planning? What instructional objectives does Alice seem to have? What instructional objectives do you think it would be desirable for her to pursue?

11. What is involved in effective classroom planning? How effective was Alice in her planning? What does she need to learn about the elements of effective planning?

12. How will Alice take individual differences into consideration as she evaluates the projects of the various pupils in each of her groups? How could she defend giving a slow pupil an *A* while giving a bright pupil a *C*? Is this a fair way of evaluating pupil progress? Why? Should Alice use norm-referenced or criterion-referenced evaluation procedures? Should she grade pupils on a satisfactory/unsatisfactory basis? Should grades be given at all in the first grade?

PART IV

INSTRUCTION AND EVALUATION

CASE 13

HERESY OR GOOD TEACHING?

Brandon Elementary School is one of five elementary schools in the city of Brandon, which has a population of approximately 18,000 people and is located in the Southwest. Residents of Brandon enjoy a high employment rate because of the large farms in the area and the numerous small manufacturing plants, which permanently employ a large number of workers.

Parents of the pupils generally support the schools and desire their children to have a high-quality education. The building is relatively old but well kept and well equipped. Brandon serves a 60 percent white, 20 percent African-American, 15 percent Hispanic, and 5 percent Asian-American population.

Joy Noska is a 21-year-old-graduate of a nearby state university who is beginning her first year of teaching. She has been assigned to a self-contained fourth-grade class with 26 pupils. It is the Friday before classes are scheduled to begin and Joy has just left the auditorium where the school principal, Mr. Dias, has had a faculty meeting to welcome the faculty back to school and to introduce new faculty. Joy is the only new faculty member. She is walking with Tanya, who has four years teaching experience and is also a fourth-grade teacher. Tanya sat next to Joy at the meeting. She and Joy are the youngest teachers in the group.

TANYA Well, Joy, are you all set for Monday?

JOY I'm not sure. The school faculty and staff seem to be very nice, but Mr. Dias didn't give out much information about school policy, teaching expectations, or educational philosophy, did he?

TANYA [Laughing] No. He's sort of a casual type of principal. But I'm glad. He pretty much lets us all do our own thing and is quite supportive. He doesn't bother us unless we get into some kind of trouble.

JOY Well, that's good news. But I'd really like to know more about the general school policies and practices.

TANYA Like what?

JOY Nitty-gritty things like what kinds of class materials are available for pupil use. Is there a school grading scale that all the teachers follow? Do we teach reading from basal readers? Are there separate textbooks for math, science, social studies, and health? Is there a separate period set aside for each subject? Does the school have a specific program for discipline that all teachers follow? I'm just curious about whether there are standard practices that teachers generally follow that I should know about.

TANYA   Wow, you do have lots of questions! I'm not sure I know the answers to all of them. Let me tell you the school's grading scale first. That's the easiest one to answer. Between 92–100 is A, 83–91 is B; 74–82 is C; 66–73 is D; and below 66 is F.

JOY   Can you adapt this scale for slower students who are conscientious and work at full capacity?

TANYA   I don't believe that's ever been discussed in a faculty meeting. I'm not aware of any teachers having to defend their grades to the principal. Occasionally, a parent's unhappy with a pupil's grade, but Mr. Diaz usually supports the teacher.

JOY   That's encouraging. Now, how about the reading materials?

TANYA   We use graded textbooks for all our classes. We have a common basal reading series for the entire school. Fourth grade has two reading books. One's numbered 4.1 and is for the slower readers, and the other, 4.2, is for the better readers.

JOY   Is the school library well stocked?

TANYA   I'm embarrassed to admit it, but I don't really know. I've generally relied on textbooks and the set of encyclopedias in my classroom for information.

JOY   Then I assume that there must be grade-level textbooks for math, science, social studies, and health and a separate period set aside for the teaching of each of these subjects?

TANYA   You've got it. Even though our classes are self-contained, I teach reading first period, language arts second, social studies third. That takes us to lunch period. After lunch I teach math and science. Health's part of science class.

JOY   Do you like that arrangement?

TANYA   [After a long pause] Yes. It's worked OK for me. When I was in college, that's pretty much the way we learned to teach. I came here straight from college four years ago and have stayed in the same position. That's why I was so glad to see you at the faculty meeting and sat beside you today. We're quite a bit younger than the other teachers, and I'd like us to be friends.

JOY   I'd like that, too. I appreciate your making me feel welcome at the meeting today.

TANYA   Anyway, back to my story about when I first came here. When I asked the other teachers what they did, they were using basal readers and basic texts for each subject, so I basically followed suit. Why? Don't you like this arrangement?

JOY   I'm not sure. Remember this is my first teaching job. But in my education classes at college all the professors seemed excited about different approaches to teaching that are being introduced in some *avant garde* classrooms—whole language, unit teaching, and individualizing instruction. In these approaches, pupils study a large theme, like the geography of the United States. Then, pupils learn all the different subjects by applying them to this theme.

TANYA   [Overwhelmed] Wow! That's really a different approach! My professors at Southwestern State didn't teach anything like that. I think that approach would be very complicated. Is that the way you want to teach here?

JOY I don't know. It's a pretty new approach. That's probably why you didn't study it four years ago. I'm not sure whether the parents or even the principal and other teachers here would know much about it.

TANYA *[Thoughtfully]* Maybe you shouldn't ask. Just do it if you want to! My Dad's first law is, "It's easier to get forgiveness than permission."

JOY *[Laughing]* That's good, Tanya! I like it! I think your Dad's my kind of a guy.

But I'm not ready to make any big decisions like that until I meet my pupils, examine the texts that the school uses, and become more familiar with the school in general.

TANYA Our school has good cumulative records of all our pupils. Maybe they'll help you to find out some of the information you want to know about your pupils. Eventually, Maria, the office secretary will send them to you to keep in your filing cabinet. If you want them now, I'm sure she'd be delighted to have you pick them up. It'd save her the time and effort of finding them for you.

JOY *[Enthusiastically]* That's a good suggestion, Tanya! I hadn't even thought of cumulative records. I'll be able to get lots of good information from those, I bet.

TANYA Yes, for one thing, you'll probably find out what level basal readers all your pupils have read since they entered school. And you'll also get a general idea of what grades they've earned in the primary grades, whether they've been in trouble at school, and if they have any special needs.

JOY Good! That'll be a big help. Thanks Tanya. Now, I gotta go. See you Monday.

TANYA O.K. Bye.

Although Joy and Tanya have seen each other every day and have become good friends, they haven't talked much about their school classes. It's Friday evening, three weeks after the teacher's meeting at which they met. Earlier in the week, Joy had suggested that they go to dinner together Friday evening. Tanya agreed. They're seated in one of the local restaurants.

TANYA This was a good idea, Joy. I'm glad you suggested it.

JOY Me, too. I get tired of my own cooking. Besides, I need to have some moral support from you.

TANYA *[Exaggerated seriousness]* This sounds quite heavy. Are you planning to commit a heresy that needs my moral support?

JOY Heresy might well be an appropriate word for what I'm planning to do.

TANYA Well, don't keep me in suspense. Reveal to me your sinister plan, whatever it is.

JOY OK. Here it is. Remember our conversation after the faculty meeting three weeks ago about teaching procedures, grading, and other practices?

TANYA Sure. You were talking about unit teaching and other teaching strategies that I don't know much about.

JOY Well, after our conversation, I went to the office and asked Maria for the cumulative records of my pupils as you suggested. I took them home and studied them very carefully. The results of last year's Metropolitan Achievement Test are included. Based on these results, the reading level of the pupils in my class this year will range from first grade through seventh grade. *[Hands Tanya a copy of class records]*

TANYA   True. There's a wide range of ability in all our classes. But don't keep me in suspense. Tell me what you're going to do about it.

JOY   Well, I distributed the basal readers and other texts to my pupils and used them for three weeks. During this time I observed the activities of all the pupils very carefully. I'm convinced that the books and materials available are appropriate for only about half of my pupils. About a fourth of them are capable of going beyond the materials, and the same fraction can't read well enough to understand them.

TANYA   Yes. I think that's probably true of my class, also. So, what did you decide to do?

JOY   That's the hard part. I'm still not really sure. But I spent a lot of time in our school library and was pleasantly surprised. There's really a good collection of books and reference materials there. And Ms. Nolan, the librarian, is terrific! She's happy to find a teacher who's interested in using the library, and I'm delighted to find a librarian willing to do hours of research for me, which she's already done.

TANYA   What kind of research?

JOY   For one thing, she's selected books that range from first to seventh grade in reading difficulty and labeled them according to grade level. These books are all related to the Southwest—history, geology, geography, biographies of famous people, demographics, parks, Native American tribes, and other related information. There are also literary selections written by or about people from this area during the different periods of its history and development.

TANYA   But, what're you going to do with all these books?

JOY   Well, that's the revolutionary aspect of my plan. I've already substituted these books for our textbooks.

TANYA   *[Taken aback]* But how can you do that? How will you manage the class? How will you grade the pupils? How will you keep track of the work that pupils do? How will you instruct them? How will . . .

JOY   *[Solicitously]* Tanya, Tanya. Slow down. It's all right. For one thing, I've assigned all my pupils books they can read on their own. I selected them from the books that Ms. Nolan set aside for me. And, as I mentioned before, these books are all related to various aspects of the history, development, and culture of the Southwest.

TANYA   I guess that's all right, if you've got books written on all those different levels, pupils should be able to read them. But how will you give them all individual assignments?

JOY   I've selected a unit on the Southwestern United States as our project for six weeks. Our history book deals with the history of our state, but it's so tied in with the development of the Southwest that it's really a book about the southwestern United States.

TANYA   Yes, that's true. But all the rest of us teachers use basal readers and single texts for the other subjects. You're really going to be different from the rest of us.

JOY Well, you already said that's heresy, right? But didn't you ever wonder why there's a special reading period with special reading books, that aren't even literature books, to teach reading? Aren't all classes in school really reading classes? Yet, in all classes but the reading class, the reading assignments are related to what the pupil is studying. In reading class, pupils seem to read for the purpose of reading. In the real world people don't do that.

TANYA But aren't basal readers especially written so that they're appropriate for the reading level of the pupils using them? That's what I was taught in my methods classes in college—basal readers are written especially for the purpose of teaching pupils specific reading skills.

JOY Yes, that's right. But that's what people say about all the textbooks in school. Yet, remember, those texts aren't appropriate for at least half the pupils in my class. But, even if they were, does it make sense to solve problems in the math book that aren't related to anything the students are interested in? Or to study history without relating it to economics, literature, geography, and culture? Why can't we study math by computing distances explorers traveled each day, or the dimensions of a plains tepee? Why can't we read literature about the Native Americans who settled in the Southwest, the people who explored it, the culture and fine arts that developed here, its economic development, and other relative topics? Why can't we draw scenes of the Southwest in art class, sing its songs in music class, write its stories in writing workshop and act them out in drama class so that all pupils share all this information that relates to this area we are studying?

Well the answer is, we can. And in my class, we are. I have just described my new curriculum.

TANYA [With concern] You're boggling my mind, Joy. I'm having trouble dealing with all your questions. And I can't imagine one teacher being able even to make assignments to the pupils in a system like that.

JOY Well, I have. And the pupils have already chosen their assignments from a wide range of choices I made available to them.

TANYA I think it'll be really hard to manage a program like that. How will you evaluate the pupils?

JOY In my college methods classes, we learned that if you combine whole language with unit teaching, the evaluation isn't that complicated. For one thing, unit teachers usually don't use objective-type tests, such as multiple choice, true–false, matching, and fill in the blanks. Many educators believe that these types of items tend to encourage memorization of isolated facts but don't evaluate pupils' broader understandings of the material presented.

TANYA Well, I guess that's true. Pupils have to memorize facts to score high on objective tests.

JOY In my class the pupils will share their work with each other. Posters, art work, models, and other types of constructions will be displayed along with an appropriate written report. Other projects involve mathematical computations, drawings, maps, geological surveys, and original plays and songs. These will all be shared with other pupils and I'll evaluate them in place of tests. The backbone of the study will involve extensive reading. Whenever the pupils read anything, they'll follow up with some kind of writing.

TANYA   Won't this just about overwhelm you with work?

JOY   I don't think so. I like dialogue journals. Pupils draw a line down the middle of each page. They write a reaction to their reading on the left side. Then I write a reaction to their writing on the right side, or suggest additional reading. This enables me to evaluate the quantity and quality of their reading and how they use the information they read to solve problems. And it doesn't really take a lot of time. Pupils don't write that fast.

TANYA   Will you keep all their writing? Won't that cause a major storage problem?

JOY   I'm encouraging them to keep copies of their best writings in a writing portfolio. Then I'll have a sample of the work that pupils think is their best. I'm not even above telling them to include certain samples in their portfolio. I'm convinced that writings and other types of projects reveal more about pupils learning than any kind of objective test can do.

I'll assign letter grades to every project based upon the length, difficulty, and quality of the project. Pupils working on group projects will be given letter grades based upon the amount, difficulty, and quality of their contribution. As you can see, the major advantage of the unit method of teaching is that all pupils can work at their own level of ability in an area of study that really interests them.

I'll base their grades on the length, quality, and difficulty of their products, and I'll have copies of them all if I need to justify a grade. I won't be able to narrow the grade down to a specific number grade, like 84. But I feel quite comfortable assigning letter grades. And I believe that my grades will better take into consideration efforts, abilities, and productivity of pupils than would two or three objective tests.

TANYA   That makes sense. But I couldn't teach that way. I don't really know enough about whole language, unit teaching, individualizing instruction, journals, portfolios and all those other things you've been talking about. I assign pupils readings from each of the textbooks we use. Sometimes I present supplementary materials that I think are important. Then I give them objective tests, usually a combination of multiple-choice and true–false tests. After I've graded a multiple–choice or true–false test over the topic they've just studied, I can tell which pupils know the most about the topic and which ones know the least. So I can really distinguish between pupil performance down to a single point.

JOY   Yes, but the information in most texts, by necessity, is extremely limited. You may just be separating good readers from the poor readers.

TANYA   Oh, I'm so overwhelmed by all this information that I don't really understand that I can't even comprehend what you're telling me. Besides, I think my pupils learn pretty well from the approach I'm already using. And I really feel comfortable with my classes.

JOY   That's great, Tanya! I'm not a very considerate dinner companion. I've spend the entire meal talking about my teaching plans. I've also really dumped a lot of information on you in a short period of time. Please don't think that I'm trying to convince you that you should teach this way. I'm not. It's just that I don't feel comfortable teaching separate subjects. If you do, more power to you. I hope I haven't ruined your dinner with all my talk about school.

TANYA   No. I've found it fascinating. It's stimulating to hear new ideas. And I enjoy talking with you. Besides, I'm really interesting in following the progress of your radical plan. *[Laughing]*

The Friday evening before Thanksgiving, Joy and Tanya are in their favorite restaurant having a pre-Thanksgiving dinner, since they're both going to spend Thanksgiving with their parents.

TANYA   How's your radical approach to teaching progressing, Joy?

JOY   I was running around like a chicken with its head cut off for about a month. But now, things have really settled down into a routine. I'm quite pleased with the class's progress so far. The pupils are reading and writing every day. And I can already see great improvement in these skills. The best part is that they seem to be really enjoying it. It seems as if we have so much more time every day for really important activities since we don't have to change subjects every 50 minutes. We spend the extra time in free reading, writing, creative activities, researching, and presenting oral reports.

TANYA   That's really great. I know you've worked hard and spent much time and effort getting your pupils organized so that they could begin working on the unit. I'm really pleased that it's turned out well.

JOY   Well, you played an important role in making it a success. You're a great sounding board and you provided the encouragement I needed when I began to get discouraged.

TANYA   Well, that's what friends are for.

JOY   Thanks for being a good friend.

TANYA   Which leads me to mention that I heard some information this afternoon that you should know about.

JOY   *[Apprehensively]* You say that as if it's bad news.

TANYA   I don't really think it's bad news, but, as the saying goes, "Forewarned is forearmed."

JOY   Now I'm beginning to worry. Please get on with it. Don't let me sit here in suspense.

TANYA   O.K. As I was driving home from school this afternoon, I stopped at the supermarket to buy a few groceries. While I was there, I heard somebody call my name. I turned around to see who it was. It was Monica Worley. Do you know who she is?

JOY   Yes, she's the elementary supervisor for our school district. She came to visit me in my class during the first or second week of school. I thought she seemed very nice.

TANYA   Yes, as far as I know everybody seems to like her.

JOY   So what did Monica have to say?

TANYA   It seems that Monica's one of the premier bridge players in Brandon, and she belongs to several bridge clubs. It also seems that several mothers of your pupils are also bridge players, and that they're represented in the different bridge clubs that Monica plays in.

JOY   O.K. I'm following you so far. It sounds as if you're about ready to get to the bottom line of this story.

TANYA   Right. It also seems that one of the topics of conversation of all the bridge clubs for the past several weeks has been all the innovations that you've implemented in your class.

JOY   Well, I've always wanted to be famous. *[Pause]* Oh, oh. You're not about to tell me that I've become infamous, are you?

TANYA   *[Laughing]* No, as a matter of fact, Monica indicated that the mothers all seemed to be delighted with their children's progress. They thought the assignments were quite creative and that their children were really learning useful information.

JOY   That's really great! Remember when we were first talking about unit teaching? That was my first goal—to make learning relevant to real life.

TANYA   Yes, I remember. And I'm glad it worked out that way because I know you really worked day and night for a while planning all the assignments, evaluation strategies, and activities.

JOY   I somehow have an idea that there's something you haven't told me yet. Am I right?

TANYA   You seem to have a way of reading my thoughts. Yes, there's more.

JOY   How long are you going to keep me in suspense?

TANYA   I'm not sure how to broach the subject. I'm also not sure what I want to say is even professional. We're good enough friends that I can tell you things without being quoted, aren't we?

JOY   Of course we are. You shouldn't even need to ask that question.

TANYA   I know that, Joy, but what I'm about to tell you is information that mustn't be repeated by either of us.

JOY   *[In mock seriousness]* Pass the steak knife and I'll cut my finger and sign an oath in blood.

TANYA   *[Smiling]* You're making fun of me.

JOY   *[Seriously]* No, I would never do that. I want you to know that my word's as good as signing an oath in blood. I'll never repeat our conversation today to anyone.

TANYA   The reason I feel so uneasy about telling you this is that Monica's conversation about your class failed to give me any clue as to her purpose for discussing it with me. She really interrogated me thoroughly about it. I felt as if she were sucking my brain dry.

JOY   That's very interesting. I wonder why she just didn't call me and ask me.

TANYA   I wondered that, too. That's why I thought I should tell you about it. I can also tell you what concerns she expressed.

JOY   You're a regular intelligence agent, aren't you?

TANYA *[Laughing]* Well, shucks, ma'am, I try to be. The first concern she expressed to me was whether your pupils were learning the reading, grammar, science, and arithmetic skills taught in the fourth-grade textbooks.

JOY That's certainly a legitimate concern.

TANYA Yes, it is. Another topic she brought up is whether you're evaluating pupils in accordance with the numerical grading scale used in our district.

JOY That might also be a concern of parents who've had this scale used to evaluate their children throughout their school career.

TANYA I'm sure it is. That's probably the only measure they know. Monica has another concern that's also related to grading. She asked whether you'll give grades to pupils in specific subjects like math, science, social studies, reading, and so forth. She also wondered how you could assess the grade level on which pupils are functioning if they're all working on different assignments.

But I didn't help her at all. I just told her that we don't talk shop when we were together, which is the truth.

JOY These are all legitimate questions. I guess the best way for her to find answers to them is to ask me directly, come to some of my classes and see for herself, or both.

TANYA I think she's planning to take Choice Number 1, because she told me that she's going to make an appointment to meet with you after school some day next week.

JOY Well, I guess I'll have to prepare answers to all her questions then.

TANYA I know—but give me a hint. What are you going to tell her?

Brandon Elementary School

Pupils' Third Grade Reading Scores*

Name	Third Grade Percentile	Reading Stanine	Reading Comp.**	Vocab. Gr. Equiv. **
1. Acosta, E.	58	6	4.2	4.0
2. Beard, A.	64	6	4.2	4.0
3. Cho, M.	25	1	1.6	1.8
4. Chun, S.	56	6	4.0	3.9
5. Esposito, R.	49	9	6.0	6.3
6. Galt, L.	56	6	3.7	3.9
7. Jarvis, K.	35	2	2.5	2.6
8. Monaco, T.	60	6	3.9	4.0
9. Ocasio, L.	50	5	3.3	3.4
10. Paz, N.	28	1	1.7	2.0
11. Phillips, R.	94	9	5.9	6.1
12. Rodriguez, C.	56	6	3.7	3.8
13. Sabas, S.	40	2	2.7	2.8
14. Shaw, L.	97	8	5.5.	5.2
15. Stout, S.	56	4	3.5	3.6
16. Su, S.	60	6	3.9	4.1
17. Sykes, K.	58	6	3.8	3.9
18. Taylor, F.	30	2	2.0	2.1
19. Tin, K.	94	9	5.9	6.0
20. Uhl, N.	60	8	4.4	4.6
21. Usuni, P.	70	8	4.7	4.9
22. Vickers, T.	55	5	3.6	3.8
23. Walker, C.	23	1	1.1	1.2
24. Weems, B.	40	2	2.7	2.9
25. Wier, J.	45	3	3.2	3.2
26. Zito, E.	68	8	4.7	4.8

*Source: Third Grade Metropolitan Achievement Test
**Decimal scores refer to months, e.g. 2.4 = 2nd grade, 4th month

QUESTIONS

1. How do Tanya and Joy's general philosophies of teaching differ? How do these differences specifically affect their classroom teaching practices? Which philosophy do you prefer? Why?

2. Do you think that Joy's pupils can learn as much English, math, science, social studies, and other subjects by using a unit plan of study as Tanya's pupils can learn by studying this information directly from the fourth-grade text for each of these areas? Why?

3. Can Joy evaluate her pupils' academic performance for the six-week period on the grading scale provided by the school system? How? Can she give letter grades for each academic subject the pupils have studied? How? Will it be easier for Tanya to evaluate her pupils' performance using this system? Why?

4. Compare and contrast the strategies that Tanya and Joy use to assign classwork to the pupils in their class. Describe what the finished products tell each teacher about her pupils.

5. Compare and contrast the strategies used by Joy and Tanya to evaluate their pupils' classwork. Do you think one of these strategies is more reliable and valid than the other? Which one? Why?

6. Did Monica violate professional ethics by talking with Tanya about Joy's classroom teaching strategies? Why? Did Tanya violate professional ethics by talking with Joy about Monica's concerns about Joy's classroom teaching strategies?

7. Based on Tanya's description of Mr. Diaz's style of administration, would you classify it as the "supporting," "coaching," "delegating," or "directing?" Explain.

8. According to Joy, Ms. Nolan, the librarian, classified more than 100 library books from Grades 1 through 7 according to level of difficulty. What criteria does one use to make such assessments? What readability formulae are available to teachers? In what ways is the information on readability useful to a classroom teacher?

9. Is the type of evaluation system used by the Brandon school system norm- or criterion-referenced? What are the advantages and disadvantages of each? How desirable is it to have school- or system-wide grading standards rather than leaving evaluation up to the individual teacher?

10. How do the instructional objectives of Joy and Tanya differ? How do their test items reflect their instructional objectives? What kind of information does each of these types of tests provide the teacher?

11. What are the basic differences between true–false, multiple-choice, matching, and fill-in-the-blank test items? How does one determine which of these items to use? What types of material can best be tested by each type of item?

12. What are the basic differences between essay and objective tests? Describe how a teacher would make up each of these types of tests. Include in your description information related to course objectives, table of specifications, item analysis, reliability, and validity.

13. From the standpoint of Maslow's need hierarchy, at what need levels do Joy and Tanya primarily seem to be operating? At what level is the elementary supervisor operating? What are the characteristics of self-actualizing teachers, and how does a person move to that level?

14. What actions can school administrators take to avoid situations in which a new teacher has no idea of the educational practices prevalent in the school with regard to teaching philosophy, grading scales, and disciplinary procedures?

CASE 14

WHOSE GRADES?

J ack Ryan is a beginning secondary social studies teacher in the medium-sized midwestern city of Grayville, population 30,000. GHS serves an 88 percent white and 12 percent African-American population. Agriculture and mining are the two major local industries. The school building was built in the 1950s, but is well-maintained. Jack grew up in a nearby small town and is a 21-year-old graduate of a small teachers' college in the state. As a first-year teacher, Jack has been assigned to teach three sections of U.S. history, two of world history, and supervise a study hall and a home room.

It is one week before the first day of classes and Jack sits in the office of Frank Conway, the social studies chair. After discussing a variety of topics, including the handling of discipline problems, the conversation turns to grading and evaluation.

FRANK   What else would you like to ask, Jack?

JACK   Well, I've started to put together my first exams and quizzes and I guess I'm not real clear on the school's grading policies.

FRANK   *[Smiling]* It would be more accurate to say the school system's grading policy, since we're the only high school. But you've seen the one on the report form, haven't you?

JACK   Yes. You mean 95–100 is an *A*, 88–94 is a *B*, 77–87 is a *C*, and 70–76 is a *D*?

FRANK   Yes. Most of us use that standard in our grading. I should also add that those of us who teach social studies use as many objective tests as we can. We do that not only to reduce subjectivity and bias in our grading but also because the state standardized achievement test is multiple choice, at least the social studies questions are.

JACK   So the exam items should be as much like the achievement test items as possible.

FRANK   Yes. We take great pride in the fact that our small school's students do so well on the state test. Last year 73 percent of our eleventh graders reached mastery on the social studies section. So it's more than just writing items like those on the state tests—it's also important to make sure that you teach and test for the basic skills covered by the test.

JACK   I remember a class discussion along those lines back in college. The dangers pointed out were that standardized tests seldom measure higher-order thinking skills and that teaching for the test can make minimums become maximums.

FRANK   No danger of that here. Every teacher is encouraged to go beyond the basic skills and encourage higher-order thinking. You should add a few essay-type questions to your exams as well. OK? But I can assure you that everyone—from the school board and superintendent to the parents—takes great pride in our school's performance on the state test. *[Pause]* What else?

JACK   I guess I'm still a little confused about how teachers use the 95–100 = A grading standard. Sometimes tests are more difficult than you expect, and the highest score might only be, say, 80. Does that mean that you don't give any A's?

FRANK   That's up to you as the teacher, of course, but always remember that learning is what it's all about, not grades. Don't let your grading scheme become an end in itself. Use it as a means to encourage learning.

JACK   Then if 80 were the highest score, I might add points on to everyone's score and make a new curve that conforms to the school's?

FRANK   I've done it many times, Jack! Other times, when I thought the kids weren't working hard enough, I just left it alone, and maybe C would be the highest grade. That's where your professional judgment and experience comes in.

JACK   I see. But, Frank, I want my kids to know more than just dates, battles, and names of famous people in history. I even want them to go beyond higher-order thinking. I guess what I'm trying to say is that I want them to love history and appreciate the contributions that ideas, institutions, and, yes, great leaders have made to their lives today. How do I construct a test to measure that?

FRANK   *[Laughing]* If you figure that one out, let me know! But, seriously, that's where your class discussions, small group projects, and essay test items come in. Don't get me wrong, Jack. We're not so rigid that we don't think such educational goals aren't important and don't encourage them. But a standardized test score is a little like the score on the scoreboard at a basketball game. It's right up there in the lights for everyone to see. Right or wrong, people judge your progress by the agreed-upon standards. But that doesn't mean that you can't go beyond it and contribute to your students' learning in ways that aren't quite so visible. *[Pause]* You're a quick study, Jack! I think you're going to do just fine here!

JACK   Thanks, Frank! I'll do my best.

FRANK   I know you will. One more thing I'd like to underscore, Jack. Grayville is really an overgrown small town and our parents are very involved in our schools. You'll undoubtedly be talking to a number of them and some of them can be quite unreasonable when it comes to their kid's grade. That's where objective test items will help you. Then they have a hard time arguing that you're biased against their child.

JACK   I'll remember that Frank. Thanks for your help.

It is the first day of classes and Jack meets his first-period U.S. History class. After a general discussion of what the course is about, textbook usage, and Jack's expectations regarding appropriate student behavior, the discussion turns to evaluation procedures.

JACK   I know that you're all wondering what your grades will be based on in this class. I plan to give you a quiz each week, usually ten items, and a large unit exam at the end of each unit. All these tests will be objective, with anywhere from 75 to 100 items on the unit tests. Because, as I said before, I'm interested in your learning more than just facts in this course, there will be a few essay items on the unit exams. Yes, you're Marianne, right?

MARIANNE   Yes, Mr. Ryan. Will there be pop quizzes?

JACK   No, they'll be announced in advance, probably mostly on Fridays, and will cover the material for that week. *[Pause]* Now, besides the tests there will be individual reports and small group projects that I'll assign. These will obviously have to be graded more subjectively, but I'll certainly make clear to you in advance the criteria I'll be using to grade them. Yes, Troy?

TROY   What kinds of individual reports will we do?

JACK   Well, take our first unit, for example—the Age of Discovery. You might want to do a report on an explorer who interests you. For example, Ferdinand Magellan or John Cabot. Yes, Marianne?

MARIANNE   What kinds of small group projects will we do, Mr. Ryan?

JACK   A little later on I'll put you—or maybe let you put yourselves—in small groups of five to six people. You'll get at least one day each week to work in class on a project of interest related to whatever unit we're working on at the time. One group might want to construct a model ship like that used by Columbus or Magellan. Another group might get into food or clothing or something like medicine or health care at the time. Whatever interests the group. Yes, Jerry.

JERRY   How will you grade the group projects?

JACK   *[Laughing]*Very subjectively, I'm afraid! I guess originality and how much work you've put into it mostly. How well you present what you've done to the class will also be important. Everyone in the group will receive whatever grade the group project earns. So you'll all want to work together and help one another. Yes, Troy?

TROY   How much weight will you give these different things?

JACK   I really haven't decided that yet. I'll let you know. I guess the unit exams and the quizzes have to get the most weight. Also, I'll probably give a bit more weight to the individual reports than I will to the group projects. We'll see. Now let's get into the first unit.

It is four weeks later and Frank is returning the first unit exam taken by the first-period U.S. History class. Apparently, the test, consisting of 60 multiple-choice, 15 matching, 11 fill-in-the blank, and 2 short-answer essay items, was difficult for the class. The highest score was 87 (Marianne's score) out of 100 possible points, so Frank added 13 points to everyone's score. Troy made a score of 81, which was the top of the B range.

JACK   Does everyone have their paper? *[Pause]* Now if you'll look at your score in the upper right hand corner of your answer sheet, you'll notice that I subtracted the number of points you missed from 100, the highest score possible, and then added 13 points back onto the remainder. That's because the highest score was 87. By adding 13 points I made the scores fit the school's grading standards that's printed on the report forms. *[Pause]* I must admit that I was a little disappointed that the scores weren't higher, but then this is our first big test. And it may also be true that some of you didn't study as hard as you could have for this test. *[A number of students laugh politely at Jack's attempt at humor]* Yes, Troy?

TROY   *[Pointing to the distribution of scores on the blackboard]* How come there are only three *A*'s?

JACK   As I said, Troy, I converted the scores to the school's grading standards. Therefore, a score of 81 would be a 94 when you add on 13 points and would, therefore, be at the top of the *B* range.

TROY   *[Without raising his hand]* That doesn't seem fair! I studied hard for this test! There were four scores in the 80s and I don't see why they all shouldn't be *A*'s. Nobody pays any attention to the grade stuff on the report cards anyhow!

MARIANNE   He's right, Mr. Ryan. Ms. Rogers, my English teacher, uses 90–100 is an *A*, 80–89 is a *B*. . . .

JACK   *[Interrupting vigorously]* All right, people! Calm down! *[Pause]* I don't know what your other teachers do, but we're going to follow the school's standards in this class! You have to draw the line between an *A* and a *B* somewhere. Also, look at the gap in the distribution between the 80s. There is an 87, an 86, and an 85. Then it drops off to 81. I had to consider that, too. This was our first test and I'm sure that we all learned something from it and will do better next time. You have your individual reports and group projects to help you pull your grade up to where you think it ought to be. *[With strong emphasis]* Also, let me remind you that I didn't have to add 13 points onto your scores. I could have let the scores stand; the highest grade would have been a *B* and 81 would have been a *C*. *[Pause]* Now, lets go over some of the test items that gave you trouble so we can do better next time. Which one do you want to look at first?

It is one week later and Jack is sitting in the teachers' lounge by himself when Allen Grimes, an English teacher with ten years experience, walks in and joins him.

ALLEN   Hello, Jack. How's everything?

JACK   Oh, pretty good, Allen. Can't complain. Except maybe for my first-period U.S. History class.

ALLEN   Is that one giving you problems?

JACK   I guess you could say so. Do you know Troy Sullivan and Marianne Briggs?

ALLEN   *[Laughing politely]* Oh, those two! Yes, I do, quite well!

JACK   *[Frowning]* What do you mean by that?

ALLEN   Well, the Sullivans are quite well-to-do professionals here in town, and they expect a lot from Troy. Troy's not much of an athlete, so he overcompensates by trying to make straight *A*'s and being active in student government.

JACK   I see. And Marianne?

ALLEN   Think, man. Her last name—Briggs. Roy Briggs is her father.

JACK   The president of the school board?!

ALLEN   *[Smiling]* I'm afraid so. So as you can see, Jack, we're not talking about average kids here. They have a lot of pressure on them at home.

JACK   I see what you mean.

ALLEN   What's your problem with those two?

JACK   They constantly challenge the way I grade. They contest every point.

ALLEN   Now do you understand why? *[Pause]* Want some free advice?

JACK   Sure.

ALLEN   This is your first year of teaching. I've noticed that a lot of beginning teachers expect too much and grade too hard at first. Maybe it's from being around college students so long and forgetting what it was like to be a high-school student. What I'm trying to say, rather badly I must admit, is to ease up a bit on the grades. Don't let them become the tail that wags the dog. There's nothing sacred about a 90, as compared to an 89. Consider how the grade you give is going to affect the student. OK?

It is Wednesday; the first grading-period-reports were sent home the previous Friday. Jack looks into the office of Don Winslow, the building principal, who motions him in and invites him to sit down. Don gets up and closes his office door as Jack sits down.

JACK   This note was in my box, Mr. Winslow, that you wanted to see me.

MR. WINSLOW   *[Smiling]* Yes, I do, Jack. I haven't been able to spend enough time with you. I guess I've been too busy with the beginning of school and all and haven't gotten to talk to my teachers, especially my new ones, on an individual basis to see how things are going.

JACK   I appreciate your interest, Mr. Winslow. I've gotten off to a good start, and I'm really enjoying my first year!

MR. WINSLOW   I'm really happy to hear that, Jack! *[Pause]* What about your first period U.S. History class? Any problems there?

JACK   *[Nervously]* Yes, I do have somewhat of a problem in that class, Mr. Winslow. Why do you ask?

MR. WINSLOW   *[Businesslike]* Some of the parents in that class have called me and complained about your grading policies. Some say that your grading procedures are vague and subjective. Others say you're just a hard grader and don't give the students the benefit of the doubt. *[Pause]* Of course, I told them that I think you have excellent potential as a teacher and believe that your grading policies have the best interests of all your students in mind. However, I did tell them I'd talk to you. What can I do to help, Jack?

JACK   Well I don't know, Mr. Winslow. Two of my students, Troy Sullivan and Marianne Briggs, do seem unhappy about my grading policies, but I have talked them over with Mr. Conway, and so far as I know, I'm just following the school's grading standards.

MR. WINSLOW   Yes, I understand that, Jack, but their argument is that you're subjective in your grading and split hairs when deciding where the letter grades fall. Troy Sullivan has introduced a student council resolution to the effect that all teachers must state explicitly the basis on which they assign grades and that they have to use objective testing procedures anywhere it's possible to use them. *[Smiling]* Of course, I'll veto the resolution even if it passes, on the grounds that it interferes with the professional rights of our faculty. That is our teachers' domain, not the students'.

JACK *[Shaken]* I had no idea all this was going on!

MR. WINSLOW *[Smiling]* Don't worry, Jack. It will all blow over. We do live in a small city and the whole community is interested in our school and how it functions. But there are some decisions that have to be left to us professionals. And, Jack, as long as you are trying to use your best professional judgment in any area, I'll back you. However, you are going to receive a call from Troy Sullivan's parents asking for a conference. They want to talk to you about Troy's grades. You may want to talk to Ann Riley before talking to them. As Troy's guidance counselor, she has his cumulative record and may give you some information that will be of help. Please let me know how the conference goes, Jack.

JACK I sure will, Mr. Winslow. Thanks for your help and understanding!

The next day, during Jack's planning period, Jack obtains Troy's folder and takes it to the teachers' lounge to study, since Ann is too busy to talk to him. In walks Allen Grimes, the English teacher.

ALLEN Hi, Jack. You look like you're hard at work!

JACK Yes, I'm taking notes from Troy Sullivan's cum folder. I've got to meet with his parents—well, I guess just his mother, since his father is too busy to come in.

ALLEN Yes, Terry, Troy's father, is a dentist with a flourishing practice. I'm not too surprised that he's too busy to come in and have a conference with you. His wife, Mary, is a clinical psychologist and does all right, I hear, especially counseling some of the ladies here in town. So my guess is that she has a bit more time for a conference. *[Pause]* Did they give you a clue as to what they wanted to talk to you about?

JACK Not really. Just that they're concerned about his grade in U.S. History.

ALLEN Yes, they would be if he's having a problem. *[Pause]* Did you learn anything from his folder?

JACK Yes, several tidbits. He's an only child for one. I'd say an overachiever for another.

ALLEN Why do you say that?

JACK Well, look at his IQ scores. He took the Kuhlman–Anderson Test in the third grade, and his verbal IQ was 108 and his non-verbal was 112. In the eighth grade he took the Otis Lennon and his IQ was 111. Looks like they gave him the Stanford–Binet in the sixth grade and his IQ was 121. That's an average IQ of 113. Fairly consistent, wouldn't you say? A little above average. Yet, look at his grades—practically all *A*'s with a few *B*'s mixed in.

ALLEN There's no doubt that his parents have put a lot of pressure on him.

JACK I'll say. His achievement is far higher than anything I would have expected considering his IQ scores. No wonder he's so uptight about his test scores!

It is Friday afternoon after school one week later. Jack sits in his classroom having a conference with Mary Sullivan, Troy's mother.

MARY   I appreciate your seeing me, Mr. Ryan. I know how busy you are.

JACK   Please call me Jack. It's my pleasure, Dr. Sullivan. From what I've heard you're quite busy, too—with a thriving counseling practice.

MARY   Please call me Mary. Yes, things get quite busy in my office around this time of the year. Singles start to worry about being alone on the holidays and become depressed and morose.

JACK   [With surprise] Really! It starts this early?

MARY   Oh, yes! And it affects a surprising number of people!

JACK   Interesting! [Pause] Well, do you want to talk to me about your son, Mary?

MARY   Yes, Jack, I do. You know, Troy is such a high need-achiever and has really been upset by the grading procedure you are using in his U.S. History class. He feels that you grade in a subjective and unpredictable fashion and is really concerned that he might make a B instead of an A because of it. Some of his friends in the class, like Marianne Briggs, who is making an A, I understand, agree with him. He feels like you're not open to hearing his position on this subject anymore and asked his father and if we'd come in and talk to you. I'm sorry that my husband was tied up today but. . . .

JACK   [Interrupting] Mary, I want you to know that I'm always open to hearing what my students have to say on any subject. Troy disagrees with my using the school system's grading standard as my basis for giving grades. It's the old business of having to draw a line somewhere, and Troy happened to be below the line. It seemed to me that Troy didn't want me to be objective in adhering to the standard and wanted me to make an exception in his case.

MARY   [Smiling, but with a slight edge in her voice] What he told me he was thinking was that you didn't have a clear procedure for where you draw the line but still weren't willing to give him the benefit of the doubt. If you only realized how important it is to him to do well in your class, Jack, then I think you might. . . .

JACK   [Interrupting] I've come to realize how important it is to Troy and frankly, Mary, as a psychologist, I'm sure you're able to understand my concern.

MARY   What do you mean?

JACK   I've had a chance to take a careful look at Troy's cum record and I see a strong overachievement pattern in it. Troy's grades are outstanding considering his IQ scores. He must put in hours studying. . . .

MARY   [Interrupting] Frankly, Jack, I'm a bit surprised to hear you labeling Troy that way! Are you saying that his IQ scores indicate that he doesn't have ability?

JACK   [Hesitantly] Well, no, of course not, Mary, I . . .

MARY   [Interrupting] Troy plans to go into the premed program at State when he finishes high school and eventually become a psychiatrist. And my husband and I not only support him in this but we think he's perfectly capable of doing it. I'd hate to think that one of his teachers won't support his efforts because of his IQ tests, that he took back in grade school and which probably have questionable validity anyhow. [Angrily] Troy is a worthwhile person, Jack, and has a right to pursue his life's dreams.

JACK   [Shocked and with hesitation] Well, of course, he's a worthwhile person, Mary! I never meant to imply . . .

MARY [*Interrupting angrily*] Jack, my husband Terry and I feel very strongly about this matter. Having talked to you I've come to feel that you are rigid in your grading and biased against my son! We are prepared to pursue this matter with the superintendent and the school board if necessary. However, we are aware that you are a beginning teacher and don't want to be unfair. We'd both appreciate your thinking this matter over and giving us a call about what you intend to do about it—not just now, but in the future as well. I'll look forward to your giving me a call at my office next week.

Distribution of Scores in Mr. Ryan's First Period U.S. History Class

UNIT 1 EXAM

(100 Points Possible)

87 (Marianne's score)		63		
86	A	62		
85 _____		62	D	
81 (Troy's score)		62		
78		58		
77	B	58 _____		
76		56		
75 _____		54		
74		52	F	
73		48		
73		36		
73		31		
73		28		
65	C	26		
65		14		
65		12		
65		8		
65				
64 _____				

QUESTIONS

1. How desirable is it to have school- and/or system-wide grading standards? How much latitude should teachers be given as professionals to set their own individual grading standards? How much commonality in grading practices should exist among teachers?

2. Evaluate GHS's grading standards. Is such a system fair? Should it be applied in all subject areas and with all types of students?

3. What is the purpose of grading? How can a teacher make the best educational use of grading in the classroom? Are there any conditions under which students might have input in determining grades? What kind of grading system is Jack using? How can Jack keep from letting grades become more important than learning?

4. What are norm-referenced and criterion-referenced evaluations? What are the strong and weak points of each, and which is Jack using? Is it best to: (1) compare the student's performance to that of other students; (2) compare the student's performance to a preset standard; (3) compare the student's performance to his/her own past performance; (4) use a combination of the above; (5) abolish grades entirely or at least move to a pass–fail grading system; (6) vary the type of grading procedure according to the instructional objectives being pursued?

5. Examine the distribution of scores for Jack's Unit I exam. How would you assign grades to the students, especially Troy? What does *grading on a curve* mean? What are standard scores, and could Jack have used them here? Should a teacher grade on a curve in some classes and not in others?

6. What are objectivity and subjectivity in scoring? What are the relative merits of objective and essay test items? How do they differ in terms of their ability to measure learning at the different levels of Bloom's cognitive taxonomy?

7. Should Jack teach to the state achievement test, as Frank Conway seems to advise? Is Jack correct about minimums becoming maximums when such tests are emphasized? How difficult is it for teachers to go beyond such tests as Frank advises, when they are emphasized by the school? How well do standardized achievement tests measure: (1) higher-order thinking; (2) creativity (as in music and art); (3) psychomotor skills (as in shop and physical education); and (4) affective variables such as self-esteem and achievement motivation?

8. What kinds of assumptions does Jack make about the relationship between IQ scores and achievement as measured by grades? Are they justified? What is an overachiever? From the standpoint of teacher expectancy theory (Rosenthal, *et al.*), is Jack in the process of creating a self-fulfilling prophecy with regard to Troy? Did Jack make any errors in the way he interpreted Troy's IQ scores?

9. What are the most effective ways to report student progress to parents? What are the components of an effective parent conference? Should parents be involved in the formative and summative evaluation of students? If so, how and how frequently?

10. How important a goal is it for students to experience competition and failure in school? From a developmental perspective, how much failure should a student face and

at what age? If failure is viewed as punishment from a behavioristic standpoint, what are the possible effects of punishment in the form of grades upon student behavior?

11. What administrative leadership style is exhibited by Mr. Winslow? Is he more of a "supporting," "coaching," "delegating," or "directing" type leader and why do you think so? How supportive of Jack do you think he'll be if the Sullivans do go to the superintendent and the school board? How directive is Mr. Winslow in communicating his expectations to Jack regarding appropriate evaluation procedures?

12. What should Jack say and do next? Who should he talk to in order to get advice and direction? Should he stick to his guns, cave in to the Sullivans, or try to work out some face-saving compromise? What do the Sullivans really want from him? What does Mr. Winslow want?

13. What advice would you give Jack about conducting conferences with parents? What skills are involved in effective parent–teacher conferences? For example, how might Jack have used a communication technique like active listening in his conference with Dr. Sullivan?

CASE **15**

DIFFERENT STROKES

S andford Middle School is in the Jackson School District, on the north side of a large metropolitan city in a southern state. The primarily middle-class population served by SMS is 65 percent white, 20 percent African-American, 10 percent Hispanic, and 5 percent other ethnic groups.

Two of the five sixth-grade teachers are first-year teachers. One of the new teachers, Maria Velez, graduated this past May with a B.A. from a private liberal arts college located within 20 miles of SMS. Maria majored in history and completed an education program leading to certification as an elementary teacher. The other new teacher, Emma Chen, graduated last May from the College of Education with a B.S.Ed., with a specialization in elementary education at State University in the eastern part of the state.

Both teachers attended the pre-school workshops held the week immediately before classes began. It is now Monday of the fifth week of school. Two weeks ago, Esther Starks, the building principal, had notified both teachers that she planned to observe their classes in accordance with the district policy that all first-year teachers be observed and evaluated three times during their first year of teaching to help administrators determine whether or not they should be reemployed the following year. She had given them the Teacher Evaluation Form designed by the Jackson School District so that they would be aware of the behavior she was planning to observe and informed each of them of the day and time she planned to visit their class. She scheduled Maria's observation for the first period today. Last Friday, she left a note in Maria's mailbox as a reminder. Esther plans to observe Emma's class during the first period next Monday.

Esther comes to Maria's room prior to the ringing of the first bell, which signals that the pupils are to enter the building and proceed to their classrooms.

MARIA   Good morning, Esther.

ESTHER   Good morning, Maria. I came a bit early so that I'd have a chance to look around your room before the pupils arrive. [*Looks at commercial posters related to Ancient Greece, such as the Parthenon, Apollo's temple, a sculpture of Zeus, and photographs of paintings by famous Greek artists, hung from the crown molding around the room. The bulletin boards display commercially prepared maps of early civilizations. No pupil efforts are displayed in the room.*]

What attractive posters and bulletin board displays! You must be planning to study Ancient Greece.

MARIA   Thank you. I bought them at the college book store my last year of college. I've always enjoyed the study of Ancient Greece and thought that, since I'm a history major, I'd someday teach about Ancient Greece and have an opportunity to use these posters. Fortunately, the fourth unit in our social studies book, which we are beginning to study today, is about Ancient Greece. I'm really excited about it! *[A bell rings and the sounds of pupils entering the building grow louder and louder. Soon the pupils enter Maria's room. They greet both Maria and Esther enthusiastically.]*

MARIA   Good morning, class. Ms. Starks is visiting our class for a while this morning.

MARTIN   *[Politely]* Welcome to our class, Ms. Starks.

ESTHER   Thank you, Martin. Thank you, girls and boys. I appreciate Ms. Velez's invitation to visit with you this morning.

[The pupils sit in their seats which are arranged in two curved rows of 15 chairs, one row in front of the other. Both rows are in the shape of a **U***]*

MARIA   *[Walking to her desk which has nothing on it except a file folder containing the lunch tally and attendance report]* Let's see now. There are no empty seats, so no one is absent. *[Marks the attendance sheet]* Now, how many of you are buying the school lunch today? *[Counts raised hands]* O.K., 21 of you are buying lunch *[Marks the lunch tally sheet, walks to the door of the classroom, and inserts both papers into the clip on the outside of the door. Then she returns to the opening at the mouth of the* **U** *and faces the class]*

    This morning we begin our study of my favorite civilization—Ancient Greece. But before we begin, I want to review with you briefly the beginnings of civilization so that we can place the development of Ancient Greece in the proper time frame.

    Martha, what do we mean by civilization?

MARTHA   *[Pause]* It's people who are advanced in the way they live.

MARIE   *[Enthusiastically]* That's right. Warren, what do advanced, or civilized, people have that uncivilized people don't have?

WARREN   *[Looks at his hands on the desk and remains silent]*

MARIE   *[Waits one second]* Warren, do you want to give an answer?

WARREN   I can't remember.

MARIE   Vernon, will you help Warren with the answer?

VERNON   *[Sits silently at his desk]*

MARIE   *[Waits one second]* Vernon? *[Waits another second]* Vernon, are you there?

VERNON   I didn't hear the question.

MARIA   How can we recognize a civilized society, Sam?

SAM   *[Looking in his book]* They have a writing system.

MARIA   Good, even though you had to look in your book! What else do they have? *[Pause]* Juan?

JUAN   They have a government to keep order.

MARIA   That's great, Juan. Can you tell me another thing they have, Juan? *[Maria looks to the back row where Vernon has just knocked Warren's books off the arm of the chair.]*

    Vernon! Get up out of your chair and move it to the side of the room over by the book case. You obviously aren't participating in the class anyway!

VERNON   But Warren took my pencil! It's his fault!

MARIA   Vernon, I asked you to move your chair, and I expect you to do so right this minute without any further discussion! *[Warren gets up slowly and moves his chair. He sits down and looks at his book.]*

Juan, have you thought of another thing that helps us identify a civilized society?

JUAN   Well, let's see. *[Pause]* Civilized people make tools.

MARIA   What kind of tools? *[Noticing a pupil dozing off]* Laura? *[Laura opens her eyes, startled, and sits up straight.]*

Were you up too late last night, or are you bored with the lesson?

LAURA   *[Embarrassed]* No ma'am, I'm not bored. We went to dinner at my aunt and uncle's home in Smithfield. It was after midnight when we arrived home. I think the lesson is interesting.

MARIA   Good. I hope you'll be able to stay awake for the rest of the day. We're doing a lot of important things today. Now, Juan just told us that civilized people have tools. Now, I want somebody to tell me what kind of tools they have? Can you do that?

LAURA   Yes. Their tools are made of metal.

MARIA   *[Enthusiastically]* That's right! Good! Now, there's something else civilized people can do that uncivilized people haven't been able to do. *[Looks around the classroom]* Tina, tell us what that is.

TINA   Civilized people are able to move supplies across the land and water.

MARIA   *[Pleased]* Bingo! These are four ways that we can identify civilized people. They have a system of writing, make metal tools, have a government that protects people and property, and are able to transport goods.

Tell us about one of the earliest civilizations, Matt.

MATT   The first one was called Mesopotamia, which meant "between two rivers." It was where Iraq is now. The two rivers were the Tigris and Euphrates. The soil was very fertile there, so the people began to farm, raise cattle, and grow many of the crops we grow today.

LAMAR   *[Speaking out]* All the early civilizations were located in river valleys. The Hebrews and Phoenicians settled in the Nile Valley, which was also near the Mediterranean Sea.

MARIA   That's right, Lamar. But please raise your hand if you want to speak! But since you brought it up, why did these civilizations spring up in river valleys?

LAMAR   I guess because there was always a water supply for their farms.

MARIA   I'd like it better, Lamar, if you remembered what we studied and didn't have to guess. What are other reasons that civilizations sought out river valleys, Tim?

TIM   Rivers bring rich soil to river valleys. And water makes the climate warmer.

MARIA   Good answer, Tim! Now, tell us what other civilizations began about that time? *[Pause]* Rosalyn?

ROSALYN   A civilization was formed along the Hwang Ho River in China, and the fourth was in the Indus River Valley in India.

MARIA   Very good, Rosalyn. That covers all four locations: in Mesopotamia between the Tigris and Euphrates, in the Nile River Valley, in central China in the Hwang Ho Valley, and in Northwest India in the Indus River Valley. *[Pauses]*

Now, what were some of the major contributions to civilization that were made during this period? Warren? [*Warren continues to stare blankly at his book and does not respond.*]

MATT   [*Calls out*] Religions. The Hebrews developed Judaism, Egyptians developed nature worship, Aryans developed Hinduism, and a Hindu named Gautama developed Buddhism. These civilizations also developed writing, medicine, and a calendar. They built pyramids, ships, and temples and used irrigation.

MARIA   Excellent! You must have been interested in this section, Matt.

MATT   Yes, I had never thought about how these things came about! It's really interesting.

ROSALYN   [*Speaking out*] Will we have a test at the end of Unit 4 covering the whole unit, like we did with the other three units?

MARIA   Yes, Rosalyn, we'll have just one test over Ancient Greece.

ROSALIND   Will the test be about the same as the tests we have had over the other units?

MARIA   Yes. Since this is a long unit, the test will probably have 50 multiple-choice questions worth two points each. The grading scale will be the same as it was on the previous three unit tests: $A = 92$–100; $B = 84$–91; $C = 76$–82; $D = 68$–75; and $F = 74$ or lower. [*Vern raises his hand*]

MARIA   Yes, Vern?

VERN   [*Haltingly*] I made bad grades on the tests we've had. Can I earn points by making some kinds of projects?

MARIA   What kinds of things do you mean, Vern? Reading about things is usually the best way to learn about them.

VERN   Well, when my brother was in this class two years ago, he made a building with steps all around it out of cardboard and tape. The Sumarians built buildings like that. They were where people had religious ceremonies. But they were also storage warehouses for grain and other food that belonged to the people.

MARIA   Are you talking about a ziggurat, Vern?

VERN   Yes, that's what they're called. I couldn't think of that name. There's a picture of a ziggurat in our book. My brother learned all about the Sumarians when he built the ziggurat. But he's like me—not a good reader, and his teacher gave him points for making projects. That way when he made a low grade in a test, he could bring it up with his project points.

MARIA   But he must have read about the ziggurats if he learned all that information about them.

VERN   Maybe, but he wouldn't have read it if he hadn't been interested in building the ziggurat.

MARIA   Well, I'd rather have you get interested in becoming a better reader. Then you wouldn't have to spend all that time building something. You can learn anything better by reading about it. Reading is our most important learning tool. Would you be willing to do that?

VERN   I don't know. I'll try. But I'm not a good reader.

MARIA   Good. And thank you for telling us about the ziggurat, Vern. Now we need to turn our attention to the magnificent civilization of ancient Greece. If you'll look at the posters I hung around the room last Friday after school, you'll see some of

the magnificent architecture used in their buildings, which are still standing today. *[Pointing]* This building is the Parthenon, which is a temple in Athens constructed to honor Athena, the patron goddess of the City. It was constructed entirely of white marble. This building is a temple dedicated to Apollo, who was
the Greek god of the sun. This is a statue of Zeus, who is the primary god who
rules over all the other Greek gods, so you can see what the sculptor thought he
looked like. These posters over here are various paintings by famous artists who
lived in Ancient Greece.

LAMAR   *[Speaking out]* Their gods looked like real people, just like us!

MARIA   Yes! Some people want to know what their gods look like, so they make them
look like humans. Other religions believe that gods are different from people, so
they don't show what their gods look like.

LAMAR   I never thought that gods would look like people.

MARIA   I think there are so many interesting questions that are answered as we study
history. That's why I love history so much.

Well, the time's really flown by. It's just about time for us to move on to
reading class. We'll end class today by talking about our history assignment for
tomorrow. *[A few of the pupils groan discreetly]*

These assignments should be interesting. First, I want you to study the
map of Greece carefully. Notice how it is surrounded by different bodies of water. Read the section of the chapter that describes the climate of Greece along
with the section that describes the early Aegean world, and be prepared to answer these questions tomorrow. Write them down in your notebooks. *[States
each question very slowly]*

1. How do the bodies of water near Greece affect its climate?
2. Locate the five areas in the world having a Mediterranean climate on the climate map in your text.
3. Explain how this climate affects the life of the people living in these areas.
4. Use the population map in the text to find where most of the people in
   Greece live. Explain why they live where they do.
5. How did the Lydians and Phoenicians contribute to the development of
   Greece?
6. Contrast the lifestyles of the citizens of Sparta and those of Athens.
7. What were the major strengths and weaknesses of the democratic government established in Athens?
8. How did personal freedom help to place the Greeks among the most original
   thinkers in history?
9. Briefly describe the three great Greek philosophers: Socrates, Plato, and
   Aristotle.
10. List who you believe are the five most important Greek statesmen and tell
    why you think they were most important.

[At that point a bell rings] All right, let's take a break. I want you all back in
your seats in ten minutes, and we'll begin our reading class.
*[The pupils get up from their chairs. Some mingle inside the room. Others go into the
hall to get a drink, go to the bathroom, etc.]*

ESTHER   *[Rising from her chair and stretching]* Thanks for allowing me to observe your class. It helped me recall interesting information that I haven't thought about for years. I'll fill out the evaluation form that I gave you a couple weeks ago. Can you meet with me after classes end a week from today?

MARIA   Yes, that's a good time for me.

ESTHER   Great! I'll see you then, if not before. *[Leaves the room]*

The next Monday, Esther enters Emma Chen's sixth-grade classroom approximately 15 minutes before the pupils are scheduled to arrive. Esther had made arrangements for the visit two weeks ago, and had left a note in Emma's mailbox in the office the previous Friday reminding her of the visit.

ESTHER   Good morning, Emma.

EMMA   Good morning, Esther. I've been expecting you. Is there anything you'd like for me to show you or tell you about?

ESTHER   Thanks. Your room is so interesting, I'd appreciate it if you could take me on a guided tour until the pupils arrive. I may not be able to absorb it all in the time available. *[All the bulletin boards are completely covered with pupils' work neatly displayed. The tables are covered with models of buildings, bridges, and other structures, along with various kinds of artwork. The chairs are arranged in circles with five chairs in each circle. A bookcase in the corner is filled with a variety of art materials and supplies.]*

EMMA   There are many hours of pupil effort represented in each of those displays. There's such a wide range of ability in my class that the only way I can encourage pupils to work at their own level is to allow them to select individual projects, as well as work in groups. These projects are usually a component of a larger project that a committee is working on.

ESTHER   That seems like quite a reasonable way to proceed. But how do you ever manage to think of all these different projects?

EMMA   Oh, I don't think of the projects. As we discuss a topic, the pupils select what they think is important information that they should learn about. They research this information and develop a strategy for presenting this information to the rest of the class.

    [Pointing to a two-feet-wide strip of wrapping paper on the floor extending from the back wall to the front wall on one side of the room] That's a time line. The first week of school we began our study of history. Barry, one of the most immature pupils in the class, thought it was important to demonstrate in some manner how many years were involved in the development of civilization. I allowed that to be his project, and he began to work with that time line. We're now beginning our fourth unit, and he extends the time line appropriately with each unit. I'm sure he'll continue it for the entire year. Eventually it will extend clear around the room. But all of us have learned from that project, especially Barry.

    I learned about teaching through the use of thematic units when I was at State College, but no one in the school at which I did my internship used this approach. When I first saw our social studies book, it occurred to me that it was organized in such a way that it could serve as the framework for a thematic unit on civilization that could continue all year. I've collected many literature books that deal with ancient history. Some are fiction based on fact and others are factual. But they serve a dual purpose. They enrich our social studies *and* they help pupils realize that they can do their own research through reading. *[At that point a bell rings]*

ESTHER   Oh, now the pupils will arrive. I was hoping to find out more about how you manage a thematic unit.

EMMA   That's no problem. Ask the pupils. Any one of them can tell you how he or she selected a project, researched it, and presented it to the class. Today, we're going to begin the study of how Greece was settled and the many contributions they made to civilization. But this will really be a continuation of many of the projects they have already begun, such as the time line and the evolution of agriculture.

[The pupils enter the classroom, go to their respective seating areas and begin to work on their projects. One pupil is taking the class roll and the lunch orders simultaneously. When she finishes, she fills out the two forms and inserts them in the clip on the outside of the door. Then she returns to her group and begins to read a book]

EMMA   Boys and girls, I'm sure that you all know our principal, Ms. Starks. She is visiting us this morning because she is interested in what we are doing in class. I hope that she'll ask you lots of questions about what you're doing and that you'll be able to answer them all. *[Some pupils groan at the last remark. Esther and Emma both smile.]*

Today, we're beginning the study of a new civilization. Have any of you looked ahead to see what it is? *[Several hands go up]* Martin, what is it?

MARTIN   Greece.

EMMA   Good. How did you know that?

MARTIN   I read the first part of the chapter last night.

CHARLIE   *[Whispering to Doug]* What a nerd, reading ahead in the book! *[Doug chortles]*

EMMA   *[Pleasantly]* Doug, do you have something you'd like to say to the class?

DOUG   No ma'am. I just coughed. *[Becomes interested in looking at his book]*

EMMA   *[Looking back at Martin]* It's good that you're reading ahead, Martin! Reading ahead shows that you're interested in learning. Can you tell us something interesting you learned about Greece?

MARTIN   Well, I read about the location and climate of Greece and learned that there are only five places in the world that have the same type of climate as Greece. I thought the geography group might be interested in that information.

EMMA   Good thinking, Martin! It's good that you're aware of what topics other people in the class are working on.

THERESA   I read part of the new chapter, too. I noticed that there are two new groups of people that the culture committee can give a report on.

EMMA   Good, Theresa. You're helping another group, too. Do you remember who these new people are?

THERESA   They are the Achaeans and the Mycenaceans. I'm not sure I pronounced them right.

MARK   *[Waving his hand enthusiastically]* Ms. Chen?

EMMA   *[Equally enthusiastic]* What is it, Mark!

MARK   I thought of another work group we'll need to have!

EMMA   OK, tell us what group we need.

MARK   We'll need an important people committee, because this unit begins to talk about important people, like Homer, Pericles, Socrates, Plato, and Aristotle. I think I've heard of some these people, but I don't know anything about them. So someone should make a book of important people in the different civilizations.

EMMA   That's an excellent suggestion, Mark. Is this a group that you'd like to work on?

MARK   Yes. I think that would be cool.

EMMA   Good! I'll appoint you chair of the important people committee. I'm sure there will be other people in the class who would like to work on that committee. If there are, they can tell you. *[Four people raise their hands]* Probably two or three others would be enough for that committee right now, but we may need more people on it when we begin to learn about more and more important people. Thanks for that suggestion, Mark.

        Now, let's all skim the entire unit on Ancient Greece to identify important information that needs to be presented to the class. By Wednesday you should be able to tell me what projects you want to do for this unit. We'll probably spend two weeks on it.

        Barry, you'll begin to have more and more entries on your time line, because more things are happening in the world now than were happening when civilization was just beginning.

BARRY   That's OK, I'll get them all recorded.

EMMA   I hope so, because that time line is important for all of us. *[Barry beams]*

        Let's see, we already have a culture group, a religion group, a geography group, and a government group, don't we? *[Pupils answer affirmatively]* Can any of you think of any other groups we need to form?

SYLVIA   There are at least two wars that I read about. Maybe we'd better form a war group.

EMMA   You're right, Sylvia. That's a good suggestion, because from now on the number of wars will increase. And wars do have a big influence on civilization. Would you like to chair that group, Sylvia?

SYLVIA   Yes, I think it would be interesting to learn about what causes wars and how they could be avoided. Consuela wants to be on the war committee, too.

EMMA   That's fine. You could use four or five people on that committee. *[Four hands go up]*

GEROME   Ms. Chen, is it O.K. if Sam and me go to the library for a while?

EMMA   You and Sam were at the library for at least two hours Friday afternoon. Why do you need to go again today?

GEROME   We found a lot of books about ancient Greece Friday, and gave them to Ms. Simpson to check out to us. But she said that there were some other books that we could use in our study of ancient Greece. She said that if we come to the library this morning she'd have them all checked out to us. And since there would probably be at least 50 altogether, she'd stack them on a library cart that we could use to bring them to our room.

EMMA   *[Pleased]* How nice of Ms. Simpson! You and Sam must behave yourselves nicely in the library for her to give you such special attention.

GEROME *[Embarrassed]* She's a nice lady. But we don't do anything bad in the library.

EMMA   Good! I'm glad to hear that. And, yes, you and Sam may go to the library. We might be able to use some of them for book reports in our English class.

Class, it's just about time for the break. When you come back, I want you meet with your groups and plan the reports and projects you want to prepare for this unit. In addition to the reports I want you all to read the entire unit on the ancient Greeks. Be aware of who settled that area, how the Mediterranean climate affected the settlers, what caused the various wars that broke out, contributions that the ancient Greeks made to civilization, what caused the Greek dark age, how Greece become a democracy, what the major cities of Greece were, what Greek life was like during The Golden Age, and who Alexander the Great was and what he did.

Members of the study groups will need to begin researching the information related to your groups and prepare reports for the class to study. *[Enthusiastically]* O.K. Break time. When you return, you'll have an hour to meet with your groups. *[Pupils get up from their seats. Some leave the room, some walk to the bookcase and look at the new books, others stand in groups and converse.]*

ESTHER *[To Emma]* This was a most interesting experience for me. I've read about thematic units and heard them discussed at workshops, but I've never seen one in operation. I'm astounded at how much work your pupils are doing. And they seem to enjoy it.

EMMA   Well, this is a brand-new experience for me, too. So far, I'm really pleased with the outcomes. But sometimes I think it's too good to be true. Maybe the pupils will become bored with it or get tired of doing so much work. But so far, they've actually become more enthusiastic as we continue to implement the unit.

ESTHER I'm really interested to see how it works out!

EMMA   Well, you're certainly welcome to come to my class. You don't have to be a spectator. You can pitch right in and work with the pupils. Drop in anytime. You don't need to give me any kind of notice. We pretty much do what you saw this morning every day. Except that in a week, the different groups will present reports to the class and turn in written work to me to be graded.

ESTHER I wanted to ask you about grades. How do you decide what they will be?

EMMA   I've examined all the pupils' records and have a pretty good idea of the level on which they function. They select their own projects and pretty much seek their own level. If they select something I think is too hard, I make suggestions that will make it easier, and vice-versa. I don't want the assignments to be either too easy or too hard. If the final report or project is really excellent, I give it an A. If it's better than average, I give it a B. Average is C. Below average, D. I don't give below D if they turn in something. This system isn't infallible, but it takes individual ability as well as effort into consideration and I think it is fair. *[At this point the bell rings and the pupils rush back to their groups]*

ESTHER Thanks for letting me observe your class. I really enjoyed it. Can you meet with me in my office next Monday after the pupils leave? I'd like to go over the evaluation form with you.

EMMA Sure, that's a good time for me. I'm anxious to see my evaluation.

ESTHER Good. I'll see you then, if not before.

QUESTIONS

1. How would you describe the evaluation system used by Maria? by Emma? Which system do you prefer? Why?

2. What are cognitive and affective behaviors as defined in the *Taxonomy of Educational Objectives* by Bloom, *et. al.*? Which teacher's questions encouraged pupils to respond on higher levels of the cognitive domain? of the affective domain? Give one example of the highest-level assignment made by each teacher for each domain related to teacher–pupil dialogue, discipline, or academic assignments.

3. In her questioning technique Maria Velez called a pupil's name before she asked a question. Emma Chang asked the question before she called the pupil's name. Which of these is the better technique? Why?

4. Both teachers provided reinforcement to pupils who answered a question correctly. How did the reinforcement differ? Which teacher's reinforcement was more effective? Why?

5. Both teachers made efforts to create an attractive classroom by displaying interesting materials related to the topic the pupils are studying. Which classroom was decorated more appropriately? How were the respective teachers' styles reflected in the classroom decorations?

6. Both Maria and Emma were studying the same historical periods and using the same textbook, yet their approaches were quite different. Compare and contrast the types of information Maria's and Emma's pupils would learn about Ancient Greece. Which information would you prefer your pupils to learn? Why?

7. Describe the types of study skills the pupils in Maria's and Emma's classes would learn. Which types of study skills would you prefer your pupils to learn? Why?

8. Compare and contrast the instructional objectives and teaching methods of Maria and Emma. What different curriculum models were involved? Which will have the greatest impact on student learning? Why?

9. Critique the Teacher Evaluation Report. Does it really relate to effective teaching? How would you change the instrument? What would you add or subtract? Should such rating scales be used to determine merit pay for teachers?

10. What research would need to be done to determine the validity and reliability of the Teacher Evaluation Report? Should such instruments be used to evaluate teachers *before* such research is done?

11. What are formative and summative evaluation? Which type of evaluation is the principal making in this case?

12. At what levels of Maslow's need hierarchy are Emma and Maria primarily operating? How does this help explain their differences in teaching procedures?

13. Compare and contrast Emma and Maria in terms of their use of academic learning time, the classroom climates, their learner accountability and monitoring strategies, and their practice and review procedures. Which is the more effective and likely to have the greatest impact on student learning? Why?

14. To which teacher would you give the highest overall ratings on the Teacher Evaluation Report above? On what categories would they be most similar? most different?

Teacher Evaluation Report
Jackson School District

Teacher's name: _____   School: _____
Evaluator: _____   Date: _____
Grade: _____   Time of observation: _____ _____
                                                        began   ended

                                     Conference time: _____ _____
                                                        began   ended

RANKINGS: Outstanding: Performance reflects exceptional quali-
                                ties of teaching and class management

              Satisfactory: Exhibits expected and desired profes-
                                sional behavior.

              Unsatisfactory: Exhibits weak performance and/or teach-
                                ing deficiencies

Mark *X* below the appropriate ranking: Outstanding (O), Satisfactory (S), or Unsatisfactory (U), after each item:

	O	S	U
I. TEACHING PROCEDURES _____			
A. Evidence of organization and planning _____			
B. Knowledge of subject matter _____			
C. Individualization of instruction _____			
D. Variety of teaching strategies _____			
E. Effective use of wait-time _____			
F. Encourages good work-study habits _____			
G. Appropriate practice/review procedures _____			
H. Evaluates learners effectively _____			
I. Effective use of class time _____			
II. CLASSROOM MANAGEMENT _____			
A. Effective classroom management _____			
B. Attractive physical setting _____			
C. Effective interaction with pupils _____			
D. Maintenance of appropriate records _____			
E. Positive classroom climate _____			
F. Appropriate use of group work _____			
G. Effective monitoring of pupils _____			
H. Is reasonable, fair and impartial _____			
I. Keeps pupils on task _____			
III. PROFESSIONAL CHARACTERISTICS _____			
A. Accepts responsibilities _____			
B. Encourages self-discipline _____			
C. Continual self assessment _____			
D. Keeps abreast of new ideas _____			
E. Professional appearance _____			
F. Develops rapport wlth pupils _____			
G. Keeps parents informed _____			
H. Follows school district policies _____			
I. Poised and self-assured _____			

CASE 16

JOAN'S MISCOMMUNICATION

Gulfview is a ten-year-old elementary school located in an upscale suburban area of a large city in the Deep South. Gulfview has an enrollment of approximately 800 middle-class pupils and is known as a good school. The school enrollment is approximately 80 percent white, 15 percent African-American, and 5 percent other.

Joan Caldwell, who is in her second year of teaching second grade, graduated from Alice S. Blackwell Liberal Arts College for Women with a major in political science and a certification in elementary education. Joan grew up in a suburb in the same city in which Gulfview is located. She is happy with her job and the school in which she teaches.

It is Monday morning during the fifth week of school. Pupils are arriving at Gulfview school in busses, in cars driven by parents, or on foot. Darlene and Penny are among the walkers, and are the first pupils to arrive. They giggle as they skip into their second-grade classroom. They smile and greet their teacher.

PENNY   Hi, Ms. Caldwell.

JOAN   *[Smiling]* Good morning, Penny. Good morning, Darlene. It's nice to see you girls this morning.
As other pupils enter the room, they take their assigned seats in the classroom. There are six round tables with five chairs at each table. Joan greets each pupil and calls him/her by name. All the pupils have arrived and most of them are seated at their assigned tables by the time the last bell rings. Brent and Sam, however, are on the floor in the play area, pushing trucks across the floor.

JOAN   *[Crossly]* Brent! Sam! Why aren't you in your seats?

BRENT   *[Innocently]* We were just playing with our trucks until school starts. *[Both boys hastily take their seats.]*

JOAN   *[Accusingly]* You both know that you're supposed to be in your seats when the last bell rings! That's when school starts! From now on, I expect you to be in your seats when you hear that bell! *[Both boys nod their heads in assent and appear to be somewhat flustered.]*
Let's see *[counting the pupils]*, there are no empty chairs, so that means that all of you are here, so there is no one absent. *[Signs the attendance report]* All right now, if you're buying lunch today, please raise your hand. *[Pauses]* Sue, are you buying lunch? *[Sue nods her head yes]*

[Sternly] Then raise your hand. You weren't paying attention, were you? *[Sue looks embarrassed and shakes her head no.]*

[Joan records the appropriate number on the lunch form, looks at Penny, and smiles] Penny, are you ready to do your job? *[Penny returns the smile, stands and walks to the front of the room, takes the forms from Joan, and leaves the room]*

PAULA   *[Speaking out]* Why does Penny always get to take the sheets to the office? Last year our teacher let us take turns. Penny takes them every day. That's not fair.

JOAN   You must remember not to speak out without raising your hand, Paula. To answer your question, since I'm the teacher it's my job to decide who takes the sheets to the office and does other jobs around the classroom. School just started a few weeks ago. I'll switch the jobs around soon. *[Paula raises her hand]* Paula?

PAULA   That's good. Its more fair when everybody in the class gets a turn at doing the class work.

JOAN   *[Smiling]* Thank you, Paula. I'm glad that you agree with my plan.

[Joan addresses the class] Do you remember that last Friday we talked about this week being a special week? *[Several pupils wave their hands in the air.]*

Good, some of you have good memories. Peggy, what special week is this?

PEGGY   *[Enthusiastically]* It's national newspaper week!

JOAN   Right. That's very good, Peggy. Now, who can tell me why we have national newspaper week? *[No one raises a hand. Pupils look puzzled.]* Let's think now. Why do we designate special days or special weeks by giving them the names of famous people, events, and institutions, Paula?

PAULA   *[Long pause]* I don't understand the question.

JOAN   Let me rephrase the question. Why do we have Presidents' Day or Martin Luther King Day?

MARK   *[Shouts out]* To show that we like Martin Luther King or our presidents.

JOAN   That's right, Mark. We name special days or weeks after important people or events to show that we like them. We honor people like Martin Luther King and our presidents. And we honor important events like Thanksgiving and Memorial Day. Why do we honor newspapers? *[No response]*

[Penny returns to the classroom and sits down.] Penny, this week is national newspaper week. Do you know why we have a newspaper week?

PENNY   *[Immediately]* Because newspapers are important.

JOAN   Good. Now, tell us why newspapers are important.

PENNY   They come every day and tell about important things that happen.

JOAN   Very good, Penny. Now who can name some of these important things that newspapers tell us about? *[No hands are raised.]* *[Waits three seconds]* Sue?

SUE   *[Flustered, Sue answers uncertainly]* What things are happening in town?

JOAN   Are you asking me, or is that your answer?

SUE   *[Embarrassed—begins to sob]* That's my answer.

JOAN   Why are you crying, Sue? That's the right answer. I can't imagine a seven-year-old crying about a thing like that. There's no reason for you to cry.

SUE   *[Emotionally]* I don't like it when you're not nice to me. You've said two mean things to me already today. I'm not doing anything bad!

JOAN   Of course you're not. But you weren't paying attention earlier.

SUE   You don't say mean things to other people who don't pay attention or don't raise their hands. You just pick on some people. You pick on me!

JOAN   *[Matter-of-factly]* Well, I'm sorry if you think I pick on you. But I don't think I do pick on you. I think you are overly sensitive. Let's just forget this morning and start all over again. I won't pick on you anymore. Is it a deal?

SUE   *[Unenthusiastically]* O.K.

JOAN   *[Although somewhat concerned about Sue's response, she doesn't think it wise to pursue the matter further at this time, so she continues the lesson.]* Now, back to the newspaper—who can name some other information that the newspaper tells us?

BRENT   *[Shouting out]* People being robbed. *[Pause]* Club meetings.

JOAN   Good, Brent. That's right. But remember to raise your hand. *[Looks around the classroom]* Who can tell us other things that the paper tells us?

MARK   *[Shouts out]* It has the comics every day!

JOAN   Are the comics important?

MARK   *[Emphatically]* Sure they are!

JOAN   And can you tell us why comics are important, Mark?

MARK   Sure. They're important because people like to read them.

JOAN   Comics are entertaining, aren't they? And people enjoy being entertained. Who can tell us where in the newspaper the most important event of the day is shown?

SAM   *[Shouts out]* The headlines.

JOAN   Sam, how many times do I have to tell you pupils not to shout out before you remember not to do it?

SAM   *[Taken aback]* I'm sorry. But other people have shouted out! Mark just shouted out a minute ago. You didn't say anything to him.

JOAN   I won't have you talking back to me, Sam Ryan. That's rude.

SAM   I didn't mean to be rude, and I said that I'm sorry for shouting out.

JOAN   O.K. Let's forget it. Tell us where the headlines are located in the paper, Jamal.

JAMAL   On the top of the front page.

JOAN   What else is on the front page, Terry?

TERRY   Pictures of things that have happened and other news stories.

JOAN   Right, Terry. That's good! [To the class] Now I have a surprise for you. The owners of our city newspaper, *The Gulfview Sun,* have offered to give all the pupils in our school their own copy of the newspaper every school day this week. *[Distributes a paper to each pupil in the class]* And we're going to learn how to use the newspaper to find out information that is important to us.

I've cut five comic strips out of each of the papers. I'm going to give each table five different comic strips that I have cut apart. I want you to arrange them in sequential order. Who knows how to do that? *[Waits three seconds]* Lori?

LORI   *[Long pause]* What does sequential order mean?

JOAN   It means to arrange the pictures in the order that they occurred

MARTIN   You mean you want us to show the picture that happened first and the pictures that happened second, and third, and fourth?

JOAN   *[Smiling]* That's very good, Martin. *[Turning to the class]* So when you work with the comic strips, you put the picture first that happened first. Then you put the second thing that happens next to the first, then the third thing that happened, then the last thing. You may help each other if you want to. Raise your hands when everyone at your table has arranged the pieces in order.

After the last class has ended on Tuesday of the following week, Frank Short, the principal, stops in the hall outside Joan's classroom.

FRANK   Knock, knock. *[Joan looks up from her desk and smiles]* Hi, Joan. Do you have a few minutes to talk?

JOAN   Yes, I do. I'm just straightening the classroom up a bit. Have a seat. *[Frank sits in a chair at the table nearest Joan.]* What's up?

FRANK   Well, I'm not sure. That's why I wanted to talk with you for a few minutes. I just finished a telephone conversation a few minutes ago with Sara Rozelle, Sue's mother. She received a letter from you in today's mail regarding Sue, and she seemed to be quite upset about it. I told her that I wasn't aware of any letter having been sent, and assured her that I would look into the situation. So here I am.

JOAN   I did mail a letter to Ms. Rozelle on Saturday. But I don't know why she would be upset by it.

FRANK   Well, apparently she was sufficiently upset to call me the day the letter arrived.

JOAN   *[Obviously annoyed]* I wonder why she didn't call me instead of going over my head!

FRANK   Actually, I don't think she had any intention of going over your head. The only telephone number listed for Gulfview Elementary School rings in my office. When my secretary answered, Ms. Rozelle asked to speak with you. My secretary explained that there are no telephones in the classroom and asked her if she would like to speak to the principal. She said that she would. And that's how I happened to become involved. I don't believe that Ms. Rozelle had any intention of going over your head. But I would like to know what made you send Ms. Rozelle a letter instead of calling her on the telephone or setting up a conference with her.

JOAN   Well, last Monday morning I found myself in a situation that I wasn't quite sure how to handle. On two separate occasions within the period of an hour I asked Sue Rozelle a question. The first time, I asked the pupils who were planning to buy lunch to raise their hands. Sue didn't raise hers, but since she typically buys lunch, I called her by name and asked if she was planning to buy lunch. She nodded yes. I asked her if she failed to raise her hand because she wasn't paying attention to what was happening in class and had not heard the question. Again, she nodded her head yes. So I put her down for lunch and went on with the class. She was embarrassed, but I believe it was because she wasn't paying attention, not anything that I said or did.

On the second occasion, I called on Sue to answer a question. She did, but her answer was so tentative that I asked her if she was asking a question or giving an answer. She became upset and said that it was an answer. Then she actually cried and accused me of picking on her because I accused her of not paying attention on the first occasion, and then pointed out her uncertainty on the second occasion. But I certainly didn't punish her or make unkind remarks about her. In fact, I apologized and told her that I didn't mean to be unkind to her. I then suggested that we start all over again and that I'd be careful not to hurt her feelings, or words to that effect. Those were the only problems we had Friday, but Sue and I didn't have any conversations for the remainder of the day. In fact, Sue is a very quiet child who doesn't have many interactions with the other pupils either. That was the main reason that I wrote the letter.

FRANK   But, again, why did you write a letter instead of just calling her parents?

JOAN   To begin with, I thought a lot during the day about the interactions that Sue and I had. She seemed more upset than the situation called for. Then I thought about how she is pretty much of a loner in the class. As I considered these things, I became more convinced that it was my responsibility to share my concern with her parents. I thought hard about whether it would be better to call them or to write them a letter. I eventually came to the conclusion that parents might attach more significance and threat to a phone call than to a letter. I sort of look at a letter as being more impersonal. Maybe I made the wrong choice.

FRANK   I guess the crux of the issue revolves around what you said in the letter.

JOAN   Well, I addressed the letter to both parents: Mr. and Ms. Frank Rozelle. I began the letter by explaining to them pretty much what I've just told you. Then I went on to explain that Sue seemed to be pretty much of a loner, didn't respond very often in class, and didn't seem to have any friends that she buddied up with in the class. I asked if she had friends in her neighborhood or in any organizations that they were members of as a family, such as church, health clubs, civic groups, etc. I ended the letter by saying that if they were interested in discussing this matter with me, that I'd be happy to arrange a time convenient to them for a meeting.

[Walks over to her filing cabinet, pulls out a folder, examines its contents and pulls out a letter.] Here's a copy of the letter if you'd like to read it.

FRANK   [Takes the letter, reads it, and hands it back to Joan] Wow!

JOAN   Would you care to translate that "Wow" for me?

FRANK   That "Wow" means that I wish you would have called the Rozelles instead of writing them a letter. It also means that I wish you hadn't suggested that Sue is under stress and implying that her school problems might be rooted in something that is happening at home. It's always more appropriate to describe the behavior and stop there instead of attempting some kind of psychological analysis to explain it.

JOAN   What should I do now?

FRANK   I guess if I were the Rozelles and read this letter, I'd be concerned enough that I'd want to meet with you. Maybe they should be concerned. However, under the circumstances, I think that the ball's pretty much in your court now. Ms. Rozelle did make an effort to reach you here at school, so I think you should at least return her call. And if they want to meet, you should set a time and place immediately so that we can put this matter to rest to everybody's satisfaction.

JOAN   O.K. I'll follow through with my offer to meet with the Rozelles. I'll call their home this afternoon and make an appointment.

FRANK   Good. Let me know what happens.

After classes have ended on the following Friday, Joan is waiting in her classroom for Ms. Rozelle to appear. After her meeting with Frank on Tuesday, she called Ms. Rozelle and suggested that they meet and talk about her plans for the second-grade class. Ms. Rozelle indicated an interest in coming to the school for the meeting. They agreed that they would meet in Joan's classroom at 4 P.M. today.

At exactly 4 P.M. a tall, attractive, smartly dressed woman appears in the doorway. She smiles at Joan and extended her hand.

SARA   I'm Sara Rozelle. And you must be Ms. Caldwell.

JOAN   Yes. Please call me Joan. I'm so glad that you were able to come. *[Indicating one of two adult chairs near one of the tables]* Please sit down. *[Smiling]* I managed to locate two adult chairs in the principal's office.

SARA   Well, Sue is our only child, and we want her to be both happy and successful in school. I was quite upset when I received your letter.

JOAN   I'm really sorry that the letter upset you. I debated with myself almost all day last Friday about whether I should call you, write a letter to you, or do nothing at all. Finally, I decided to write the letter. Looking back, it might have been better to call. But Sue was definitely upset Friday morning. I didn't think that my pointing out that she wasn't paying attention would have motivated such an intense response. I wanted to check with you to learn whether there was something else that I should know about affecting her behavior.

SARA   *[Defensively]* Like what?

JOAN   *[Pause]* Any number of things happening outside of school can negatively affect a pupil's behavior—pets die, family members become ill, parents get divorced, dad loses his job, hundreds of other events.

SARA   I see what types of things you're talking about. *[Long pause]* There's nothing like that affecting our family life. In fact, I definitely got the idea from Sue that she was upset basically by your behavior towards her.

JOAN   *[Dismissing the possibility]* Surely my asking her whether she had been paying attention and, later, asking if she was asking a question or giving an answer shouldn't bring a seven-year-old child to tears.

SARA   *[Defiantly]* Well, it did. Sue isn't a shrinking violet at home. She participates very well in give-and-take with her playmates. And when she engages in behavior that doesn't fit in with our family values, we point it out to her immediately and discuss the reasons we don't approve of that behavior. She's never responded to our punishment in the way that you described in your letter. In fact, the tone of your letter seemed to suggest that Sue is emotionally unstable. Sue is seven years old, and you are the first person to have suggested that she has some kind of adjustment problem.

JOAN   I can assure you that I didn't mean to suggest that at all. Sometimes a pupil has a bad experience out of school that affects the pupil's behavior in school the next day or next few days. If the teacher is made aware of the situation, she can often provide additional support in school to help defuse the situation. That's all I had in mind.

SARA When we asked Sue what happened, she said that you were cross with her because she hadn't held up her hand when you were counting the number of pupils who were buying lunch. And she said that you called on her for the answer to the question about the newspaper after no one else volunteered an answer. She wasn't sure what type of answer you wanted, so she was a bit tentative about her answer. She didn't think it was necessary for you to ask whether her response was a question or an answer. It was obviously an answer.

JOAN It wasn't my intention to be cross with her. I guess Sue and I interpreted the situation differently.

SARA Let me ask you something. Do you scold some of the pupils for speaking out without raising their hands, and then allow other pupils to speak out without censure?

JOAN If I do, I'm not aware of it. I want all the pupils to raise their hands to be called on. That practice helps prevent situations in which all the pupils are trying to talk at once.

SARA Do you allow Penny to deliver the attendance record and meal orders to the office every day?

JOAN *[Defensively]* I told the class last week that all the jobs like that would be shared by members of the class.

SARA But wasn't that in response to another pupil's complaint that Penny did it every day?

JOAN *[Angrily]* I really suggested this meeting to discuss Sue, not to defend my practices in the classroom.

SARA But maybe your practices in the classroom affect your pupils' behavior.

JOAN I think it goes without saying that every teacher's behavior in the classroom affects pupils' behavior. So that isn't really a topic that we need to debate.

SARA I was just suggesting that if some pupils are allowed privileges that other pupils are denied, it may affect the behavior of both groups of pupils—the first group positively and the second group negatively.

Do your pupils complain sometimes that they don't understand your questions?

JOAN I think that I've shared all the information with you that I wanted to share. I informed you of my concerns regarding Sue's behavior. There don't seem to be any out-of-school events that are causing her stress. The behavior that I was concerned about last week hasn't recurred. So I don't think we really have anything more to discuss. *[Standing up and walking toward the door]* Thank you very much for coming. If I think there is further need for me to discuss Sue's behavior, I'll call you. And if you have any concerns about her school experiences, I'd appreciate it if you called me.

SARA *[Also stands and walks toward the door]* Thank you for your interest in Sue. But I'm still not satisfied that the source of her problems aren't in the classroom rather than at home. Since you seem reluctant to answer some of my questions regarding your classroom procedures, I plan to make an appointment with Mr. Short. Good-bye *[She walks down the hall before Joan can think of any reply.]*

Two weeks later, Joan checks her mailbox at the end of the day. In it, she finds a note from Mr. Short stating that he has had a conference with John and Sara Rozelle and would like to have an opportunity to discuss the results of the conference with her at her earliest convenience. Joan walks to his office and sees that he is still at his desk.

JOAN   Frank, I just read your note and came to make an appointment to talk with you about your conference with the Rozelles.

FRANK   Good. Do you have any plans right now?

JOAN   No. I'm free for the rest of the afternoon. Besides, I'm anxious to find out what happened.

FRANK   Come in and sit down, then, and I'll tell you all about it. *[He walks across the office and closes the door]* I'm afraid it isn't good news.

JOAN   *[Emotionally]* Oh, no! What did they say?

FRANK   Well, they said a number of things. But I can give you a quick summary of the major points. They said that you don't treat all the pupils in the class equally—that you are solicitous of some and impatient with others. Unfortunately, Sue was one of the pupils you were cross with, but this has stopped since your conference with them.

JOAN   Well, at least that's good news. I've been trying to be especially nice to her since this issue was raised.

FRANK   The Rozelles have talked with several parents of other pupils in your class, and they say that there's general agreement among these other parents, based upon the reports of their children, that some of your classroom procedures are quite questionable.

JOAN   *[Discouraged]* Oh, no! Like what?

FRANK   Well, Sara said that she mentioned to you the fact that some of the pupils said that you play favorites; for instance, that Penny has taken the attendance and lunch sheets to the office every day. It that true?

JOAN   Yes, but I told Sara that I was going to have pupils take turns doing that job.

FRANK   Have you named another pupil to do that job yet?

JOAN   No, not yet.

FRANK   When do you plan to begin doing this? If Penny's done it for six weeks, and you allow others to do it for that same period, only five other pupils will be picked this year.

JOAN   I'll have to think of enough other tasks so that every pupil will have a chance to do something.

FRANK   Another questionable practice they mentioned is that you use language that many of the pupils don't understand. Is this true?

JOAN   I wasn't aware of this until Sara mentioned it. But I have noticed some instances when that was true. I'm working hard to correct that.

FRANK   Evidently one of your most blatant practices, according to the pupils interviewed, is that you insist that some pupils raise their hands to answer questions and others consistently are allowed to speak out without any sort of redress.

JOAN   *[Very uncomfortable]* I guess I'm guilty of that, too. It isn't a deliberate thing. I guess I just enforce the rule sometimes and don't enforce it at other times. I don't think there are pupils who are allowed to speak out all the time and others are never allowed to speak out. Whenever I am conscious of someone speaking out, I correct that.

FRANK   I specifically asked this question, and, according to the pupils the Rozelles talked with, there are pupils who are always allowed to speak out and others who are never allowed to do it.

JOAN   I'm really embarrassed. I didn't even realize that I've been doing some of those things you've mentioned until I talked with Sara. She asked me about some of them, too. Are there more things that you haven't mentioned?

FRANK   That's about it.

JOAN   I just don't know what to say. What should I do? *[Emotionally]* This is the worst thing that has ever happened to me!

FRANK   Ms. Rozelle told me that when she had begun to ask you about some of the practices I just mentioned, you politely terminated the interview. She believes that these things I just mentioned are serious matters and should be dealt with seriously.

JOAN   Have you decided how they should be dealt with?

FRANK   It's obvious that the complaints that I've mentioned must be dealt with somehow, and they must be dealt with immediately. At the end of our conference, I told the Rozelles that I would have a conference with you and discuss these matters thoroughly. Then I assured them that I would be back in touch with them and explain how we were going to remedy the undesirable situations that they had described to me. If I can describe some very specific solutions that we are going to apply to remedy these situations, I believe that the Rozelles will be willing to give the solutions a chance to work before they decide whether or not to take any further action.

JOAN   And how are you going to do that?

FRANK   *[Emphatically]* I'm not going to do it! You are! It's basically your problem! You're going to think seriously about all these complaints that your pupils have expressed to their parents. Then you're going to describe in detail and in writing specific strategies that you will apply to remedy all these complaints.

When you have proposed these strategies and made arrangements to implement them in the classroom, I want you to tell me. Then I'll conduct several random observations of your classes to convince myself that the strategies are successful.

JOAN   What do you think will happen then?

FRANK   I think that the Rozelles and their friends will be satisfied. And I think that you will be a better and a wiser teacher.

JOAN   When you say that I should describe the corrective strategies in detail in writing, how much detail do you mean?

FRANK   Let me give you an example. Many of the parents accused you of favoring some pupils and ignoring others in the assignment of classroom duties, such as taking the attendance and lunch purchase sheets to the office. This criticism would be laid to rest if you wrote what we used to call in the army a duty roster. Think of all the different duties pupils in the class could perform. Then make a chart showing these duties. After each duty, list the pupil that will be in charge of this duty each week, or for whatever length of time each pupil will perform this duty. Make sure all pupils have an equal amount of time for each duty. I will take a copy of this chart to the Rozelles and you can give a copy to each pupil to take home. This will prove to the parents, beyond any question, that you are treating their children equally.

JOAN   That's a good idea. And I could do that quite easily. But how can I document some of the other criticisms that are less structured, such as using language that some pupils don't understand?

FRANK   In that case, I think you can make a list of intentions or resolutions, or whatever you want to call them, to describe how you plan to improve your classroom discussions and your relationships with your pupils. This should be given to me in writing. Then I can use the list of resolutions when I come in to observe.

JOAN   That's fair enough. I really appreciate your support in this situation. I think I can be a better teacher now that we've talked. The first of next week, Monday or Tuesday, I'll give you a written statement on how I plan to proceed in revising my classroom procedure. I'll implement the plan immediately in my class. You're invited to come to my class anytime you like and to stay as long as you wish.

FRANK   Thank you. I'll look forward to taking you up on your invitation. But first, I want to see your written statement.

JOAN   O.K. I'll work on it over the weekend and have it for you Monday. And, Frank, thanks again for going to bat for me.

October 3, 1995

Mr. and Mrs. Harold Rozelle
3210 N.W. Silver Drive
Gulfview, USA

Dear Mr. and Mrs. Rozelle,

As Sue's second grade teacher, I am writing this letter to inform you of some conversations that Sue and I had this morning. I pondered most of the day about whether or not to write, but decided that I should.

Each morning, as soon as the pupils come into the room, I take attendance and count how many of the pupils plan to buy their lunch in the cafeteria. This morning, when I asked the pupils buying lunch to raise their hands, Sue didn't raise hers. I know that she usually does buy lunch, so I said, "Sue, aren't you buying lunch today?" She said that she was. I responded that she should have raised her hand. Then, half jokingly, I said, "You weren't paying attention, were you?" She acted really embarrassed and said "No."

I didn't think much about this until later in the morning, when I was introducing a unit of study on the newspaper. I asked a general question about what kinds of information appear in the newspaper. No hands were raised, so I called on Sue. She answered very uncertainly, "What things are happening in town?" Because of her uncertainty, I responded, "Are you asking me, or is that your answer?" Immediately, Sue burst into tears and replied, "That's my answer."

At that point I became very concerned and asked her why she was crying since her answer was right. She replied that I'm not nice to her and that I'd said two mean things to her: that she's not doing anything bad but that I pick on some people in the class, and she's one of them.

At that point I tried to explain that I was not trying to be mean to her. Earlier, when she hadn't ordered lunch, I asked her if she wanted to order lunch since she usually did. I was trying to be nice and make sure she had a lunch to eat. Later, I asked her if she was asking or answering a question because she seemed so tentative. I wanted her to act more self-confident because she usually answers questions correctly.

Then I assured her that I didn't mean to pick on her, and I apologized for making her think that I was. I suggested that we both forget our differences and start over again. She agreed to do this. The remainder of the day went without any other problems.

Maybe I'm making a mountain out of a mole hill, but it seemed to me that Sue seemed to over-react to both situations. I wonder if she is having some kind of pressure outside of school that may be stressful to her. If this is the case, there may be something I could do here in class to provide her with more support. Please let me know if you would like to discuss this situation further. I will be happy to meet with you or have a telephone conference if you would like to explore this matter further.

Sincerely,

Joan Caldwell

Joan Caldwell
Second-Grade Teacher

QUESTIONS

1. Evaluate Joan's proficiency in communicating with her pupils. What are her strong points? her weak points?

2. How has Joan grouped her class for instruction? Is she using the child-centered or subject-centered approach? Compare and contrast these two approaches to curriculum.

3. Did Joan use poor judgement in writing the letter to Sue's parents? Should she have telephoned them instead? Or should she have done nothing? Why?

4. What administrative leadership style does Principal Frank Short use? Is he more of a supporting, coaching, delegating, or directing leader?

5. What are the elements of a good teacher-parent conference? How could Joan have conducted her conference with Ms. Rozelle differently?

6. What are the different kinds of questions that teachers can ask in the classroom? What are open- and closed-ended questions? What are higher- and lower-order questions? How can Bloom's Cognitive Taxonomy be applied to teachers' questions?

7. What is wait time? How effectively did Joan use wait time?

8. What is a sociogram? How could Joan have used the sociogram to get a more accurate picture of pupil interactions, especially Sue's, in her classroom?

9. Examine Joan's use of social reinforcement and punishment from the standpoint of operant conditioning. How might B. F. Skinner have critiqued her performance? What kind of classroom climate has she created? How might it be changed?

10. How did Joan, Sue, Sara, and Frank view what was going on in Joan's classroom? From the perspective of humanistic psychology, how do their perceptual fields differ? How did the events in Joan's classroom affect Sue's self-concept? How would a humanistic teacher have handled things differently?

11. Examine the events in the classroom and the teacher–parent conference from the framework of Teacher Effectiveness Training [TET]. Whose problem is it? What communication problems exist? What type of conflict exists? What TET procedures could have been used instead?

12. What techniques can be used to involve parents in schools? If Gulfview Elementary used such parent involvement procedures as parent volunteering in the classroom, home visits, or parent participation in school advisory councils, how might such events as the ones described in this case have been prevented or handled differently?

13. Construct an observation schedule for Frank to use in observing Joan's teaching. What items would you put on it and how often should Frank observe? What advice would you give Frank about sharing the data with Joan, and how should he conduct his conferences with her? How much and what kind of information should he share with the parents?

CASE **17**

PARENT POWER

est Hills Elementary School is located in a residential area outside a large urban area in a northeastern state. The district this K–6 school draws from consists of 67 percent white, 20 percent African-American, 10 percent Hispanic, and 3 percent Asian-American students. Roughly 60 percent are from low-income families. The school building is eight years old and is well maintained.

It is the first day of a two-week preplanning session for teachers, prior to the opening of school. Ann Riley, a white fourth-grade teacher, and Tara Hill, an African-American third-grade teacher, are sitting in Ann's classroom talking during the afternoon. The two teachers have become close friends during their five years of teaching at West Hills.

ANN   I tell you, Tara, I've never taken a course that I've gotten so much out of! My head is just brimming with ideas!

TARA   What did you say the course was called? I never get in a course like that!

ANN   "Parent Involvement in Education."

TARA   Who was the professor?

ANN   Dr. Saunders. Boy, was he full of information! It has to be the best summer course ever!

TARA   Well, what did you learn?

ANN   For one thing, did you know that there have been a lot of studies done that show that when a child's parents are involved in school, the child is likely to learn more in school and be more motivated? Programs for involving parents have existed for a long time, especially in elementary schools, but we just haven't heard about them.

TARA   Why not?

ANN   I wasn't real clear on the answer to that. I think a lot of the programs have been experimental, and they just haven't done a good job of disseminating the information about them.

TARA   Who hasn't?

ANN   Well, I guess the federal government and other agencies that have funded them and teacher education institutions.

TARA   That sure sounds right! I never heard of a course like the one you took *or* of a parent involvement program. I mean, I guess I've heard of the ideas but I've never visited a school that actually had such a program. *[Pause]* Well, tell me, Ann. What did you learn about parent involvement that we could be doing here?

ANN   Plenty. I learned that parent involvement can take many forms besides the traditional ones of classroom visitation, open houses, and parent–teacher conferences. Parents can be encouraged to help their children with their schoolwork at home through home visits. They can work in the classroom as volunteers or as paid paraprofessionals. Parents can participate in school decision-making activities through parent advisory committees, and they can become adult learners through school-based classes on topics like literacy and parenting.

TARA   *[Excitedly]* Whoa! Stop, Ann! I can't follow all that! Just tell me about home visits. Wouldn't they take a lot of a teacher's time? And how often would you make home visits? What would you take to the parents, homework?

ANN   It turns out that people other than teachers make good home visitors, maybe better.

TARA   Really?!

ANN   Yes. For example in one federal program they put two teacher aides in each classroom. Each aide worked in the classroom half-time and made home visits half-time. That way, there was at least one aide in the classroom at all times and every child's home got visited every week.

TARA   Then the teacher didn't actually make home visits?

ANN   No, although she could go with the aide any time she wanted to, and usually did two or three times a year for each child. But the aides were selected so that they came from the same backgrounds as the parents they were visiting. If the children were low-income Blacks, for example, then a low-income Black aide was selected and trained to make the home visits. The teacher's role was to plan the visits with the aides and help develop the home learning activities that the aide demonstrated to the parent each week.

TARA   What kind of activities?

ANN   They grew out of what was being taught in the classroom at the time but weren't just homework. They were more like enrichment material—games, puzzles, and other kinds of follow-up activities.

TARA   That is an exciting idea, Ann! But what were you talking about involving parents in decision-making? What kinds of decisions?

ANN   Through parent advisory committees. I didn't know that some states have passed laws requiring school districts to set up such committees involving parents in making decisions about things like school budgets, zoning issues, curriculum changes, and the like. The interesting thing was some of the parents who become leaders were from low-income backgrounds.

TARA   You mean low-income Black parents were involved?

ANN   Not just low-income Blacks but, yes, many of them were Black.

TARA   That *is* exciting. You say it helped the Black children's achievement test scores?

ANN   Yes, it helped the achievement test scores of a lot of the low-income children to have their parents involved.

TARA   Well, why aren't we doing some of these things here at West Hills? We pride ourselves on being progressive.

ANN   I guess it comes down to a lot of teachers and administrators either not know-
      ing about or being afraid of parent involvement programs. Probably a lot of them
      think they know more about education than the parents. In other words, they're
      the experts and don't want to be challenged by people with less education. Then
      too, I guess some teachers just don't want any other adults in their classroom.
      Can you imagine Bessie Moran working with either aides or parent volunteers in
      her classroom?

TARA   *[Chuckling]* No, I really can't. She doesn't even like it when Marie Allen, the
      music teacher, shows up once a week.

ANN   *[Laughing]* That's right.

TARA   *[Seriously]* But you know, Ann, I think she's the sole exception here at West
      Hills. I think most of the teachers here would appreciate more parent involve-
      ment. *[Pause]* Why don't we go talk to Marguerite about it and see if we can't
      bring it up at the next teachers' meeting to see how many teachers would want
      to get involved.

ANN   *[Smiling]* Now wait a minute, Tara! You're trying to get me in trouble again,
      aren't you? I've got enough to do as it is!

Tara and Ann sit in the office of Marguerite Fleming, the building principal, and
discuss with her some of the ideas that Ann disclosed to Tara the day before.

MARGUERITE   *[Frowning]* Saunders. Is that Richard Saunders?

ANN   Yes, I believe Richard is his first name.

MARGUERITE   I remember him well. We were in an educational administration course
      together when I was working on my Ed.D. *[Pause]* A bright man, at least when it
      comes to theory. But you'll notice he went on to become a college professor in-
      stead of getting down here on the firing line like us. *[Pause]* So he really im-
      pressed you, Ann?

ANN   Yes, he did, and so did his ideas.

MARGUERITE   Well, to be honest with you I've seen a lot of these theoretical ideas come
      and go. Personally, I think parents need to be involved by visiting the school,
      through conferences, and as supporters of our activities. We certainly couldn't put
      on our annual school carnival without parent help. And our new softball diamond
      wouldn't exist if it hadn't been for some of the dads, especially Billy Oeffer's father.
      But I'm not too sure about some of these ideas, like home visits, parent volunteers,
      parent advisory committees, and the like. Not only do we not have enough money
      for a lot of these ideas but I wonder if you two realize how much work would be in-
      volved in trying to involve parents in these ways.

ANN   What do you mean?

MARGUERITE   Well, suppose we found the money somewhere to put two teacher aides
      in each classroom, for example. Do you have any idea what it would take to
      train such parents? Do you realize how much time you'd have to spend planning
      with them for home visits and developing the home learning curriculum materi-
      als? Ideas like that may work in federally funded programs but just aren't cost
      effective in the real world.

TARA   But, Marguerite, most of us already have one aide. Can a second one cost that much? Some of the parents of our children would jump at the chance at being employed as a teacher's aide. As for the training, I think Dr. Saunders would help us with that at very little cost. I had him for a course once too.

MARGUERITE   Even if we got a home visitation program going, why would you want the aides to make the visits instead of doing it yourselves?

ANN   Because they are from the same backgrounds as the parents they are visiting. They share the same values, language, and subculture. I sometimes don't know what to say on a home visit after being introduced to a low-income parent. We don't dress alike, we don't share the same problems, and often our values about school are different. Sitting in a home without rugs, with dirty furniture, and a number of dirty children running around, often leaves me speechless.

MARGUERITE   [Chuckling] I see what you mean. But do you really think that such parents should be advising the building principal regarding such things as the school budget? We have a very active PTA, which does a good job of supporting our activities. But, frankly, the real leaders of that organization are white, upper-middle class housewives who have the time and know-how to get the job done. Many of them are also active in other community organizations as well. How can you expect low-income parents who haven't had that kind of experience—and many of whom didn't even graduate from high school—to take an active decision-making role?

TARA   Marguerite, just because many of those parents don't have high-school diplomas does not mean that they don't have any ideas about how the school is affecting them or their children. It might do us good to listen to low-income as well as middle-income parents. It might also help the parents develop a different view of school. The only time we contact some of them is when their child is in trouble.

MARGUERITE   Yes, I see what you mean. Perhaps I could talk to Mary Clark, the current PTA president, and see if we can figure out how to encourage a few low-income parents to attend meetings. But I'm afraid that transportation and babysitting will be big problems.

ANN   [Interrupting] Marguerite, can we present our parent involvement ideas to the other teachers at the first teachers' meeting and see how many of them might want to try out some of these ideas? If you want, I could even call Dr. Saunders and see if . . .

MARGUERITE   Ladies, I think we're being a bit premature. I'll agree that the two of you can go ahead and try out some of these ideas, provided you work with me as you develop them. But I don't want to make this a school project this year. I don't want to jump into the development of such a program on a school-wide basis without exploring it more. You two can develop a kind of pilot program and present it to me and we'll go from there. I do want to support teacher innovations like this but I'm not prepared to involve the entire school staff at this time.

It is the next-to-last day of preplanning and five other teachers spontaneously join Ann and Tara in the teachers' lounge during the late afternoon. These teachers are teaching children at the K–2 and 5–6 grade levels.

MEG So, Tara, what's this thing you're doing with the parents? Everyone's talking about it! How come Marguerite didn't bring it up at the teachers' meeting?

TARA Well, it's as much Ann as me, maybe more so. She took this parent involvement course this summer and we got the idea of going beyond open houses to involve parents. In the course, she learned that there are parent involvement techniques that work with low-income parents and increase achievement. Marguerite agreed to let Ann and me try them out this year and see how they work.

CORRINE *[With much indignation]* Well, I like that! How come we all get left out! Anything that gets the home and school working together to benefit the child sounds like something I want to try too!

OTHER TEACHERS *[Chorus]* Yes. Tell us about it Ann. What Marguerite doesn't know won't hurt her. Yes. Tell us.

ANN Well . . .

It is the first regular faculty meeting of the new school year. Marguerite presides over the meeting in the school library.

MARGUERITE I think that pretty well covers my agenda, folks. Are there any questions before we adjourn? Yes, Meg?

MEG I'd like to hear more about the pilot project that Ann and Tara are doing this year.

MARGUERITE *[Slightly flustered]* Yes, well, I didn't plan to bring it up since it's a project that involves only the two of them. I thought we'd see how it worked before I reported on it to you.

MEG Several of us, I would say most of us, heard about their project and are eager to try out some of the parent involvement procedures. I, for one, think the home visitation and parent volunteering ideas are great! I also think that more parents, especially those from low-income backgrounds, should be involved in school decision-making. After all, it's their school as well as ours. *[Many teachers nod their heads in agreement at Meg's remarks.]*

MARGUERITE *[Recovering quickly]* I agree with the concept as well, Meg. But I feel that we should try out these new ideas slowly and see what the problems and costs are before we make it a school program.

CORRINE Couldn't some of the rest of us participate in the experiment, as well? After all, only two teachers isn't a very large study.

MARGUERITE Well, I know, but the bottom line is that I'm not going to commit our staff and financial resources to a large-scale parent involvement program until we do all our homework. Such a program may be quite costly in more ways than one. *[Many teachers frown or look away]* Look, I'll tell you what I'm going to do. We'll bring up our pilot program at the parent open house and tell them what we're trying to do. *[Looking at Ann]* Ann, would you and Tara do that?

ANN Yes, Marguerite. We'd be glad to.

MARGUERITE Also, the room across from the library, Room 121, is large and not being used right now. We'll turn that into a "parents' room" and it can serve as a meeting and organizing place for our parent involvement activities this year. I'll let Mary Clark know about this and ask her to help us organize it. Also, let's all do some research on these programs so we know what we're talking about before we get too far along. *[A general chorus of teacher approval and agreement.]*

It is November of the same school year. Marguerite sits in the office of Dr. Brad Sutton, the superintendent of schools.

BRAD   What's up, Marge?

MARGUERITE   Brad, some of the teachers at West Hills have gotten bees in their bonnets about involving parents. Seems one of them took a course and has convinced most of my teachers that unusual kinds of parent involvement will improve student learning. I've tried to get them to try out a limited version of the program but a large number of the teachers are demanding to be involved. I just wanted you to be fully informed as to what is going on.

BRAD   Whoa, Marge! What do you mean by "unusual kinds of parent involvement?"

MARGUERITE   Well, it grew out of a course taught by Rich Saunders . . .

BRAD   *[Interrupting]* Oh, yes, I know him. A bright guy!

MARGUERITE   *[Frowning]* Yes, well, he advocates involving parents through home visits, as volunteers in the classroom, in parent advisory committees, and as adult learners in school-based programs.

BRAD   Well, that's a bit unusual, but it sounds innocent enough. Open houses, PTAs, and parent–teacher conferences aren't enough for Rich, huh?

MARGUERITE   It's more than that, I'm afraid, Brad. He especially advocates reaching out to low-income parents and getting them involved. The kind of home visitation he advocates involves putting two teacher aides in each classroom as home visitors. My teachers, especially Ann Riley and Tara Hill, the two ringleaders, don't seem to realize the costs and training problems that would be involved if the whole school adopted this program.

BRAD   *[With a twinkle in his eye]* What's the real problem, Marge?

MARGUERITE   *[With anger]* Brad, those parents aren't capable of advising me on how to run my school! I feel like the teachers are railroading me into a potentially dangerous situation. I've talked to Mary Clark, our PTA president, and she agrees with me that some of these parents could be real troublemakers if given half a chance. What do you think I should do, Brad?

BRAD   *[Soothingly]* Marge, how many times have I told you that things are never as bad as they seem? I've seen these kinds of movements come and go before. Just go along with it as best you can and drag your feet. Both the parents and teachers will tire of this before the year's over. I don't see any problem, budget-wise, with you putting an extra aide in the classrooms of the teachers that insist on having one. If you've got an empty room, tell the parents they are welcome to meet and organize their activities there. Put a big "Parents' Room" sign over the door.

MARGUERITE   I've already done that.

BRAD   Good. Call Rich Saunders and ask him to come work with them for free. Tell him we have no consulting money, but the staff will be eternally grateful.

[Pause] Don't worry about the low-income parents. After a little flurry of interest, they'll get tired and fade away. Maybe Mary Clark can help you with that.

MARGUERITE   *[Smiling]* Brad, you're wonderful! I knew you'd know how to handle things! I feel better already.

BRAD   *[Smiling]* Just remember that half the things we worry about never come to pass.

It is half-way though the school year, and Ann sits in her classroom at the end of the school day planning with her two African-American teacher aides, Rose Brown and Vanette Sanders.

ANN   I really feel good about the way we have been able to organize things this year so that you can make your home visits in the mornings, Rose, and you can do yours in the afternoon, Vanette. That way, I have one of you here in the classroom all day. Can we keep to that schedule the rest of the year? *[Rose and Vanette nod in the affirmative]* Good.

ROSE   What did you think of the home learning activity we did on reading, Ann?

ANN   *[Picking up and looking at a sheet of paper]* Good. Very good. This follows up nicely on the vocabulary activity you took into the homes last week. How is Mrs. Jackson responding to your home visits, Rose?

ROSE   Great! She even has punch and cookies ready for my visits now. She told me last week that although she enjoys working with Jerome on the home learning activities during the week, the thing she likes best is my telling her what's going on at school. She said she didn't know much about the school before. Now she even knows who Mrs. Fleming is when she sees her. The other day Mrs. Fleming recognized her as she passed the parents' room and called her by name. It just thrilled her to death. She says Mrs. Fleming is the first principal she has ever really gotten to know.

ANN   *[With eyes watering up]* That's a sad and wonderful story at the same time! *[pause]* Do you think she'll come to a parent advisory group meeting and maybe get involved?

ROSE   I asked her and she said yes, if I would pick her up and give her a ride.

ANN   *[With emotion]* That's wonderful! I don't know how I ever taught without the two of you!

Seven teachers, including Ann, Tara, Corrine, and Meg, sit in the teachers' lounge after school one month later.

CORRINE   *[Excitedly]* I just can't believe how involving the parents has affected the behavior of the children this year! Even though I only have one teacher aide and she can only make biweekly home visits, it has made all the difference in the world! I've never seen such a hard-working and happy bunch of kids! *[Other teachers voice their pleasure and agreement with this report.]*

MEG   I hear from the grapevine that a lot of parents, including a number of low-income parents, are really getting involved and vocal in both the PTA and the school advisory committee. I understand that Mary Clark is having a real problem trying to keep PTA from becoming more of a political group than a support group. *[Laughter and exclamations of surprise follow.]*

ROYANE   *[Conspiratorially]* Do you know what I heard last night? The SAC elected a low-income parent, Arlene Jackson, as its president, or is it chair? *[Exclamations of surprise]*

MEG   Chair. That's true! Isn't change wonderful and exciting? *[Exclamations of agreement and delight]*

ROYANE   And the parents' room. Talk about a beehive of activity, with Dr. Saunders in and out of there all the time!

CORRINE   You know what else I heard? I heard that Marguerite got him to help without giving him a consulting fee. How do you suppose she did that?

MEG   *[With a puzzled look]* That's a good question. Maybe the man is just dedicated to getting parent involvement going.

ANN   *[Assertively]* Definitely. Doesn't surprise me at all.

MEG   *[Looking directly at Ann and Tara, who are seated next to one another]* You two! You really got something going, didn't you? *[Exclamations of praise and support]*

It is seven months into the school year and Marguerite has asked Ann and Tara to meet her in her office after school. After the two are seated she closes her office door, sits down at her desk, and tries to control her anger.

MARGUERITE   Are you two aware of what happened at the Board meeting last night? I didn't see either of you there, so I'm not sure.

TARA   *[Puzzled]* No, what happened?

MARGUERITE   A whole block of your new PTA and SAC parents showed up and accused, in rather vulgar language I might add, the school board of being racist. They demanded rezoning of the schools. I would have liked to have disappeared when Dr. Sutton asked them to introduce themselves and tell what school their child attended, mainly to reduce the tension, I think, and about three-fourths of them were West Hills parents. Dr. Sutton and the members of the school board all looked at me and glared! I would liked to have died!

ANN   *[Sympathetically]* That was terrible for you, Marguerite!

MARGUERITE   *[Angrily]* Well, don't you two think you had something to do with it? I told you that I wanted to move slowly with this thing and just try it out in your two classes! But, no, you two had to get the rest of the teachers involved and now look at what has happened!

TARA   *[Both surprised and angry]* That's not fair, Marguerite. We did tell the other teachers what we were doing, but *you* agreed to let the other teachers develop their own programs.

MARGUERITE   I agreed reluctantly and now I wish I hadn't. But that's not all!

ANN   *[Anxiously]* What else?

MARGUERITE   Mrs. Jackson, the chair of the SAC, came in to pay me a visit this morning. The SAC is demanding, let me emphasize *demanding*, that they be allowed to go over every inch of the school budget and be given a summary of West

Hills' students' test scores in relation to other schools. Finally, ladies, they want to assist me and Dr. Sutton in developing procedures for evaluating teachers, with a view toward implementing merit salary procedures in this county. *[Ann and Tara look at one another with shock and surprise.]* *[Marguerite pauses as she struggles for self-control]* It's all happening too fast!

TARA   What are you going to do, Marguerite?

MARGUERITE   *[Controlled]* Well, let me ask you two a question. You two who started this whole thing. Do you see any reason why I shouldn't close down the parents' room? Can you give me any reason why I shouldn't ask you two and the rest of the teachers to stop this experiment in parent involvement right away? Don't you agree that the whole thing has been one tragic mistake?

Home Learning Activity for Ann Riley's Class

A READING WE WILL GO

Why?   For development of vocabulary.
What?   Several short story books.
How?

   1. You and the child should look through the books, checking the pictures to see which one appeals to the child.
   2. After he has decided on one, find a quiet time and place for you and the child to be alone so you may read it to him.
   3. Have him tell you something about the cover picture.
   4. Let him discuss the pictures in the book as you read to him.
   5. Read about two pages. Then ask him questions about what has been read. Give him time to think about his answers. Accept his answers only if they have been given in complete sentences.

After you are finished with the complete book, ask:

- Who was the main character in the story?
- What was he trying to do? Why?
- Which part of the story did you like best? Why?
- Do you suppose you would have liked another book better?
- Why?

What   Have the child write his own story from an experience he
then   has had. Encourage him to use new words and use your
or   dictionary to check the spelling of them so he will learn
what else?   that it's always good to use the dictionary to find new words.

QUESTIONS

1. What is parent involvement in education, and how strongly is it related to student achievement? What are the different forms that parent involvement can take and how effective is each (for example, home visits, parent volunteering, parent advisory committees, adult learning activities, parent–teacher conferences, etc.)?

2. What is socio-economic status (SES)? What is its relationship to racial and ethnic differences? How do upper and lower SES groups differ in their participation in various types of parent involvement activities? Why is it more difficult to involve parents from low SES and culturally different backgrounds? What attitudes and values do they hold toward the school? How can parent involvement programs help change negative attitudes?

3. What home and parental variables have been found to relate to a child's success in school? How can the school and other community institutions help compensate for the lack of such influences in a child's life?

4. What federally sponsored research and development programs, like Project Head Start and Project Follow Through, have been developed to help compensate for home and parental differences in children's lives and their success in school? What are the components of such programs, especially with regard to parent involvement? How successful have they been?

5. What are the barriers to getting successful parent involvement programs started in schools? What kinds of things can teachers and administrators do to help get such program started and to sustain their growth? What kinds of contributions can successful parent involvement programs make to the school and the school district?

6. What kinds of school-sponsored parent involvement activities are most effective in helping parents as learners? For example, are classes such as parenting, human growth and development, literacy, and employment skills successful? How well does involving parents as classroom volunteers work? as paid paraprofessionals? Can field trips include as many parents as possible and impact on parents as well as the children?

7. What is the purpose of home visitation? What are the characteristics of a successful home visitor? If the purpose of the home visit is to encourage the parent to work with the child at home, what kind of home learning material is most appropriate? What is the best way to deliver such material to the parent? How can such home visitation activities affect other children in the family? How could such material be delivered to a parent who is illiterate or who doesn't speak English?

8. How would you describe the principal's leadership style? What type of school climate has she helped create and why? How might a different principal have functioned differently, especially in relation to parent involvement? How might personnel at the district level have helped?

9. Who are the key persons in this case? What primary need levels explain their behavior from the standpoint of Maslow's motivational need hierarchy? Under what conditions can people and schools become more self-actualizing?

10. What response should Ann and Tara make? Can and should the school's fledgling parent involvement program be saved? Does its potential benefits outweigh its problems? What changes will have to be made if the program is to be saved?

PART V

INDIVIDUAL DIFFERENCES AND EXCEPTIONALITIES

CASE **18**

IT TAKES ALL KINDS

anet Hoy is beginning her fifth year as an English teacher at Putnam High School, having just received tenure. PHS is ten years old, located in a middle-SES suburban area in a New England town with a population of 25,000. PHS has an enrollment of approximately 400 pupils. The pupil population is approximately 70 percent white, 15 percent African–American, 8 percent Hispanic, and 7 percent Asian–American.

The English program at PHS begins with a survey of literature in freshman English (English 1). Sophomore English (English 2) has a heavy writing emphasis and includes a survey of world literature with a focus on ethnic literature. Junior English (English 3) is a study of American literature, and senior English (English 4) concentrates on English literature. Pupils are required to take all four English courses unless they qualify for the honors program. Honors students have the option of enrolling in honors sections, which have the same content but require pupils to go into greater depth in their reading and writing.

Throughout the four years she has been at PHS, Janet has taught three sections of English 1 and two sections of English 3. She takes pride in the fact that she has been able to maintain rigorous academic standards in her English classes and generate a love of literature in most of her pupils.

During the first two weeks of school Jan made an effort to become acquainted with the pupils in her classes, especially those in English 1, since all of them were new to Putnam High School. Some of the pupils in her English 3 classes were unfamiliar to her, but she had already met most of them either by having them in class or by meeting them at school functions. However, something about all her classes seems different this year. The behavior of some of the pupils seems more out of control, their work in class is below the standard Jan expects of pupils, and their interest in learning generally seems lacking. This seems to be particularly true in her third-period English 1 class.

On Monday of the following week, Jan greets the pupils of the third-period English 1 class, and begins to discuss the lesson assigned for the day.

JAN   Yesterday, I asked you to read the selection from *Tom Sawyer* called "The Cat and the Pain Killer." Now, I'd like us to discuss this story in class. *[Sam and Eric both burst out laughing]*

]Jan smiles and walks to their desks.] Sam, Eric, what seems to be so funny?

219

SAM   Eric said the cat is a pain. *[He and Eric break out in another spasm of laughter]*
[Several pupils look at each other and shake their heads. One boy rotates his finger in a circle next to his right temple. Jan frowns at him.]

JAN   *[Puzzled]* Well, maybe Tom thought the cat had a pain, but I'm not sure there's anything in the story to suggest that the cat *was* a pain. Eric, can you tell us why that part of the story is called, "The Cat and the Pain Killer"? *[Eric just faces Jan with a blank stare and makes no response.]* Sam, how about you? Can you answer the question?

SAM   *[Laughing raucously]* Maybe because the cat was a pain!

JAN   Thank you, Sam. Alice, can you tell us why?

ALICE   Because Tom Sawyer poured some of the pain killer in the cat's mouth.

JAN   That's right, Alice. And what did the cat do? Mark?

MARK   It jumped up in the air, twisted, ran around the room—just about went crazy.

JAN   Right! Good answer, Mark. Tell us why the cat acted that way, Dora.

DORA   I don't remember.

JAN   Did you read the story, Dora?

DORA   Yes, I did. But I don't remember why the cat did that. I can read OK, but then I can't remember what I've read.

PAUL   *[Soft whisper to Julie]* That's because she's a dumb Dora. *[Laughter from the class]*

JAN   *[Angrily]* Paul, I don't ever want to hear that type of comment in this class again. It's rude to make unkind comments about other people anytime, but it's especially out of place in a classroom! Now, you apologize to Dora and the rest of the class right now!

PAUL   *[Embarrassed, in a soft voice]* Yes, ma'am. I'm sorry everybody. I'm sorry, Dora.

DORA   That's OK, Paul.

JAN   Thank you, Paul. Now, can you tell us why the cat acted so wild when Tom gave it the pain medicine?

PAUL   Yes. From Tom's description it was bad tasting and it also burned his mouth.

JAN   That's right. But if that's true, why do you think Aunt Polly gave it to Tom? Alice?

ALICE   She was trying to make him better.

NED   My mother gives me medicine out of a spoon every morning before breakfast, Ms. Hoy.

JAN   That's interesting, Ned. What kind of medicine is it?

NED   I don't know. *[Laughter from class]*
[Angrily] Well, the doctor wrote out what it is and we bought it at the drug store. I take it every day. I don't really need to know what it is!

JAN   *[Smiling]* That's true, Ned. All you need to do is take it when you're supposed to, right?

NED   Right!

JAN   Now class, how did Tom avoid taking the medicine? Sara?

SARA   He pretended to like it and kept asking Aunt Polly if he could take some. She got tired of getting it for him and told him just to get some medicine whenever he wanted to. Then, he began to pour it down through a crack in the floor so he could get rid of it fast.

ERIC   I don't see why he'd ask for it all the time if he didn't like it.

MARK   *[Softly]* Because the cat is a pain, Eric. *[Laughter from the class]*
           [Jan frowns at Mark and he looks down at his desk]

JAN   *[Distributing a sheet of questions to each pupil]* Here are some other questions
           about this reading selection. I want you to spend the rest of the period rereading
           the selection and writing the answers to the questions. If there are questions you
           don't finish in class, answer them at home tonight.

The following Thursday after school, Jan enters the office of Patsy McNab, the resource teacher, to inquire about the pupils in her English 1 class who seem so imma-
ture.

PATSY   Nice to see you, Jan. We seem to have been missing each other since classes
           started. How do things seem to be shaping up for you this year?

JAN   Nice to see you, too, Pat. I'm here to ask you for some information that might
           help me to answer the question about how things are shaping up. They seem to
           be shaping up a little differently this year than they have in previous years.

PAT   How's that?

JAN   Well, for the first time since I've been teaching at Putnam, I have pupils that
           need special help in dealing with English 1.

PAT   *[Sympathetically]* I'm sorry to hear that. Give me some examples of the kinds of
           troubles you're having.

JAN   Specifically, the problem is that some of my pupils don't function at the high-
           school level. They seem to have some kind of learning difficulties.

PAT   You do have some pupils with learning difficulties in that class.

JAN   *[Astounded]* Do you mean that I have exceptional pupils in my regular English 1
           class?

PAT   Yes. That's exactly what I mean.

JAN   How can I have exceptional pupils in my class and not be informed of it?

PAT   Well, as you know, Public Law 94–142 requires that all children with disabili-
           ties be educated in the least restrictive environment. This means that whenever
           possible they should be mainstreamed into a regular classroom. Some of the
           children in your class have been placed in special classes for some types of in-
           struction. This is indicated on each of their IEP's along with the special instruc-
           tion they'll receive. The pupil, parent, the school psychologist, and I have signed
           off on the special programs. They're being mainstreamed into your class because
           that is part of their IEP. You aren't required to sign off on the program.

JAN   *[Obviously annoyed]* That makes me angry, Pat. Even though I didn't need to sign
           the IEP, common courtesy would dictate that you or Sam Darst *[building principal]*
           inform me of this decision. If I'd have known I was going to have special pupils, I
           could have planned for them! That's just administrative arrogance! In fact, it's not
           even professionally ethical to place special education pupils in regular classrooms
           without giving the teachers advance notice. I resent being deceived in this manner!
           You're these children's resource teacher! School's been on for a month and this is

the first I've seen of you! Even if you would've dropped by my class the first week of school and told me about the special pupils, I would have had three week's more planning time, which would have been a big help.

PAT   *[Solicitously]* I'm sorry that you're angry with me, Jan, and I can understand why. But the county administrators and special education staff wanted the pupils included in the regular classes without the teachers knowing it. We resource teachers were specifically asked not to inform the regular teachers of the change in policy.

JAN   *[Angrily]* That makes it even worse! It just reflects the general lack of respect that our administrators have for classroom teachers!

PAT   *[Calmly]* The administration has a very good reason, which I'll explain. In reading about the experiences of other school districts with mainstreaming, our district staff members found evidence that when special education pupils are put into regular classrooms without being identified as special education pupils, they seem to be accepted more readily by both teachers and other pupils. In many cases, they're not even recognized as being special education pupils.

JAN   I've read that also. The problem is the self-fulfilling prophecy effect.

PAT   Yes! Exactly! That's the major reason why nobody told you or the other teachers that these pupils were being placed in your classrooms. Since there is evidence that exceptional pupils feel more at home in classes where nobody recognizes them as exceptional, we decided not to tell the teachers. We believe that will reduce biases and stereotyping.

But I can see your point, too. Had you been informed of the special pupils before classes began, you would have had more time to prepare specific lessons for these mainstreamed pupils.

Just as a matter of interest, I'd like to check you out on your recognition of the special pupils, if it's OK with you. Will you tell me the pupils you think are the exceptional pupils?

JAN   *[Smiling]* I see. You're giving me a test. OK. There's Eric Ames, Sam Baker, Alice Sliger, and Lynn Thut. I think these pupils are slow learners, or whatever you call them in special education.

PAT   They're now called educable mentally challenged. I'm really impressed! You're batting a thousand so far!

JAN   The other two pupils I've noticed are Dora Ulmer and Ned Whitt. I think they're intellectually capable of learning, but they seem to have some kind of intellectual short circuit.

PAT   Bingo! I must admit that I'm impressed! Dora and Ned are classified as learning disabled. They're able to learn normally, but they both have some type of neurological dysfunction that makes it difficult sometimes for them to remember information.

But I've worked with those pupils for the past two years. I know their reading levels and exactly where they are in the basal text workbooks. Even though these pupils are mainstreamed into your classroom, I'll be glad to work with them if you think you don't have the time to do it. As a classroom teacher working with exceptional pupils, you have the right to request my services in preparing lessons and/or teaching these pupils.

JAN   Thanks for the offer, but these pupils are doing fine in my class. I'm just annoyed that I wasn't been told in advance so that I wouldn't be in such a rush now.

PAT   Well, I can save you time if you want me to help. I can form the special education pupils in your class into a group and come in and teach them.

JAN   Then the pupils would be in the same situation that you just told me the county staff is trying to avoid. If you did that, every pupil in the class and probably in the entire school would know that these are exceptional pupils. Even though they'd be in a regular class, they'd be segregated into a special group. Isn't this the exact situation that the county staff is trying to avoid?

PAT   But exceptional education is my specialty. I could give them special assignments and they could work on them individually while the other pupils are working on their assignments. No one would need to know.

JAN   I think everyone would know. And aside from that, the class is an English class. And English is my specialty. I think that I'm better qualified than you to teach English—even to exceptional pupils.

PAT   I'm not really convinced of that. I'm quite well qualified in strategies for teaching exceptional pupils.

JAN   But you just told me that the parents of the exceptional pupils and the district administrators found that these pupils performed better when they were assigned to regular academic teachers who didn't even know that they have exceptional pupils in their class.

      I'm a regular academic teacher who knows her field. Since I became aware of the limitations of the exceptional pupils in my class, I've already planned activities that allow the exceptional pupils to work in groups with the regular members of the class. And, if I understand the protocol, I have the prerogative to ask you to help me with the exceptional pupils if I want you to. But I don't have to if I don't want to. Am I correct?

PAT   [Unsettled] Yes, that's right. You have the authority to request my services if you want me to work in some capacity with the exceptional pupils. But I'm not authorized to work with pupils assigned to your class unless you request my help.

JAN   [Sweetly] The exceptional pupils have been totally integrated into my class. The other pupils have accepted them as regular class members. They're all successfully working together in groups. I'll let you know if I need any help.

      The only distinction that I've made between the special education pupils and the regular pupils is in the individual assignments that they have to do for the group projects. Of course, you're welcome to visit my class at anytime.

The following week, Jan checks her mailbox in the principal's office after her last class. The box contains a note from the principal, Sam Darst, requesting her to stop in his office after school. While she's reading the note, he sees her, gets up from behind his desk, and walks to his office door.

SAM   Jan, do you have time to talk with me?

JAN   Sure, I don't have any plans until after dinner this evening.

SAM   Great. Come on in.

     [Jan enters the office and sits in the chair offered by Sam.]

     The reason I wanted to see you is to ask you to tell me how things are going with the exceptional pupils assigned to your class.

JAN   Good! I'll be happy to tell you anything you want to know.

SAM   First, I've heard that the exceptional pupils are integrated into groups with the regular ninth graders. Is this true?

JAN   Yes, it is. When school began in the fall, I didn't know there were special education pupils in my class. But I soon realized that there were six of them. I talked with Pat McNab about this, and she explained that these pupils had been mainstreamed into my class. She also explained the administrative decision not to inform regular teachers that the exceptional pupils had been placed in their classrooms. I told her in no uncertain terms that I think this is a prime example of administrative arrogance and that I deeply resent it!

SAM   *[Taken aback]* Didn't she explain the reasons for making this decision?

JAN   Of course. She said that there is some evidence that exceptional pupils tend to do better in regular classrooms when neither teachers nor the other pupils are told that exceptional pupils are in their rooms. Evidently, the implication is that both the teachers and regular pupils won't figure out who the exceptional pupils are. This notion was not supported by the articles I found at the University Library, however. Sooner or later teachers and regular students identify the exceptional students, and I don't see how trying to deceive them for a while is going to help.

     I'd like to point out, just for the record, that I identified all the exceptional pupils in my class, along with their exceptionalities, during the first week of school. And I'm reasonably certain that their classmates did, too.

SAM   I'm certain that none of the staff members who made that decision think that our own teachers would be unable to figure out who the exceptional children are.

JAN   Oh? Well, maybe Pat was mistaken about the reason we weren't informed about the situation. Why don't you tell me the real reason?

SAM   I'm sure that you've heard of the research on the self-fulfilling prophecy idea. The results of those studies provided the basis for the decision not to tell the teachers about the exceptional pupils in their classes. Pat's told me that she's already offered to teach the exceptional pupils in your class. She's really obligated to plan lessons for the exceptional pupils.

JAN   I know that she's obligated to teach them if I request her to, and she's willing to do so. But I believe that I'm a good enough English teacher that I can teach English to exceptional as well as regular high school pupils.

SAM   But most exceptional pupils aren't able to work on the same level as average pupils.

JAN   That's true.

SAM   But you just said that they study the same material as the other pupils in the class.

JAN   Yes, they do. But all my assignments over the material are on not on the same level of difficulty. I adapt them to the students' ability levels.

SAM   I don't understand.

JAN   For instance, right now, the English 1 class is studying different types of literary fantasy—folk tales, fairy tales, and legends. I've divided the class into six groups of five members each. Each group had a choice of more than fifteen selections of literary fantasy. And for each fantasy, there are ten to twelve activities pupils can choose as a project. I've deliberately planned some activities that are on the appropriate level of difficulty for the special education pupils in the class.

SAM   Wouldn't it have been easier all the way around just to have asked Pat to plan special assignments for the special education pupils?

JAN   No, I think it would be harder. That would segregate the exceptional pupils into a separate group, which is exactly what you told me the school district's trying to avoid. Isn't that right?

SAM   *[Hesitantly]* Yes, it is.

JAN   You should know me well enough by now to know that in teaching, I'm not really looking for the easiest way. I'm looking for the best way. And I'm positive that being isolated in a separate group would make the special education pupils feel like second-class citizens. That's what mainstreaming is all about, isn't it?

SAM   Why would they feel like second-class citizens?

JAN   Why wouldn't they? Let's think about this for a minute. First you take six pupils that are the same age as all the other pupils in the class, and you require them to sit in a little group all by themselves. Then you bring in Pat, who indicated to me that she would assign these fourteen year-old high school pupils stories to read from a fifth-grade basal reader and then complete the accompanying workbook assignment. These assignments are certainly different from those of their classmates. Do you really need to ask me why they'd feel like second-class citizens?

SAM   Is that why you decided to give them the same types of assignments as the other pupils in the class?

JAN   I decided to do that because that's exactly what the Individuals with Disabilities Education Act (IDEA) requires, isn't it? In fact *[digging in her purse]* here are some notes I made when I went to the library and found information regarding this act. *[Hands them to Sam]*.

SAM   *[Reads the paper]* Well, I, uh, see your point.

JAN   Pat told me that the superintendent and county staff met last summer and designed this plan not to inform the teachers that special education pupils are in their class. Is that right?

SAM   Yes, the county staff did agree that this would help exceptional pupils from being identified and segregated.

JAN   Then what I'm doing in class is what all the teachers who have special education pupils in their classes should be doing, isn't it?

SAM   *[Uncomfortably]* The problem is that the parents of some of your pupils have complained to me about your class.

JAN   Oh, so now we get to the real reason that you wanted to see me. And were the complaints from the parents of the exceptional pupils or the parents of the regular pupils?

SAM   From the parents of the regular pupils.

JAN   So this conference really has nothing to do with the education of the exceptional pupils.

SAM   No. It's about the other parents. One of their main complaints is that you assigned their children to a group in which there are slow learners.

JAN   And they're right. I have done that. But their children are not working on the same assignments as the slow learners.

SAM   The parents also said that their children were required to tutor the slow learners.

JAN   That's not true. In each group I ask one of the good readers to read aloud the literary selection so that all the members of the group can hear the entire story before they begin their assignments on the story. But I don't consider that to be a situation in which a smart pupil is required to tutor a slow one. In English 1, I believe that pupils should develop skills in oral reading. Do you think that this is an inappropriate requirement?

SAM   No. I don't.

JAN   Well, what did you tell these irate parents?

SAM   I told them I would talk with you and find out exactly how you were conducting the class and then I would get back to them.

JAN   [Assertively] Why didn't you ask them to call me directly? I would have been glad to explain it to them.

SAM   I wanted to check out their complaints by talking with you directly so that I will be informed as well. I don't like parents complaining directly to teachers without my being involved. Besides, they had other questions that they wanted answered.

JAN   Such as?

SAM   They wanted to know how you can use any kind of standard grading strategy when pupils are working on different assignments. They also wanted to know whether their children are being held back by working in groups with special education pupils. They think that it's not good practice to mix the special education pupils into groups with the regular pupils when they could be working effectively in their own group.

JAN   Did you tell them that the district administrators decreed that those pupils would be put in a regular classroom so that they could be mixed with regular pupils?

SAM   No, I could have answered their questions, but I didn't. However, after talking to you, I'd like for you to answer them because you can explain the exact details about what you are doing in the class and why.

      I'm sorry if you're upset because I asked the parents what their concerns are about your class. But as the principal of this school, I want to keep everything working harmoniously in the entire school district—the district office, the teachers, the pupils, and the parents.

JAN   Well, I think relationships with teachers like me would have been more harmonious if I had been informed about the placement of the exceptional pupils in my class. But I can live with that if that's the way it has to be. You set up the time and place that I can meet with the parents of my pupils, and I'll come and answer their questions.

SAM   [*Relieved*] Good. I appreciate your willingness to do that. But first I'd like you to review for me what you're going to tell them. For instance, do you have a uniform grading scale that you apply to all pupils in English 1? Describe to me what it is. How are you able to challenge the bright children as well as the exceptional children? Give me some of the assignments that you give to the bright pupils. Then give examples of some assignments you give to the slow pupils. What strategies do you use to evaluate the assignments of the bright pupils as well as the slow pupils? What rationale do you use to mix the smart and slow pupils in the same groups? How do you keep the slow members of groups from imposing on the study time of the bright pupils? How do you challenge the bright pupils without neglecting the slow pupils? Let's take a few minutes right now and you tell me how you will answer each of these questions.

Education for all Handicapped Children Act (Public Law 94–142) This act guarantees to all children with disabilities a free and appropriate public education. This law, which outlines extensive procedures to ensure that exceptional students between the ages of three and eighteen are granted due process in regard to identification, placement, and educational services received, applies to every teacher and school in the country.

Individuals with Disabilities Education Act (IDEA) Extends the availability of a free, appropriate education to disabled youth between the ages of three and twenty-one years of age. It also requires:

- *Least restrictive environment.* All children with disabilities must be educated in the *least restrictive environment.* This means that a student must be mainstreamed into a general education classroom whenever such integration is feasible and appropriate and the child would receive educational benefit from such a placement.
- *Individualized education program (IEP).* Every child with disabilities is entitled to a written *individualized education program (IEP)* that meets this child's needs. This IEP must specify educational goals, methods for achieving those goals, and the number and quality of special educational services to be provided. The IEP must be reviewed annually by (1) the parent or guardian, (2) the pupil, (3) a teacher, (4) a professional who has evaluated the pupil, and (5) the principal or a special education resource person from the school district.
- *Confidentiality of records.* Parental permission is required before any official may look at a pupil's records. Parents can have their child's records amended if they believe the information therein to be misleading, inaccurate, or in violation of the child's rights.
- *Due process.* Parents have the right to protest an IEP or an evaluation of their child's abilities through an impartial due process hearing presided over by an appointed state official. If parents or the school district are not satisfied with the outcome of the hearing, the case may be taken to the civil courts.
- *Mental exceptionalities.* The two types of mental exceptionalities dealt with in this case study are *mentally challenged* (which is characteristic of pupils who have general learning problems associated with all their intellectual functioning both in and out of school), and *learning disabled* (which is characteristic of pupils who have a disorder in one or more of the basic processes involved in understanding or in using language, spoken or written).

QUESTIONS

1. Jan was able to identify the educable mentally challenged and learning disabled pupils in her classroom by their behavior. Compare and contrast the types of behavior that would be characteristic of each of these groups of exceptional pupils.

What other categories of exceptionalities have been identified under PL 94–142 and IDEA? What are the characteristics of each? What treatment works best with each?

2. What do the terms *least restrictive environment, mainstreaming,* and *IEP* mean? Who develops the IEP, and who is responsible for implementing it?

3. According to the research, how does mainstreaming affect the achievement of both the exceptional and regular students? How does it affect the biases and stereotyping of exceptional children by regular students and teachers? How are the self-concepts of the exceptional children affected?

4. What are the respective roles of the resource teacher and the regular teacher for dealing with exceptional children who are mainstreamed? Who's responsible for planning and assigning grades? What are some problems that can create conflicts between the regular and resource teachers?

5. Administrators of the Putnam School District made the decision to mainstream educable mentally retarded and learning challenged pupils into the regular high school classes. On what logic was this decision based? List the advantages and disadvantages of such a strategy.

6. Who writes the IEP for each exceptional student? Whose job is it to implement the plan? What are the child's parents' rights with regard to the IEP?

7. Based on his conference with Jan, would you consider Sam Darst to be an effective educational leader? Would you classify Mr. Darst's administrative style as supporting, coaching, delegating, or directing?

8. Jan integrated her exceptional pupils into the class by organizing the class into heterogeneous groups. Explain how this organization enabled Jan to meet the needs of all the pupils in the class. Suggest some other strategies that a high-school teacher could use to meet the educational needs of a wide range of pupils.

9. How appropriate were the resource teacher's lessons for the exceptional pupils in Jan's third-period English 1 class. What are some other strategies that Jan could have used to teach English literature effectively to all the pupils in her third-period class?

10. What is cooperative learning, and how effective is it in working with classes containing mainstreamed students? How could Jan have used these techniques in this situation?

11. What are parent involvement techniques? How effective would such techniques as classroom volunteering, parent advisory committee work, and home visitation be in working with the parents of exceptional children?

12. How should Jan answer the questions that Mr. Darst poses to her at the end their meeting? What should she say to the parents when she meets with them?

DIVISION AND FRACTIONS

Dean Goodman is 22 years old and is in his first year of teaching mathematics at the middle school level. He teaches in a medium-sized (population 60,000) suburb of a large urban center in the southwestern United States.

It is fourth period of the first full day of classes as the new school year begins. The bell has rung and the 32 students in Dean's Math 8 class become quiet and wait for Dean to begin class. Dean smiles as he looks at the mixture of white, African-American, and Hispanic faces that attentively wait for him to begin.

DEAN   Welcome to Math 8! I hope we've all adjusted to the fact that summer vacation is over and that it's time to get back to work. *[Several students groan, while others laugh.]* There, now. I hope you got the last of that out of your systems. *[More laughs.]* Now. If you open your books to the table of contents, you'll notice that we're going to cover a lot of important material in this class—math concepts that should be valuable to you no matter what you do in life. We'll get into ratios, proportions, percents, decimals, dividing and multiplying fractions, working with positive and negative numbers, taking square roots and so forth. These may sound mysterious to you now but I guarantee you that once you understand them, you will find them quite useful whether you end up as a mechanic, a cook, or a banker. Don't worry about understanding the material just because it's math. We're going to take it slow and have fun as we learn it. *[Sees a hand raised.]* Yes, what's your name?

PATTI   I'm Patti Williams, Mr. Goodman. How will we be graded in here?

DEAN   Thanks for asking, Patti. I was just coming to that. Each Monday I'll introduce and explain the math concepts that we'll be working on. We'll start with proportions of whole numbers this week. When I do that, it will be real important for you to pay attention to the explanations and examples that I give. Then I'll give you some assignments for you to work on your own. If you do a good job on these weekly assignments, you'll get Friday off to have fun! *[All hands go up.]* Yes, aren't you Bill?

BILL   Yes, Billy Carter. What do you mean have fun on Friday? Do we get out of class?

DEAN   No, not exactly. If you do the weekly assignments that I mentioned and turn them in on Friday and get a good grade on them, then you get to spend your class time on Friday in my math lab. *[Smiles and speaks teasingly.]* You're going to love the math lab! It's full of all kinds of math games, math puzzles, interesting filmstrips, records, tapes, and computers. If there isn't something there that you'd like to do, like your favorite hobby, I'll try to make it available if it doesn't cost too much. *[Hands go up.]* You're Gerardo, aren't you?

GERARDO   What happens if we can't finish the assignments or don't get a good enough grade on it?

DEAN   *[Tauntingly]* Don't even think that way, Gerardo! It's a fate worse than death! *[Opens his eyes wide and speaks slowly for emphasis].* You have to work on your assignments while the other students have fun in the math lab. *[Everybody laughs.]* And you have to do something else worse than death: you have to sit down and write your parents a letter explaining to them why you didn't finish or got a low grade. *[Several students groan.]* It gets worse. If I don't get the letter back on Monday, signed by your parents, then I'll call them and see what happened. Remember, I'd rather be having fun in the math lab, too, instead of working with students on their assignments. And you don't want to make me mad because I give the grades around here. *[Many students laugh.]* Now. Let's all open our books to page 1.

Two months later, Dean sits in the classroom of Janet Justice, a fellow math teacher that Dean has been dating for some time. The school day is over and the classroom is empty except for the two of them.

JAN   How's your fourth-period class going, Dean?

DEAN   Why do you ask, Jan? Did somebody say something about it?

JAN   You did just yesterday. You really seem preoccupied with that class.

DEAN   Yes, well, I've got to admit that my fourth-period class is more trouble than my other four combined.

JAN   I don't understand what the problem is, Dean. You said that they are fairly well behaved. What's going on?

DEAN   It's a weird combination of things. First, there seems to be two distinct groups of kids academically: roughly half of them are bright and the others are relatively slow. But mixed in with this are real differences in family backgrounds.

JAN   You mean the bright kids are from upper-income families while the academically slower ones are from disadvantaged homes?

DEAN   Yes. That's for openers.

JAN   There's more?

DEAN   Yes and I don't quite know how to describe it.

JAN   Well, give it a try.

DEAN   I guess I'd say that some of the kids have a lot of initiative and prefer to work independently. They don't need or even want much help from me in grasping math concepts or doing their assignments. The other group, though—the slow group—shows no initiative at all. It seems like they need total organization and structure all the time. They are constantly running to me or other kids in the class for help. I guess they're afraid of not getting to go to math lab on Fridays.

JAN   So you have a sort of water and oil type of mixture?

DEAN   It's even more of a difference than I've tried to explain, Jan. Like I said, it's hard to describe.

JAN   Well, keep going, you're doing fine.

DEAN   The bright half don't even think the same way as the slow half. The bright kids are good analyzers and grasp the main points quickly. But the slow group, well, they just can't seem to see the trees because of the forest. They just can't get beyond the big picture and break things down into their parts. Like the other day, I was trying to explain proportions and used a pie chart that I drew on the blackboard. The slow kids just couldn't grasp the idea of breaking the pie down proportionately. And need I say how the bright kids were giving them a hard time when they asked questions or gave answers that the bright kids thought were dumb? It really tested my patience with both groups.

JAN   Dean, you just can't let things get to you that way!

DEAN   I know. But when I try to work with some of the slow kids individually, I get this "I can't do math, Mr. Goodman." Like when I was tutoring Patti Williams after school yesterday.

JAN   Oh, Yes! Patti's such a cute girl!

DEAN   I agree, but she keeps telling me that she can't do math because her mother and grandmother couldn't do math. Like it's a hereditary thing or something. It doesn't do me any good to point out to her that she's successfully gotten to go to math lab for two months now. She still insists that she can't learn the next math concept you try to teach her.

JAN   I think a lot of girls have that problem. I remember a professor in a course that I took saying that female math anxiety has generated a lot of research.

DEAN   That may be, but its not just Patti who thinks that way. Several of the boys in the slow group don't believe they can do math. Gosh, I must have a dozen kids like that.

JAN   You really do have a problem, don't you, Dean? What are you going to do?

DEAN   I don't know! [Smiling] I thought I'd ask you and you'd tell me what to do.

JAN   [Smiling] Well, it seems like you have one of those "providing for individual differences" situations that they talk about in education courses.

DEAN   But, Jan, I've tried to provide for individual differences with my math lab approach.

JAN   Well, I really don't know what to tell you. If it were me I guess I'd try to figure out a way of working with the bright and slow kids in groups somehow.

DEAN   [Brightening up] Hey, yes! Homogeneous groups. Putting the kids in groups according to their ability. I'm not sure how to set that up or work with the groups differently but that's a good idea, Jan!

JAN   [Teasingly] Hey, if you've got any problems just ask me! I'll tell you how to solve them!

Two more months have passed and Dean sits in the teachers' lounge talking to Bill Ryan, the middle school curriculum director for the school system. Bill, who dropped

by to talk with the building principal, has stopped by the teachers' lounge to say hello
to whoever was there. Dean and Bill are alone as the other teachers leave at the sound
of the bell to teach their classes.

BILL   Is this your planning period, Dean?

DEAN   Yes it is, and I'm real glad that I've lucked out and caught you alone. I need
        your advice.

BILL   I apologize for not contacting you earlier to see if I can help in any way, but you
        can't believe how busy I've been, Dean, with the district-wide curriculum revi-
        sions that we've got underway!

DEAN   Hey, no need to apologize. I know how busy you must be.

BILL   How can I help?
        *For the next ten minutes Dean describes the situation in his fourth-period Math
        8 class just as he did for Jan two months earlier.*

BILL   So you formed the kids into ability groups? How did that work out?

DEAN   It hasn't. That's the problem. At the beginning I thought it was going to work.
        But over time all that's really happened is that the bright groups have moved along
        much faster and work on more advanced material than the slow groups. Further,
        the kids in the bright groups resent the fact that they have to work on harder and
        more advanced material than the slow groups to get to go to the math lab on Fri-
        days. Needless to say, the bright kids take their resentment out on the slow kids in
        a number of subtle ways, razzing them and calling them names at every opportu-
        nity. The slow kids fight back as best they can, but all that belittling can't help their
        self-concepts. They know they're in the slow groups without my ever telling them
        so. *[Pause]* And to be truthful, Bill, it takes me so much more time to work with the
        slow groups that I get frustrated as well. I have to explain things over and over and
        sometimes act like a cheerleader. So many of those kids honestly believe they just
        can't do math, both the boys and girls alike. Any advice, Bill?

BILL   Well, it looks like homogeneous groups haven't worked. Have you considered
        heterogeneous groups?

DEAN   No, I haven't. How would I do that?

BILL   Did you study anything about cooperative learning in your college work?

DEAN   Well, yes, of course. But I'm not sure how I could get that to work in my
        fourth-period class.

BILL   In a nutshell, what's involved is putting the kids in heterogeneously grouped
        teams, mixing bright and slow kids in together so they have to work as team-
        mates. Then you set it up so the teams have to compete against one another. You
        convert the grades that the kids get on your assignments and tests into team
        points. The bright kids have to tutor the slow kids so their team can win.

DEAN   *[Pondering]* I see, but I'm not sure how to work that with this class. That
        might mean that some teams would get to go to math lab and others wouldn't.
        What would I do with entire teams that didn't get to go?

BILL   Remediation work, I would say. Help them so they get to go next time. Perhaps
        you could get some parents to come in as volunteers or even ask for a teacher aide

so you can do remediation work with the losing team or teams as well as work individually with the kids in your math lab. *[Pause]* You can work it any way you want to, maybe so that you have only a few teams. You could set it up so that only one team loses at a time. The point is that getting the bright and slow kids working together might help the situation and make your life better as well.

DEAN   *[Pondering]* Yes, I guess I can figure all that out, but how to group them is only part of the problem, Bill.

BILL   You're referring to the differences in the way they think and whether they believe in themselves or not.

DEAN   Yes. I found it difficult myself to work with the slow groups. They're so dependent and nonanalytical, almost the opposite of the bright kids who are take-charge types and see right to the core of things quickly. It's like you're mixing together a bunch of self-confident entrepreneurs with dependent groupies. If *I* had a hard time working with the slow kids, how can I expect the bright kids to work with them? They'll get frustrated when the slow kids can't grasp the math concepts quickly and break them down into their elements.

BILL   Well, Dean, that's where your professionalism as a teacher will come into play. The kids may get frustrated, and so might their parents when their kids confide in them that they're tutoring slow classmates. But as a teacher you have to control your biases and remain tolerant of individual differences in your students. After all, just because a student is more assertive, self-confident, and a good analyzer of math concepts doesn't mean he's a more worthwhile human being or more deserving of our time and attention as teachers.

DEAN   *[Smiling contritely]* Thanks, Bill. I guess I deserved that. I guess I wasn't consciously controlling my biases and objectively trying to deal with this problem situation I'm facing.

BILL   *[Smiling]* That's what I'm here for, Dean. That's why they pay me the big salary they do. *[Both men laugh.]*

It is one week later and Dean meets his fourth-period Math 8 class.

DEAN   OK guys, settle down. The bell has rung. It's Monday and you know what that means—a new math concept. This week we're going to work on positive and negative numbers. Negative numbers are hard for some people to understand *[a few groans from slow students]* but I'm going to explain it real clearly and give lots of examples. Before I begin, let me pass out your weekly assignment sheets for positive and negative numbers. Would you take a few of these and help me, Patti? Yes, Gerardo?

GERARDO   Are we supposed to work in our groups now?

DEAN   I'm glad you asked that, Gerardo. We're going to reorganize our groups this time. *[Many shouts of protest.]* Settle down now and let me explain! *[Pause]* I think it's getting a little boring in here. We need to make some changes and liven things up a bit. You need to work with some different people, that's all. Yes, Patti?

PATTI   But I really like my group. We all work together real well and help one another. I don't think I can learn some of this stuff without their help, especially Sarah Samuelson.

DEAN   Now I don't want you to worry. We're going to put good people in our new groups and everything's going to work out fine. Back at the beginning of school, Patti, when I first put you in groups, I'll bet you had no idea that you were going to get along so well with your group members and look how well it turned out. Have a little faith in me. *[Pause]* OK, please stop talking. *[Pause]* And guess what else, gang! We're going to jazz things up a bit and pretend that our groups are like athletic teams and compete against one another. *[Shouts of protest.]* Now settle down! Look, your grades on your assignments and tests will earn points for your team. It will be like making touchdowns in football. Yes, Gerardo?

GERARDO   What do the winning groups get to do?

DEAN   To go to the math lab, of course.

GERARDO   Then the losers don't get to go?

DEAN   That's right. They get me as a prize! I'll spend time working with them so they can win next time. Maybe we can sweeten the pot a bit more by allowing the winner special privileges for the week like taking the roll, repairing some of the math lab equipment, or assisting me with record-keeping. *[Protests]*

GERARDO   And who's going to be in these new groups?

DEAN   I thought I'd divide the groups equally in terms of ability. In other words, I'll spread the good players around.

GERARDO   And the weak players as well?

DEAN   Yes, Gerardo, and I'd appreciate it if you would raise your hand instead of just speaking out. *[Grumbles and protests]* Yes, Patti?

PATTI   Mr. Goodman, can't we please keep the groups we have? Do we have to have contests? Math is real hard and I just want to make a good grade in here. *[Shouts of agreement]*

DEAN   *[Displeased]* Well, OK, look guys. Maybe I should think this over some more. We'll keep things the way they are for a week while I think about it. *[Cheers, applause, and shouts of approval.]*

Dean sits in his classroom talking to Janet Justice, his friend and fellow math teacher, after school on the same day.

DEAN   Jan, I am totally confused. First I tried grouping the kids by ability and that didn't work. Bill Ryan suggested heterogeneous groups using cooperative learning methods, but the kids want to keep their ability groups even though they're not working. What do I do, Jan? Do I just go in there and tell the kids that I'm the boss and in my professional opinion we have to go to heterogeneous grouping whether they like it or not? I guess the problem is that the slow kids may be too insecure to make the change at this point. The train has already gone down the track, as they say. Yet, how can I keep things the way they are? What I'm doing just isn't working. What can I do now, Jan?

Student Information Assembled by Dean Goodman on his Fourth-Period Math 8 Class

Name	Eligible for School Lunch	Group vs. Individual Work Preference	Math Anxious	I.Q.*
1. Adams, Jennifer	No	Individual	No	110
2. Anderson, Willie	Yes	Group	Yes	87
3. Bailey, John	Yes	Group	No	98
4. Butler, Latesha	Yes	Group	Yes	86
5. Carter, Billy	Yes	Group	No	87
6. Dennis, Wayne	No	Individual	No	102
7. Ferguson, Scott	No	Individual	No	110
8. Gil, Maria	Yes	Group	Yes	103
9. Gonzalez, Donna	Yes	Group	Yes	91
10. Greene, Laura	No	Individual	No	115
11. Harris, Mark	No	Individual	No	120
12. Hernandez, Rita	No	Individual	No	133
13. Herrera, Gerardo	No	Individual	No	131
14. Jackson, David	Yes	Individual	No	116
15. Johnson, Tyrone	Yes	Group	Yes	97
16. King, Jerome	Yes	Group	Yes	94
17. Landry, Greg	No	Individual	No	124
18. Lewis, Jamal	Yes	Group	Yes	88
19. Martin, Debra	No	Individual	No	135
20. Martinez, Luis	Yes	Group	No	118
21. Miller, Tekha	Yes	Group	Yes	95
22. Mitchell, Cynthia	No	Individual	No	123
23. Murphy, Iris	Yes	Group	Yes	94
24. Ramos, Hosea	No	Individual	No	128
25. Samuelson, Sarah	No	Group	No	121
26. Sanchez, Elena	No	Individual	No	142
27. Sullivan, Roy	No	Individual	No	138
28. Valdez, Julio	Yes	Group	No	113
29. Washington, Cassandra	Yes	Group	Yes	83
30. White, Dannette	Yes	Group	Yes	90
31. Williams, Patti	No	Group	Yes	111
32. Young, Karen	No	Individual	No	123

*Total I.Q. score on California Test of Mental Maturity, Level 3, given in seventh grade.

QUESTIONS

1. What are the characteristics of field dependent and field independent learners? To what extent do the students in Dean's fourth-period class exhibit such characteristics? What teaching procedures are most effective with such students?

2. From the standpoint of observational learning, what is a high or low sense of efficacy? How does this differ from a positive or negative self-concept or sense of self-esteem? To what extent do these constructs fit students in Dean's class? What can be done about a low sense of efficacy or a negative self concept?

3. What are internal and external attributions? To what extent do these constructs apply to the students in Dean's class? What are attribution training programs and could Dean use the elements of such programs with his fourth-period class?

4. What are the advantages and disadvantages of homogeneous vs. heterogeneous grouping? Which would be the best for Dean to use in this situation?

5. In the case of homogeneous or ability grouping, what is the best way to assign grades? For example, in determining the grade point average of a student, should a B in an advanced placement class be considered the equivalent of an A in a regular class?

6. What is cooperative learning and what are the advantages and disadvantages of the various cooperative learning programs? Would any of the cooperative learning programs have worked best in Deans' class?

7. What are disadvantaged students, and how do they differ from exceptional learners? What programs have been developed for increasing the achievement of disadvantaged students? Would any of the techniques developed in such compensatory education programs have worked in Dean's class?

8. What are the characteristics of high vs. low achievers? How do they differ in terms of such variables as SES, home environment, and motivational patterns? What are overachievers and underachievers and what are their characteristics?

9. What is parent involvement, and how do such parent involvement techniques as home visits, parent volunteering, parent participation on school advisory committees, and parent participation in school events relate to student achievement? Could Dean have used any of these procedures?

10. What is contingency management? To what extent is Dean's use of the math lab an example of contingency management? Are there ways that Dean could have used it more effectively?

11. What research has been done on teacher expectations regarding the ability of students to achieve? How does this relate to the self-fulfilling prophecy notion and teacher biases? Does Dean have any biases as a teacher?

12. At what level of Maslow's need hierarchy do Dean, Patti Williams, and Gerardo seem to be operating? How could Dean have taken the different need levels of the bright and slow groups into consideration?

13. What is math anxiety, and what can be done to reduce it? Why do female students generally seem to have more problems with math anxiety than male students?

14. What advice should Jan give Dean about what he should try next? Where could Dean go to get help with his problem?

CASE 20

GUYS AND DOLLS

Patricia Renfroe is a doctoral student at Midwest State University. She has completed all her course work, passed her qualifying exams with flying colors, and is making arrangements to collect the data she will need to complete her dissertation, "An Investigation of Teacher Gender Biases in Elementary School Instruction." Shortly after school started in the fall, Pat made an appointment with Dr. Lois Freeman, principal of Shadyside Elementary School, which Pat would like to use in her data collection.

Shadyside Elementary School is located in an upper-middle/lower-middle class community of 20,000, approximately fifty miles from Midwest University. There are three classes at each K–6 grade level, with a school population of 600 pupils of which approximately 65 percent are white, 25 percent African-American, 5 percent Hispanic, and 5 percent Asian-American.

PATRICIA I'm Pat Renfroe, a doctoral student in educational psychology at Midwest State. I appreciate your seeing me this morning, Dr. Freeman. As I told you in my letter, the title of my doctoral dissertation is "An Investigation of Teacher Gender Biases in Elementary School Classrooms." I've drawn a stratified random sample of elementary and secondary schools based on size, ethnic composition, and geographic location. Your school met our criteria. And perhaps even more significant is the fact that Dr. Thomas Riley, the chair of my doctoral committee, said that he's worked with you and knows you'd be interested in the results of the study.

LOIS It's nice to meet you, Pat. Please call me Lois. I'm delighted that you're working with Tom Riley. I earned an Ed.D. Degree in Educational Leadership from Midwest State several years ago, and Tom was my favorite professor. I enrolled in two of his courses, and they were the best courses of my entire college experience.

PAT That's interesting! He's the best teacher I've had, too! And when he said that he knew you, I just knew that you would certainly be a good person to work with.

LOIS Thanks for the compliment. I've always tried to run a good school, and I'd be pleased to have you collect your data here, if it would help you. Your study sounds really interesting and should certainly make an important contribution. I think all professional women should be interested in gender issues. But if you're looking for gender bias in instruction, you'd probably find more at another school. I'm quite aware of gender stereotyping and can assure you that you'll find very few such practices in my school.

PAT   It will be wonderful if that happens. The major purpose of my study is to investigate instances of gender discrimination, classify them as to type, and then attempt to determine whether gender bias has increased, decreased, or remained relatively constant since we became aware of its existence several years ago. I'd like to be able to conclude that it's decreased.

LOIS   Well, let's make arrangements then. Here's an application to conduct research in this school district, and a copy of the procedures which must be followed. If you'll fill out and sign the application, along with the enclosed agreement stating that you'll follow the procedures stated in the procedures booklet, I'll sign to indicate that I'm willing to have you work in this school. Then I'll forward both documents to the superintendent's office. When he signs it, approved copies will be sent to both of us. Then you're in business. I'm certain that the superintendent will sign it, providing the research and evaluation people approve.

PAT   You've really been a big help, and I appreciate it. I'm sure I'll enjoy working with you and hope that the data I collect in your school will be of use to you, the teachers, and the pupils.

LOIS   I hope so, too. Let me know when you'd like to begin collecting data in the classes and we'll plan a schedule together.

Near the end of the school year, Pat is in Dr. Riley's office with the first draft of her completed dissertation.

DR. RILEY   You were really efficient in your dissertation research, Pat, and you've done a good job of writing it up.

PAT   I couldn't have been so efficient without all your help.

DR. RILEY   It's always a pleasure for me to have a student like you who knows what she wants to do and how to go about doing it. It's one of the great rewards of being a professor.

PAT   It's nice of you to say that. Thank you. I still have some loose ends to tie up. I've shared the results with most of the principals who allowed me to observe in their schools, but I haven't talked yet with Dr. Freeman at Shadyside Elementary School. And I promised her that I'd do that.

TOM   Yes, you should at least let her see the observational data you collected in her school. In fact, she'd probably appreciate a copy of the entire study if you have an extra one.

PAT   I'll make her a copy and talk with her this week about a convenient time that I could visit with her.

Two weeks later, Pat and Lois Freeman are sitting in Lois's office at Shadyside Elementary School. Pat has just presented Lois with a copy of her study, and they are going over it together.

PAT   The classrooms I used in the study have been identified by grade level, but I didn't identify the schools, teachers, or students. In your copy of the study, I put a tab on each page that contains Shadyside Elementary School data. Thanks again for allowing me to make observations here. It helped me tremendously and contributed significantly to my study.

LOIS   I'm glad it did. I believe we should all support research in our profession whenever we have an opportunity to do so. Can you stay for a few minutes until I read the observational data? I'm interested in gender issues. There may be some things in the study that we can discuss.

PAT   Yes, I'd like to do that. In fact, I was going to suggest it.

The following are transcripts of "raw" observations made at Shadyside Elementary School before systematic analysis.

Observation One: A kindergarten class taught by a female teacher. The bell has rung and the pupils are entering the classroom.

TEACHER   Good morning, Girl One and Girl Two. Don't you look pretty this morning. Is that a new dress, Girl Six?

GIRL SIX   Yes, I got it for my birthday.

GIRL NINE   I got my dress to wear to Mary's birthday party.

TEACHER   Well, you both look very pretty. Good morning, Boy Four. I see you're wearing new basketball shoes. Do you think you'll play basketball for our school when you get to fifth grade?

BOY FOUR   Maybe. *[After all the pupils have entered the room and gone to their seats, the teacher begins class.]*

TEACHER   I'm glad to see all of you this morning. The first thing we'll do is to go to the centers for a while. You girls can go first. Ladies first, you know. *[Girls all select centers.]* Now, its the boys' turn. *[Boys go to various centers, including the doll center.]*

　　　Boy Ten, you and Boy Seven would probably enjoy the building center more than the doll corner. Here, let me take you there with the other boys.

BOY TEN   Why can't we stay here?

TEACHER   You don't see men playing with dolls, do you? But men do build roads and buildings and other things.

BOY TEN   My dad takes care of my baby sister a lot.

　　　[Teacher A ignores the comment and takes the boys to the building center. While there, she sees Girls Three and Four in the building center.]

TEACHER   You girls come with me to the art center. You'll probably use art skills much more than you'll use building skills.

　　　[Now the building and science centers are occupied by boys only. The doll corner and kitchen are occupied by girls only. Both boys and girls are working in the art center, reading center, toy center, and water table. Pupils work in the centers for approximately 45 minutes.]

TEACHER   Now, let's sit in the reading circle and I'll read you a story. Boy Three, would you bring the chair behind the desk to me?

GIRL NINE   I can get it, teacher.

TEACHER   No, Girl Nine. Carrying heavy loads is an easier job for a boy. *[Boy Three brings chair to the teacher and she sits in front of the reading circle]*

Observation Two: A male physical education teacher has taken a fourth-grade class of 18 boys and 12 girls to the playground for physical education.

COACH   O.K., class, I want all the girls on the grass over there in front of the gym. Girl One, take four jump ropes out of the carton sitting over there. There are 12 of you so you'll all have something to do. You'll work in four teams. Each team will have two turners and one jumper. Four teams of three are 12, right? Take turns jumping and turning the rope so that everybody will have a turn at both jobs.

You boys go out to the field. We're going to have a game of kickball. It has the same rules as baseball, but it's a little easier because the ball's bigger. Each team will have nine players: three fielders, three basemen, a short stop, a pitcher and a catcher. Three strikes and you're out; four balls and you walk.

GIRL ELEVEN   Why can't we play kickball too, coach?

COACH   With all that running around, I worry that one of you might get hurt. Besides, if you girls played, there would be too many players to deal with. Baseball and kickball teams have nine members. That's the number we have if the boys play. Each team would have 15 if the girls played, and that's too many.

GIRL ELEVEN   Well, you could let the boys jump rope and let us play kickball.

COACH   Then, there wouldn't be enough players on the kickball team. Anyway, boys don't jump rope. That's more of a girl's game. Besides that, I'm going to coach the boys' baseball team in the spring. I want to watch the boys in the different classes play so that I'll be able to pick out the ones who can catch, throw, run fast, and understand the game. Then I'll know who the real players are.

GIRL SIX   My Dad said there's a baseball program for girls in the spring, too. Will you watch the girls in this class to pick out the girls who are good players, too? My dad showed my brothers and me how to play.

COACH   I don't know anything about a girls' team. There wasn't one last year. But if there is one this summer, I won't work with it, because I'll be working with the boys' club. What's wrong with jumping rope? Jumping rope is good exercise for you. It makes your muscles strong, improves your breathing, and helps you to work in rhythm.

GIRL FIVE   It might be good for the boys, too. It might help them be good baseball players.

COACH   It might. One of these days I might have the boys skip the rope. Maybe you can demonstrate how to do it right when I do.

Observation Three: A fifth grade science class has a female teacher. In this class the boys are all seated on one side of the room and the girls are on the other. The teacher is using a reading strategy known as KWL, which is designed to help pupils comprehend written selections more effectively. She has written the following diagram on the chalkboard:

KWL STRATEGY

K—What we know   W—What we want to know   L—What we learned

TEACHER   Now, I'm going to ask you to give me some information that can be put under *K*. This is information you already know about bats. That's what this *K* stands for, *know*—what we know. If you know something that we should list under *K*, "What we know," raise your hand. When I call on you, you can tell me what it is. O.K., who wants to tell us something about bats? [*Several girls and a few boys raise their hands.*]

BOY TEN   [*Shouting out*] Bats aren't birds. They're animals.

TEACHER   That's right, Boy Ten. Bats are mammals. Who else knows something about bats? [*More pupils raise their hands.*]

BOY TWO   [*Shouting out*] They sleep in the day and come out at night.

TEACHER   Good, Boy Two. Do you know what we call animals who sleep in the day and come out at night?

BOY EIGHT   [*Shouting out*] Nocturnal.

TEACHER   Right. That's a big word, Boy Eight.
          [*The teacher is standing in the aisle that separates the boys' and girls' side of the room, but she's facing the boys' side and not looking at the girls.*]
          Who else knows something about bats that you can tell us?

GIRL SIX   [*Shouting out*] Bats eat insects.

TEACHER   That's right, Girl Six, but let's remember to raise our hands if we want to talk.
          [*The pupils continue to list things they know about bats until they can't think of anything else. The teacher continues to face the boys' side of the room and allow the boys to shout out information. Only one girl shouted out. The teacher called on three girls, but eight boys shouted out answers.*]

TEACHER   That's very good. You know many things about bats. Now, let's move on to the *W* part of the chart. The *W* stands for *Want*—things that we don't know now, but *want* to know.
          Now who can think of something you would like to know about bats that you don't know now? [*No response*] Sometimes it's hard to think about what we don't know, isn't it? Boy One, tell us something that you could learn about bats that you don't know now. [*Waits for about 5 seconds.*]

BOY NINE   Do bats really attack people?

TEACHER   Good. There are books and movies about bats who do attack people, aren't there? [*Writes question on the board below the W section*] Who else can think of something to list under *W*?
          Girl One? [*Waits about one second, then calls on another pupil*] How about you, Boy Five? [*Waits for six seconds*]

BOY FIVE   Where do bats live?

TEACHER   That's an interesting question, Boy Five. I'm sure we'll find out the answer when we read the selection. *[Writes question on board]*

BOY THREE   *[Shouting out]* I'd like to know what bats eat.

TEACHER   It seems to be an important question that should be included, doesn't it? Boy Three? *[Writes question on the board]*

[The teacher continues to stand in the center aisle facing the boys' side of the room. Two boys shout out questions. Four more raise their hands. Eight girls sit with their hands up, and two are called on. One shouts out successfully. All questions are listed on board.]

TEACHER   Now, we'll take turns reading aloud the article on bats. After each section of the story, we'll list all the information that we learn below the L, which stands for what we *learned*. Girl Two, please read the first two paragraphs of the article.

[For the remainder of the period, the teacher faces the girls' section and calls upon girls to read. But when she asks questions, she turns to the boys' section and calls on them to answer the questions about what they learned from the reading selection.]

Observation Four: A male sixth-grade teacher is beginning a social studies unit.

TEACHER   Today, we begin a study of famous Americans. You'll remember that last week I asked each of you to list three Americans whose contributions have made them famous.

As you contribute your names, you'll list them on the board. If someone else gives a name that's on your list, cross that name off. We don't want to list any name more than once. When all the names are on the board, you'll all vote to decide the fifteen famous Americans we'll study in depth. Boy Seven, tell us your three choices.

BOY SEVEN   I picked George Washington, Abraham Lincoln, and Bill Clinton, because they were all presidents. *[Writes names on board]*

TEACHER   Yes, Boy Seven, those are good choices. Tell us the names of your three famous Americans, Girl One.

GIRL ONE   I think that Martin Luther King, George Washington Carver, and General Colin Powell are good Americans.

TEACHER   Yes indeed. I agree. Girl Two, who are your famous Americans?

GIRL TWO   I chose John F. Kennedy, Robert Frost, and Garth Brooks.

TEACHER   A president, poet, and singer, a variety of different talents. Good choices. Who are your famous Americans, Boy Two?

BOY ELEVEN   Magic Johnson, Muhammad Ali, Arthur Ashe.

TEACHER   Aha! A sports fan—basketball, boxing, and tennis. And those are three great athletes.

[As the pupils present their choices, the teacher lists them on the chalkboard. Duplicate choices are eliminated. After 15 of the 27 pupils have responded and more than 40 names have been listed, the teacher makes an observation.]

TEACHER   Wait a minute. What's happening here? Do you see what I see? There's something unusual about this list. What is it? *[There is a long silence. Finally a boy raises his hand]* Boy Three, what have you noticed?

BOY THREE   There aren't any women on the list.

TEACHER   Bingo! That's right. Look at that! Forty names of famous Americans and not a woman among them! Have you all learned to be prejudiced against women? Do any of you have women on your list? *[Two girls raise their hands]* Good for you! What women do you think are famous Americans, Girl Twenty?

GIRL TWENTY   I have two women on my list: Eleanor Roosevelt and Hillary Clinton. Then I listed a male poet, Robert Frost. He's my favorite poet.

TEACHER   Let's get those names up here on the board, especially the women, before someone passes by in the hall and thinks that I'm brainwashing you to ignore women. *[Students laugh]* Tell us who your famous Americans are, Girl Twenty-four.

GIRL TWENTY-FOUR   I selected three African-American women: Coretta Scott King, Rosa Parks, and Maya Angelou.

TEACHER   *[Writes the names on the board]* And all of them wonderfully talented. Thank you, Girls Twenty and Twenty-four. You saved our class from being guilty of gender discrimination. Now, let's discuss why only two of us listed women as great Americans.

GIRL FIVE   When you asked for famous Americans, I think you cut down the choices. In the past famous people were mostly men. Most of the books tell about men who were presidents, explorers, politicians, inventors, and athletes. I think we did the same thing. Maybe we've been taught to think like that.

TEACHER   Thank you, Girl Five. Your comments show much insight, and I agree with you. You've been taught that famous people are people who do the things men typically do. And I was taught the same thing when I was in school.

BOY THIRTEEN   But that idea seems to be changing now. We have women astronauts, soldiers, athletes, and politicians. Hillary Clinton is a politician.

GIRL FIVE   But doesn't that mean that women have to do men's jobs to be famous? What about Rose Kennedy? I heard on TV that Rose really influenced all the members of her family. All her sons became what they are because she was such a strong person in their lives. Doesn't that make her a famous American? Coretta Scott King helped Martin Luther King at tough times. Abraham Lincoln said his mother helped him a lot. We have a book of sayings at home. One goes, "All I am or ever hope to be I owe to my mother." All through history there are examples of women helping their husbands and sons. Aren't these women as famous as some of the men in history? *[A bell rings]*.

TEACHER   There's the bell. I'm sorry that we have to stop. However, you certainly raised some issues that are important to our society and, I might add, I didn't expect to come up in class today. You're a good class, and I promise you that we'll continue this discussion later.

Lois finishes her reading of the raw observations that Pat made in the four classrooms at Shadyside.

LOIS   Well, I've read these observations several times, but they don't seem to get any better no matter how many times I read them! *[Pause]* I'm sure that I don't need to tell you how disappointed I am and how ashamed I am that some of my teachers are so insensitive to gender differences! I had no idea. I'm shocked! *[Pause]* In fact, I remember suggesting to you when we first met that perhaps you'd be better off observing in another school if you were looking for gender discrimination. And here you have found blatant examples of it in all four of the classrooms you visited in my school. I'm mortified!

PAT   Would it be of any comfort to you to know that your school was about average in comparison with the other schools I observed?

LOIS   *[Smiles wanly]* Not very much. For years I've taken pride in the fact that I spend at least one meeting each year with my faculty discussing school problems. We always talk about avoiding any kind of discrimination based on gender. It appears that my time and effort have been wasted!

You must think that I'm a really poor principal! Please help me! Tell me what I can do about these gender problems!

PAT   It just so happens that as I analyzed the data from the various schools, I grouped them into different categories. Then I suggested ways that these categories of teacher bias could be reduced. I titled this document, "Strategies Teachers Can Use to Reduce Gender Bias." *[See list on next page]* I hope to be able to expand it into a short article for one of the educational journals. Here's a copy that you may have. It might at least be a starting point for you to work from.

LOIS   *[After reading the page with the five strategies]* Well, the examples of gender bias that appeared in my classes certainly fall into these categories. It's a good list. But how can I apply these strategies here at Shadyside? How can I get the teachers to become aware of what they're doing and begin to use strategies like these every day? And the parents, the homes that children come from—doesn't gender bias begin there? How can I change the behavior of the parents? I just feel overwhelmed!

Strategies Teachers Can Use to Reduce Gender Bias

Research studies and observations of gender bias in classrooms have clearly identified inequities that exist in the treatment of boys and girls. The following suggestions for classroom teachers are based on the results of these studies:

1. Assume that both boys and girls are equally capable of learning all subjects. Currently, after Grade 4, girls are less likely to have an interest in science and math, elect a science or math class, or experience success in these fields. Women now represent only 9 to 10 percent of the science and engineering work force in the U.S., Great Britain, and Canada.

2. Provide boys and girls with equal amounts of attention and recitation time in class. Research indicates that boys are currently called on up to three times more frequently than girls, and are given as much as one-third more wait time to answer questions.

3. Avoid gender biased actions or comments, such as "throw like a girl," "boys don't cry," "girls are pretty and frilly," "boys are tough and manly," "girls clean house, cook, do laundry, and raise children," "boys play sports, bring home the pay check and discipline the children," "girls are sweet and docile," and "boys are strong and assertive."

4. Avoid using books that have strong gender bias. Research conducted by Women on Words and Images, Princeton, N.J. (1972) included an analysis of 2,760 stories from 134 children's books. The ratio of boys' stories to girls' stories was 5 to 2. The ratio of adult male main characters to adult female characters was 3 to 1. Male biographies outnumbered female biographies 6 to 1. Male animal stories outnumbered female animal stories 2 to 1. Male folk or fantasy stories outnumbered female folk or fantasy stories 4 to 1. Although this research resulted in a general reduction of these ratios, more recent research indicates that pupils are still exposed to more stories about men and boys than about women and girls. Teachers should make a conscious effort to expose pupils to literature that describes both successful men and women. Avoid using textbooks that stereotype gender roles.

5. Provide equal recreational opportunities for boys and girls. At present, public schools and universities have approximately 70 percent more athletic teams and intermural activities for men than they do for women.

Questions

1. What are the origins of gender discrimination? What role does the family play? How do schools, especially teachers, reinforce such discrimination? Why are the teachers biased?

2. What type of administrative leadership style would be most effective in reducing gender bias in Shadyside Elementary School? Should Dr. Freeman assume a supporting, coaching, delegating, or directing style in this situation.

3. How do ethnic, racial, and social class influences differ with regard to gender biases? When do gender biases begin and who is responsible for them?

4. What types of parent involvement techniques can Dr. Freeman and her teachers employ in this situation? How could parent volunteering, parent classes at school, home visits, and parent participation in advisory committees, open houses, and parent-teacher conferences be used to reduce gender bias?

5. Are all gender biases against females? Are there courses and types of teachers that favor girls over boys?

6. What kinds of things can teachers do in the classroom to reduce gender biases? Can you suggest curriculum and textbook changes? What subjects lend themselves to the greatest amount of bias? Why?

7. How does the kindergarten teacher express gender bias through her comments about pupils' attire? through asking the boy rather than the girl to bring her chair?

8. How did Boy Ten innocently reject a gender stereotype suggested by the kindergarten teacher's remark that men don't play with dolls?

9. What message did the physical education teacher send to the pupils by his assignment of activities? How did the fourth-grade girls challenge the physical education teacher's gender bias?

10. Explain why KWL is an effective strategy for helping pupils comprehend reading selections.

11. What message did the fifth-grade teacher send to the boys by calling on them more frequently and allowing them to shout out answers to questions without raising their hands? by the way she positioned herself in the classroom? What message did these practices send to the girls?

12. What is the significance of wait time (time allowed to students to answer a question) in sending messages to the boys and girls in the fifth-grade class?

13. What is the significance of the fact that neither the boys nor girls in the sixth-grade class noticed that their list of famous Americans included no women? React to the explanation of Girl Five regarding why the class did not include women in their choices of famous Americans. What criteria does she believe should be used to designate famous women?

14. Describe what kind of program Principal Lois Freeman should implement to reduce gender bias in her school. Describe some specific activities that would be appropriate in such a program.

GO TEAM!

San Juan High School is a large downtown urban high school located in a large city in the southwestern United States. The school was built during the early 1950s. In the 1980s, when the upper-middle class began moving to the suburbs, the socio-economic level of the surrounding area slowly began to drop, and the cultural diversity increased. In the past few years, this trend has accelerated rapidly, so that now the school attendance area is approximately 60 percent white, 15 percent African–American, 15 percent Hispanic and 10 percent Asian–American. The 2,500 students of San Juan High School generally live in the area surrounding the school.

Despite the change in population, there is still strong neighborhood and parental support for the school. This support has been maintained in part through winning athletic teams (especially football) and in part by effective public relations practices by the school administration and teachers.

Chet Daggett is beginning his first year as a history teacher at San Juan High School. Two years ago he graduated from a state university located in the southwest with a B.S.Ed. degree with a major in history. Last year he taught history at Ft. Concho High School, in the central part of the state. While there, he decided that he would like to live in a large city in the Southwest, so he applied for the opening in history at San Juan High School.

Irene Santos has taught at San Juan for 15 years, is recognized as an excellent teacher, and has been chair of the history department for ten years. She was chair of the selection committee which interviewed Chet for the history position. Since he was the first choice of all the members of the committee, he was given the job. He teaches three American History and two World History classes

School began two weeks ago, and Chet has just given his first test in American History. Chet and Irene are having coffee in the teachers' lounge during their free period.

IRENE   You look as if you just lost your last friend, Chet.
CHET   That's the way I feel this morning, Irene. My classes are obviously unhappy with both the subject and me. My first-period American History class was a total disaster this morning when I returned the first test of the year. The students generally did not do well on the test. Naturally, they blamed me for their poor showing. I'm afraid this is shaping up to be a very unhappy school year.

IRENE   That surprises me, Chet. Your recommendations from Ft. Concho High School indicated that your classes ran smoothly, and that you were one of the most popular teachers in the school. What's different about this year?

CHET   Well, there's a number of differences. For one, all the classes at San Juan are much more culturally diverse than those at Ft. Concho. Almost half of my students here are from minority groups. There was such a wide range of scores on the test! This tells me that there is a wide range of ability among the members of the class.

IRENE   That's true of the entire school population.

CHET   Yes. I guess it would be. Most of the students at Ft. Concho were upper-middle class. My approach to teaching there was typically to assign readings to the students. Then I would supplement the readings with related information that I had learned in my classes at college. The students wrote a paper each semester on a historical period, person, or event which they selected with my approval. They all seemed to enjoy my classes, learned a lot about history, and scored high on the social studies section of the state test.

When I moved here in August, I learned that the school used different history and government textbooks from those I used at Ft. Concho. I was in such a rush to make course outlines for my classes this year that I didn't take the time to look at the cumulative folders of my students. I just assumed that their socio-economic backgrounds, test scores, and academic backgrounds would be the same as my students in Ft. Concho. I guess I followed the same style of teaching that I used there.

IRENE   Fortunately, the year has just begun. Now that you realize that there is a problem, you have time to do something about it before the students become alienated. Tell me what happened in your class this morning that upset you so.

CHET   I'd like that. Perhaps you can make some suggestions that can help me reach these students better. Obviously, I'm not doing that now.

As Chet tells Irene what happened, he flashes back and sees himself standing at the door of his classroom as his first-period eleventh-grade American History class enters.

CHET   Students, you will find the test you took Friday face down on your desks. Many of you did very well, but I am quite disappointed in some of your scores.

CLINT   That test weren't fair, Mr. Daggett. You didn't go over all of the stuff on the test in class. Some of my answers that you marked wrong were what it said in the book.

CHET   We'll go over every question on the test, Clint. If I made any mistakes in grading your paper, I'll give you credit.

ALPHONSO   I don't think some of the answers were even in the book!

HUNG   You're wrong, Fonsie, I found the answers to all the questions when I went back over the chapter.

MARIA   You would, Hung. You ace every test you take. You don't do nothing but study.

CHET   Why do you say that, Maria? There's nothing wrong with studying hard, is there? Isn't that why we're all here?

MARIA   That's not why I'm here. I'm here 'cause its the law. Wasn't no law, I wouldn't be here!

CHET   Maybe we can change the class so that you will enjoy it, Maria.

MARIA   I don't think you could do nothing to make me like school.

CHET   Well, there are many different ways to study a subject. Maybe after we talk about the class this morning, I can think of a way to study that you will like better. If I do, will you be willing to try it?

MARIA   I guess so.

CHET   Good!

MARCUS   That textbook is too hard for me to read. I read the whole chapter and can't remember nothing it said.

LATRICIA   That's right! I ain't never had to read no textbook hard as this. Why we read such a hard book, Mr. Daggett?

CHET   This book was adopted by the school district's textbook selection committee. One of the reasons they adopted it is that it's the most widely used high school American History textbook in the country.

MARIA   That don't mean it's the best book for us, man. Some of us don't read as good as those other students.

CHET   Good point, Maria. In fact, all of you have made good points. But since you have asked so many questions about the test, let's go over the questions and answers now and make sure all the papers are graded correctly. We can also discuss the questions that you don't understand. In the meantime, I'll think about what all of you have said and think of a way you could study American history that would make it easier and more interesting. Monday morning I'll tell you what I've planned.

IRENE   Well, it's obvious that you have enough rapport with your students that they feel comfortable being truthful with you.

CHET   I think it's a mistake to stop talking with students for any reason. As a teacher I want to know what students are thinking. The only way I can do that is to let them know that I am interested in their opinions.

IRENE   I'm sure that's the reason your students feel free to tell you what they think. The message came through loud and clear, though, that some of them didn't like the test. What kind of test did you give?

CHET   It had 50 items. There were 30 multiple-choice items, 10 true–false items, and 10 short-answer items. The items were generally factual and were taken directly from the first chapter of the book, which deals with major events during the four thousand years leading up to the discovery of America. It mainly covers the settling of the 13 original colonies.

I took them through the chapter slowly. The students read a section of the chapter silently. Then we discussed the content of the selection. Two or three times I supplemented the information in the book with related information that I thought might interest them. Then we went on to the next section and followed the same procedure. I plan to assign written projects later in the year. But now my major interest is getting to know the students and giving them an opportunity to get to know me and each other.

IRENE   What was the grade distribution on the test like?

CHET   It was unusual. Basically it was two distributions—one at the high end of the scale and one at the low end. I think you call that type of distribution bimodal. Anyhow, the top 15 scores ranged from 80 to 98, with an average of about 88. The low 15 scores ranged from 20 to 78, with an average score of 56.

   I deliberately made the test easy, Irene, because it was the first one. I wanted all the students to do well on it so that they'd feel good about themselves, the class, the subject, and me. I'm really disappointed at the way the scores came out.

IRENE   I can understand your disappointment. But maybe you should be pleased. After all, it's just the beginning of the school year, and you've found out some very important information about that class. The same information will probably be true of your other classes also. Now you're in a position to do something about it.

CHET   That's right. And I've already decided what to do.

IRENE   That's quick work. What have you decided to do? And how were you able to decide so quickly?

CHET   Well, I decided that the two major causes of learning difficulties in the class are the wide range of abilities and cultural diversity. About half the class is above average and is made up of white and Asian–American pupils. The other half is made up primarily of African–Americans and Hispanics, who are considered to be "high-risk learners." And I failed to use strategies that are considered to be appropriate for "high-risk learners" to teach and test this half of my class.

   Students seem to hang out with their own groups and don't have much to do with other groups. I haven't noticed any hostility among groups, but the members of each group don't seem to understand or have much in common with the members of other groups.

IRENE   That's a pretty accurate description of most classes here. What do you plan to do?

CHET   In one of my education classes in college, we studied cooperative learning methods. The one that appealed most to me divides the class into teams of four or five. Each team is made up of both high and low achievers, boys and girls, and minority and nonminority students. One of the reasons I like this method is that research indicates students working in small groups develop strong friendships over time with team members who are considered to be high-risk learners. This feeling of acceptance then generalizes beyond the group. I think this is a terrific bonus for working cooperatively.

IRENE   Yes, it would be. The separation of cultural groups, socioeconomic levels, and ability groups is a major problem in this school. And, from what I have read, it's a major problem for most schools like ours. Although I've read about cooperative learning techniques, I've never actually used them. Specifically, what do you do? I know there are different forms of cooperative learning.

CHET   The teacher introduces a unit of study and makes study guides, books, work-sheets, and other resources available to the teams. Team members work together most of the time, tutoring each other by using available resources and applying their learning to problem-solving activities. The teacher then tests students over the materials studied.

IRENE   Do all students take the same test?

CHET   Yes, they do.

IRENE   Then won't high achievers still test high and low achievers still test low? I don't understand how the team concept will really change student performance.

CHET   That bothered me at first, too. Although students take the same test, they are graded on different scales. I'll establish a base score for each student, which will be five points below the score he/she received on last week's test. Students will earn up to a maximum of ten points on the next test for each point they score above their base score. Those students who make perfect scores will receive a ten point bonus regardless of their base score. Their base score will then become five points below the average of their two tests, and so on.

IRENE   That's neat! That way students who've made low scores on a test can have success if they improve their scores even a little!

CHET   Yes, I think so. And I plan to use this bonus idea to start a friendly competition between the teams to stimulate motivation. After each test, the group whose members show the greatest gain will be named the champion group for the week. I have an appointment with the editors of the *San Juan Messenger* to see if the name of the winning team can be published in each weekly issue.

     At the end of each grading period we'll have a ceremony to honor the winning team for that period. During this ceremony, I'll formally present small gifts to all members of this team as an additional honor.

IRENE   It's obvious that you've given a lot of thought to your classes. When do you plan to start the cooperative learning groups?

CHET   I plan to explain the idea and divide the class into groups next Monday. I'll make up the resource materials over the weekend so that I can distribute them as soon as the groups are formed. Then they can begin working.

IRENE   Wow! You don't fool around, do you?

CHET   Well, what I did last week obviously didn't work. I think cooperative learning will work. I want to get it under way as soon as possible, before the students become more restive than they already are.

IRENE   It sounds like a good idea. I hope it works well. I'd appreciate it if you would keep me up to date on your progress during our free time. Have a good weekend.

CHET   Thanks, Irene. I'll keep you informed on my progress. You have a good weekend, too.

CHET   Good morning, class. When I returned your tests last Friday, some of you shared some things you didn't like about the test and about the class. I told you that I'd think of a different way to study American History that might be more interesting for you and help you to make better grades on the test. I've come up with a plan that I'll tell you about now. Instead of each of you studying the material on your own, you'll belong to a team that will study together.

MARIA   What kind of team? Like a football team?

CHET   Yes, your team would be kind of like a football team. It won't be as large, but your team will practice together every day working on the lesson. Then, on Fridays, you'll play the other teams and one of you will win.

CLINT   You mean the teams will have names like the Dallas Cowboys, and we'll have training rules and do things together in class?

CHET   Yes, Clint. Each team will choose a name for itself. You'll spend time together in class and learn to work together as a team, just like a football or basketball team. Instead of running plays, you'll practice different strategies for studying. You'll probably become good friends with your teammates.

MARCUS   I want to be on the Thunderbolts. That's the best name for a team.

CHET   That's fine with me, Marcus. But if your team is going to work together, the other members of the team will have to agree to that name.

CARLOS   How do we keep the teams alike so that one doesn't win all the time? And how'll being on a team change what we do in here? I don't understand how the teams will play against each other on Fridays.

CHET   Good questions, Carlos. Each team will have both boys and girls, students of all ability levels from A through F, and members from the different backgrounds represented in our class. Every team will be very much like every other team in its make-up, just like professional athletic teams.

The difference that the teams will make in learning about history is that your team members will work together. Good readers can help poor readers learn what the textbook says. Poor readers can make maps, charts, or posters, construct objects, and do other jobs that the team needs for a project. Everyone on the team will help everyone else on the team learn all the information that they need to learn. And everybody on the team will contribute to the team.

Playing against each other will be taking the test over the American History assignment. The team that does the best job of practicing will make the best scores on the test and win the game for that time period.

MARCUS   Whoever gets me on their team will lose every time. I got 20 on the last test—the bottom of the class for that test.

CHET   I'm glad you brought that up, Marcus, because that isn't really the case. In fact, since you made the lowest score on the last test, you have a good chance to make the most points for your team. The number of points you earn will be the number of points you make above what I'm going to call your base score on the last test, which is 15. So if you make the same score as you made last week, you will earn five points for your team. If you make five points higher, or 25, you earn ten points for your team, which is the most anyone can make.

CLINT   Wow! Good show, Marcus. I wish I'd made a lower score. That way I could make points for the team without making a very high score.

CHET   You can do exactly the same thing as Marcus, Clint. Take five points off your test score and that's your base score. If you make the same score you made last week, you can earn five points for your team. If you score five points higher than your last week's score, you can earn ten points. That is what is so neat about this plan. You compete against yourself, not against anybody else.

This is how everyone in the class will be graded. Grades will not be given on the basis of 100 points. They will be given on the basis of how many points you score above the average of your past test scores. Since we've had only one test, you'll get credit for each point you score above your base score, which is five points lower than your last week's test scores. The number of points above your base score becomes a part of your team's score.

The most points that any team member can score is 10. We'll have five members on each team. So the highest score that any team can make is 50 points—10 for each student.

GERARDO   I don't like this idea. I don't even understand it.

CHET   What don't you understand, Gerardo?

GERARDO   Nothing. How do you study history in a group? I don't understand how we know what to study if you don't tell us what'll be on the test. What'll I do if I'm in a group?

CHET   Probably a number of people have those same questions, Gerardo. In the group, you'll work with a study guide that I'll give you. It'll help you to learn the important information about the period of history you're studying. The advantage to working in a group is that if you have trouble understanding the book or a question in the study guide, someone in the group will help you to understand it. If you understand something that someone else in the group doesn't, you can help that person.

LAVERNE   I like this plan Mr. Daggett. I like the scoring part. I think it's fair for everybody. It gives people like me who make bad grades credit for doin' better.

MARCUS   Let's do it. I want to be on the Thunderbolts.

CLASS   It's worth a try. It's better than what we usually do. Yes! Sounds like fun! I want to be on Hung's team.

CHET   I agree. Let's try it. I think you'll all learn to like history better, learn more, and get to know people in your group much better.

To get started, we need to select the teams. I've selected two people to represent each of the six teams. These representatives will choose the other three members of the team.

The representatives of each team will take turns choosing members. You'll choose one member each turn. After each group has three turns, the teams'll have all their players. Then you can select a name for your team, read over the study guide, pick the job you want to do for the team, pick a teammate to work with today, and begin work.

Here are the representatives for each team. Team 1: Diana Bush, Gerardo Perez. Team 2: Michael Chen, Latricia Perkins. Team 3: Consuela Diaz, Clint Walker. Team 4: David Gage, Sing Su. Team 5: Wan Ho, Alphonso Perkey; Team 6: Hung Ong, Alice Reynolds.

On the Monday following the second history test, Chet and Irene are talking in the teachers' lounge during their free period.

IRENE   I hoped you'd come for coffee today. I'm interested in how your first-period class made out on their test Friday.

CHET   They did great! I'm really pleased. Four students made slightly lower scores than they did on the first test, but all the students in the class exceeded their base scores. Michael Chen and Latricia Perkins' team, the Red Devils, scored the most points. We had our first ceremony this morning, and the Red Devils will be written up in the *San Juan Messenger*. All the teams are excited because the scores are really close.

IRENE   I don't understand how your students could improve their learning so quickly. What did they do?

CHET   Basically, the study guides showed them exactly what they needed to know. Group members worked together and saw to it that every member of the group could respond to the study guides correctly. Here is a copy of the study guide for our lesson on "The Struggle for Independence (1775–1793)."

Monday morning of the sixth week of the cooperative learning plan, Chet is having a coffee break in the teachers' lounge with Irene.

IRENE   Your cooperative learning program must be going well, Chet. I'm hearing very positive comments from some of your students. Many of them are from people who are usually pretty negative about school.

CHET   I'm really pleased with the program. In fact, I'm now phasing it into one of my World History classes, and I plan to implement it in all my classes by the end of the first semester.

IRENE   You must be pleased! What are the greatest improvements cooperative learning has brought about in your classes?

CHET   In my first-period class, the average base score of the class has increased by five points. Members of all the teams have become more comfortable working with each other. Students also seem to be more enthusiastic about learning and are more attentive to their assignments. They're really excited this week, because their scores on Friday's test determine the winner for this six-week period. The teams are so close in their scores that any of them could win. We'll have a big ceremony Monday with refreshments. I've bought pens and notepads for members of the winning team. The *San Juan Messenger* will have a big write-up about the members of the winning team.

IRENE   That is quite a change from the first week of class, as I recall.

CHET   Yes. That first week was a frustrating experience, but I'm glad it happened, because it motivated me to try cooperative learning.

The next morning Chet stops in the office on his way to the teachers' lounge during his free period. Harry Crews, the building principal, sees Chet and motions for Chet to sit down.

DR. CREWS   I'm glad I saw you, Chet. It saves me time in trying to get together with you. I wanted to talk to you about the new program you've initiated in your American History class.

CHET   [*Warily*] Yes, well I'm using cooperative learning. I have the students working in teams. The purpose of the program is to improve student motivation and performance by evaluating students on their improvement rather than on an arbitrary standard. The results have been good so far.

DR. CREWS   That's very interesting. Unfortunately, some of the parents don't think the program is good for their child. During the past two weeks I've had several calls. Although some parents like the program, most have been unhappy. In fact, there's a delegation of parents who want to meet with me next Friday. Can I count on you to attend the meeting as well?

CHET   I'm sorry that the parents didn't come to me. I'd have invited them to come to my class and see the program for themselves. But I'll be happy to come to the meeting, of course.

DR. CREWS   Good! I have messages from some of the parents. I'll read them to you so that you can prepare to answer their questions.

Mrs. Bush writes, "My daughter is spending much of her time reading the history book to a student named Gerardo. Diana is planning to attend college upon graduation from high school. She needs to learn all she can in high school to prepare herself for college. It isn't fair to take study time away from the best students by requiring them to tutor poor ones."

Then there's Dr. Chen's note: "Mr. Daggett is reducing all the students in his class to the lowest common denominator. Michael is serving as a tutor for lower achieving students. This punishes Michael for being a good student. In a democracy all people are encouraged to perform to the maximum of their capacity. Why can't Michael be grouped with the most able students and be more intellectually challenged?"

Mrs. Diaz says, "Mr. Daggett puts the needs of the slower students above the needs of the better students. This practice punishes the students who should be rewarded. I believe that it is a dangerous practice, and I am not going to have my daughter in a class where it takes place."

On the other hand, Chet, some parents like the program.

Mrs. Walker writes, "Clint is doing better in Mr. Daggett's class than he has ever done in school before. He was wanting to drop out of school at the beginning of the year, but now he is planning to graduate. Mr. Daggett has made his class interesting to all the students. Clint's making better grades than he has ever made before."

Mrs. Mohammed agrees. She wrote, "Lavern is a different girl. For the first time in her life, she studies every night. This year she really looks forward to going to school. God Bless Mr. Daggett."

DR. CREWS   So you can see, we've got a bit of a problem on our hands, Chet. I'd like for us to resolve it so that some of these parents don't end up going to the superintendent and members of the school board with it.

CHET   [*Angrily*] I do, too, Dr. Crews. But it just doesn't seem fair!

DR. CREWS   What doesn't, Chet? The parents?

CHET   Dr. Crews, the students in my class were unmotivated—turned off to learning. Cooperative learning has begun to turn things around. And now this!

DR. CREWS   *[In a conciliatory tone]* I want to commend you for your fine effort. But the parents of your more able students feel that their children are being short-changed when they have to spend time working with the less able ones. We've got to reassure them. *[Pause]* We can do that, can't we, Chet?

San Juan High School, El Paso, Texas

American History, First Period, Chester Daggett							
Name	I.Q.	Reading level	GPA	Test 1	Team	Base	Test 2
Acton, Mary	89	10.0	2.1	82	R	77	85
Brown, Marcus	70	4.8	1.1	20	TB	15	25
Bush, Diana	122	14.2	3.5	97	TB	92	97
Chen, Michael	118	13.2	3.6	90	RD	85	94
Clark, Lucille	96	9.6	2.0	69	S	64	70
Dale, Edgar	110	12.5	2.9	94	GH	89	91
Diaz, Consuela	113	12.8	3.4	91	R	86	91
Dyer, Patricia	105	11.4	2.0	64	GH	59	67
Ellis, Martin	100	11.0	2.2	74	C	69	75
Gage, David	78	9.0	2.1	78	S	73	78
Gonzales, Maria	85	10.6	2.8	80	RD	75	81
Hamilton, Sarah	100	11.2	3.0	80	C	75	82
Ho, Wan	115	14.0	3.6	94	GH	89	92
Jacobs, Jerry	90	9.5	2.0	85	RD	80	90
Johnson, Samuel	105	11.2	2.0	85	GH	80	86
Kelly, Katherine	100	11.0	2.5	87	S	82	85
Kirkpatrick, Evan	93	9.2	2.3	87	R	82	90
Kroger, Lois	95	9.0	2.1	87	TB	82	88
Mohammad, Lavern	80	8.2	1.5	63	S	58	72
Nunez, Carlos	85	8.8	1.8	69	RD	64	68
Ong, Hung	115	13.5	3.6	92	C	87	95
Patina, Verdi	105	11.0	3.0	89	C	84	90
Perez, Gerardo	60	4.2	1.0	35	TB	30	41
Perkey, Alphonso	68	5.5	1.2	41	GH	36	47
Perkins, Latricia	65	6.5	1.3	49	RD	44	51
Reynolds, Alice	68	6.8	1.5	50	C	45	55
Rusk, Ruth	70	7.2	1.8	60	TB	55	59
Su, Sing	120	13.0	3.8	96	S	91	95
Tang, Merav	90	8.5	2.2	68	R	63	70
Walker, Clint	75	6.2	1.6	64	R	59	68

Team Key:
TB—Thunderbolts
RD—Red Devils
R—Rattlers
S—Slashers
GH—Green Hornets
C—Conquistadors

QUESTIONS

1. How do cooperation and competition affect learning and motivation? To what extent do cooperative learning techniques address the problems created by competition? Do all cooperative learning techniques shortchange the more able students?

2. Chet seems to use cooperative learning as a remedial technique for dealing with cultural diversity. Would cooperative learning be as effective in a class of all high achieving students? Which cooperative learning methods would be most effective for that program?

3. Is there a conflict between "tracking" or teaching high achieving students separately in homogeneously grouped or advanced placement classes and cooperative learning methods? Can the two concepts be combined?

4. Do cooperative teaching techniques foster intrinsic or extrinsic motivational patterns among participating students? Do such students come to value learning for its own sake or for more extrinsic reasons such as not letting the team down? If they learn, does it matter?

5. What is cultural diversity? What are the most effective ways for teachers to take such student differences into consideration? How effectively has Chet handled cultural diversity?

6. What stereotypes exist in this case? Does the use of names like *Trish* and *Fonsie* suggest prejudice? How well does Chet deal with such issues?

7. Does Chet have low expectations for some of his students? If so, which ones? From the standpoint of teacher expectancy theory and the self-fulfilling prophecy model, how do teacher expectations impact on student performance?

8. Evaluate the testing strategies that Chet used for the first exam. How do they compare with the evaluation procedures that he used when he initiated cooperative learning?

9. How well did Chet handle his students' complaints about his class and the first test? How good a communicator is Chet?

10. What could Chet have done to communicate with the parents more effectively before he fully implemented cooperative learning? How well did Dr. Crews handle the parents' complaints? Did he interact with Chet effectively?

11. What are the educational philosophies of Mrs. Bush, Dr. Chen, and Mrs. Walker? How do they contrast with those of Chet? How do they contrast with the principles underlying cooperative learning?

12. Analyze Chet's cooperative learning approach and his original teaching method in terms of Bloom's Cognitive Taxonomy. What teaching methods might Chet have tried other than cooperative learning methods?

13. Cooperative teaching can take a variety of forms. What are the essential components of cooperative teaching? Does cooperative learning have to be used all the time as the exclusive teaching method with all projects, or can it be used with certain projects and not with others? What particular cooperative learning model does Chet seem to be using?

14. What students seem to learn best in cooperative learning activities? For example, is cooperative learning equally effective with African–American, Native American, and white students? Does it work equally well with students at all grade levels?

15. What should Chet say to Dr. Crews? to the different parents? to the superintendent and members of the school board, if necessary? Should Chet stop using cooperative learning in his classroom?

WITHDRAWN WANDA

aren Young has taught social studies at Fairmont Middle School for five years. She also taught for two years at another middle school in the same city, Midland, which has a population of about 60,000 in a midwestern state. Fairmont's attendance district is approximately 75 percent white and 25 percent African–American.

It is sixth period of the second day of classes, and Karen leads a discussion of prehistory with her ninth-grade world history class. There are 32 students in the class.

KAREN   We've all had a chance to read this interesting chapter on prehistory. I know that dinosaurs always fascinate people, because of movies like Jurassic Park, but today we want to focus on people, or to be more technical, Homo sapiens. Let's review a little from yesterday. Roger, how old is the earth?

ROGER   Four and a half billion years.

KAREN   Right! Now how long have human beings been on the earth? *[Several hands go up]* Gloria?

GLORIA   About a million years, but I'm not sure that all those prehistoric people were human beings.

KAREN   Good answer, Gloria. Certainly, Homo sapiens haven't been on earth that long. What are the names of some of Homo sapiens' predecessors? Wanda? *[Wanda stares down at the floor and shakes her head no.]* You don't remember any of them, Wanda? *[Wanda continues staring at the floor.]* Barry, can you remember any of the names of our prehistoric ancestors?

BARRY   Yeah, Neanderthal man, Java man, and, what's that, oh, yeah, Peking man.

KAREN   Yes, Barry, very good! I'll bet you all remember Neanderthal man from *The Clan of the Cave Bear.* But the Neanderthals weren't our immediate ancestors, were they? *[Hands go up]* Yes, Marilyn?

MARILYN   No. Cro–Magnon man was, and he lived about 25,000 years ago.

KAREN   Excellent, Marilyn. You people have really been working hard, I can tell! But think about this, people—Homo sapiens hasn't been on earth very long. If the earth is four and a half billion years old and Cro–Magnon man has only been here for about 25,000 years, we are real new on the scene. Barry?

BARRY   Yeah, but my dad says that we've probably done more damage to the environment and killed more animals and people than all those early guys combined.

KAREN   I couldn't agree with your dad more, Barry. Homo sapiens may be a relatively new species on this planet, but we sure have caused a lot of trouble in that short period of time. [A few laughs] What do you think, Wanda? Can you think of some ways that Homo sapiens has either helped or harmed the earth? [Wanda looks down and shakes her head. Karen counts off five seconds to herself as she waits for Wanda to answer.] OK, Kristen, what do you think?

It is one week later. Karen has noticed Wanda's failure to participate in class in any way. She has resolved to draw her out during class discussion.

KAREN   OK, people. We talked the last time about the end of the New Stone Age around 5000 B.C. Around that time civilization began. Wanda, do you remember that we talked a little about the rise of civilization? We said that certain developments took place that brought about the beginning of civilization. Can you name one of those for us? [Wanda frowns and looks down at the floor. Several hands go up. Karen counts off five seconds to herself.] OK, think about it, Wanda, and I'll come back to you in a minute. Yes, Donna?

DONNA   The development of writing was one of them.

KAREN   That right, Donna, and maybe that's the most important one. Ray, what's another?

RAY   The development of metal tools.

KAREN   Absolutely! Wanda, have you thought of one yet? [Wanda stares down at the floor.] Maybe one relating to what we would call business today? [Wanda just frowns.] OK, the development of trade, weren't you thinking of that, Wanda? [No response.] Well, uh, Gloria, can you give us a more exact date for the beginning of civilization besides 5000 B.C.?

GLORIA   Yes, 4241 B.C. is the oldest date in recorded history.

KAREN   Very good, Gloria. What is that date from?

GLORIA   I'm not sure—I've forgotten.

KAREN   [Moves directly in front of Wanda] I'll bet you can tell us where that date comes from, Wanda. Think now. [Wanda stares down at floor as Karen counts off five seconds to herself.] OK, Barry?

BARRY   It's from the first calendar. It was developed by the Egyptians.

KAREN   [Still in front of Wanda, speaks quietly] I'll bet you knew that, didn't you, Wanda? [Wanda nods her head yes.] OK, then, Toni Sue. Besides writing, metal tools, and the development of trade, what else had to develop before civilization could begin?

TONI SUE   Government.

KAREN   Absolutely. And we've had problems ever since, haven't we? [Several students laugh.]

It is Friday after school during the same week. Karen sits in her classroom talking to Mark Harris, a school psychologist in the local school system.

KAREN   Thanks for coming, Mark.

MARK   My pleasure, Karen. You said that you wanted to talk to me about Wanda Loveless. Are you considering referring her? I didn't get a chance to look at her cum record. We had a long staff meeting about farming out some of our testing and I came directly here from the meeting. I do know a little about Wanda though. Several of her teachers consider her very shy and withdrawn. Is that the problem?

KAREN   I'll say! I've tried every trick in the book to draw her out and she just won't participate. I sense she knows the answers but she just won't talk!

MARK   Have you given any tests yet?

KAREN   Yes, and she does just fine on them—low B, high C range.

MARK   Sounds like she primarily has a social problem then.

KAREN   Yes, I guess so, but we're going to be working in groups soon and I wonder if Wanda is going to be able to contribute.

MARK   That will be a good test, won't it? My guess is, based on her past behavior, that she won't participate much more working in a group with her peers than she did during class discussion.

KAREN   That's discouraging, Mark! But what do you think is going on here? Should she be referred to some program?

MARK   Let me look into her case a bit, Karen, before we do anything. Between you and me, it's possible that she's emotionally disturbed. But I don't want to jump the gun. Once you label a child as exceptional, the stereotype can be as bad as the disease, if you know what I mean.

KAREN   Not really.

MARK   What I mean is that teachers, other students, and sometimes even parents begin to relate to the child differently.

KAREN   I see what you mean.

MARK   I just want to take my time and be certain before we do anything.

KAREN   Of course. However, I have done one thing I hope you approve of.

MARK   What's that?

KAREN   I called Wanda's mother and asked her to come in for a conference.

MARK   Oh, boy! Mrs. Loveless?

KAREN   Yes. Why do you say it that way?

MARK   Did she agree to come see you without any protest?

KAREN   Yes, of course. Parents don't usually object to having a conference about their child. I guess she thinks it's about grades. But why, Mark?

MARK   Mrs. Loveless is a real battle-axe. Talking to her is a little like talking to a truck driver who's busy and in a hurry. Good luck!

KAREN   [Smiling] Well thanks, Mark, for your good wishes! But seriously, she didn't protest, seemed reasonable enough, and I just don't expect any trouble.

MARK   [Smiling] OK. Well, let me know how it comes out and meanwhile I'll look into Wanda's situation.

It is Wednesday of the next week and students are working in small groups of six to nine members. Each group is focusing on a different cradle of civilization that developed around certain river valleys during the dawn of civilization around 5000 B.C. One group is working on Egypt, another on the Fertile Crescent, a third on India, and a fourth on China. As each group busily works on its report, Barry leaves the Ancient Egyptian group and comes up to Karen's desk.

KAREN   Yes, Barry? What is it?

BARRY   Ms. Young, you said that everyone in the group will get the same grade for the group report?

KAREN   Yes. That's right.

BARRY   Well that doesn't seem fair! Some people aren't hardly doing anything and they're going to get the same grade as me!

KAREN   Who are they, Barry? I'll talk to them.

BARRY   Well, it's mostly one person. Wanda.

KAREN   Really? Wanda? Well, you go back to your group and in a little bit I'll call Wanda up and talk to her about it. And I'd appreciate it, Barry, if you'd do your very best to work with Wanda. I think she's shy.

BARRY   *[Leaving]* I think she's lazy! *[Five minutes later Karen calls Wanda up to her desk. Karen motions for her to sit in a chair next to her desk. Wanda looks away from Karen's eyes as Karen talks to her.]*

KAREN   Wanda, I've been wanting a chance to talk to you and this is the first real class time we've had. *[Pause]* Wanda, I've tried to call on you in class several times and I'm certain you know the answer but you just don't seem to want to talk. Why is that?

WANDA   I don't know.

KAREN   But you do know the answers, don't you, Wanda? Like the other day when I asked you who developed the first calendar. You knew the answer, didn't you? *[Wanda nods her head "yes".]* Is it hard for you to talk to me, Wanda?

WANDA   *[Speaks barely above a whisper]* No.

KAREN   Wanda, I want you to do well in here and I know you are capable. Can't you tell me why you won't talk more?

WANDA   I don't know the answers. I can't remember all this stuff! It's too hard!

KAREN   Wanda, you've been getting good grades on the tests. You got nine out of ten on the last one. Don't you remember that?

WANDA   Yes, but I really didn't understand it. Sometimes I just seem to get it right.

KAREN   Well, Wanda, tell me about your group. Do you like working with the other students? *[Wanda shakes her head no.]* Why not, Wanda?

WANDA   They just don't like me. They don't really care what I think.

KAREN   Well, Wanda, when you don't say anything, the group may begin to think that you don't know anything when you really know as much as any of them. Why don't you try to contribute more? Why don't you go back to the group now and see if you can't contribute at least three ideas. Will you do that for me?

WANDA   If I can.

KAREN   Did your mother tell you that she's coming in to have a conference with me next week?

WANDA   *[With fear in her eyes]* No! Why? I haven't done anything wrong, have I?

KAREN   *[Taken aback]* No, Wanda, you haven't. But I like to meet the parents of as many of my students as I can. Since your mother has known you longer than I have, I thought that she might tell me some things that might help me get to know more about you so I can do a better job of teaching. That's all. Nothing to worry about.

WANDA   [Frowning] Can I go back to my group now?

KAREN   Well, yes, I guess so. But Wanda, don't be afraid to speak up and let other people know what you know. OK?

WANDA   OK.

It is Friday of the next week after school. Karen meets Wanda's mother in her empty classroom. Ms. Loveless is a tall, heavy woman, dressed in jeans. She shakes Karen's hand and takes a seat next to Karen's desk.

KAREN   Thanks for coming, Ms. Loveless. I wanted to talk to you about Wanda.

MS. LOVELESS   Is she doin' something wrong? Don't remember her bringin' home any bad grades.

KAREN   No, that's not the problem. Wanda can make B's when she applies herself.

MS. LOVELESS   Well, that's just it. Wanda can be lazy when she wants to. You just have to keep after her and not cut her any slack. I'll guarantee you she's not lazy around home. It's just her and me, you know. Her dad ran off with some young chick when Wanda was four.

KAREN   Oh, I didn't realize that you were divorced.

MS. LOVELESS   Yes, and I love it that way. I don't have to listen to some man tellin' me how to live my life. But I work at Central Electric and I get a lot of overtime. So Wanda has to pitch in and do her share. Of course, from what I've seen of a lot of kids these days, it's clear that a little discipline would do them good. So I guess what I'm tellin' you is that if Wanda slacks off in her work, just let me know. I'll back you up at home. I didn't get to be the only female foreman at Central by bein' lazy, and I'm not goin' to let Wanda learn bad habits.

KAREN   Well, Ms. Loveless, it isn't laziness that worries me. Wanda is just so shy and withdrawn. She just won't answer questions during class discussions and she even seems to have trouble talking with other students when they are working in small groups.

MS. LOVELESS   *[Pondering]* Well, I guess I can see how she might be a bit shy. She and I don't get out much—maybe to church some Sundays. We mostly stay home nights and watch TV. She doesn't have any regular friends that come over. But I always make her do her homework first before she does her chores around the house. *[Pause]* But I think all you need to do is tell her that it's important to talk out and draw her out a bit. If that doesn't work, let her have it. I'll back you up.

KAREN   Yes, well, I have talked to her and have tried to draw her out as you put it. But, Ms. Loveless, she acts fearful, like she's scared of making a mistake all the time. I guess she doesn't try talking so she won't fail.

MS. LOVELESS   Well, like I said, just explain to her that it's important for her grades that she talk and don't mince any words. Really crack down on her if she doesn't do what you want. I'll guarantee you that it'll work. I do it at home with her all the time.

KAREN   *[Hesitantly]* Well, Ms. Loveless, I was wondering if that might not be part of the problem. Your coming down so hard on her at home all the time might be causing her to be fearful around other people.

MS. LOVELESS   *[Angrily]* It sounds to me like you're telling me I'm a poor parent! Well I'd like to point out to you that you don't see Wanda goin' around beating up, insulting, and robbin' other folks! There are a lot of parents out there not doin' their jobs, but I'm not one of them! Even though I have to do the job alone, I do it right, and I don't need you tellin' me otherwise! You take care of the teachin' and I'll take care of the parentin'. *[Storms out]*

KAREN   Ms. Loveless, I . . .

It is Tuesday of the next week, and Karen meets with Wanda in her classroom alone after school.

KAREN   Wanda, I just wanted to compliment you on the score you made on the test that I gave Friday. I guess that you know by now that I talked to your mother that same day, and I would have told her about your good grade if I'd had a chance to grade them.

WANDA   Yes, I guess I got real lucky on that one.

KAREN   Wanda, do you really think that getting 87 of 100 points was just luck? Don't you think your hard work had something to do with it?

WANDA   That's just it. I have to work twice as hard as the other kids because I'm just so dense. I'm so envious of someone like Gloria Ashton—she doesn't need to study hardly at all and gets straight A's.

KAREN   Wanda, you're smart too. It exasperates me that you keep putting yourself down like that all the time. Believe me, as your teacher who has taught a lot of students, you're not dumb! *[Silence]* Did your mother say anything about our conference?

WANDA   Yes.

KAREN   What did she say? Won't you tell me?

WANDA   She said that you told her that I'm as lazy at school as I am at home and that I'd better get busy and get my grades up or she'll come down on me. I don't think she likes you either.

KAREN   What did she say?

WANDA   She said that you're a know-it-all and she doesn't want any more to do with you.

KAREN   Oh, Lord! Now I wish I'd had some really good news to share with her like your test score. Maybe that would have helped.

WANDA   No, she really wouldn't have cared. She would just have told me that I should try to do better. I really wish you hadn't talked to her.

KAREN   Why not, Wanda?

WANDA   Because she blames me for causing trouble and making her come to school to talk to you. It always turns out to be my fault! I just wish everybody would leave me alone!

     Karen meets with Mark Harris, the school psychologist, in his office located in the district school board building downtown.

MARK   Come in, Karen. I'm sorry that you had to meet me here but I had an important staff meeting before our appointment. Finances, you know. Thought we were never going to finish!

KAREN   Mark, I needed to talk to you about Wanda Loveless so badly that I would have agreed to meet you anywhere!

MARK   *[Laughing]* Sounds really serious! What's going on?

KAREN   Well, I met with Wanda's mother and the conference turned into a real disaster. I think I may have hurt Wanda more than I helped her by talking to her mother.

MARK   I was afraid of that. What happened?

KAREN   I tried to discuss Wanda's withdrawn behavior with her and she thought I was criticizing her parenting skills.

MARK   *[Smiling]* Were you?

KAREN   *[Laughing]* Yes, I guess maybe I was. She's so demanding and thinks punishment is the solution to every problem.

MARK   *[Seriously]* Do you think there's physical abuse going on there?

KAREN   Not physical—mental maybe. But I'm not real sure what abuse is anymore.

MARK   Well certainly the scars of mental abuse are sometimes more difficult to detect than those of physical abuse.

KAREN   I just don't know what to try next, Mark. Ms. Loveless has certainly made it clear that she doesn't want anything more to do with me. I had some idea about involving her as a classroom volunteer but that will never work.

MARK   I agree. At least, I'd hate to try that if I were in your position.

KAREN   Mark, I wonder if Wanda would be better off in another class, like a class for exceptional children? Wouldn't you say she is emotionally disturbed, or handicapped, or whatever the current label is?

MARK   Honestly, I'm not sure yet, Karen.

KAREN   How do you determine that?

MARK   It isn't an easy evaluation procedure. There are behavior checklists that we use, and I plan to evaluate Wanda as soon as I can schedule it. But what it comes down to is a matter of degree. Is the problem behavior a consistent and persistent pattern, or not? Is Wanda over-inhibited, or not? That is, is she excessively withdrawn and shy? Once we label her and put her in a special program, it is likely to follow her the rest of her school days. So it's a serious call. Based on what you know now, Karen, what call would you make?

KAREN   I'm not certain, Mark. But what am I going to do with her in the classroom if you decide she isn't emotionally disturbed?

Name: Wanda M. Loveless
Address: 1423 Herera Avenue*
Father: Dewey J. Loveless
    Occupation: Unknown
    Address: Unknown
Mother: Rita L. Loveless
    Occupation: Forewoman
               Central Electric
    *Mother's Address: parents
    divorced

Home Phone: 384-5768
Former School: Rawlings Elementary
General Heath: Good
Handicaps: None
Date of Birth: 9/14/82

TEST RECORD
INTELLIGENCE TESTS

Test	Form	IQ	Date	Grade
	Elementary I	116	9/8/84	3
Otis-Lennon School	Intermediate	106	9/14/88	7
Ability Tests	Advanced	111	9/1/90	9

ACADEMIC RECORD

	Grades 1–6 (Year Averages)						Grades 7–9 (Year Averages)				
	1	2	3	4	5	6	7			8	9
Reading	B	B	B	B	B	B	English	B	English	B	
Mathematics	C	C	C	C	C	C	Geography	B	U.S. History	B	
Science/Health				B	C	C	Mathematics	C	Mathematics	C	
Social Studies				B	B	B	Science	C	Earth Science	C	
Language Arts	B	B	B	B	B	B	Phys. Ed.	C	Phys. Ed.	C	
Spelling	A	A	A	A	B	B	Conduct	A	Conduct	A	
Music/Art	C	C	C	C	C	C					
Citizenship	A	A	A	A	A	A					

QUESTIONS

1. What is self-concept? How does it differ from self-esteem? Is it a unidimensional or multidimensional construct? How is self-concept formed, and under what conditions can it change? How does this relate to Wanda's self-concept?

2. What is self-efficacy and how does it differ from self-concept? In what areas does Wanda have a low sense of self-efficacy? How can the sense of self-efficacy be raised?

3. What are internal and external attributions? Are Wanda's attributions external? Does Wanda exhibit a learned helplessness pattern of beliefs? What are attribution training programs, and do they have implications for Wanda's situation?

4. What is child abuse? Is Wanda a mentally abused child? Why?

5. At what level of Maslow's need hierarchy is Wanda primarily functioning? Wanda's mother? How could Karen have taken advantage of that information?

6. What is discipline? Does it differ from punishment? What relationships exist between punishment and withdrawal behavior? What forms can punishment take? At what point does corporal punishment begin to become physical abuse?

7. What are Baumrind's parenting styles? What parenting style best fits Ms. Loveless? How do parenting styles relate to the child's success in school?

8. What is a withdrawn child? Are such children usually viewed as discipline problems? What teacher strategies are most effective in working with withdrawn children? In working with the parents of such children?

9. What are the characteristics of an emotionally disturbed child? What are the characteristics of an over-inhibited child as opposed to a child that is just unusually shy? What techniques work best with such children?

10. What is wait-time? How effectively did Karen practice wait-time? Why didn't it seem to work in Wanda's case?

11. What are the principles involved in conducting an effective parent–teacher conference? How good a job did Karen do? What could she have done differently?

12. Would it be best for Wanda to be placed in a program for emotionally disturbed students? What are the pros and cons? If Mark decides against such placement, how should Karen deal with her in the classroom? How should Karen deal with Wanda's mother?

CASE 23

TO BE OR NOT TO BE

Nicole Lewis is beginning her sixth year of teaching at San Luis High School, which is located in a large urban area on the Pacific Coast. The school's attendance area is approximately 35 percent white, 30 percent Hispanic, 25 percent African–American, and 10 percent Asian-American. The school's physical plant and grounds reflect the gradual deterioration that characterizes the surrounding neighborhood, resulting from the migration of the middle class to the suburbs. Nicole commutes 56 miles each way in order to live in the suburbs.

It is the first day of classes and Nicole meets her 36-member third-period general business class. The bell rings; students scramble to their seats. Nicole smiles as she faces the class.

NICOLE   *[Assertively]* All right, people, let's find a seat and settle down. *[Pause]* This is general business and I'm Ms. Lewis. How many of you are sophomores? *[All hands go up.]* Good! I'll bet you're glad you're not freshmen anymore! *[Shouts of agreement and laughter.]*

STUDENT   You've sure got that right, Ms. Lewis!

NICOLE   *[Smiling]* Without a doubt, general business is my favorite course. I like working with students on practical things like learning how to budget your money and how to do your income taxes.

STUDENT   What money? *[Laughter]*

NICOLE   Well, maybe you'll learn a few things this year, Angelo, about getting a job and earning some money: how to prepare a resume, dress for an interview, conduct yourself during the interview, and, I guess, how to search for a job in the first place.

ANGELO   Killer!

NICOLE   *[Smiling]* I'm glad you approve, Angelo, but please raise your hand before you speak!

ANGELO   Right!

NICOLE   Well, anyhow, I've lined up some interesting speakers this year and we'll see some excellent films. Now, how many of you think you'll learn something in this class this year? *[All hands go up but one.]* Now let me begin by calling the roll. *[After calling five names]* Kirsten Bell? *[No response]* Kirsten's not here? *[A girl taps Kirsten on her arm.]*

KIRSTEN   [To girl] Stop that!
GIRL   She called your name!
NICOLE   Are you Kirsten Bell?
KIRSTEN   Yes.
NICOLE   [Noticing glazed look in Kirsten's eyes] Are you O.K., Kirsten?
KIRSTEN   Yeah, I'm fine.
NICOLE   O.K., well then, let's all pay attention! James Birch.

The next day, Nicole drops by the office of Karen Thurmond, one of the school's guidance counselors, during her planning period.

KAREN   [Smiling] Hi, Nicole. How's everything going?
NICOLE   Everything's great! I'm teaching my favorite courses with only two preparations.
KAREN   Got a good bunch of kids this time?
NICOLE   Yes, I really do. However, I wanted to ask you about one of them— Kirsten Bell—kind of a heavy-set dishwater blonde.
KAREN   Oh, yes, I know Kirsten. I tried to counsel her for a while but she just wasn't open to me. Of course this system we have of a teacher sending a kid to the dean's office and then the dean referring the child—or should I say requiring the child—to see me is part of the problem. The child sees me as an extension of the dean's office and just clams up. Kirsten just wouldn't tell me anything.
NICOLE   So you don't know much about her?
KAREN   I didn't say that, now. I always try to find out as much as I can about a child before I meet with her. I went over her cum record rather carefully and talked to a number of teachers about her. I even talked to her mother on the phone at some length. Also, I have a friend, Marge, who knows Kirsten's mother rather well—well, I should say as well as anyone knows her, since she doesn't seem to have many friends.
NICOLE   Well, so tell me. What did you learn about Kirsten?
KAREN   Why, what's she done?
NICOLE   She didn't do anything. But I got the impression that she was high on something in class yesterday. She seemed like she was a thousand miles away and her pupils were really dilated.
KAREN   Yes, she's been known to use drugs and alcohol. Her mother says that she uses pot regularly. [Pause] Her home life is rather unstable. She lives with her mother, Donna, and her stepfather, Bruce, and two sisters. They had a son but I think he was killed in an automobile accident. Anyhow, rumor has it that there may be abuse going on there and Kirsten stays away from home as much as possible. Have you ever heard of a gang called the Felindae?
NICOLE   Yes, I believe I have. Don't they wear the black and white jackets with the name on the back?
KAREN   That's the one. Kirsten belongs to that group.
NICOLE   Really! [Pause] Seems like I see more girls wearing that jacket than boys.

KAREN   Yes, I think it originated as a girls' gang but it has a large number of guys in it
        now. Most of the members come from the east side of San Luis around the Third
        Street area.
NICOLE   The low-income area?
KAREN   Yes. A lot of unemployed there, including Kirsten's father the biggest part of
        the time.
NICOLE   Not a pretty picture but I guess it sheds a lot of light on the situation. *[Bell
        rings]* Oh, oh, there's the bell. I've got to go to my next class. Thanks for the in-
        formation, Karen.
KAREN   Anytime.

It is one week later and ten minutes into Nicole's third-period class. As Nicole is
passing out an assignment, Kirsten staggers into class late and walks close to Nicole on
her way to an empty seat in the front row. Some of the students chuckle to themselves
and roll their eyes at one another. Nicole smells the odor of alcohol as Kirsten passes by
her. Nicole asks a student to finish passing out the papers, walks over to where Kirsten
is sitting, and talks to her in a low, confidential tone.

NICOLE   Kirsten, you're late to class today. What's that odor I smell?
KIRSTEN   *[Defiantly]* I don't know!
NICOLE   Then why don't you just go on down to the dean's office and see if Ms. Jobe
        can figure out what it is.
KIRSTEN   *[Meekly]* Please don't send me. I'm sorry!
NICOLE   Go ahead and start this assignment (hands her a copy). However, I want to
        talk to you right after your last class.
KIRSTEN   Yes, Ms. Lewis.

The last period has ended and Nicole is sitting at her desk grading papers as she
waits for her conference with Kirsten. Twenty minutes later, Kirsten arrives wearing
her Felindae jacket and sits down in a chair next to Nicole's desk.

KIRSTEN   You wanted to talk to me, Ms. Lewis?
NICOLE   Yes, Kirsten, I do. *[Puts down her papers.]* Kirsten, I want you to do well in
        my general business class this year. However, I've noticed your poor attendance
        in your classes in the school records and, I'll be totally honest with you, I have
        zero drug tolerance. I don't appreciate your coming to class under the influence
        of alcohol, or any other drug for that matter, the way you did today.
KIRSTEN   *[Hesitantly]* I have lots of friends, Ms. Lewis, and they like to party a lot.
NICOLE   *[Angrily]* That's not much of an excuse, Kirsten! There is a time to party and
        a time not to party! Let me make this real clear to you. If you come to my class
        again under the influence, I'm going to send you to the dean's office. Do you
        know what that means?
KIRSTEN   *[Sheepishly]* Yes, they'll suspend me and tell my parents. They'll really be
        mad!

NICOLE   I decided to let you stay in class today for that very reason. However, don't count on it next time!

KIRSTEN   *[Getting up to leave]* I'm sorry. It won't happen again.

Two months later, Nicole runs into Karen Thurmond, the guidance counselor, outside Karen's office.

KAREN   Well, hello, Nicole. How've you been?

NICOLE   A whole lot better than I was last time I saw you. All my classes are really going well this year.

KAREN   That's wonderful! Does that include Kirsten Bell?

NICOLE   Actually, yes. I had a conference with her right after I talked to you about her and I read her the riot act. She's really straightened up and I think we've become friends. Oh, she's had a few slips but I just frown at her and send her to the bathroom to straighten herself out. *[Pause]* I guess what I really feel is that she's better off in school than out and we've sort of developed an understanding. She's really trying!

KAREN   That's marvelous! Maybe almost unbelievable!

NICOLE   Why do you say that?

KAREN   Yours must be the only class in school that she isn't in trouble in. How about her grades?

NICOLE   O.K., nothing exceptional. Mostly C's, but she's made some B's lately.

KAREN   You're a miracle worker, Nicole! How did you do it?

NICOLE   I just talk to her a lot and we're totally honest with one another. I guess you might say that I usually talk to her like a Dutch uncle but I get the feeling that she trusts me because of it. *[Pause]* However, she's been acting very depressed lately and she's been very sharp with me when I try to get her to open up. Sometimes she just lays her head down on her desk and doesn't participate in class. She wasn't like that a month ago. Something must be going on at home. Have you got any clues?

KAREN   Not a one. Like I told you before, Kirsten doesn't confide in me, or, as far as I know, anyone else. Your class is the only one that she attends regularly. She's constantly down for one illness or the other but never sees a doctor. I've asked the school nurse about her, and she says that Kirsten sometimes has a temperature but never anything serious. It's a real puzzle.

NICOLE   Yes, well I guess I'll have to try to get through to her. Right now I've got to get down to my room and get the overhead projector set up. See you later, Karen.

KAREN   Bye, Nicole. Have a good one.

Two weeks later, Kirsten asks to talk to Nicole after school. Kirsten sits down in a chair next to Nicole's desk. Kirsten's appearance is disheveled, her eyes are puffy and discolored, and her demeanor suggests heaviness and depression.

NICOLE   Kirsten, I'm so glad that you asked to talk to me. I was going to suggest it myself. We don't get much time to talk in class.

KIRSTEN   I know. I've got to talk to someone, Ms. Lewis. And you're the only one I feel like might help me.

NICOLE   *[Sympathetically]* You know I'll do anything in my power, Kirsten. But can't you talk to your parents about whatever's bothering you?

KIRSTEN   You don't know my parents, Ms. Lewis. My stepfather, Bruce, is a scum-bag. I hate him!

NICOLE   *[Quietly]* What about your mother, Kirsten?

KIRSTEN   Mom—well I guess she tries. She's just so weak. She can't help herself, much less me.

NICOLE   I talked to Ms. Thurmond, the guidance counselor, the other day and your name came up. She said she used to talk to you. Wouldn't you feel good about talking to her? After all, she's a trained professional.

KIRSTEN   *[With animation]* No! I don't trust her! *[Pleadingly]* Please, Ms. Lewis, won't you just listen and tell me what you think and not tell anyone else—especially Ms. Thurmond?

NICOLE   *[Surprised]* Well, of course, if that's what you want. What do you want to tell me?

KIRSTEN   You don't really know me, Ms. Lewis. You think you do but your life isn't like mine.

NICOLE   What do you mean, Kirsten?

KIRSTEN   Nobody really cares about me—no one in the world. *[Begins to tear up]*

NICOLE   You don't feel like anyone loves you?

KIRSTEN   No one. My parents are totally into themselves and my friends aren't really my friends.

NICOLE   What do you mean, "your friends"?

KIRSTEN   I've been part of what you'd call a gang for a long time. At first it felt good to be part of a family and always have people to have fun and laugh with. But after a while you find out that they only like you as long as you do what they want. If you cross them they don't want to have anything more to do with you.

NICOLE   Are you talking about Felindae?

KIRSTEN   Yes.

NICOLE   And you crossed someone important in the gang?

KIRSTEN   Not just one, they're all like that. All the guys want is for you to party with them whenever they feel like it.

NICOLE   Are you talking about drugs and sex?

KIRSTEN   Of course; that's basically what all the guys want.

NICOLE   And the girls? I hear there are a lot of them in Felindae.

KIRSTEN   They're two-faced. They tell you they're your friend but they'll drop you in a minute if some guy tells them to.

NICOLE   Let me ask you something personal, Kirsten. Do you practice safe sex?

KIRSTEN   I need to, but I don't worry about it anymore. And the guys don't want to bother with it. I just really don't care anymore!

Nicole   Kirsten, surely you know that you'll eventually graduate from school and leave behind your family and friends and, who knows, you might meet a wonderful man and have a much better life than you do now. Things change, you know.

Kirsten   Wonderful man! I wish! I don't think I've ever known one—not really. Well, except maybe for Renaldo.

Nicole   Where's Renaldo now?

Kirsten   He's dead. Committed suicide a year ago.

Nicole   Really?! Oh, you mean Renaldo Chavez. I do remember reading about him in the paper. You and he were close?

Kirsten   Yes. He was the closest friend I ever had. He and I would stay up, do pot, and talk for hours. He had this wonderful philosophy! And I know he believed it, because he died for it.

Nicole   What philosophy was that, Kirsten?

Kirsten   I can't say it like he did—he was so smart! But he made me see that we all die, that we only live 80 or 90 years at most. He used to say, "Kirsten, quit fooling yourself. There is no future, only now. Live the moment." He used to say that people spend their whole life trying to grab on to something that makes them feel good inside. It might be a lot of money, or a certain job, or a church, or another person. But in the end you end up alone and die anyhow. "It's all an illusion," he'd say. He said you can leave it all behind any time.

Nicole   [Anxious] You mean suicide?! Didn't he believe in an afterlife?

Kirsten   I used to ask him about that. He said that he honestly didn't know what happens after death. But he figured that it would either be like becoming unconscious forever or else finding out that you still live in another form. If you still live, then you would just have to take it as it comes and deal with it, just like here. He never worried about Hell or the devil because he figured that the churches made those up to keep control of people.

Nicole   Kirsten, are you telling me that you believe these things that Renaldo told you?

Kirsten   Yes, I do. I just wish he was here to tell me what to do! [Begins to cry quietly.] But I think I know what he'd say.

Nicole   What?

Kirsten   He'd say it doesn't matter whether I stay here or go. It's all an illusion anyhow.

Nicole   Kirsten, are you telling me that you're considering committing suicide like Renaldo did?

Kirsten   Yes, but not the same way. I've been reading books on how to do it. It's real easy to do if you take some sleeping pills and tie a plastic bag over your head so you breath carbon dioxide instead of oxygen. It's real painless. . . .

Nicole   [Interrupting anxiously] Kirsten, you have to promise me that you won't do this until I have a chance to think about this and we have a chance to talk again! Promise!

Kirsten   Well, yes, Ms. Lewis, if you want me to. I wasn't planning on doing it today exactly. That's why I wanted to talk to you. I guess I really wanted to see if you can give me any real reason why I shouldn't.

NICOLE   *[Losing it]* My Lord, Kirsten! You're so young! You've got so much to live for!

KIRSTEN   I'm sorry, Ms. Lewis. I just don't buy that line! I don't see anything good in my future! I don't see any way things are going to change.

NICOLE   *[Firmly]* Kirsten, I want you to meet with me day after tomorrow right here after school!

KIRSTEN   O.K.

NICOLE   Promise?!

KIRSTEN   I promise. *[Kirsten gets up and begins to shuffle slowly and dejectedly out of the room.]* Goodbye, Ms. Lewis.

It is the next day after school. Nicole sits in Karen's office with the door closed.

KAREN   What's this all about, Nicole? I've been wondering all day what was so important that you said you absolutely had to talk to me today without fail. What's up?

NICOLE   It's Kirsten. She's talking about killing herself and I think she means it!

KAREN   Oh, boy! Well listen, we'll get her professional help. Let me do some calling today to see who would be the best one to work with her. Of course, I'll have to get hold of her parents first and get their permission. Does Mr. Buxton *[building principal]* know about this?

NICOLE   *[Anxiously]* You don't understand, Karen! She won't talk to anyone but me. And I've got to meet with her again tomorrow after school. She's extremely depressed and thinks no one in the world really cares whether she lives or dies but me, I guess. She made me promise I wouldn't contact her parents. All the things you're talking about will just put more pressure on her!

KAREN   They often say those things but don't really mean them. She's only 15, Nicole, and we have to have her parents involved. Mr. Buxton has to be told what's going on. Don't try to take this thing on yourself. If she would try to kill herself, her parents could sue you for all you're worth!

NICOLE   *[Angrily]* Karen, I hear what you're saying but you're not helping me! She's a human being who's only 15 years old and worth saving! I've got to meet with her again tomorrow night and tell her something that will make her want to go on living! Now help me! Tell me what I should do!

SAN LUIS HIGH SCHOOL
Cumulative Record

Name:	Bell, Kirsten Ann*	**Home Phone:**	375-4235
Address:	324 East Spruce St.		
	Apt. 38B		
Father:	Bruce M. Bell		
	(Stepfather)		
Occupation:	Gas station attendant		
Mother:	Donna Martin Bell		
Occupation:	Clerk		
Siblings:	Josephine F., Age 11		
	Deanna S., Age 2		
Former Schools:	Wilson Elementary	**Handicaps:**	None
	Jackson Middle S.	**Date of Birth:**	6/14/79
Date Entered SHS:	9/15/92	**Age:**	15
General Health:	Fair		
	*Student approved for free lunch		

TEST RECORD

Intelligence Tests	Form	I.Q.	Date	Grade
Otis-Lennon Mental	Level 1H	111	10/14/87	3
Ability Tests	Level 3	108	10/20/91	7
	Level 4	98	10/18/94	10

ACADEMIC RECORD

Grades 1–6 (year averages)

	1	2	3	4	5	6
Citizenship	A	A	A	B	B	B
Lang. arts	C	C	C	C	C	C
Reading	C	C	C	C	C	C
English			C	C	C	D
Spelling	B	B	B	C	C	C
Writing	B	B	B	C	C	C
Social studies			B	B	C	C
Arithmetic	B	B	C	C	D	D
Music	B	B	B	B	B	B

Grades 7–9 (year averages)

Grade 7		Grade 8		Grade 9	
English	C	English	C	English	D
Geography	B	U.S. History	C	World History	D
Arithmetic	D	Arithmetic	D	Algebra	F
P.E.	C	P.E.	C	P.E.	D
Band	B	Band	B	Biology	F

PERSONAL AND SOCIAL DEVELOPMENT
CODE: 1 = SUPERIOR
              5 = UNSATISFACTORY

	Grade 7	Grade 8	Grade 9
Emotional stability	3	4	5
Initiative	3	4	5
Leadership	3	3	5
Social attitude	3	4	5
Integrity	3	4	5

QUESTIONS

1. What are the causes of adolescent suicide? What gender differences exist regarding suicide? What are the signs that a teacher should look for?

2. What are the signs that a teacher should look for that indicate that a student is using drugs or alcohol? What is the most effective way for a teacher to handle such problems?

3. If you were Kirsten's teacher, how would you use the information presented in Kirsten's cumulative record?

4. Why do adolescent groups form? What ethnic/racial/social class groups join gangs? Why would an adolescent like Kirsten join a gang? What can be done about gangs in schools?

5. Why did Kirsten confide in Nicole, rather than other professionals in the school? What are the characteristics of teachers whom students feel they can trust?

6. In what way has Kirsten's home environment influenced her behavior of joining a gang, using drugs, engaging in sexual activities, and considering suicide?

7. At which of Kohlberg's stages of moral development does Kirsten seem to be operating? How can Nicole take this into consideration in her efforts to try to work with Kirsten during her crisis?

8. At which level of Maslow's need hierarchy does Kirsten primarily seem to be operating? How could Nicole take this into consideration in working with her?

9. From a humanistic (i.e., Rogerian) perspective, how does Kirsten perceive her life situation? her self? How is the self-concept formed, and under what conditions does it change? What counseling techniques might Nicole have used to help Kirsten?

10. What are the legal, professional, and ethical considerations if Nicole decides to handle this situation herself without notifying Kirsten's parents, the building principal, etc.? Did Nicole get too close to Kirsten and fail to keep a respectable social distance from one of her students?

11. In light of the rise in adolescent suicide rates, the prevalence of groups, and the high rate of drug usage and adolescent sex, should schools provide students information on these problems? If so, what form should this take? Should schools provide free contraceptives to students, for example? How effective are drug and sex education programs?

12. Should guidance counselors like Karen be part of the line or staff in school systems? How should the role of the school guidance counselor be defined so that professionals like Karen can encourage students like Kirsten to bring their problems to them?

13. It has been suggested that teachers' responsibilities in cases like Kirsten's include appropriate "intervention and referral" procedures. What courses of action should Nicole follow in dealing with this situation? What should she say to Kirsten at their next meeting and how should she say it? Who else, if anybody, should Nicole involve in helping Kirsten?

14. Which agencies should be notified in cases like Kirsten's? What federal, state, and/or community agencies deal with problems like potential suicide, drug and alcohol abuse, and gang activities?

VICTORIA'S SECRET

Caitlin Evans is a 24-year-old second-grade teacher in Madison Elementary School, which is located in the Madison County Consolidated School District. Madison was the first of three elementary schools built in the town of Madison, which is located in a midwestern state. This rural community has a population of approximately 6,000, which is 80 percent white, 15 percent African–American, and 5 percent Hispanic. Since Madison is located in the center of a large agricultural area, a majority of its residents are farm owners, farm workers, or manufacturers/suppliers of farm equipment and supplies.

Two years ago, Caitlin graduated with a major in elementary education from a large state university in the Midwest. She then applied for and was offered several teaching positions, but she accepted the one at Madison because she had grown up on a farm and felt at home in Madison. Four weeks ago she began her third year of teaching second grade.

On Monday afternoon after the final bell rings, Caitlin works at her desk for almost an hour reviewing her class roll and jotting notes about each pupil's progress during the first four weeks of school. She seems to have quite a bit of information about all her pupils except for Vicky Warden, a cooperative but reticent pupil who sits at the front desk in the first row of seats. Vicky does average work, seems to know the other pupils, and responds when called upon. But there is something about her that makes her seem different in some way. But Caitlin can't put her finger on the problem.

Caitlin puts her class records in the desk drawer, clears the top of her desk, takes her purse, and leaves the building. As she is walking out to the parking lot, she sees her best friend, Nora Whittin, a first-grade teacher who is also in her third year of teaching.

CAITLIN   Hey, Nora. Don't you know it's cheating to work for an hour after school's out? It gives you an unfair advantage over the rest of us.

NORA   Hi, Caitlin. Looks like you're trying to get an unfair advantage, then. Why are you here so late?

CAITLIN   I'm just reviewing some of my pupils' records.

NORA   Are you reviewing them just to familiarize yourself with your pupils, or do you have a specific reason for doing so?

CAITLIN   Both, I guess. It seems like a really good class. They're enthusiastic, cooperative, and an easy group to work with. I'm just trying to assess their progress for the first four weeks of school. But I'm also looking for information on a particular pupil.

NORA   I don't want you to think I'm nosy, but I know a lot of the pupils in your class because I had most of them in first grade last year. I asked the question because I think I might be able to help if you are looking for some specific information. I agree, they really are a nice group. Who's the particular pupil you want information about? And what type of information do you want?

CAITLIN   That's right. You would know most of my pupils. *[Pause]* Was Vicky Warden in your class last year?

NORA   Yes, I had Vicky. Surely she isn't giving you any trouble. She was really quiet and cooperative last year.

CAITLIN   No, she isn't giving me any trouble. And she is quiet and cooperative. But she seems so passive and withdrawn. She knows the other pupils' names and they all know her, but there isn't any interaction between her and the others. She seems to live inside a shell.

NORA   Yes! It was pretty much the same situation with her last year. But, there are quiet introverted people in the world, Caitlin. Vicky always completed all her work on time and well even though she was absent quite a bit. She didn't have trouble with anybody. I've had many pupils in the past that I'd trade for Vicky any day. I really don't think she has any problems.

CAITLIN   Why was she absent so much?

NORA   Just the usual first-grade things—mainly colds, but she also had measles, and broke a couple of fingers.

CAITLIN   How did she break her fingers?

NORA   Some kind of accident on the farm as I remember.

CAITLIN   Maybe I'm making a mountain out of a molehill. There just seems to be something worrisome about her that I can't put my finger on.

NORA   Maybe as the year progresses she'll warm up to some of her classmates. She might just be really shy. I have to run. Gotta go shopping. Bye. See you tomorrow.

CAITLIN   Bye, Nora. Thanks for the info.

The following day in class, Vicky is working in a group of pupils who are drawing individual pictures. Caitlin pulls a chair over and sits beside her.

CAITLIN   That looks like an interesting picture, Vicky. Tell me about it.

VICKY   That's the farm. *[Pointing]* This is our house. There's the barn. These are peach trees. This green's the wheat field. There are lots of other things on the farm but the paper's not big enough to put them all on.

CAITLIN   It must be fun living on a farm. Do your mother and daddy run the farm by themselves?

VICKY   No. It's Mr. Bloomquist's farm. Lots of people work there. Mom works at the big house and Dad works in the fields. Sometimes I help Dad work with the animals.

CAITLIN I bet that's fun. I think I'd like to do that. What things do you get to do?

VICKY Sometimes I feed chickens and hogs. They really use machines to milk the cows, but Dad taught me how to do it with my hands. *[Enthusiastically]* He's teaching me to ride a pony, too.

CAITLIN Wow! It sounds like you have fun with your dad.

VICKY I do. I like to help him.

CAITLIN Do you help your mother in the big house sometimes?

VICKY No.

CAITLIN Do you have brothers or sisters?

VICKY No.

CAITLIN That's a good picture, Vicky. Thanks for telling me about it.

Several days later, Caitlen's class is on the playground engaging in free play during recess. Vicky, by herself as usual, is climbing on the jungle gym. Caitlin notices that she's wearing a long-sleeve sweater even though it's a very hot September afternoon. As Caitlin wonders why Vicky is wearing such a warm outfit, Vicki steps towards a bar across from her on the jungle gym. Her foot slips off the bar and she drops down through the inside bars to the ground, hitting her forearm hard just below the elbow hard, directly on a bar. She cries out and holds her elbow as she lies on the ground in the center of the jungle gym. Caitlin rushes over to her.

CAITLIN *[With concern]* Vicky! Are you all right?

VICKY *[Trying to hold back the tears]* I hurt my arm real bad! It might be broke!

CAITLIN *[Reassuringly]* Vicky, I'm going to take you out from under the jungle gym very carefully. I'll put my hands under your shoulders and slide you out on your back. Do you think you can help me by pushing with your feet?

VICKY Yes, ma'am. *[With feeling]* But my arm hurts awful bad!

CAITLIN I know it does, honey. But after we get you out, we can look at it and see how to make it better.

VICKY *[Pleading]* Can't you just take me home?

CAITLIN *[As she slides Vicky slowly out from under the jungle gym]* Is your mother or daddy at home now?

VICKY *[After a long pause]* No, they're both at work.

CAITLIN *[Calling to the other second-grade teacher]* Ms. Walker, will you watch my pupils while I see about Vicky's arm?

MS WALKER Sure, we'll be all right. Go ahead.

CAITLIN Thanks. I'll be back soon.

Caitlin and Vicky enter their empty classroom. Vicky holds her left elbow as she walks along.

CAITLIN Now, Vicky. Lets see what your arm looks like. Here, let me help you take off your sweater.

VICKY *[Apparently terrified]* No! No! I don't want my sweater off!

CAITLIN   [Taken aback] Vicky, Vicky. It's all right. We have to take off your sweater to see how badly your arm is injured. Here. I'll close the door so no one can see into the room.

VICKY   [Hysterical] I don't want my sweater off! I can't have my sweater off! No! No! No!

[Caitlin is astounded at Vicky's behavior. She hugs Vicky to her side and talks quietly to her in an attempt to calm her down. Eventually, Vicky stops sobbing and looks up at Caitlin.]

CAITLIN   [Soothingly] Vicky, we have to find out what type of injury you have on your arm. I must see it so that I know what to do about it. Why don't we unbutton the front of your sweater. [She begins to unbutton the sweater] Then I can help you slip the hurt arm out of the sleeve. You can keep the sweater over the rest of you. [Encouraging] Come on now. Slip the arm slowly out of the sleeve. That's fine. Easy does it.

[As Vicky pulls her arm out of the sleeve, the sweater pulls away from her side. Her side is a mass of red and purple bruises.]

CAITLIN   [Shocked] Vicky! What happened to your side?

VICKY   [Beginning to cry] Nothing.

CAITLIN   [Pulling the sweater away from Vicky's body] You're bruised all the way around your body! That must be awfully sore! How did you get bruised all around your rib cage like that, Vicky? The marks are shaped like the end of a table spoon. Did somebody hit you with a large spoon? There are scars from other welts and cuts.

VICKY   [After a long pause] No. Nobody hit me. I fell off the horse. Daddy was helping me learn to ride, and I fell off the horse.

CAITLIN   It doesn't seem that you'd be bruised all around both sets of ribs like that if you fell off a horse. How did you get those other scars?

VICKY   [Another long pause] I hurt one side of me when I fell off the horse. I rolled against the fence and hurt the other side of me. [Pause] I sometimes hurt myself when I help out with the farm work. That's what those other scars are.

CAITLIN   Well. Let's look at that arm. [Examines the arm] It doesn't have any marks on it. Can you bend it up and down?

VICKY   [Moving the arm up and down] Yes. It moves OK. It doesn't hurt when I move it.

CAITLIN   [Pressing gently on the portion of the arm that Vicky was holding]. Does that hurt?

VICKY   No. It doesn't hurt at all. But it really hurt when I bumped it.

CAITLIN   Yes. I could tell that it did. But sometimes bumps are like that. They hurt when they first happen, but then they stop hurting pretty fast.

VICKY   Yes. That's what happened to me. Can I go back outside?

CAITLIN   All right, Vicky. If you feel OK you may go back to the playground until recess is over.

After classes are over that afternoon, Caitlin goes to Nora's room to discuss Vicky's situation with her. She describes the accident and the discovery of the spoon-shaped bruises and the scars from other injuries, along with Vicky's explanation for them.

NORA   Her explanation that she got those bruises from falling off a horse and that farm accidents are responsible for the other scars doesn't seem logical to me.

CAITLIN   No, I don't see how the rib cages on both sides of her body could be bruised that severely by a fall from a horse. More likely she would have injured arms or legs. And there were too many other scars to have been caused by accidents. Beside that, she behaved as if she weren't telling me the truth.

NORA   What are you going to do about this?

CAITLIN   I don't know. That's why I wanted to talk with you. I haven't been in this situation before.

NORA   In this state, all schools have a child advocate who handles situations like this and is responsible for reporting them to the Child Protective Services. In our school, it's our assistant principal, Harold Carris.

CAITLIN   Unfortunately, the thought of Mr. Carris being in charge of this situation doesn't generate a great deal of confidence in me.

NORA   He's not really a ball of fire, is he? But, I think that if child abuse does take place, he's required to report it to the Child Protective Services. Of course, you'll be right in the middle of the situation.

CAITLIN   Yes, I know. And I'm not really excited about that. In fact, I can't be absolutely sure that Vicky really is being physically abused.

NORA   Maybe you should talk with Vicky's parents before you report it to Mr. Carris.

CAITLIN   I'm planning to do that. I wouldn't feel right reporting them for child abuse until I've talked with them. I'll call them as soon as I get home and make arrangements to visit with them as soon as possible.

NORA   Lots o' luck!

The following evening, Caitlin is sitting in the main room of the small, poorly furnished cabin in which the Wardens live. The cabin has an old-fashioned kitchen which is heated only by an iron stove. It has a wood plank floor, bare except for two small, worn throw rugs.

After Caitlin had met with Nora yesterday, she called the number of the Bloomquist farm since the Wardens do not have a telephone and arranged a meeting with the Wardens. Unfortunately, when she arrived, Mrs. Warden was the only family member there. Caitlin is surprised by Mrs. Warden's appearance. She is a most attractive woman who appears to be unusually young for having a child in the second grade.

She apologizes for the absence of Vicky and Mr. Warden, and explains that there is a plumbing problem at the big house and Mr. Warden had been asked to fix it. He took Vicky with him.

CAITLIN   As I told you when I called, I wanted to visit with you and Mr. Warden to talk about Vicky.

MS. WARDEN   Well, if she's in any kind of trouble, you don't need to come here to visit about it. Just call on the phone and let us know and we'll take care of it. Our motto is, "Spare the rod and spoil the child."

CAITLIN   *[With emphasis]* Oh, no. That's not the reason I'm here at all. Vicky's a model pupil. She's quiet, obedient, well-liked by the other pupils, and does all her work regularly.

MS. WARDEN   That's good. We expect her to do them things. Why are you here then?

CAITLIN   Mainly, I came to see how Vicky's feeling. As you know, she fell off a piece of playground equipment yesterday and hurt her arm.

MS. WARDEN   Yeah. I heard about that. She's OK.

CAITLIN   Even though it was very hot yesterday, Vicky wore a heavy long-sleeve sweater to class.

MS. WARDEN   *[Forced laughter]* Yes, I let Vicky dress herself. Sometimes she gets into some pretty strange get-ups.

CAITLIN   When I helped her take off the sweater so that I could look at her arm, I saw horrible bruises clear around the upper part of her body. They were shaped like the end of a tablespoon. There were many other kinds of scars on her upper arms and body. How did she get bruised so badly and how did she get all those other scars?

MS. WARDEN   *[Responding slowly]* Well, *[pause]* uh, she went to the *[pause]* uh, barn with my husband to pitch some hay into the loft. She *[pause]* uh, was playing up on the tractor and *[pause]* uh, fell off. She *[pause]* uh, lit on a lumber pile layin' on the floor there. But those bruises are almost better.

CAITLIN   What about all those other scars and welts on her back and shoulders? How did she get those?

MS. WARDEN   *[Angrily]* You know how kids are always falling around. I don't even remember how she got most of 'em. Why do you need to know about all this? Your job's to teach her readin', writin' and 'rithmetic, not to pry around about how she got scars and such. Did you find out what you need to know? I got work to do.

CAITLIN   Yes, I did. Thank you for allowing me to visit with you. Vicky is a nice girl. I'm sure you and your husband are proud of her.

The next day after school, Caitlin is in the office of Assistant Principal Harold Carris. She's just described in detail how Victoria fell off the jungle gym, how she noticed the bruises, and how she had visited the Warden home. She placed special emphasis on the discrepancy between Vicky's and her mother's explanations of her bruised body.

MR. CARRIS   Well, that's strange, all right. Might be that one of them was lyin'. Or might be that one of them forgot what really happened.

CAITLIN   Or it might be that we have a physically abused pupil in our second-grade class, who might be seriously injured or killed before she finishes second grade unless we do something about it.

MR. CARRIS   *[Thoughtfully]* Yes, that's a possibility too. *[Pause]* But somehow that possibility doesn't seem quite as reasonable as the others.

CAITLIN   Yes, but the results of *that* possibility are terminal. Maybe we should make an effort to prevent that possibility.

MR. CARRIS   But, on the other hand, if we report the Wardens for child abuse and it can't be proved, they could sue us for a lot of money. If Vicky is being abused, the abuse certainly will continue. I'm not interested in making serious accusations without having really convincing evidence. Then our report will have more teeth and the Child Protective Services will have a better case. What do you think of that idea?

CAITLIN   I'm not satisfied with it. I believe that child is in danger of being seriously injured or killed.

MR. CARRIS   Well, it's my responsibility to report it, and I'm not satisfied that the child is really being abused.

CAITLIN   Does your being responsible mean that if you don't report it and Vicky is seriously injured or killed, that you're responsible for it? After all, I have reported this to you.

MR. CARRIS   I'm not sure. Let me check some more, and I'll get back to you.

The next day after school, Caitlin and Nora are having a drink in a fast-food restaurant after school. Caitlin has described Mr. Carris's response to her report on Vicky's situation.

NORA   What a guy! It's really hard for him to make a decision, isn't it?

CAITLIN   Yes, especially on something he is accountable for.

NORA   Have you learned any more about Vicky's home situation?

CAITLIN   Yes, I've learned some really interesting information. Yesterday after school, I went over Vicky's school records. Then last night I went to the library and read some books on child abuse.

NORA   And what did you find out?

CAITLIN   Well, the most startling thing I learned is that more children are physically abused and/or neglected by their mothers than any other person.

NORA   *[Emotionally]* That *is* startling! Why would a mother abuse a sweet child like Vicky? How could any mother abuse her own child?

CAITLIN   I found that out, too. Children are frequently abused either by mothers that are unusually young or unusually old. Some young mothers get pregnant before they are married. Whether or not the father marries them, they're not in a position to support themselves and their child very well.

When older mothers get pregnant, they often don't want the responsibility of a child during a period in their life that they want time and money to enjoy themselves. Both groups of mothers often take out their disappointment and frustration on their child.

NORA   And Vicky falls into the first category.

CAITLIN   Yes. Vicky's school records indicate that both her mother and father are high school drop-outs. I would guess that her mother got pregnant while she and her husband were dating in high school. The records indicate that they married, dropped out of school, and obtained below-minimum-wage jobs as farm workers. I'd be willing to bet that her mother blames Vicky for their poverty and takes it out on her when she becomes depressed.

NORA   That sounds reasonable. What do you think about her father?

CAITLIN   I think he is nice to Vicky, but isn't willing to challenge his wife. Vicky always speaks of him as if she really likes him. He didn't meet with me when I visited their home. I'm guessing that he feels guilty because he thinks that he's responsible for his wife's pregnancy and their poverty-level existence.

NORA   Wow! You've found quite a bit of information in a very short time!

CAITLIN   Yes! And there's more. Look at this list of characteristics of physically abused children [Hands sheet to Nora]. Vicky has many of these characteristics.

NORA   What are you going to do now?

CAITLIN   I'm really not sure. I'm in a real dilemma. While I was reading about abused children, I found a section in one of the books that said that teachers report more than twice as many abused pupils as do representatives of any other agency, but that they report only a small percentage of the pupils who are abused. That's frightening!

NORA   Yes, it is! It's can be disastrous for the abused children! Are you going to give this information to Mr. Carris?

CAITLIN   Not right now. I don't think it would make any difference to him. He's really scared to get involved in controversy. I'll just have to think about this whole situation for a while before I do anything.

The following week, Vicky doesn't come to school. By Wednesday, Caitlin is concerned. She calls the Bloomquist number. Ms. Bloomquist says that the Wardens are out in the fields. She agrees to ask one of the parents to return the call to Caitlin. No call comes.

Thursday, Vicky is still absent. After school on Thursday, Caitlin drives to the Bloomquist farm. No one is at the Warden's cabin. Vicky gets back in her car and drives toward the big farm house. As she approaches the farm house, she catches sight of a figure playing in the creek near the cornfield. It's the section of farm that Vicky drew in her picture. And the figure is Vicky.

CAITLIN   [Shouting] Vicky! Vicky!

[Vicky turns, sees Caitlin and begins to run in the other direction. Caitlin notices that she can move her legs only with great difficulty and apparently is in pain every time she takes a step. She continues to run after Vicky, and draws near to her very quickly. She sees why Vicky has difficulty running: both of her legs are circled with angry red welts that begin at her ankles and continue on up under her skirt. As Caitlin approaches, she holds out her arms to Vicky. Vicky turns and runs into her arms.]

CAITLIN   Oh Vicky! Tell me what's happening to you!

VICKY   [In tears] Oh, I can't Ms. Evans! I just can't! Please don't ask me to tell what's happening to me! I just can't tell! I'm afraid to!

Caitlin   *[To nobody in particular]* Oh, please help me! I just don't know what to do now!

Identifying Signs of Physical Abuse in Children

Physical Indicators
- Bruises and welts that are:
  in unlikely places on the body: face, lips, mouth, torso, back, thighs, buttocks, or genitalia;
  in various stages of healing;
  clustered or form regular patterns;
  reflective of the shape of article used to inflict, such as electric cord or belt buckle;
  on several different surface areas of the body;
  evident regularly after absence, weekend, or vacation.
- Questionable fractures:
  to skull, nose, facial structure;
  that are multiple or spiral.
- Questionable burns:
  Cigarette or cigar burns on soles, palms, back, or buttocks.
  Immersion burns that are sock-like, glove-like, or donut-shaped on buttocks or genitalia
  Pattern burns reflecting shape of burner or iron, or rope burns on arms, legs, neck or torso.
- Questionable lacerations or abrasions to mouth, lips, gums, eyes, or external genitalia.

Child Behavior Indicators
- Uncomfortable with physical contact;
- Frightened of parent(s);
- Afraid to go home;
- Complains of soreness or moves uncomfortably;
- Wears clothing inappropriate to weather to cover body;
- Reluctant to change clothes (attempts to hide injuries);
- Turns to strangers indiscriminately for affection;
- Does not look to parents for relief of discomfort;
- Exhibits extreme anxiety.

QUESTIONS

1. What should Caitlin do now? If she reports the latest incident to Mr. Carris, what should he do? Trace what you think the progress of this case would be from the school to the appropriate state agency. What do you think will happen to Vicky?

2. Evaluate Caitlin's handling of this suspected child abuse situation. Comment on her effectiveness in working with Vicky, Mrs. Warden, and Mr. Carris. What other actions do you think she should have taken?

3. There are four types of abuse that are typically inflicted on children: physical abuse, neglect, emotional abuse, and sexual abuse. Define and give an example of each of these types of abuse. How can teachers recognize signs of these types of abuse?

4. Describe procedures in your state for reporting and disposing of cases of child abuse.

5. Can a parent who has been reported by a teacher for abusing a child bring legal action against the teacher if the charges are not true? Can legal action be brought against school personnel who have reason to believe that a child is being abused but do not report it?

6. Why do parents abuse their own children? List some of the reasons for child abuse that are not mentioned in this case.

7. Comment on the historical development of child abuse. Has the frequency of child abuse increased or decreased since the time of ancient civilizations? How do you explain this tendency? Suggest specific steps society can take to reduce the incidences of child abuse.

8. On what level of Maslow's need hierarchy does Mr. Carris seem to be operating? What about Vicky? Vicky's mother? What does this suggest about ways of working with them?

9. Does Mr. Carris exhibit a supporting, coaching, delegating, or directing style of leadership?

10. How can Caitlin as a teacher and the school system go about involving parents so as to reduce child abuse? How well might techniques such as home visits and adult education programs work?

C A S E 25

THE EXCESSES OF YOUTH

Ray McBride has taught social studies at Van Buren High School for five years, ever since completing his B.S. at the College of Education of the state land-grant university. The Van Buren Vikings are a perennial powerhouse football team that has won the championship in their division several times in a football-happy state in the Eastern part of the United States. The high school is located in a large city and draws from an attendance district that is approximately 60 percent white, 25 percent African–American, 10 percent Hispanic, and 5 percent other assorted racial and/or ethnic groups.

It is Monday, two weeks after classes have begun, and the Vikings have already won their first two games by large scores. As Ray meets his seventh-period U.S. history class, the students are all abuzz, discussing last Friday's game.

RAY OK, people! Settle down! Refocus your attention from last Friday's game back to the Age of Discovery in Europe, where we left off last Friday. Besides, those first two games we played were easy ones. Now this Friday we'll find out how good we are when we play the Southport Spartans. If we beat them on their home turf then I'll be impressed. *[Laughter and shouts of agreement]* Now think back to the days before there was a United States, before there was even a Van Buren High School. *[Shouts of protest]* In fact, before the game of football was even invented! *[Mock shouts of despair]* So, Jerry, what three European nations led the way in discovering the new world?

JERRY Uh, Portugal, Spain, and England.

RAY Right, Jerry! But don't forget that little old Genoa in what is now Italy played an important role. Can anybody remember what? *[Silence for about five seconds then one hand goes up.]* Yes, Maurine!

MAURINE Weren't both Columbus and Cabot from Genoa?

RAY Excellent, Maurine! While Columbus sailed for Spain and Cabot for England, both were natives of Genoa. A minor fact in history, but you remembered it, Maurine! Yes, Maurine?

MAURINE But why was that, Mr. McBride? Why didn't they sail for Genoa?

RAY *Ah*, a good question. And why might that be, ah, Don?

DON I don't know. Probably because of money.

RAY   *[Walking back to where Don and his ever-present friends, Billy, Mike, and Tyrone sit]* That's right, Don! Can you tell us about it?

DON   Not really. I haven't read the chapter yet.

RAY   Well, that was still a good guess. Why did you think that was the answer?

DON   Doesn't money always make the world go around?

RAY   *[Smiling]* I guess so, Don. It certainly determined who Columbus and Cabot decided to sail for. *[Looking at Billy, Mike, and Tyrone]* Can any of you tell me what happened? *[Billy and Mike shake their heads no, and Tyrone lays his head down on the desk.]* All right then. How about you, Donna? *[Paces back up to the front of the class.]*

DONNA   Didn't Columbus try Portugal, but then end up sailing for Ferdinand and Isabella of Spain?

RAY   Right you are, Donna. Good answer. Now let me ask another question. How many of you have read this chapter? *[All hands go up but those of Don, Billy, Mike, and Tyrone.]* OK, thanks. Remember that we covered this stuff last week. If you haven't read the material by now, you are really behind. How many of you read today's chapter on exploring the New World? *[All but the same four hands go up.]* OK, thanks. Now let's start with the American Indian tribes that were already living in the New World when the Europeans came over here to explore it. Please turn to the map on page 22 of the text which shows where the various American Indian or Amerind tribes were located in the sixteenth century.

Ray sits in his classroom after school where he is joined by his friend, Jim Turpin. Jim was a guidance counselor at Van Buren, but has recently been promoted to assistant principal.

RAY   Well, look who's here! The new assistant principal!

JIM   *[Smiling and bowing]* Yes, well, someone has to provide leadership in this school!

RAY   *[Smiling]* And I can't think of a better person for the job! Sit down, Jim, and talk a bit.

JIM   *[Sitting down]* Personal or professional?

RAY   Well, give me your personal advice on a professional matter.

JIM   I gotcha! What's the problem?

RAY   Jim, it's some of the boys in my seventh-period U.S. History class—four to be specific.

JIM   Discipline problems?

RAY   No, not really. They don't read the assignments and haven't done well on the quizzes that I've given so far, but that's not the real problem.

JIM   What is this—twenty questions? Am I suppose to guess what the problem is? One of them is pregnant?

RAY   *[Laughing]* No, I think you've been to one movie too many lately, Jim. *[Seriously]* I think there's a serious drug or at least alcohol problem with these guys. No, I think it's both.

JIM   As far as I am concerned, alcohol is a drug too, even if it is legal. But what makes
       you think there's a drug problem? And who are these kids anyhow?

RAY   They are a kind of gang. Not in the formal sense of an organized juvenile gang,
       you understand, but they are always hanging out together and they even sit to-
       gether in my class. There's Mike Mason, who sort of seems to be the leader, Billy
       Reardon, Tyrone King, and Don McCabe. Don doesn't seem to fit in as naturally
       as the others—seems to be a kind of a fringer. But I see him more with those
       guys than anyone.

JIM   Oh, yes, I know that crowd! Tyrone King used to be one of my counselees. He
       used to talk about Mike and Billy a lot. Yes, I would guess that they do their
       share of drugs. Do you think they are on drugs when they are in your class?

RAY   Definitely. I've been watching them carefully for over a week now, and often
       move close to them as I pace around the room during classroom discussions.
       The signs are there.

JIM   Such as?

RAY   Odor. I can smell pot on them. And their eyes are often quite dilated. Often they
       just sit around drowsy and inactive with their heads on their desks. One day I
       got too close to Mike and I could smell it on his breath as he talked. And
       Tyrone—he always has a bottle of cough syrup in his pocket. I've always won-
       dered what's really in that bottle. In fact, maybe I don't really want to know, Jim.
       I'm not sure what I should do about this. But just ignoring it, like a lot of teach-
       ers and parents choose to do, won't help much.

JIM   Yes, it's a difficult situation for a teacher to be in. Yet all the workshops I've been
       in on adolescent drug usage see the teacher as being in an ideal position to serve
       as an information and referral agent. Do you want me to work on this, Ray?

RAY   What do you advise?

JIM   I could do some discreet information gathering and maybe you could work with
       Don a bit, since you seem to feel that he is the one that is most salvageable.

RAY   That makes sense. I'll line up a conference with Don.

It is three days later and Ray meets with Don McCabe after school alone in his
classroom. They sit in chairs facing one another in front of Ray's desk.

DON   You wanted to see me, Mr. McBride?

RAY   Yes, Don, I do. Don, I think you have the potential to be a good student in my
       U.S. History class but you never seem to have read the material or come to class
       prepared. I'd like to know why.

DON   I don't know.

RAY   I can't remember one day in the last three weeks that you or your friends have
       read the assignment before coming to class.

DON   You mean Mike, Bill, Tyrone, and I?

RAY   Exactly. Why don't you read the assignment before you come to class?

DON   I guess the truth is, Mr. McBride—no offense—we just aren't interested in his-
       tory.

RAY   In history or in any of your classes? I've checked with your other teachers and you guys don't come to their classes prepared either.

DON   *[Surprised]* Really! Well, I guess we're just not that into school right now.

RAY   What are you into, Don? Drugs and alcohol?

DON   No, of course not!

RAY   Don't give me that, Don. I'm not as stupid as I look. I've smelled pot on your clothes, noticed how dilated your eyes are, seen Tyrone's ever-present cough syrup bottle . . . .

DON   *[Nervous laugh]* Yeah, well, I guess you've got us, Mr. McBride. What are you going to do? Report us to the police?

RAY   I don't have a plan at the moment, Don. What I'd like to do is help you become a better student. But I'm not sure I can help you as long as you're using that stuff all the time.

DON   "That stuff" is just alcohol and pot, Mr. McBride. Oh, except maybe for Tyrone, who uses crack sometimes. It isn't like I do it every day. Just when I need to.

RAY   And when do you need to, Don?

DON   Look, Mr. McBride. Alcohol is perfectly legal. My dad drinks it all the time and the liquor really flows at all our family gatherings. You should have been at my sister's wedding last month!

RAY   OK, tell me about pot. That's not legal.

DON   Well, yeah. But I only take three or four hits a day. It relaxes me and helps me think.

RAY   It sure doesn't help you read your history text.

DON   Believe me, it's not the pot, Mr. McBride. I'm just not much of a student.

RAY   What does motivate you, Don?

DON   I mainly just like to hang out with the guys and our friends.

RAY   By the guys you mean Mike, Billy, and Tyrone?

DON   Yeah, and our girlfriends.

RAY   Some of our girls here at Van Buren use pot too?

DON   Of course, and some of the girls from other schools. Pot really helps you break down barriers and makes it real easy to get to know another person.

RAY   *[Smiling]* It makes the girls real affectionate?

DON   *[Smiling]* Yeah, it sure does. I just don't see why alcohol's legal and pot's not. I'd rather be around a guy who's high on pot than I would one who's drunk. Drunks always get mean and nasty after awhile, but potheads are real easy to get along with. Some people even need to use pot for medicine but the government's too stupid to let them, even when their doctor says so.

RAY   I hear what you're saying, Don. But isn't life best when you're clear-headed and fully aware of what's going on?

DON   Maybe for you, but definitely not for me. Like I said, it's not like pot is my whole life.

RAY   What about Mike, Billy, and Tyrone?

DON   What are you going to do with the information if I tell you? Report them?

RAY   Like I said, Don, I'm interested as a teacher. Maybe if I understand you four better I can figure out how to motivate you to learn history.

DON   *[Laughing]* I'm afraid that's hopeless.

RAY   Why's that?

DON   Talking Mike, Billy, and Tyrone out of using drugs would be quite a chore.

RAY   Why do you say so?

DON   Look, Mr. McBride, Mike's used drugs since he was seven and Billy's almost as bad.

RAY   Seven?!

DON   Yeah, He started out sniffing glue and paint and finally got on pot and alcohol. Same for Billy, only he started in the sixth grade. You understand I'll deny I said any of this if you mention it to anyone else?

RAY   I understand. What about Tyrone?

DON   Tyrone drinks a lot, but he also uses crack. Since he's from the neighborhood over on 84th street, he can get stuff for us real easy.

RAY   So, Don, what's your goal in life? Grow up to be a dealer?

DON   *[Laughs]* No, that's a rich but dangerous life, Mr. McBride. Tyrone might, but not me. Look, I'm not good at much. I'm not good at sports and you know I'm no class brain. I don't figure I'll get a chance to go to college. My dad's a salesman and makes a lot of money at times. He says that I have a likeable personality and can be a salesman too. But that's later, Mr. McBride. Right now I just want to be a high school kid and have a good time. I hope I can make C's and graduate, but whatever.

RAY   What's to keep you from becoming a pothead and not wanting to do anything the rest of your life?

DON   It's not like that, Mr. McBride. I use some pot and alcohol, sure. From time to time we party big and really get stoned. But usually it's just enough to get through the day. I'll tell you what, Mr. McBride, I'll think about all you've told me and I'll try to start reading your assignments before I come to class. But I can't do anything about Mike, Billy, and Tyrone. They're their own people and it would be a waste of time. They'd kill me if they knew that I'd talked to you.

RAY   Don't worry. I won't tell them.

DON   *[Stands up]* Thanks, Mr. McBride. I'll try to do better.

RAY   OK, Don. Thanks for being honest with me.

DON   *[Smiling]* It was real easy, Mr. McBride. You're a nice guy! *[Sticks out his hand, and Ray, remaining seated, smiles and shakes it.]*

It is after school the next day and Ray walks down to the office of Jim Turpin, the assistant principal. Jim greets Ray, motions for him to take a seat, closes his office door, and takes the seat behind his desk.

JIM   Ray, how's it going?

RAY   Great, Jim. I talked to Don McCabe, as you suggested.

JIM   How did it go?

RAY   Surprisingly well. He was suspicious of me at first, but he finally opened up and told me quite a bit about himself and his friends.

JIM   What did you learn?

RAY   In confidence, Jim, Tyrone King is the dealer. At least he gets the drugs, and Mike and Billy are heavy users. Don seems to be on the fringe of the group. He doesn't drink and use pot as heavily as they do, at least not yet.

JIM   So it's primarily alcohol and pot.

RAY   Yes, although apparently Tyrone does some crack. I guess Don is up to taking a hit of pot three or four times a day and gets drunk when they party down. He claims he's not addicted, but I think he might be kidding himself. If he keeps up this pattern he'll sure get there.

JIM   I agree. What are you going to do?

RAY   That's what I wanted to talk to you about. Don's attitude toward life and his drug usage is clearly affecting his grades. If something isn't done now, by somebody, I think he'll just end up as another failure. Maybe I'm wrong, but he's the only one in that group that I feel like there is any chance of saving. I'm not sure what role I should play in all this. I'd like to work with Don and see if I can help him. But I realize that something needs to be done for the others. Should they be referred to one of the guidance counselors or to the state division of human services? If that is done, Don will know that I've broken the confidentiality between us and may quit relating to me. Also, take the homes of these boys. Shouldn't someone contact their parents and get them involved in all this? But again, it's the same problem. While the parents may be the ultimate cause of this whole thing in the first place, I may terminate any chance I have to help Don if I contact them. I know I can tell you all this in confidence, Jim, because you're my friend. But the problem is, Jim, what do I do?

JIM   You're "caught between the devil and the deep blue sea" all right, Ray. I don't know. Let me think about it, check into some possible courses of action, and get back to you. OK? Meanwhile you keep working with Don.

RAY   [Standing up] Thanks a million, Jim. I knew you'd help.

It is near the end of seventh period, two days later. Ray looks out at the class as they quietly prepare for their upcoming exam on the European discovery and exploration of the New World by answering some self-test questions that Ray has handed out to them. He catches Don's eye as he looks up and motions for Don to come up to his desk.

RAY   [Speaking quietly] How's it going, Don? Are you having any trouble with the questions?

DON   To tell you the truth, Mr. McBride, I am, and it's my own fault. I've just barely skimmed the chapters and these questions are pretty in-depth.

RAY   Would you like some help?

DON   [Brightening up] I sure would!

RAY   If you'll read these chapters, and I mean really read them, Don, I'd be willing to tutor you a bit for this test.

DON   That would really be cool, Mr. McBride! When would you want me to come see you?

RAY   It's got to be tomorrow after school. The test is the next day.

DON   I'll do it. I'll read the chapters real good and come here tomorrow after school. Thanks! I appreciate your help!

It is seventh period three days later, and Ray passes back the tests to the students by calling out their names and handing them their test papers with their answer sheets inside.

RAY   I want you to look your tests over carefully, especially your multiple choice answer sheets where I've calculated your scores. We'll go over the answers and then I'll tell you what I looked for on the essay part. We'll discuss a few of the objective items that bothered you, so you can improve on the next test. I want you to particularly look at the red marks on your answer sheets to see if there is any pattern to the multiple choice items that you missed. Are they evenly distributed over the answer sheet or are they in clusters? It may be that certain material covered by the test was more difficult, or maybe you studied some chapters differently than you did others. Look at that and try to figure out how you might do things differently next time. *[Pause]* Now before we go over the answers, let's talk about the overall grade that you received. The objective part was worth 50 points and so was the essay part. So you could have received a total possible of 100 points. The average score was 74.2 points. As is always the case, there are always those students who work real hard and get a perfect score. I don't like to embarrass people but Maurine Sullivan really worked hard for this one and made a perfect score. Stand up and take a bow, Maurine! *[Maurine stands and smiles while students applaud, cheer, and kid her all at the same time. She sits back down.]* Yes, Jerry?

JERRY   Maurine may be the winner but who was the first runner-up?

RAY   A nice line, Jerry. From the Miss America contest, I assume. Well, believe it or not, the first runner-up was a boy, not a girl. And his name, folks, is Don McCabe. Don made a 96. Don, stand up and take a bow! *[Don stands up, smiles, and puts his hands together to make a gesture of victory while the students, somewhat surprised, applaud and cheer loudly, especially Mike, Billy, and Tyrone.]*

DON   I owe it all to the good tutoring I received.

RAY   *[Waiting for the applause to recede]* There's a moral to this story, folks. Hard work always pays dividends. Nice job, Don!

Two days later Ray sits in his classroom alone after school, working on his lesson plans. Jim Turpin walks into the room quietly with a serious look on his face.

RAY   *[Looking up]* Hi, Jim. What's the matter? You look like you've just lost your best friend.

JIM   No, but we have lost a good friend of yours.

RAY   *[Stunned]* What do you mean?

JIM   I hate to be the one to tell you this, Ray, but one of your students was killed in an automobile accident just off the school grounds—Don McCabe.

RAY   *[Stricken]* Oh, God, no! What happened?

JIM   It was a drunken driving accident right after school was out. Mike Mason was driving, and Don, Billy, Tyrone and two girls were in the car. They plowed right into a van with four cheerleaders and a mom who was driving. Two of the cheerleaders and Don were killed. Mike, Billy, and Tyrone were barely scratched.

RAY   Poor Don! And he seemed to be making such progress.

JIM   Maybe academically, but he just hung around with the wrong crowd.

RAY   Do you know if Don was drunk?

JIM   No, I don't.

RAY   Jim, I've got to ask you something and I want an honest answer.

JIM   Sure, Ray.

RAY   Jim, I know that hindsight is always better than foresight, but surely there must have been something I could have done to have kept this thing from happening. Are there people in the school system or in state agencies that I should have involved, instead of trying to handle this myself? Should I have tried to talk to Don's parents? And what, if anything, should I try to do about Mike, Billy, and Tyrone? What is a teacher like me suppose to do in a situation like this, Jim?

Information Compiled by Mr. McBride from School Cumulative Records

Student	School Lunch Eligibility	Parent(s)/ Guardian Present in Household	Parents' Occupations	Parents' Education	No. of Siblings	Cumulative G.P.A
Don McCabe	No	Mother, Father	Salesman (F) Sales Clerk (M)	12th 12th	2	2.23
Billy Reardon	Yes	Mother	Waitress (M)	11th	3	1.07
Mike Mason	Yes	Mother, Father	Construction Worker (F) Housewife (M)	10th 12th	4	1.21
Tyrone King	Yes	Guardian (Aunt)	House Cleaning (G)	5th	5	0.78

QUESTIONS

1. What are the causes of drug usage in adolescence? What are the drugs of choice? Do gender differences exist? At what age does usage begin?

2. What role do the home and parents play in drug usage? What are the most effective programs for helping drug users?

3. What state and federal agencies provide assistance in the case of drug usage? What community assistance is available? What personnel in the school system normally work with drug users? At what grade level should such assistance begin?

4. What student characteristics are the best predictors of drug usage? How closely related are SES, race, ethnicity, family size, family dysfunctionality, school achievement, and I.Q. to drug usage? Are students who are "at risk" of dropping out of school more likely to be drug users?

5. What signs indicate that a student has a drug or alcohol problem? What signs did Ray respond to? How effectively did Ray handle the situation? What should he have done differently?

6. How has Don's home environment affected his behavior with regard to alcohol and drugs? Have Tyrone's neighborhood norms regarding the availability and sale of drugs affected the other three boys and their girlfriends as well? What can be done about such neighborhoods?

7. What would be the most effective intervention with the boys' parents? Who should handle the intervention? What role should Ray play?

8. What is the most effective role that the school's administration, faculty and students can play in reducing the consumption of alcohol and drugs? How effective are drug education courses and speakers? Should tobacco be considered a drug?

9. At which of Kohlberg's stages of moral development does Don seem to be operating? What about Mike, Billy, and Tyrone? How can the stage of moral reasoning be raised?

10. At what level of Maslow's need hierarchy do Don, Mike, Billy, and Tyrone seem to be operating? How could Ray have taken this into consideration in working with them?

11. What, if anything, should Ray do to help Mike, Billy, and Tyrone? What is the appropriate role for a teacher to play in such cases? What does it mean to say that a teacher should serve as an "information and referral agent?"

PART VI
CONDITIONS OF WORK

C A S E **26**

PLAN OR BE PLANNED FOR

B radley Middle School is located in the city of Patton in a southern state. Patton has a population of 85,000, and BMS draws from an attendance area that is 73 percent white, 25 percent African–American, and 2 percent Hispanic. The school is relatively new, with a physical plant that was built just three years ago.

Keri Larson is a beginning teacher who graduated from the College of Education at a large university about 40 miles away. She sits in the office of the building principal, James Downes, discussing arrangements for a field trip that she wishes to take involving her eighth-grade science classes.

MR. DOWNES   What did you say the purpose of the field trip is again, Keri?

KERI   We want to help the kids learn how to identify edible plants, to increase their survival skills. Sherri *[a social studies teacher at Bradley]* will be working with part of them to increase their awareness of environmental problems resulting from all the construction around Possum Hollow.

MR. DOWNES   Yes, I remember how wild Possum Hollow used to be when I was a kid growing up here. Boy, has all that changed!

KERI   Yes, exactly, Mr. Downes.

MR. DOWNES   So, I'll need to get subs for both you and Sherri for a full day. *[Pause as he writes]* I've already lined up the bus, Keri. Ray Grimes will be your driver.

KERI   Good.

MR. DOWNES   Now, Keri, Ray tells me that the bus has a capacity of 65 students. Is that going to do it?

KERI   Yes. I have 31 from one class and 29 from the other. That's 59, so we'll be O.K.

MR. DOWNES   Have you gotten back signed permission slips from all the parents?

KERI   I have all but five, and those five promise to get them into me right away.

MR. DOWNES   Be sure they do, now. They're important.

KERI   Do they really protect you if anything goes wrong?

MR. DOWNES   Yes and no. A parent can't really sign away any rights guaranteed under the law, but it does show that you're doing some planning and involving the parents in the process.

KERI   Oh.

MR. DOWNES   Now, Keri, that's a lot of students. Do you have enough sponsors lined up to supervise them? You know how wild they can get on a field trip if you don't have the people to keep them in line.

KERI   Oh, yes. I've gotten ten parents, most of them men, lined up, in addition to Sherri, Ray, and me.

MR. DOWNES   Now, Keri, don't expect Ray to help once they're off the bus. He's just the driver. *[Pause]* Keri, if you have 59 students plus 12 adults, how are you going to get them all on a bus with a seating capacity of 65?

KERI   *[Frowning]* Well, I guess we'll have to get some of the parents to drive their cars.

MR. DOWNES   No, that won't do, Keri. You all need to be together at all times. That's important. *[Pause]* I'll tell you what. I'm going to ask Ray to try to get one of the big school buses that can hold 84. I don't think there will be any problem with that, so you can count on it unless I let you know otherwise. *[Pause]* Do you really need Sherri to go along too? That's two subs all day, you know.

KERI   Oh, yes, Mr. Downes. I definitely need her.

MR. DOWNES   *[Interrupting]* But her area is social studies. How can she help you?

KERI   Her interests have been environmental issues for a long time. We were Girl Scout leaders together for a long time and she really knows the environmental problems in Possum Hollow. She'll lead one group and I'll lead the other.

MR. DOWNES   Well, all right then, Keri, but make sure that you and Sherri keep a firm hand on those kids.

KERI   *[Smiling]* We will. Thanks so much for your help, Mr. Downes.

Keri is discussing the field trip with her second-period eighth-grade science class the next day.

KERI   *[Animated]* Mr. Downes is going to get us one of the big buses so both classes can go. Yes, Barry?

BARRY   *[Frowning]* Do we have to go with the third-period class? Why can't we go by ourselves? They are a bunch of creeps in there!

KERI   *[Smiling]* Why, Barry! I had no idea there are so many weird students in the third-period class. As I recall, they did better than this class on the last exam. *[Moans and protests]* Yes, Reba?

REBA   Well, why do they want to go?

KERI   For the same reason this class does. They want to learn how to increase their survival skills and become more aware of mankind's increasing encroachments upon nature.

REBA   *[Blurting out]* Right! More likely they just want to cause trouble. They're a bunch of boozers and potheads, to quote my dad. *[Chorus of agreement]*

KERI   *[Raising her voice]* All right, people! Now they have as much right to go as you do. Mr. Downes, Ms. Reardon, and I have put a lot of work into this and I'd appreciate it you'd try to get along with the third-period class for one day!

BARRY   We will, but will they try to get along with us?

KERI   That's enough, Barry! Now Barry and Reba, I still don't have your signed parent permission forms, do I? If you don't get them into me soon you won't have to worry about the third-period class at all that day! *[Moans]* Yes, Melanie?

MELANIE   Ms. Larson, I have a friend that almost went crazy when I told him about our field trip! His name is Troy, and he believes that all these earth changes are going to happen in the next few years and we've got to learn about edible plants and things like that if we're going to survive!

KERI   Well, I'd say he's a bright guy, Melanie. I guess I agree with him.

MELANIE   Is there any way he can go along, Ms. Larson? I know he'd get a lot out of it and he'd appreciate it so much!

KERI   Well, I don't know. We only have, let's see, I think it's 85 seats and we have 59 students plus 12 adults, let's see, 71—yes, I guess we can take one more, if its that important to him. But only if it's OK with his parents and teachers. I'm not going to get into that! And he'll have to get his parents to sign a permission slip. Yes, Marsha.

MARSHA   Ms. Larson, I have this really good friend, Lorrie, and she's really a nature freak. She's just die for a chance to go on a trip like this!

It is Thursday evening of the third week in April. The field trip is the next day. Keri sits in the living room of her home talking to her long-time friend, Sherri Reardon, a social studies teacher at Bradley who is co-sponsor of the field trip.

KERI   It's just not working, Sherri! Everything is just falling apart! Frank *[Keri's fiancee]* got sick on me and five of the parents have backed out!

SHERRI   Keri, the kids are going to be so disappointed if you cancel out! This field trip is all I've heard about at school this week!

KERI   But Sherri, it will just be you and me and four parents supervising all those kids!

SHERRI   Look, Keri, we'll just have to get them organized like we used to in the Girl Scouts. You and I will take the lead, and we'll put one parent in the middle of each group and one bringing up the rear for each group. We'll just explain the situation to the kids and tell them that we need their help. They're good kids! They'll cooperate!

KERI   Do you think so? Oh, I hope you're right!

It is 6:30 A.M. the next morning. The bus has arrived. The students mill around in a group at the side of the big bus, while Keri and Sherri stand apart talking to one another as they prepare to check on last-minute details and begin the boarding of the bus. Ray Grimes, the driver stands in the main doorway of the bus preventing boarding until Keri gives the word.

KERI   *[Whispering]* Lord, Sherri, can you believe it! Only two parents! Mr. Johnson and Ms. Parmalee didn't even bother to call and say they weren't coming!

SHERRI   I know it. We'll just have to go with what we have!

KERI   *[Shouting]* Would Barry, Reba, Sarah, Jerry Joe, and Sam—Sam Crittenden that is—please come over here a minute. *[Five students walk over to Keri and Sherri.]* People, I need your signed permission forms.

REBA   Please, Ms. Larson, my parents said its OK for me to go, but my father lost the form! Please let me go! It's O.K. with them, I promise! *[Other students chorus a similar response.]*

KERI   *[Looking at Sherri]* Lord! What do you think!?

SHERRI   *[Hesitantly]* I don't know! It's your call, Keri.

KERI   Well, I should have collected them before now, so I guess it's my fault as well as theirs. Mr. Downes said they really don't give you any legal protection anyhow.

KERI   *[Loudly to students]* All right! Do all five of you promise that your parents gave verbal permission for you to go? I want all the other students to hear your answer. *[A "yes" choral response.]* I can't hear you! *[All shout "yes" loudly.]* All right. Everybody get on the bus. *[Students and two parents board the bus as Ray moves to the driver's seat. Keri and Sherri get on last, next to the driver.]*

SHERRI   *[Standing up and looking toward the back of the bus.]* We can't start until you three sit down.

KERI   *[Standing up]* I can't believe it. Count the number of people, Sherri, will you?

SHERRI   *[Counting]* There's 87 counting you and me.

KERI   *[Agitated]* That doesn't make sense! This bus holds 86 people!

RAY   I'm afraid not, Ms. Larson. Its maximum load is 84. I can't carry 87 people. It's against the law.

KERI   *[Angry]* Now Ray, don't you become a problem too! You don't know how much Sherri and I have gone through! (Begins to cloud up.) If three people have to get off to make things legal, you decide which ones and tell them, Ray!

RAY   *[Gently]* Now, Ms. Larson, you know I can't do that! I'll tell you what. I'm just going to act like I didn't hear what Ms. Reardon said about how many. Let's just go!

KERI   *[Smiling wanly]* Thanks, Ray. *[To three students.]* You three will have to sit down somewhere or not go with us! Your choice! *[Boy sits on floor, two girls sit on boys' laps.]* All right! Let's go!

The bus arrives at a dirt road on the edge of Possum Hollow. Keri has all the kids get off the bus and she and Sherri divide them into the two groups that had been determined in advance. Keri and Sherri stand apart from the two groups talking.

KERI   *[Angrily]* Lord, Sherri, what a bunch of brats! I can't believe it! (Turns to address students.) Now listen, people! I don't mind telling you that we really didn't appreciate your behavior on the bus coming over here! All you did was argue, fight, and molest one another the whole time! Now if this is the way you're going to behave today, let's just head back now!

STUDENT   We're sorry, Ms. Larson! We'll behave! *[Chorus of agreement.]*

KERI   *[Turning to Sherri]* I hope so! *[Turning back to students.]* Listen up then. We really don't have enough adult help today, so we need your cooperation. I'll lead the edible plants group down that path *[pointing]* and I'll ask Mr. Normandy *[a parent]* to bring up the rear. Mrs. Reardon will lead the environmental group down that path *[pointing]* and Mrs. Simonetti *[parent]* will bring up the rear of that group. *[Pause]* Now please stay with your group and don't get separated. We'll all meet back here at noon and eat lunch together in that clearing. *[Students express surprise.]* Yes, Mr. Grimes has food and a table stored in the luggage area of the bus and I think you'll be surprised at what it is.

STUDENT   Pizza!

KERI   *[Laughing]* No, not pizza but I guarantee you'll like it. After we eat we'll discuss what we've learned today and then we'll start back. (Raises voice) Now remember this! We must start back at 2 P.M. sharp! Yes, Raymond?

RAYMOND   Ms. Larson, what if we have to, well, you know, go to the bathroom?

KERI   *[Smiling]* Well, you'll just have to separate from your group briefly, Raymond, and go behind a tree or something. There are no portable toilets here, I'm afraid. *[One female student says "Yuk," and Keri ignores her.]* Now remember people, stay with your group!

Keri and Sherri's groups go down separate paths. As the two teachers stop at various points, point out items of interest, lecture about each, and answer student questions, each groups spreads out more and more. Some of the students sneak away from the main group quietly and move into the woods. About 45 minutes after Keri's group started down the path, Keri is in the middle of explaining how to eat an edible plant she has pointed out. A core group of sixteen students, mostly females, stay very close to her and hang on her every word. Suddenly, one student, Bob, runs from out of the woods right up to where Keri is standing and shouts her name.

BOB   *[Excitedly]* Ms. Larson! Ms. Larson!

KERI   What's the matter, Bob?! What's wrong?

BOB   It's Steve Shea! He fell out of a tree and he's hurt bad! He broke his arm for sure! You can see the bone! And he can't walk!

KERI   Oh, my God! What was he doing in a tree?! Where is he?

BOB   *[Pointing]* Way over there! Hurry! I'll take you there! *[Entire group follows Bob through the woods to where Steve lies lying in agony on the ground under a tree. His girlfriend, Sharon, is bending down trying to help him as another boy and girl stand around helplessly watching.]*

SHARON   *[Crying]* Oh, Ms. Larson, help him. He's hurt bad!

KERI   *[Both furious and terrified]* My lord, Sharon, how did . . . ? *[Calming down.]* Bob, I want you to run to the bus and get Mr. Grimes. Tell him to bring a blanket to make a stretcher with.

SHARON   Should we move him? Can't we call an ambulance?

KERI   How Sharon? There's no phone out here. No, we've got to get him back to the
       bus and drive him in ourselves, at least until we can get help. Barry?
BARRY   Yes, Ms. Larson?
KERI   Barry, I want you to go find Ms. Reardon's group and tell her what's happened.
       Tell her to meet us back at the bus as fast as she can. O.K.?
BARRY   Yes, Ms. Larson. *[Runs off.]*

Ray joins Keri's group and he and two of the boys make a stretcher for Steve. They
slowly carry him, moaning and crying, back to the bus, which Sherri's group has already boarded. Keri and Sherri get the rest of the students on board and sit up front to
try to comfort Steve, who is stretched out on a pile of blankets in the aisle. His girlfriend, Sharon, sits in a seat just above him crying.

KERI   *[Whispering to Sherri]* My, God, Sherri, can you believe this? All we wanted to
       do was have a simple field trip!
SHERRI   *[Tearing up]* I know! I can't believe. . . . *[Suddenly a girl sitting in the back of
       the bus moves away from the boy she was sitting with and begins to shout obscenities
       at him.]*
KERI   *[Angrily shouting]* What's going on back there?! Don't we have enough trouble
       without . . . Melanie, is that you?!
MELANIE   *[Shouting and crying]* Yes, Ms. Larson! He raped me!
KERI   *[Stunned]* What! Who raped you?! You were just sitting next to him. How
       could he . . .
MELANIE   *[Interrupting and crying]* Back in the woods! Troy raped me!
KERI   Troy! Who's Troy?
TROY   *[Holding up his hand]* I'm Troy, Ms. Larson, and I didn't rape her! She wanted
       to have sex.
MELANIE   *[Shouting]* He's a damned liar!
TROY   *[Calmly]* Believe me, Ms. Larson, all we did was smoke a little pot and have
       sex. I didn't rape her.
MELANIE   I hate you, you. . . .
KERI   My God! Don't we have enough trouble without this! You two just stay away
       from one another and we'll sort this out later!

It is the next day, and Keri and Sherri sit in Mr. Downes office with the door
closed. He speaks to Keri with controlled anger.

MR. DOWNES   Keri, you should never have let that group get on the bus! You used
       terrible judgment! I can't tell you how disappointed I am in both of you! *[Both
       teachers hang their heads.]* I just got off the phone with the superintendent. Steve
       Shea's parents are threatening to sue, and the girl who says she was raped—
       Melanie Larrison, is it?—
KERI   Yes.

MR. DOWNES   Well, her parents have called the police. Both parties will accuse you of negligence. And, something you didn't know. Do you know a Mark Lotz?

KERI   *[Surprised]* Yes, he's in my third-period class.

MR. DOWNES   Well, it seems that you pulled off and left him behind. He had to walk and finally hitchhiked his way back home. His parents are furious!

KERI   *[Sobbing]* Perfect!

MR. DOWNES   Keri, crying won't help! Three members of the school board have called here already and are asking for facts about what went on. You've got to get yourselves together and do some explaining! I don't know how this is going to come out! *[Pause]* I've notified George Burkett, the union rep, about what's happened. He'll meet with both of you after school tomorrow in your room, Keri.

It the next day after school. George Burkett, the portly, aging, white-haired local teachers' union representative walks calmly into Keri's classroom and introduces himself to Keri and Sherri. They form their chairs into a circle to talk.

KERI   George, I'm so glad to see you! I'm in big trouble and don't have anyone to turn to except for Sherri here, and I'm afraid that I've gotten her into as much trouble as I am!

GEORGE   *[Smiling]* Well, things aren't all bad, Keri. You both had the good sense to join the union, and that means that you are automatically covered for malpractice for up to a million dollars.

KERI   Really! That's wonderful!

GEORGE   Not entirely. This is your first year of teaching and you don't have tenure. They can let you go without giving a reason. Sherri has tenure, so it would be very hard for them to get rid of her.

SHERRI   But it can be done?

GEORGE   Tenure really guarantees you due process, Sherri. They'd have to prove you were negligent.

SHERRI   How do they do that?

GEORGE   Well, I'm not an attorney, but I've been involved in enough cases over the years to know what goes on. You see, as a teacher you stand in *loco parentis*, or in place of the parents, in case of a situation like this field trip. Therefore you're responsible for them. Generally, the court uses the test of foreseeability, I believe they call it, in cases like this. What that basically comes down to is whether or not you tried to anticipate the risks and situations that might come up and planned for them. All this starts, of course, by informing the parents and getting them to sign permission slips.

KERI   George, I just wish I had known all this before we went on this field trip! I sure would have done things differently!

GEORGE   Keri, since you don't have tenure, I don't honestly know whether you'll end up losing your job over this or not. But if you do, I think from what I've heard about your teaching ability, you'll end up as a teacher somewhere else. I always say that after you make mistakes, all you can do is learn from them. So tell me,

Keri what have you learned from all this? If you had to do this field trip all over again, what would you do differently?

School Board of Patton County Curriculum Division, Parental Field Trip Permission

School _____ Teacher: _____ Grade: _____
Date: _____
Permission is requested for your son/daughter to go on a field trip to:

_____
with his/her class on _____, 19 _____.
We will leave the school at _____ ( ) a.m. ( ) p.m., and return to the school
at approximately _____ ( ) a.m. ( ) p.m.
*Emergency phone: Daytime _____ Evening _____ Other _____
If your son/daughter has permission to go on this trip please sign below:
        Please accept this form as a consent signature for a physician or hospital staff
to give emergency treatment of an injury or illness to my son or daughter if medical
attention is needed.

METHOD OF TRAVEL

School Bus _____
City Bus _____   _____
Walking_____   Student Name (please print)
Private Vehicle _____
Driver:_____   _____
Other: _____   Signature of Parent of Guardian
                (Specify)

*Your student cannot go on the trip unless emergency phone number(s) are listed.

QUESTIONS

1. What mistakes did Keri make in planning and executing this field trip? How could she have handled these things differently? Make a list of things that Keri should have done in planning for a field trip.

2. Would you like to work for a principal like Mr. Downes? Why or why not? Would you describe his administrative style as one of supporting, coaching, delegating, or directing? How supportive will he be of Keri and Sherri when their case is dealt with by the school system?

3. What educational objectives does Keri seem to be pursuing in arranging the field trip? What curricular purposes do field trips serve? If the field trip had worked out well, what would have been some appropriate follow-up activities in the classroom? In general, what educational values do field trips serve?

4. From the standpoint of school law, what kind of protection do parent permission slips provide the teacher? What does it mean to say that the teacher stands in loco parentis when teaching students? What is the test of foreseeability and how would it apply to teacher activities such as a field trip? What are malpractice and negligence as applied to teaching?

5. How do you feel about teachers' unions? Do they help or hinder teaching from becoming a profession? In what areas are they most effective? least effective? Why? Why do teachers' unions exist in the first place?

6. What does it mean to call teaching a profession? What are the characteristics of a profession? How is Keri's job different from that of a physician or attorney in private practice?

7. What is tenure as it applies to teaching? What does it mean to guarantee a teacher due process in deciding whether or not a teacher should be fired due to such grounds as malpractice, incompetence, or moral turpitude?

8. How does Maslow's motivational need hierarchy help explain the motives of key persons in this case, such as Keri or Mr. Downes? How would schools have to change in order to become institutions that foster self-actualization in students?

9. What classroom management model could Keri have used in developing and conducting the field trip, so as to avoid the problems that occurred? How could these procedures have grown out of, or been integrated with, those used in the classroom? For example, how might she have used contingency management techniques from behavior modification theory?

10. What is parent involvement in education and what parent involvement techniques are most highly related to student success in school? What parent involvement procedures might Keri have used in increasing parent support for and participation in the field trip? How many parents is it desirable to involve on a field trip and what are the most effective ways to use their help?

WELCOME ABOARD!

erry Russell is beginning his first year of teaching science at Fletcher Middle School. FMS is located in a large urban area in the eastern part of the United States and draws from an attendance district that is 60 percent white, 25 percent African–American, 10 percent Hispanic, and 5 percent other racial/ethnic groups. All the teachers in the city's school system are meeting in the large auditorium of Woodrow Wilson High School to participate in the annual welcoming and orientation meeting that kicks off the teachers' two-week pre-planning session prior to the opening of school.

Terry has a B.S. degree in science education from the College of Education of the state's large land-grant university and is eager to begin his first year of teaching. He has already made plans to begin work on his master's degree the following summer. Terry is married and has three small children, the oldest child being five years old.

As Terry enters the auditorium, he feels quite alone, since he doesn't see anybody he knows. He accepted the job without visiting either the school or the school district. While the personnel office of the school district wasn't especially helpful in helping Terry and his family find a house, they at least advised him on which neighborhoods to avoid. However, he hasn't had a chance to meet any of his fellow teachers yet. Terry chooses a seat near the front of the auditorium.

TERRY   Is this seat taken?

JOHN   No. Help yourself.

TERRY   [Sticking out his hand] I'm Terry Russell. I'm a new science teacher at Fletcher Middle School.

JOHN   [Shaking Terry's hand] Hi, Terry. I'm John Newell. I've taught mathematics here at Wilson for eleven years. Is this your first year?

TERRY   Why, yes it is. How did you know?

JOHN   [Smiling] Just a lucky guess.

TERRY   [Smiling] It shows that much, huh?

JOHN   [Smiling] Not at all, Terry. You just look young and you aren't sitting with any of the Fletcher teachers.

TERRY   To tell you the truth, I don't know any. I haven't had the opportunity to meet any yet.

JOHN   You'll find most of them at the back of the auditorium. [Pointing]

Terry   Really? Why is that?

John   I don't really know. So they can duck out without getting noticed, I suppose.

Terry   *[Pointing to a number of people sitting in chairs up on the stage.]* Are those the building principals?

John   Yes, and other school district administrators.

Terry   Which one is my principal?

John   *[Smiling]* You haven't met your principal yet? Well, I guess that's not too surprising.

Terry   What do you mean?

John   They call your principal the ghost. Old Bixby is never around, and *[looking intently at the stage]* it would appear today is no exception. I don't see him up there anywhere.

Terry   *[Frowning]* You mean he's not accessible to his teachers?

John   I'd say that's a fair statement! His family has long had a lot of political clout. Rumor has it that he hates being principal and so he's around as little as possible.

Terry   That's terrific!

[At that point, Dr. Chester Gunn steps up to the podium to begin the meeting.]

Dr. Gunn   Welcome, ladies and gentlemen. For those of you who might not know me, I'm Chester Gunn, the superintendent of schools. Let me begin by introducing the administrative staff of our school district that are seated on the stage with me. Then I'd like to take a few minutes to acquaint you with some of the new programs that we have underway in the school district for this school year.

It is the afternoon of the first day of pre-planning. The morning was spent in the school library where Jim Rafferty, an assistant principal, led the meeting. When the new teachers were introduced, there was rather quiet applause. When Rafferty introduced Terry he mentioned that he was replacing Ray Hanna, who had retired.

After the meeting Terry met with Mr. Rafferty as instructed, in order to receive his teaching and room assignments. Rafferty was friendly to Terry and said to let him know if he could be of assistance in any way. Since Rafferty's office was adjacent to the principal's office, Terry walked into that office and up to the desk. An older woman, Martha Jamison, was clearly the boss, as she gave orders to two younger women. After a while she looked up at Terry without smiling.

Martha   Can I help you?

Terry   *[Smiling]* You sure can. I'm Terry Russell, the new science teacher. I just met with Mr. Rafferty and he suggested that I come in here and get my supplies before I go to my room.

Martha   *[Icily]* Well, Mr. Russell, as you can see we're really very busy right now. When we have some time I'll have one of the girls get your supplies together. I'll send someone down to let you know when they're ready and you can come in and get them.

TERRY   *[Controlled anger]* Well, I'd appreciate that very much. I'm going to need my
supplies so I can get ready for my classes. Do you have any idea when you'll be
able to help me?

MARTHA   Not really! Like I said, I'll let you know!

TERRY   Let me ask you this, Ms. Jamison. Mr. Rafferty mentioned that I might be able
to get some information pulled from student records to help me understand my
students' abilities better. Was he right in saying that I should see you about that?

MARTHA   *[Angrily]* He knows better than that! We don't have time to put that kind of
information together for every teacher who wants it! We wouldn't be able to get
anything else done around here! You'll have to go to the counseling office about
that!

> *[Terry walks out of the office very rapidly so he won't explode in anger.]*

It is the first day of classes. Terry has fifth period for planning. He walks into the teachers' lounge in order to get to know some of his fellow teachers better. Five teachers are
already seated in the lounge and a sixth walks in behind him and introduces himself.
The other teachers remain seated.

TERRY   Hi, I'm Terry Russell, the new science teacher.

GERTRUDE   Hello, Terry, I'm Gertrude Ayres. I teach English. And these people are
Lester Felling, mathematics, Charles Einhardt, science like yourself, Donna
Chalos, social studies, Bill Tregor, geography, and Leroy Johnson, physical
education.

> *[Terry shakes each of their hands in turn as he is introduced. They all remain
> seated. Gertrude and Terry take seats.]*

GERTRUDE   As you can see we have a very culturally diverse faculty.

TERRY   *[Noting that Donna is Hispanic and Leroy is African–American]* Yes, I see.

CHARLES   *[In a serious tone]* So, Terry. You're replacing Ray Hanna? They gave you
Ray's room?

TERRY   Yes, that's right.

CHARLES   Isn't that just like Rafferty? Always trying to build his power base by getting
leverage on the new teachers.

TERRY   What do you mean?

CHARLES   Ray's room is the largest, best-equipped room in the school. I've been here
fourteen years, Terry. By rights he should have given that room to me, but no,
he gives it to you. Now you owe him. He'll point that out to you sometime when
he needs something.

TERRY   *[Nonplussed]* I don't know anything about all that!

BILL   You're going to have to learn fast to survive around here, Terry. You're just
lucky that your planning period is the same as ours. *[Laughter and statements of
agreement.]* So, Terry, have you joined the union yet?

GERTRUDE   Of course he hasn't, Bill. They just mentioned the union during pre-
planning. They haven't even put the membership information and applications
in the new teachers' boxes yet.

BILL Well, let me give you a little free advice, Terry. Join as soon as you can. It's the only protection you've got around here.

TERRY Tell me about it, Bill. Where I grew up and went to school, teachers generally didn't belong to a union. Mostly blue-collar workers joined unions.

CHARLES *[Snorting]* That might be fine for small towns, but not here. Don't let people like Rafferty feed you that line that teachers are professionals like doctors and only blue-collar workers join unions. Think about it. Doctors, dentists, and lawyers have their own private practice. They are in a private, fee-taking position. They don't have school boards and superintendents telling them what to do. Teachers, on the other hand, are paid out of tax revenues and are part of the socialized end of the economy. They have bosses who tell them when and what they're going to teach, when they can go to lunch, and what extra-curricular activities they're going to supervise. Believe me, we're more blue collar than we'd like to admit, and we need the protection of a union just as much as a blue-collar worker.

BILL That's right. We've all been here a long time and remember what it was like before we unionized. The administration had turned teachers into slaves. They had us coming back at night and doing unpaid labor like selling and taking tickets for school events. And the high school teachers had it worse than we did. Unionization ended all that stuff. *[Nods of agreement all around]*

TERRY I hadn't heard about all that. I guess I experienced a little of that myself on the first day of pre-planning.

GERTRUDE What happened, Terry?

TERRY Well, Rafferty told me to go see Martha Jamison in the principal's office to pick up a plan book, grade book, red marking pencils, and other supplies that I needed, and you would have thought that I was putting her out or something. She was totally uncooperative, to say the least. Made me feel real welcome!

CHARLES *[Sharing smiles with the other teachers]* That's sounds like our Martha, all right. She can be a real witch until you start to give it back to her. Then watch her melt. You just have to let her know that you're not going to put up with her crap. Just because Bixby's never here doesn't mean that she's the boss.

TERRY Yes, and what's that business about Bixby never being there? Believe it or not, a teacher from another school told me that and that he was called the ghost. *[All teachers laugh aloud.]*

CHARLES Sounds like you're a quick learner, kid. Frank Bixby has a lot of political clout because of his brother and family connections. *[Looks at his watch]* He's probably out playing golf at the West Side Country Club right now. Rafferty really does all the work and runs the school. Bixby gets a free ride and nobody says anything.

BILL Which is good for Rafferty, too. If you bring Rafferty a serious problem that he doesn't want to handle, he tells you that you have to take it up with the principal. Since Bixby's hardly ever here, that means nothing will get done about it. If you would happen to catch Bixby in his office, he'll just tell you that that's part of Rafferty's job and you'll have to take it up with him. It's the old catch-22.

TERRY   (Frowning) Boy, you people make this place sound like a very unhappy work-place.

CHARLES   *[Smiling]* You don't know the half of it, kid! Just stick with us and we'll steer you right! And first of all, get that union membership form filled out and turned in to Bill.

TERRY   To Bill?

CHARLES   Yes, he's our local rep.

It is Friday of the same week. Terry has had a problem with the temperature in his classroom due to a broken thermostat, which he reported to Mr. Rafferty on Tuesday. Rafferty said that he'd tell the custodians to fix it. Terry decided to walk down to the basement of the school and talk to the head custodian, Fred Wilson. Fred is the only non-Hispanic white custodian in the building. On the way down to the basement, Terry walks up to another custodian to get directions.

TERRY   Pardon me. I'm Mr. Russell, a science teacher. Can you tell me where Mr. Wilson's office is?

CUSTODIAN   *[Interrupting his work]* Down on the next level, but you can't go down there.

TERRY   Why not?

CUSTODIAN   Insurance reasons. No teachers or students are supposed to go down there.

TERRY   Well, can you tell me how I can see Mr. Wilson?

CUSTODIAN   Nope. Mr. Rafferty takes care of that.

TERRY   Thanks.

> *[Terry waits until the custodian goes back to his work and then quickly walks down the stairs to the bottom level. He soon sees a door marked HEAD CUSTODIAN and, since the door is open, walks up to the room and looks in. He sees one man in a white shirt giving orders to three others, one of whom is an African–American female. The man in the white shirt turns and looks at Terry.]*

TERRY   Are you Mr. Wilson?

MR. WILSON   Yes, I am. Who are you?

TERRY   I'm Terry Russell, the new science teacher up in Room 311. I wanted to talk to you a minute, if I could, when you're through.

MR. WILSON   *[Turning back to the three workers]* OK, any more questions? *[Pause]* Then let's do it that way then. *[They leave and Wilson walks over to Terry.]* How can I help you, Mr. Russell?

TERRY   I was wondering if Mr. Rafferty had had time to let you know about my thermostat problem in 311?

MR. WILSON   Nope. Need fixing?

TERRY   It sure does. It's very hard to teach in there.

MR. WILSON   We'll take care of it, but in the future I'd appreciate it if you'd relay your requests through Mr. Rafferty.

TERRY   I did, Mr. Wilson, but the message apparently didn't get down to you. I told Mr. Rafferty last Tuesday and nothing got done.

MR. WILSON   *[Angrily]* Mr. Russell, did you serve in the army?

TERRY   No. I haven't.

MR. WILSON   I didn't think so. One of the things you learn in the army is that it works better when you get your orders from one person. Around here that's Mr. Rafferty. I can't be taking orders from every teacher.

TERRY   *[Angrily]* I believe I explained that I tried to go through channels and it didn't work! What's more, Mr. Wilson, I not only have a broken thermostat, I don't have the minimum equipment that I need to do a decent job of teaching. I don't have enough chalk, most of the audio-visual and laboratory equipment is broken, and. . . .

MR. WILSON   *[Interrupting angrily]* That's too bad, Mr. Russell! Like I said, tell Mr. Rafferty, not me! And what's more, my people tell me that the chairs in your classroom are always out of order. Other teachers try to help us out a bit by having their last-period classes put the chairs back in order. But I guess you're just not the type to try to cooperate with other people! Now I've got work to do!
[Goes into his office and shuts the door.]

It is one week later. Terry has given his third-period class time to work on an assignment. It is halfway through the period and he sits at his desk grading papers while he keeps one eye open for students who raise their hands in order to ask for assistance. He has noticed that the third-period English class across the hall has been consistently noisy since the first day of classes. He also noticed that the teacher, Juan Martinez, often leaves the class and returns during third period. Terry has heard Mr. Martinez frequently shouting at the class during class time as well. However, the noise was far enough away that Terry couldn't hear exactly what was being said or determine what was going on.

Terry gets up from his desk and walks to the door of his classroom to try to figure out the nature of Mr. Martinez's exceptionally loud shouting. He is able to see and overhear Mr. Martinez shout at a female student as the rest of the class sits in stunned silence watching.

MR. MARTINEZ   I'm just not going to put up with your lazy crap anymore, Marissa! You think that just because you have a great-looking body and are a female that you can turn in any kind of sloppy work you want to! Well, you can't! I'm going to treat you like any other lazy student! If you don't want to do any work in here, then you need to leave and get out on the street like the rest of the losers! And I'm sure you'll be able to use your good-looking body to survive very nicely out there, at least for a while! Then one day when you're older you'll lose your looks and will wish you had decided to stay in school and get your diploma! If this is the best you can do then get out!
[A female African–American student walks out of the classroom slowly, obviously upset and in tears. Terry walks out of his classroom and over to her.]

TERRY   I'm sorry. I know that you don't know me but I'm the teacher across the hall. I
just heard everything that happened to you. Are you OK?

MARISSA   [Crying] I just turned in a bad paper! He just hates me!

TERRY   [Puts his arm around her as they walk down the hall] What's your last name,
Marissa?

MARISSA   Jackson.

TERRY   Where are you going? Don't you want to go to the counseling office? Maybe
someone there can help!

MARISSA   Nobody can help! I guess I just better go home.

TERRY   Are you sure? Is there anything I can do?

       [Marissa just shakes her head no and continues walking slowly down the hall-
way sobbing uncontrollably. Terry watches her for a while, then walks angrily back
to his classroom.]

It is the end of the last period of the schoolday, and Terry walks down to the counseling office. A secretary looks up as Terry enters.

SECRETARY   Can I help you?

TERRY   Yes, I'm Terry Russell, the science teacher in Room 311. I need to see or get
an appointment with Marissa Jackson's counselor.

SECRETARY   Who?

TERRY   Marissa Jackson.

       [The secretary types Marissa's name into the computer and waits for the infor-
mation to come up.]

SECRETARY   Can you give me her social security number? We have three Marissa
Jacksons.

TERRY   Well, this one's in Mr. Martinez's third-period class.

SECRETARY   [Brings up class records] OK, that helps. Her counselor is Mr. Daggett.
[She gets up and goes to an office and has a conversation with the occupant and returns.] He'll see you now. Go on back.

       [Mr. Daggett walks out of his office, introduces himself and shakes Terry's
hand. He then motions him toward a chair and sits down behind his desk. He leaves
his office door open.]

MR. DAGGETT   How can I help you, Mr. Russell?

TERRY   I hope what I am about to share with you will be kept in confidence, Mr.
Daggett.

MR. DAGGETT   Of course.

       [Terry describes to Mr. Daggett the events that occurred outside his classroom.
Mr. Daggett listens but makes no comment.]

MR. DAGGETT   I see. So Marissa was obviously very upset when she left. I also gather
that you are very upset and that's why you came to see me.

TERRY   I'd say that's a pretty accurate summary.

MR. DAGGETT   This is your first year of teaching, isn't it?

Terry   Yes. That's right.

Mr. Daggett   Let me give you some advice, then. If I were you I wouldn't try to get involved in this situation. You just don't have enough information about what was going on there. You don't know anything about the relationship between Mr. Martinez and Marissa.

Terry   That's true, of course, but no matter what's happened in the past, I just don't think that a teacher should talk to a student like that! He was downright abusive.

Mr. Daggett   Be careful now. *Abuse* is a dangerous word, Mr. Russell. May I call you Terry?

Terry   Of course.

Mr. Daggett   Terry, it has been my experience that getting in the middle of situations like this is a bit like getting involved in a quarrel between a husband and his wife. As an outsider, you really don't know what dynamics are operating between them, and even if you manage to stop the quarrel somehow, they may both turn on you and resent the interference. The quarrel represents something different to them than it does to you.

Terry   I hear what you're saying, Mr. Daggett but . . .

Mr. Daggett   *[Interrupting]* Please call me Chet.

Terry   OK, thank you, Chet. Like I said before, I just don't think any teacher should yell at a student like that.

Mr. Daggett   Nor should a husband and wife yell at one another in public. But you know it happens.

Terry   Well, Chet, is there anything you can do as Marissa's counselor? Maybe you could talk to her.

Mr. Daggett   We're awfully busy right now with course changes and reports, but I'll discreetly look into the matter. I'll think of a pretext, maybe course scheduling, and get Marissa in here. I'll just ask her how everything's going and we'll see what happens.

Terry   Could you do that soon, Chet? You should have seen how upset she was and how hostile Martinez was to her. He practically called her a prostitute.

Mr. Daggett   As soon as I can, Terry. Most teachers don't realize how little time we counselors have for actual counseling work with students. Most of what we do is administrative. I probably spend more time at course scheduling and filling out forms than anything else. But don't worry about it, Terry. I'll take it from here. You've done your job and done it well, I might add. I think you'll make a fine teacher.

Terry sits in his favorite chair in the living room of his home that same evening. On his cordless phone he dials the home of John Newell, the math teacher at Wilson High School that he met at the teacher's orientation meeting at the beginning of the school year. So much has happened to Terry in the meantime that the meeting seems like it took place a long time ago.

JOHN   Hello?

TERRY   John, this is Terry Russell, the science teacher at Fletcher Middle School.

JOHN   Oh, yes, Terry. We met at the teachers' orientation meeting.

TERRY   John, are you busy now?

JOHN   No, not at all. I was just relaxing and watching a little TV. It's just an old movie that I've seen several times. Let me turn the set off. *[Pause]* So, Terry. How are things going?

TERRY   John, you can't believe all I've been through since that orientation meeting! Let me bring you up to date. I really need your advice!

   [For the next half hour Terry tells John about the major events in his professional life as a teacher.]

JOHN   Well, Terry, I knew you'd figure out the situation at Fletcher soon enough. When a principal like Bixby leaves a power vacuum, someone like Rafferty is bound to move in and fill it. Bixby needs Rafferty to do his job for him so he can spend his time as he likes. Rafferty is ambitious and his goal is to move up in the administrative hierarchy as fast as he can. His goal, and everybody in the school system knows it, is to become superintendent some day. Not necessarily in this school district, of course.

TERRY   And Martinez?

JOHN   Scum of the earth, Terry. A bad teacher. He has a reputation of trying to coerce good-looking young girls into having sex with him. Chet Daggett knows that.

TERRY   What about Daggett? Do you think he'll try to help Marissa?

JOHN   It's hard to say. Chet is ambitious too. He's using the position of guidance counselor as a stepping-stone to an assistant principalship. No doubt he wants to be principal of his own school one day.

TERRY   All that ambition is fine but what about students like Marissa? Don't these people like Rafferty and Daggett care about them?

JOHN   That's the sixty-four-thousand-dollar-question, isn't it, Terry? Why become a superintendent or a principal if you don't really want to help students? After all, isn't that what we're all here for? But I've noticed, Terry, that those noble sentiments too often get lost in the pursuit of money, power, and position. Chet might call her in and talk to her. He might even move her to another class. That won't cost him much effort. Then he'll let you know what he's done and you'll think he's great and will owe him one.

TERRY   What about Fred Wilson, the head custodian, and Martha Jamison, the principal's secretary. Why are they so hostile?

JOHN   They figure you are just a foot soldier, a teacher. You have no real power and they don't have to listen to you. They certainly don't have to put themselves out for you and do their jobs the way they should be done. *[Both men laugh.]* What you don't know is that Rafferty and Wilson are in-laws and Wilson owes his job to Rafferty. Wilson doesn't like his job or do it well, but at least it's an income with good fringe benefits and he has some people under him he can boss around. And he sure doesn't have to take any crap from a beginning teacher! *[Both laugh again.]*

TERRY   Is Martha an in-law of Rafferty too?

JOHN   No, she's just been there forever. She has played the game well. She's kept all she has learned about running the office, financial procedures, personnel policies, etc., to herself. She has made herself indispensable. Rafferty can't run the office without her and she sure isn't going to impart what she knows to a new trainee. Knowledge is power, Terry.

TERRY   Yes, I've heard that before.

JOHN   And Terry, watch that fifth-period union gang in the teachers' lounge, especially Charles Einhardt and Bill Tregor. They are just as power hungry in their own way. Now don't get me wrong! I'm not saying that teachers' unions are bad or that you shouldn't join ours. But unions provide access to power, and sometimes people like Tregor and Einhardt get into leadership positions. They are not much different than Rafferty in their own way.

TERRY   Well what do they want from me? What should I worry about?

JOHN   I'm afraid that you are just a raw recruit to them. They'll try to use you in any way that might benefit them. I really don't know what the union is up to at the moment, so it's hard to say.

TERRY   Well, John, all of this has been very enlightening, but very upsetting at the same time. Let me ask you something, John. Are all the schools in the school district like Fletcher Middle School?

JOHN   No, they're not, Terry. Most are better, but maybe one or two that I can think of are actually worse. Your big mistake, Terry, was in not getting more information before you took a job at Fletcher. I believe you told me that you took the job sight unseen. Isn't that right?

TERRY   Yes, it is.

JOHN   I'll bet you don't make that mistake again! And when you go for your job interview, be sure to talk to a lot of teachers, including those from other schools. *[Both laugh.]* How are your classes going, Terry?

TERRY   Oh, everything's just fine in the classroom. My problems are with things outside the classroom. I find that the kids at Fletcher are generally quite interested in science.

JOHN   I didn't figure you'd have much trouble in the classroom.

TERRY   John, I'm really upset. On the one hand, I ask myself how anyone would want to teach in a school like Fletcher. But on the other, who's going to help the students if all the teachers jump ship. John, do you think I should work on trying to get transferred to another school next year, or do you think I should stay at Fletcher and try to become a change agent?

Statement of School's Goals on the Wall of the Principal's Office at Fletcher Middle School

---

THE PURPOSE OF OUR SCHOOL IS TO:

1. Prepare our students for the world of work.
2. Discover and nurture our most creative and talented students.
3. Strengthen the moral and ethical values of our students.
4. Help our students become wise consumers.
5. Enlighten our students as to their rights and duties as citizens of a free democracy.
6. Encourage our students to make wise use of leisure time.
7. Develop in our students the ability to think rationally and to communicate their thoughts clearly.
8. Strengthen our students' respect for cultural, ethnic and racial differences.
9. Encourage in our students the appreciation of arts, music, and literature.
10. Develop our students' understanding of science and the nature of man.
11. Reinforce in our students the understanding of the conditions necessary for successful family life.
12. Develop our students' habits of good health and physical fitness.
13. Help our students make intelligent use of natural resources.
14. Prepare our students to think critically and become effective problem solvers.
15. Encourage our students to develop positive self concepts and effective human relations skills.

QUESTIONS

1. What are the characteristics of an effective school principal? What administrative leadership style is exhibited by Mr. Bixby and Mr. Rafferty: supporting, coaching, delegating or directing? What type of school climate have they helped create?

2. At which of Kohlberg's stages of moral development are the following people operating: (1) Mr. Martinez, (2) Mr. Daggett, (3) Mr. Rafferty, (4) Bill Tregor, and (5) John Newell? How does this help you to explain their behavior?

3. At which level of Maslow's need hierarchy do the following people seem to be primarily operating: (1) Fred Wilson, (2) Mr. Bixby, (3) Martha Jamison, (4) Charles Einhardt, and (5) Terry Russell? How does this help us understand their behavior?

4. From a social psychology perspective, what is power? What different kinds of power do Mr. Rafferty, Mr. Martinez, Fred Wilson, Martha Jamison, Bill Tregor, Marissa Jackson, Chet Daggett, and Terry Russell have? How is power lost and gained?

5. What are the characteristics of a profession? To what extent does teaching exhibit those characteristics? Do teachers' unions move teaching toward or away from professional status? Can and should teaching become a profession?

6. In an effective school, what type of role relations would exist between teachers, administrators, custodial staff, secretarial staff, and the counseling office? Why do less than ideal relations exist at Fletcher Middle School?

7. What are teacher stress and burnout? What are the primary sources of stress impacting on Terry at Fletcher Middle School? What coping styles best explain differences among teachers in handling stress?

8. What is teacher morale and what are the sources of high and low teacher morale? How is it measured? Does low teacher morale affect teacher effectiveness in the classroom?

9. What is the role of the guidance counselor in the school system? What role should the counselor play with regard to discipline problems? with regard to teacher malpractice? How appropriate were the courses of action proposed by Chet Daggett?

10. Examine the school climate from an operant conditioning perspective. What behaviors (teacher, administrative, staff) are being reinforced? Which ones are being punished? What are the reinforcers that are operating, and how should the pattern of reinforcement be changed?

11. From an observational learning perspective, what models are being imitated and why? What vicarious reward and punishment patterns are prevailing and why? How should these patterns be changed?

12. What are the elements of an effective job-seeking process for a teaching position? What kinds of questions should be asked about a prospective teaching position, and what people should the candidate for the position try to talk to?

13. What is nepotism? In what ways can it be detrimental to the effective functioning of a school system? What examples and effects of nepotism can you identify in this case?

14. What are conflict, conflict management, and assertiveness training? How might they apply to this case?

15. Teaching always occurs in a context (e.g., state, community, school system, school). As a result, a number of extra-classroom influences impinge on the classroom teaching process. A classroom teacher like Terry can do something to mitigate the effects of some of them but not all of them. Should Terry try to transfer to another school or should he stay and try to become a change agent? Or is it possible for him to insulate himself within his classroom from such external factors by just ignoring them and concentrating his efforts totally on doing a good job of teaching? If he chooses to move, is it easier or more difficult for a beginning teacher like Terry to move than a more experienced one like John Newell?

SIXTEEN TONS

S am Goodman is 21 years old, married, and his first child is on the way. He has just completed his B.S. degree in social studies education at State University. Sam is interviewing for an opening at Jackson Senior High School, which is located in a southern city of approximately 75,000 people. JHS has about 1,200 students in Grades 10–12 who are crowded into a physical plant built in 1948 to hold 1,000 students. The student population is approximately 70 percent white, 25 percent African–American, and 5 percent other.

The interview for the social studies position takes place in the office of the building principal, Jim Dunfey. Jim and Sam are joined by John Boyd, the assistant principal. All three are seated as they talk.

JIM   I asked John to join us today, Sam, because he's involved in all the interviewing we do here. We've known one another since the first grade and I've come to trust his judgment about people. *[Smiling]* After all, he had the good sense to choose me as a friend for all these years. *[All three men laugh.]*

JOHN   Where are you from, Sam?

SAM   Oh, I grew up in Farmington, about 40 miles from here. I can remember my parents driving over here to shop when I was just a kid.

JOHN   Yes, I've been through Farmington many times. Must be different growing up in a town that small.

SAM   Yes, but this whole area is home to me. When I finished my degree in teaching, I knew I wanted to come back to this area to teach.

JIM   To tell you the truth, that's why we're interested in you. We think that your credentials look real good, but the fact that you're from this area gives you the advantage of understanding the parents and students better. We think you're our man, Sam.

SAM   Thank you very much! That's good to hear. My wife also thanks you and my child to be thanks you as well! *[All three laugh.]*

JIM   Your wife is expecting? That's great!

SAM   Thanks. I just hope the child's healthy.

JOHN   I know what you mean.

SAM   Well, tell me about the job.

JIM   Sam, as you well know, these are hard economic times around here. This old building wasn't built to hold 1,200 students. The boys downtown keep cutting our budget. So the position that we're offering you will involve teaching a fairly heavy load of courses. But we just have no choice in that, Sam.

SAM   How heavy will my teaching load be?

JIM   Probably only five classes, but with maybe three preparations.

SAM   Well, I guess I can handle that OK.

JIM   Well, we appreciate your being willing to do it, Sam, and, of course, I'll try to cut you back to a more reasonable load as soon as the ole boys downtown will let me. *[Pause]* Oh, by the way, I forgot to mention that you'll need to help us out with one of our extra-curricular activities as part of your load. I usually don't ask new teachers to do that, but frankly, Sam, we're short on staff.

SAM   I'll do it. What activity do you want me to work with?

JIM   Oh, one of the student clubs. I'll let you know. *[Stands up and sticks out his hand.]* Welcome aboard, Sam.

JOHN   *[Smiling and shaking Sam's hand]* Glad to have you with us, Sam.

JIM   Now, do you remember where you fell on the salary schedule?

SAM   Yes, I do. Do I go back to Personnel now?

JIM   Yes, you do. I will have called them before you get there to let them know that we're giving the job to you.

JOHN   By the way, Sam, it isn't unusual for a new young teacher like yourself who is expecting a child to be interested in making some extra money.

SAM   I sure am!

JOHN   Do you like sports?

SAM   Sure.

JOHN   You may want to talk to our athletic director, Roy Williams, about working our ball games. We pay extra when you sell or take tickets or anything else that Roy needs for you to do.

SAM   Thanks. I'll look into that.

JOHN   And, as long as you're going back to Personnel anyhow, you might ask them to put you on the list for homebound teaching. You can pick up quite a bit of extra money that way.

SAM   *[Walking toward the door]* Thanks so much for everything, gentlemen. I'm sure that I'm going to enjoy it here at Jackson.

It is the first day of the teacher pre-planning session before classes actually begin. The day begins with a teachers' meeting in the school auditorium. Jim Dunfey, the principal, begins the meeting by welcoming the teachers to a new school year and then introducing the new teachers. Following this, Jim hands each teacher a teaching schedule.

JIM   As all of you old-timers know, I generally let you know at the end of one school year what you'll be teaching the following year. However, until the school board, the politicians, and the voters finally decided what our budget was going to be for this year, it was impossible for me to finalize your teaching schedules. As you can see, there is good news and bad news. The good news is that, in spite of our overcrowded conditions, we didn't have to go on double sessions. The bad news is that most of you have to teach a heavier-than-usual load. Most of you had to give up your planning period, and we generally had to go to three preparations. There may be some other sacrifices that I'll have to ask you to make. All I can say is that the teachers' lounge won't be the same without you. *[Laughter]*

I wish I could assure you that things will change soon, but I can't in all good conscience do that. Until the economic and political climate changes, we'll just have to struggle along as best we can, but if there is one thing that I've learned over the years, it's that I can count on this faculty to get the job done no matter what the difficulties. In my judgment, you are the finest group of teachers in this city! *[Smiles all around.]*

Now, down to some more mundane business. Let's talk about homeroom for a minute. Let me emphasize that Tuesdays and Fridays are set aside for guidance. Don't let students out of homeroom on those days. Work with them on guidance activities. If you need additional materials or assistance, please see Mr. Malloy, Head of the Guidance and Counseling Center. Let me urge you to read and discuss the announcements carefully on Mondays. Make sure all the students are present and listening. On Wednesdays and Thursdays, and on those days only, students will be permitted to leave homeroom for clubs and activities. Please make no exceptions to this schedule. Okay? Yes, Charles?

CHARLES   Jim, are you going to bring up the matter of the new teachers joining the union?

JIM   Oh, yes. Thank you for reminding me, Charles. I certainly don't want to forget mentioning to the new teachers that they should consider joining their professional organization. The forms and information will be in your mailboxes, but I'm going to give Charles Gibson, our local building representative, a few minutes right now to explain the matter to you and answer any questions that you have.

It is the next morning and Sam sits in the classroom of Roy Moore, a fellow social studies teacher with seven years of teaching experience. Sam and Roy met and sat next to each other at the teachers' meeting the day before, and the two men took an instant liking to one another.

SAM   Roy, I just can't believe my teaching load. They talked about three preparations when they hired me, but can you believe I've got four and a study hall? All five of my classes have at least 38 students in them.

ROY   That's really a rotten thing to do to a beginning teacher.

SAM   And that's not half of it. Jim asked me if I'd sponsor an extra-curricular activity. Can you believe he gave me Tri-Torch? It's the biggest student club in school.

ROY   Unbelievable! Tri-Torch sponsors a dance every Friday night and has always had to put on the Football Queen's Prom.

Sam   And don't forget, they have to build a float for the merchants' downtown Christmas parade.

Roy   You are really going to be putting in a lot of hours at night. I'm sure you'd rather be spending the time at home, with your wife being pregnant and all—or at least grading papers.

Sam   And he's got me scheduled to eat lunch during third period! It's bad enough that I'm not hungry that early, but I also have to give up the last 15 minutes of my lunch period for hall duty!

Roy   That's awful! I'm really sorry, Sam.

Sam   When am I supposed to do my planning, Roy? And then when he told us that we had to buy our own grade books and red marking pens and give at least two weeks advance notice for the duplication of tests and handouts so they can cut costs, I wanted to walk right into Dunfey's office and resign!

Roy   You know you can't do that, Sam. You've got to make the best of it at least for this school year.

Sam   And those old outdated textbooks—there aren't even enough for all my students! And the broken-down audio-visual equipment in my room! *[pause]* Tell me, Roy. Do I have to buy my own chalk?

Roy   *[Laughing]* No, you don't have to buy your own chalk. Just go down and see Maggie in the office and she'll give you a box. But you'll have to convince her that you've used up the entire box before she'll give you another.

Sam   Oh, brother! Roy, what am I going to do?! Seriously. Besides all Dunfey has assigned me to do, I have agreed to sell tickets at all the ball games and teach a homebound student. We really need the money. But, Roy, how am I going to have time to do all this?!

Roy   *[Shaking his head]* I don't really know, Sam. All I can suggest is that you organize your courses so that you minimize your load as much as you can. Plan every assignment carefully.

Sam   What do you mean?

Roy   Just use your common sense, Sam. If you give essay tests or assign written projects, you've got to grade them. Ask yourself if each thing you assign is really necessary. With around 200 students in your classes, you'll kill yourself if you don't watch what work you give your students.

Sam   *[Frowning]* I know you're right, Roy, but somehow that feels like I'm cheating the kids.

Roy   Maybe in some ways it is. But if you don't, you may not survive as a teacher and be available to teach them at all. Difficult times call for hard choices.

It is the first day of classes, and Sam sits on top of his desk as he talks to 36 (3 are absent) juniors in his seventh-period U.S. History class.

Sam   So now we come to how I'll figure your grades in this class. Every Friday we'll have a quiz over the assigned readings in the text. We'll also have either two or three exams each six-week grading period. They will be over the text and your classnotes. All exams will be announced in advance and will be objective in format—mostly multiple choice, but with a few matching, true–false, and fill-in-the-blank items thrown in. *[Pause]* Now, in addition we may do things like map work, and I'll give you credit for bringing in items for our current events bulletin board. All of that will be announced in advance too. No surprises. Yes, Charles?

CHARLES   What kinds of things will be on the tests?

SAM   Oh, important people, events, battles, dates—the usual. When you read the text you should write down the topic sentence in each paragraph as well as the names, terms, and so forth.

CHARLES   Can we underline in the book?

SAM   No, Charles. Other students will have to use those books, so don't mark them up in any way. Things are so tough now money-wise that we can't buy many new books. So don't mark them up. But look at the good side of it—you didn't have to buy your books yourself, like they have to in some school districts. Yes, Suzanne?

SUZANNE   Are we just going to have objective items on all our tests? No essay? I have a lot more trouble with objective tests that I do with essay. It just doesn't seem fair.

SAM   Well, Suzanne, if you study testing like we have to do to become teachers, you learn that both types of tests have advantages and disadvantages. One of the main advantages of objective tests is that you can cover, or sample as they call it, more of the content that the student is asked to study. Essay tests just focus in on a few topics, so they don't sample as much of the material as I'll be asking you to learn. So for that reason I've decided to go with objective tests.

SUZANNE   But couldn't you at least use both types when you test us?

SAM   I thought about this but decided that there really isn't enough time to use both types of items. Yes, Rick?

RICK   Mr. Goodman, will you be willing to work with kids after school if they need help? If Mr. Carson hadn't done that for me last year in world history, I don't think I would have passed.

SAM   I don't know, Rick. It's doubtful. With the schedule I have this semester, I probably won't be able to. *[Several students groan.]* I'm sorry, guys. Tell your parents that we're so overcrowded and underfunded here that the students are beginning to suffer. I hate it, because I would enjoy working with you after school. There just isn't time. *[Sam gets down off the top of his desk and begins to pace.]* Now, let's talk a little U.S. history. *[Students take out pencils and paper and get ready to write.]* To really understand how our country came into being, we first have to go back to Europe and understand events that were taking place there.

It is that same day after classes have ended. Students have left, and Sam sits alone at his desk in his classroom deep in thought. In walks his friend, Roy Moore.

ROY   Well, hello, Sam. How are things going?

SAM   Hi, Roy. Please sit down if you have a minute. I need to talk to someone.

ROY Sure. I'm in no hurry. But don't you have a homebound student you have to teach in a little bit?

SAM *[Looking at his watch]* Yes, but I've got a few minutes before I have to leave. I only have to go to 39th and Main.

ROY Oh, that's not going to take you more than fifteen minutes unless you get caught in traffic.

SAM Roy, I feel like a hypocrite!

ROY *[Smiling]* Sounds like your conscience acting up again, Sam. What's the matter?

SAM *[Smiling]* You've got a point about my conscience. I don't deal with guilt well.

ROY So what are you feeling guilty about now, Sam?

SAM I'm shortchanging my kids. I stood right up there in front of my seventh-period class and told them that I was justified in not giving them essay tests. I've given them no assignment that involves their doing any serious writing of any length or engages them in critical thinking of any kind. I'm basically just asking them to memorize facts and regurgitate them. Worst of all, I don't have the time—or I'm not willing to give up my moonlighting money, I don't know which—to work with the kids who need it after school. Roy, I'm not happy with myself at all!

ROY Sam, quit beating yourself up like that! Do you think that you're the only teacher who is teaching his kids differently than he would if the situation were different? I'm doing the same thing. You know Hal Sutherlin, in English? He should be assigning compositions right and left, but he's not doing it. He keeps it down to a manageable minimum, just as you and I do. You get what you pay for, Sam, and right now the public just doesn't want to pay for good public education. They call the tune and we do the dance accordingly. Right now the tune is "I ain't got no money." If you overload yourself, you'll just burn out and quit. Then where will your kids be?

SAM Maybe they'll be better off with a more dedicated teacher. I took a second homebound student just for the money!

ROY You and Rita *need* the money. Teachers' salaries have gotten better in the last decade or so, but not enough to allow teachers to break out of their lower-middle-class living standards. Gosh, Sam, when I see what they are paying actors, professional athletes, and politicians in our society, I really get angry. The public clearly values show biz more than it does education. Yet, the first solution to any problem that plagues society—whether it's drugs, child abuse, or drunken driving—is supposed to be education. But do the politicians put any money with it? No! They just give the school a new problem to solve for society while shouting "no new taxes!" All the politicians really do, Sam, is force good teachers like you into a position where they can't do the kind of job teaching that they feel they should.

SAM So what do I do, Roy?

ROY You ask yourself whether you can remain a teacher under these circumstances. If the answer if yes, you do the best job of teaching that you can do under the circumstances. You cut back so you can survive. And you tell yourself that when things change, you'll do things differently.

SAM And what if things don't change, Roy?

ROY   Have a little faith, Sam. Things always change. And how can they go anywhere but up.! [*Both men laugh*] Seriously Sam, don't you think that the public will eventually see that their kids are being short-changed, and insist that things be different? Consequences, Sam. When the politician cuts the budget and there are no consequences, he says "See, you can do the job for less." When teachers cut back on what they do, and parents finally figure out what's happening, voters put pressure on the politicians to change things. It will happen, Sam! Have faith! Meanwhile, quit worrying and look forward to a better day for education.

It is six weeks later, and Sam has just returned unit exams to his seventh-period U.S. History class.

SAM   So that's how I figured the grades. Any questions? Yes, Suzanne?

SUZANNE   Mr. Goodman, can we do anything for extra credit to bring up our low grades?

SAM   Not really, Suzanne. We just need to learn to study harder for our exams and quizzes.

SUZANNE   I studied real hard, Mr. Goodman. Just ask my mother! But I just have trouble with these kinds of tests. Can't we do a paper or something to bring up our grades?

CHARLES   Yeah, Mr. Goodman. Memorizing all these dates and terms is hard. I can't remember all this stuff!

SAM   I know it isn't easy. Studying is hard work. Yes, Rick?

RICK   I couldn't get anyone to study with me. Couldn't you give us some handouts or something for us to study so we can do better on these tests? [*Shouts of agreement*].

SAM   The school has rules that make it difficult to get things like handouts duplicated, but I'll check that idea out and see what I can do. Yes, Rick?

RICK   Is there anyone that could help us study for the exams? Are there any other teachers or students that we can work with?

SAM   I can't think of any right off, Rick, but I'll ask around and see what I can find out.

It is the end of the first semester and Sam sits in the office of Jim Dunfey, the building principal.

JIM   It's always a pleasure to meet with my teachers, Sam. How can I help you today?

SAM   Mr. Dunfey, as a beginning teacher, I have some concerns I want to discuss with you. Frankly, I have to make some decisions about next year and I want to begin working on them right now.

JIM   Next year? I thought you were going to be with us next year. John Boyd tells me you're doing just fine in your classes, and that you've done a fine job getting Tri-Torch organized and going. Roy Williams tells me he couldn't run his athletic programs without you taking care of ticket sales. Says he just basically turns that area over to you and doesn't worry about it. Sam, I've got to be honest. As good as you may be as a teacher, you've got real administrative ability. You have really taken hold of these things and run them well. Have you thought about what you're going to get your master's in yet?

SAM   No, not definitely. I guess I was going to take it in my field.

JIM   Well, if you'll allow me to put my two cents worth in, I think you ought to take a serious look at secondary administration. You're principalship material if I ever saw it, Sam. And who knows, then maybe you can go on and work toward your superintendent's certificate. Heck, I may be working for you one of these days, Sam. [Jim laughs, Sam smiles.]

SAM   Thanks for the vote of confidence, Mr. Dunfey, but all that outside the class-room work, plus my heavy teaching load, is about to do me in. As you probably know, I'm a father now, and I hardly have time to see my wife and son. And what's worse, Mr. Dunfey, is that I don't feel like I'm doing as good a job teaching as I could be.

JIM   Yes, I believe John did tell me that you had a son. Congratulations, Sam, and give Rita my best. What did you name him?

SAM   Ronald. Ron for short.

JIM   Ron Goodman. That has a nice sound to it! But Sam, I've heard only good things about your teaching.

SAM   Mr. Dunfey, I'm just not able to spend the time with the kids that I know I need to. I'm not focusing on their learning the kinds of things that I know they should be learning. I feel like I'm cheating them.

JIM   I know things are hard now, Sam. They're hard for all of us. But things will change for the better. They always do. We're just in a down cycle right now economically. It's like my Daddy used to say, life is like a ferris wheel. Sometimes you're on top and sometimes on bottom. But when you're on bottom, like we are now, you know you're going to be back on top again. Sam, you have a real future in education. I hope you'll stay with us. I can't promise you exactly when the ferris wheel will start up again, but I can promise you that it will happen.

SAM   Thanks very much, Mr. Dunfey, for your confidence and advice.

Sam and Roy walk toward their cars, which are parked next to one another in the parking lot. They talk as they walk slowly.

SAM   I just don't know, Roy. I like working here and it certainly is exciting and full of variety!

ROY   But you're just not able to do as good a job of teaching as you know you should do.

SAM   Exactly! Oh, Dunfey tells me how things are bound to get better, and promises me the moon if I just hang on. But when I read in the newspaper and watch on TV what the state legislature and our local school board actually do in funding and managing our schools, I not only want to leave this school district—I want to move to another state.

ROY Do you think the grass is really greener somewhere else, Sam?

SAM It's got to be, Roy. There have to be school districts and states that really value education and put their money where their mouth is.

ROY So Sam, what are you going to do? Are you going to be back next year? If you do stay, are you going to do anything differently?

Schedule of Classes For Sam Goodman
Jackson Senior High School

Period	Time	Subject	Grade	Enrollment
HR	8:05–8:35	Homeroom	11	36
1	8:40–9:35	World History	10	39
2	9:40–10:35	U.S. History	11	39
3	10:40–11:35	Lunch		
4	11:40–12:35	Civics	12	38
5	12:40–1:35	Economics	12	38
6	1:40–2:35	Study Hall		153
7	2:40–3:35	U.S. History	11	39

QUESTIONS

1. What administrative leadership style is exhibited by the principal, Jim Dunfey? Is he more of a supporting, coaching, delegating, or directing leader? What kind of school climate has he created? To what extent is the school climate a product of internal vs. external forces?

2. What is teacher morale, and what are its causes? Would you describe Sam and Roy's morale as high or low? How does teacher morale affect the teacher's behavior in the classroom?

3. What are teacher stress and burnout? What sources of stress are impinging on Sam? What are the most effective techniques available to teachers for dealing with stress?

4. At what levels of Maslow's need hierarchy are the following people primarily operating: Sam, Roy, and Jim Dunfey? How would knowledge of their need levels help in dealing with them?

5. What are the advantages and disadvantages of essay and objective tests? Should Sam have given both types of items? Is Sam right about his belief that he is shortchanging his students if he doesn't give them essay as well as objective tests?

6. What are Sam's instructional objectives for his seventh-period U.S. History class? Do his objectives relate to the higher or lower levels of Bloom's Cognitive Taxonomy? Is Sam right about his feelings that he should have given written assignments and projects to his classes?

7. Would you describe Sam's sense of efficacy as a teacher as high or low? Would you describe his attributions for success and failure as a teacher as internal or external? How would this information about Sam's belief system as a teacher help in advising and communicating with him?

8. Sam is concerned about his effectiveness as a teacher. What is teacher effectiveness, and how does it relate to student learning? What changes do you feel Sam should make to become a more effective teacher?

9. If Sam decides to stay at JHS next year, what changes should he make so he can accomplish his objectives? For example, should he consider peer tutoring? parent volunteers?

10. Should Sam look for another job? If so, should he get out of the school district and/or state in which he is teaching? Should he get out of teaching and enter another profession?

CASE 29

THE REBEL

ohn Yuma is a young, unmarried, beginning teacher from the Southwest. He is applying for his first teaching position in the city of Braxton, which has a population of approximately 30,000, in a midwestern state. John has applied for a position at Wiley Middle School, which has a student population that is 77 percent white, 22 percent African–American, and 1 percent other. In preparing to become a teacher at Southwestern State University, John read avidly about the middle school movement in the 1970s, and has eagerly looked forward to working with middle-school students.

The interview for the position takes place in the office of the building principal, Alice Cole.

ALICE   John, I don't mind telling you that I was very impressed with your credentials from Southwestern State. Your GPA was quite high, but it was really the combination of your good grades and the leadership roles that you played in service and student government activities on campus that caught my eye. It was clear to me that you would know how to work with people as well as study.

JOHN   Thank you, Ms. Cole. You'll notice that I spent a lot of time, especially the last two years, volunteering at middle schools and tutoring middle-school-age children.

ALICE   Yes, I read in your comments how much you wanted to teach in a middle school. Why is that, John? A lot of men your age want to teach in a senior high school, or get a Ph.D. and work at the college level.

JOHN   I'm not completely sure. Maybe it was all the material that I read about the middle school, or maybe it was the fact that, as I look back on my own childhood, I just had the most fun during that time of life. But to me, the middle-school period is a time of exploration for children. It's a time when they have to examine themselves and their lives—explore their potentials, if you will—so they can make the big decisions they'll have to in senior high about a college major or an occupation. It's that last period of childhood before society starts laying its life burdens on you. And I guess the bottom line is that I just want to work with kids that age.

ALICE   It's wonderful to hear your enthusiasm, John! I think you're just the person we need. Now you're aware, aren't you, that Wiley has Grades 7–9, not Grades 5–8, as was in vogue a number of years ago?

JOHN   I know, but I've heard good things about Wiley and your leadership as a principal. A lot of middle schools are really just junior high schools, in my judgment.

ALICE   I agree. But again, you know that we are organized along separate subjects lines like a junior high school and not into pupil-centered teaching teams the way most middle schools were originally, don't you?

JOHN   Yes, but I feel the middle school spirit here. The philosophy that kids this age have a unique set of needs different from senior high students, and that they should be allowed to relate what they are learning to themselves and their lives—not just memorize facts for their own sake.

ALICE   I believe you've captured our philosophy quite well, John! Of course, there is considerable pressure on us to prepare our students to take the SAT when they get to the eleventh grade. Many of our ninth graders take the PSAT, and we are proud of the fact that so many of them do well. But the reasons that you have stated for wanting to be a middle school teacher match our goals perfectly. I've just made a decision, John! The job is yours if you want it!

It is two months later, and John meets with Mae Carlson, the social studies chair, the second day of pre-planning. They are seated alone in Mae's classroom.

MAE   John, I haven't had a chance to tell you how happy we are to have you with us. Alice thinks very highly of you.

JOHN   Thanks, Mae. I like it very much here.

MAE   *[Serious tone]* John, I like to meet with all our new social studies teachers and do what I can to help orient them. What questions do you have?

JOHN   Well, after getting my teaching schedule from Alice, I was particularly curious about my third-period U.S. history class. It's for eighth graders, isn't it?

MAE   Yes, it is. It's your standard U.S. history course that goes up to 1890.

JOHN   1890? It doesn't go up to the present time?

MAE   No. But of course you can have your kids bring in current events and discuss them to make tie-ins.

JOHN   To tell you the truth, Mae, if I had my way I'd use a text that starts with the present and goes backwards. That way, I think the kids would not only be more motivated to learn the material but would see its relevance to the present.

MAE   I believe that idea was proposed a few years back when the curriculum was revised. Perhaps you can serve on the next curriculum revision committee. But for the present time, the course goes up to 1890 and the text is organized in chronological order.

JOHN   Perhaps I can figure out a way to stay in that format and still make it interesting. What evaluation procedures are generally used in that course, Mae?

MAE   Oh, most teachers give objective tests—you know, multiple choice, matching, and fill-in-the-blank. Both the teachers and the parents are quite aware of the PSAT in the ninth grade, and we try to use a testing format that will help our students pass it.

JOHN   Then the emphasis is on learning facts—famous people, terms, dates, places, and the like?

MAE   Yes.

JOHN   I'll be honest with you, Mae. I want my kids to learn more than facts. I want to emphasize problem-solving and encourage the kids to think in logical and organized ways and become creative in their approaches to problems.

MAE   I think that's wonderful, John. We probably don't do enough with problem-solving and higher-order thinking. But again, don't neglect the basics. They are the building blocks for higher-order thought.

JOHN   I couldn't agree with you more, Mae. It's just that some of my teachers never went beyond the basics.

MAE   Yes, I know what you mean.

JOHN   Is there a school grading policy?

MAE   Well, just the usual grading standards printed on the report card. You know, 95 to 100 is an A, and 88 to 94 is a B, and so forth. We've used that for years.

JOHN   And most of the teachers try to approximate it?

MAE   Yes, that's generally true.

JOHN   I understand. Well, I've been planning while we've talked, Mae, and I think I can work within those guidelines and still develop a course that will be interesting for the kids.

MAE   That's wonderful, John! I'm looking forward to seeing how it works out. Let me know if you have any more questions and, again, we're happy to have you with us.

It is third period of the first day of classes, and John meets with 31 eighth graders in his U.S. history class.

JOHN   To tell you the truth, class, if I could organize this course any way I wanted to, I would begin with the present and move backwards. Students your age often don't see the value of history when it's organized chronologically from the European beginnings of our country. And then to stop at 1890—well, let's just say that going from the present backwards allows you to see better how we got here. Also, I know that a lot of you are good students, from fine families, and both you and your parents look forward to your doing well on the PSAT and later the SAT. And I know that you need to learn facts to do that. But I also think that it's important for you to learn how to solve problems in life and how to think things through in an organized and logical way. How to think creatively. What I'm really telling you is that I think essay exams are as important as objective ones and that I plan for you to engage in problem-solving activities in this course. Yes, Diane?

DIANE   How will we be graded in here, Mr. Yuma?

JOHN   *[Passing out handout]* I was just coming to that, Diane. I am going to use what's called the contract plan in this course. I've tried to spell it out in this handout. There, does everybody have one? *[Pause]* The first thing that you'll notice is that you have a decision to make each time we start a new unit. Namely, what grade do you want to contract for? If you just want to make average grades on tests, come to class regularly and participate, and keep a notebook of important people, terms, events, and map work, you can contract for a C. If you want a B, however, you have to do those things and more. Your test score will have to be above average and you will have to participate in either a current events report project, which can be either individual or small group, or a small-group problem-solving project, and it has to be of good quality. Your choice. And a small group is no more than four students besides yourself. I forgot to put that down. Yes, Roy?

ROY   What if we do some of the things well enough but not all of them? Oh, I see. Here at the bottom. Then we'll get a C+.

JOHN   Right, Roy. Now, for an A. All the B activities plus your test scores have to be exceptionally good, and you have to do a small group construction project. This will test your creativity. As you can see, examples of each kind of project are given on the handout. Yes, Marcia?

MARCIA   It says here that our big tests will be essay questions and our weekly quizzes will be objective.

JOHN   That's right, Marcia. Essay questions make you analyze, organize, and think reflectively. Objective items cover memorization of facts more, but you can test more content with them. I'll use both, since both are important.

MARCIA   But the big tests will be essay and they'll count more.

JOHN   That's right.

MARCIA   But how will you grade them? I mean, will a C be 70 to 79 and a B 80 to 89?

JOHN   I believe that's 77 to 87 for a C and 88 to 94 for a B. That's what's on the report card.

MARCIA   Whatever. I mean how will you grade the essay? Will you figure points and put them on a curve?

JOHN   Essay tests of the kind I'm going to give have to be graded subjectively. I might ask you to compare and contrast an event in U.S. history with a current event, for example. I will either compare your answers to what I think a model answer should look like, or I'll read all your papers and put them in piles according to their quality. Then I'll read them a second time to make sure they are in the right pile and decide how far apart the piles are quality-wise. The bottom line is that I'll give each paper a letter grade based on my subjective opinion and not try to reduce everything to points. The objective tests will be curved and then converted to letter grades. The decision as to whether a test or a project is of A, B, or C quality will be a subjective one. But I assure you that I am a fair grader and always try to give the student the benefit of the doubt. OK?

It is five weeks later, and John's third-period U.S. history class is working on settlements in the New World, particularly in the English colonies. John has been using the contract plan in all his classes and the results have exceeded his expectations. The students are highly motivated, well-prepared, enjoy working and talking together, pay attention and participate in class, and display few discipline problems. This is especially true in John's third-period class.

JOHN   OK, gang, you may recall that today Diane, Marcia, and Roy are presenting their small group problem-solving project on the exploration and settlement of the New World, especially focusing on what the English did in relation to a current event. Now I have to tell you that they had to do some convincing to get me to let them use the exploration of outer space as their current-event comparison. Yes, Jack?

JACK   Why? What's wrong with that?

JOHN   As you'll see in a minute, they didn't want to confine their current-event comparison to what the U.S. and the Russians have done in outer space. In a minute they'll give us all a list of all those space flights: when, where, the purpose, the cost, and so forth. They will also give us a list of all the explorations of the New World on a comparative basis.

JACK   So?

JOHN   Well, my problem, Jack, is that they wanted to extend their current event definition to include certain popular TV shows about the exploration of outer space. For example, they thought shows like *Star Trek, Deep Space Nine,* and *Babylon Five* should be included, as well as movies like *Star Wars* and *Stargate.* Since all those are fictional rather than factual I had some problem.

JACK   So what did you decide?

JOHN   Well, let me ask the class. How many of you feel that I should have allowed them to use the fictional materials as well as the factual? *[All hands go up.]* So committee, what did I decide?

DIANE   You told us to go ahead and use the fictional material, just as long as we made clear what it was and presented it separately from the factual material. *[Shouts of acclamation and support.]*

JOHN   All right, gang, are you ready? *[Dramatically]* Are you ready to go back to those scary days when some people still believed the world was flat and ships might fall off the edge? But men believed that there were gold and riches out there and took to their ships to find out. Although they found land and were disappointed at first, they began to see how living in the New World might allow them to escape some of the problems in Europe at that time. Thus, they started colonies. And then the fun began. And believe me, at the time there was no prime directive to be obeyed, by either the explorers or colonists. OK, are you guys ready to take it from there? Yes, Jack?

JACK   But aren't they going to get into UFOs exploring *our* world?

JOHN   *[Slapping his head exaggeratedly with his right hand]* Wow, I never thought of that! *[Looks at committee of three seated together in front of class.]* Did you guys? *[All three shake their heads no.]* Sorry, Jack. You're just way ahead of us and maybe, just maybe, the information on UFOs is even more flimsy than that on TV shows and movies. *[Shouts of protest.]* OK, guys, I hear you, but the committee didn't go into that. So, are you ready? *[Shouts of affirmation.]* Take it over committee! *[John sits down.]*

It is three days before the end of the first semester and John has received a note in his mailbox to drop in and see the principal, Alice Cole, as soon as he can. After his last class he stops by Alice's office and, seeing Alice working behind her desk, knocks at the office door, which is open. Alice smiles and beckons him to enter her office and take a seat.

ALICE   John, how are you?

JOHN   Just great, Alice. All my classes are going great, I look forward to coming to work each day, and I've started to put part of every paycheck in a mutual fund. How could life be better?

ALICE   *[Laughing]* I'm sure I don't know, John. My, you must be an entertaining teacher! *[Pause]* Well, John, I wanted to talk to you about some parent concerns that have come to my attention.

JOHN   *[With surprise]* About my teaching?!

ALICE   Yes. But now, John, I don't want you to get all upset about this! Parents usually haven't had any training as teachers and often don't see things the same way that a teacher does.

JOHN   How many parents are we talking about?

ALICE   Oh, probably a half dozen have contacted me.

JOHN   *[With strong emotion]* A half dozen! What do they say I'm doing wrong, for Pete's sake?!

ALICE   John, to boil it down, they seem to be concerned that you're ignoring the basics. They worry whether their kids are going to be able to score high on the PSAT. Apparently, when some of their children told them about some of the interesting things you are having them do in class . . . well, one parent called them fun and games and wondered when you are going to have them get down to work.

JOHN   Don't they know that I have the students keep notebooks with the kinds of facts that will be tested on the PSAT?

ALICE   Yes, but they say that you give them essay tests, except for your quizzes, and that you don't grade objectively. They are concerned that most of your test items aren't multiple-choice items like those on the PSAT.

JOHN   *[Frustrated]* That's true, of course, Alice! But in my judgment, I'd be cheating my kids if all I gave them was multiple-choice tests. Believe me, it would be easier and I wouldn't have to grade all those essay tests. But if I didn't challenge my students to organize their thoughts, think a problem through logically and analytically, and force them to critically examine ideas, I just couldn't live with myself. And let's face it, Alice, a child doesn't do much of that if all he takes is multiple-choice tests. Those kinds of tests just don't measure higher-order thinking. Don't they know that?!

ALICE   *[Soothingly]* Of course not, John. They just want the best for their children and to them that means their doing well on those standardized tests that get them college admission and scholarships. Like I say, they don't have the same perspective that you do as a teacher.

JOHN   Well, how do you feel about this, Alice? My kids are motivated and learning, and I frankly don't know how to do a better job. Do you want me to go to all objective tests?

ALICE   No, John, I don't. I told them that I'd look into the matter and get back to them. I've done that and I'm satisfied with what you're doing. I'm almost sorry that I wasn't a student in your class. But, John, I must point out that this won't end parent complaints, especially if one of their children doesn't do well on the verbal portion of the PSAT. So don't be surprised if one of the parents calls you and ask for a conference about the matter. You'll need to handle any such complaints professionally. Don't get mad at them and tell them that they don't know as much about teaching as you do. That may be true, but it's not productive to use that as an argument.

JOHN   *[Sheepishly]* OK. I hear you, Alice. I'll treat them with kid gloves.

It is the end of the second grading period of the second semester. Again, John has been summoned to Alice Cole's office. He nervously takes a seat.

JOHN   Have more parents complained, Alice? As I'm sure you remember, I had conferences with three parents and I thought all three went well.

ALICE   No, John. I have had a couple of parents contact me after our earlier conference. But I'm afraid this is another matter entirely.

JOHN   What?

ALICE   I don't want to get into names but three teachers have come in independently to talk to me about your teaching.

JOHN   *[Incredulously]* Other teachers?!

ALICE   Yes. They complain that you are grading too easy to curry favor with the students and are not following the school district's grading standards.

JOHN   You mean the 95 to 100 is an A thing?

ALICE   Exactly.

JOHN   Well, I guess I don't, to tell the truth. I convert everything to letter grades and don't try to curve my grades at all. I record the letter grades in my gradebook and average them to get the final grade. Alice, do you mean all these teachers follow the grading standards on the report card?

ALICE   Yes, I'd say they do. They give objective tests and generally adjust points to make results fit the school district's grading standards.

JOHN   What did you tell them?

ALICE   I told them that I think you are a fine teacher and are doing a good job in the classroom. But I suspect that more is going on here than how you grade. Most of them use the lecture–discussion method and emphasize the memorization of facts. The kids in your classroom are motivated and enjoying themselves. The kids like you and your classes. Some of the parents think what you're doing is fun and games and not work. Nevertheless, the kids in your classes are telling both their parents and other kids how much they like your classes. Some of the kids in the classes of the complaining teachers wish they were in your class instead. Also, your students aren't making grades as good in those other teachers' classes as they are in yours. Now, are kids in your classes making higher grades because you are an easy grader, or because they are more motivated and learning more? All these other teachers know is that they are being accused of grading harder, and kids are wanting to get out of their classes and into yours. So they come to me to complain about how easy you are and how difficult you are making their lives as teachers.

JOHN   *[Depressed]* I just can't believe all this is happening! I thought I was a good teacher but just look at this mess!

ALICE   You *are* a good teacher, John. That may be part of your problem. You get compared to other teachers who teach differently from you and these older, more experienced teachers don't look nearly as good in comparison. They get angry, blame you, and strike back.

JOHN   So what happens next?

ALICE   I don't know. That's why I wanted to talk to you. It all depends on what happens next.

JOHN   What do you mean?

ALICE   John, I don't want to scare you, but you don't have tenure in this school system. I talked to each of the teachers and tried to calm them down. I pointed out to them that we should wait and see how your kids do on the PSAT before anybody decides that you are too easy as a teacher. I even told them that you are new and they should give you a chance to examine your teaching practices and change those that aren't working. I think I succeeded. But one of them is a favorite niece of the superintendent of schools.

JOHN   Oh. Molly Barton!

ALICE   Exactly. And if she goes crying to her uncle, who knows what can happen? He *is* my boss, John. If he decides to let you go, I can argue with him, but in the end all I can do is salute and obey his orders. I'm not trying to scare you but it could happen, John. And yet, I wouldn't have you change the way you teach for the world. You've got to be yourself and do it your way.

JOHN   *[Sullenly]* What's my great crime? To do the best job of teaching I know how? I just don't fit in around here!

Contract Grading Plan for Mr. Yuma's Eighth-Grade U. S. History Class (Third Period)

C GRADE

1. Pass exams and weekly quizzes with "C" average.
2. Keep an individual notebook at the "C" level. For each chapter studied, notebook must include: (1) history-makers (what did he/she do and why was it important?); (2) definitions of key terms (such as Mercator projection, circumnavigation, Amerind); (3) ten most important events in the chapter. (Put time intervals involved on a time line); (4) map locations of key places and their distances from Braxton.
3. Regular class attendance and active participation in class discussions.

B GRADE

1. Pass exams and weekly quizzes with "B" average.
2. Keep individual notebook at "B" level.
3. Regular class attendance and active participation in class discussions.
4. Produce an individual or small group current events report at "B" level (Making analogies and discussing comparisons and contrasts between current events and an event being studied. For example, comparing the European conquest of the Amerind with current conquests.)

or

A small group problem-solving project at "B" level. (For example, explaining the U.S. government's Indian policy at various stages and offering alternative solutions.)

A GRADE

1. Pass exams and weekly quizzes with "A" average.
2. Keep an individual notebook at the "A" level.
3. Regular class attendance and active participation in class discussions.
4. Produce an individual or small group current events report at "A" level.

or

A small group problem-solving project at "A" level.
5. A small group construction project at "A" level. (For example, construct a model of Magellan's ship *The Vittoria*.)

Notes

1. Exams will be primarily essay and quizzes will be objective in format.
2. Partial completion of a contract may result in a plus (+) being added to the grade (teacher's choice).
3. Failure to complete the "C" contract will result in a "D" or "F" at the teacher's discretion. Exam and test scores will be the primary consideration.

QUESTIONS

1. What administrative leadership style is exhibited by Alice Cole, the principal? Is she more of a supporting, coaching, delegating, or directing leader? How would you describe the school climate at Wiley Middle School? To what extent have external vs. internal forces contributed to the school climate?

2. What is nepotism, and how does it affect schools and school systems? How does this apply to this case?

3. What is intrinsic motivation? To what extent has John utilized the principles and procedures for capitalizing upon the intrinsic motivation of his students?

4. John says that he is interested in higher-order learning as well as basic skills learning. How do these differ? What levels of Bloom's Cognitive Taxonomy relate to these differences?

5. What are problem solving, creative thinking, and critical thinking? What teaching strategies encourage these kinds of thinking in children? To what extent was John successful in creating an environment conducive to their production?

6. Contrast John's instructional objectives and teaching methods with those of the teachers who complained to the principal. Which do you prefer and why? Which produces the greatest amount of student learning?

7. What is teacher tenure, and how does it relate to due process and teacher evaluation? What would happen if tenure were abolished in education? Would teaching become more or less of a profession?

8. What is teaching effectiveness and how is it measured? How could the teaching of John and the teachers who complained about his teaching be evaluated and compared?

9. John prefers essay tests. What are their advantages and disadvantages? Does either lead to greater student learning?

10. What are norm-referenced and criterion-referenced evaluation? Which is John using with his contract plan? Which approach relates to the greatest amount of student learning?

11. The Braxton School District has district-wide grading standards. Is this wise, or should each school (or even each teacher) be allowed to develop and use its own?

12. Considerable emphasis is placed on PSAT and SAT scores by the Braxton school district, the parents, and some teachers. To what extent should such considerations determine curriculum and testing procedures? instructional objectives? To what extent should individual teachers like John be allowed to de-emphasize such tests in their classes?

13. Alice raises the question of whether John's students are more motivated or John is just an easier grader. Which do you think is the case and why? How well do you predict John's students will do on the PSAT compared to other teachers' students?

14. What advice would you give John if you were Alice? Would you advise him to change and conform, or keep doing what he's been doing in spite of the possible consequences? What might the consequences be if he does conform?

THE OVERSTRESSED DISCIPLINARIAN

Lane Baxter is a secondary English teacher with 16 years of teaching experience. He will soon be 39 years old and has spent the last 8 years teaching at Whitmore High School, which is located in a large urban area in a southeastern state. The attendance district served by WHS is 36 percent African-American, 2 percent Asian–American, and 62 percent white.

It is one week before Lane has to report for teacher pre-planning to begin his seventeenth year of teaching. He sits at home with his wife, Lois. They have just finished discussing their trip to Europe, from which they just returned two days ago.

LOIS   What's the matter, Lane?

LANE   What do you mean?

LOIS   You can't fool me! You were so happy and animated just a minute ago, when we were talking about our trip, then you clouded over all of a sudden. What's wrong?

LANE   Well, to tell you the truth, it suddenly hit me that vacation is over and I have to go back to the salt mines next Monday. God, I hate that place!

LOIS   *[With concern]* Lane, do you really hate it that much?! I though you loved teaching!

LANE   I'm not a kid fresh out of teachers' college any longer, Lois! You just don't know what it's like at Whitmore!

LOIS   What do you mean?

LANE   It's the kids. They're so—disrespectful. It isn't like it used to be. They not only don't care about learning, they don't care about anything. They'll cuss you out right to your face in class! You can kick them out all you want to, they just don't care! And you know what, Lois? I've gotten to the point where I don't care either!

LOIS   Lane, can't you transfer to another school? Maybe a school like Vanguard High School?

LANE   Wouldn't make any difference. Charlie Haskins has taught at Vanguard for years, and he says the same thing goes on over there. *[Pause]* It's just symptomatic of our whole country, Lois. Crime is everyone's number one concern today. The police and the courts can't or won't do anything about it. People don't feel safe in their own homes anymore. Everyone we know is either buying a gun for self-defense or looking into a home security system. Why should the schools be any different?

LOIS   I knew you weren't happy at Whitmore, but I had no idea you felt this bad about your job! *[Pause]* Lane, have you ever considered getting out of teaching?

LANE   *[Angrily]* And do what?! Write poetry? There's a lot of people out there who are out of work now and would love to have a job with a steady paycheck and fringe benefits like mine. But, God, the price is high! *[Pause]* I really envy my dad, the way he served as a principal for 28 years.

LOIS   Yes, your dad was a wonderful man and educator.

LANE   But those were easier, simpler times, Lois. I wonder if he could do it today?

LOIS   Lane, I only know that I want you to be happy! If you decide to change jobs, we can get by on my salary until you're able to make the change.

LANE   *[Moving next to her and putting his arm around her]* Thanks, dear! Hearing that means a lot to me! *[Smiling]* But don't worry—I'll get over this bad mood! It'll pass like always.

It is the first day of pre-planning and all the teachers file into the school auditorium for their first meeting of the year. As Lane looks for a seat down front, he runs into his old friend and fellow English teacher, Charles Allen.

CHARLES   Why hello, Lane. How have you been?

LANE   Hi, Charles. Good to see you. Is that seat empty?

CHARLES   It sure is. We've been saving it for you. *[Pointing to the young, well-dressed man sitting next to him]* Lane, I'd like you to meet Darryl Wilson. This is Darryl's first year, and we're looking for big things from him.

DARRYL   *[Shaking Lane's hand]* It's certainly nice to meet you, Lane. Charles has been telling me all about you.

LANE   *[Smiling]* Really? All good, I hope.

DARRYL   Oh, yes. He says that your favorite course is American literature and that's my favorite, too. I can't wait to meet my first class. It's really going to feel different, knowing they are my classes and that I'm not just an intern!

LANE   *[Winking at Charles]* Yes, well, you'll get used to it real quick!

DARRYL   When I was interviewing for the job, Mr. Cookson *[building principal]* told me he'd give me a shot at teaching the journalism classes and taking over the school paper, maybe by next year. He said I could assist Mr. Swaby with it this year and learn the ropes.

LANE   *[Smirking]* Yes, I'll bet Cookson will be happy to have you take over the school paper—and Swaby will too!

DARRYL   I hope so! Journalism is my second love! *[Frowns]* I've just got one worry, though.

CHARLES   What's that, Darryl?

DARRYL   It's probably silly, I know, but I'm afraid some of the students will know more about American literature than I do and I won't know how to handle it!

LANE   *[Rolling his eyes at Charles]* Darryl, let me assure you that won't be a problem! It'll be the last problem you'll need to worry about!

DARRYL   What do you mean?

LANE   I think you'll find out very quickly that you'll be way ahead of even advanced placement students as far as subject matter is concerned. Your problems will be discipline and student apathy.

DARRYL   I sure hope you're right. I think I'm ready for discipline and motivation problems. We spent a lot of time learning classroom management strategies and motivational techniques. But it would really embarrass me to death if a student knew more about, say, a piece of prose I was teaching than I do!

LANE   Trust me, Darryl. You don't need to worry about that!

The teachers' meeting is over, and Lane stands outside the auditorium talking to Charles.

CHARLES   Well, what did you think of Darryl, Lane? Don't you think he'll make a good one?

LANE   He's really something, Charles! I can remember being naive and idealistic like that when I first entered teaching, but I'm afraid that he's going to get a rude awakening. I just hope the students don't eat him alive! *[Pause]* At other times, though, I wish I was back there starting all over. I can't say I'm looking forward to this school year.

CHARLES   Why is that, Lane? Is something going on that I don't know about?

LANE   No, it's just that, well, like I was saying to Lois the other day, I guess I'm just tired of teaching. You could say they've worn me down, I guess.

CHARLES   I'm surprised to hear you say that, Lane. Gosh, I can remember a few years back when you won the district teacher of the year award and how happy you were.

LANE   Charles, that was 11 years ago! I don't feel that way today.

CHARLES   What's bothering you, specifically I mean?

LANE   Oh, I guess it's the kids more than anything. The lack of respect, the apathy, the constant bickering and negativity. It just wears you down 'til you wonder if it's worth it. *[Pause]* Then there's the constant pressure to teach to the test so the standardized test scores will look good. And the administration never backs you in anything. Send a student down to the office, and the Dean not only sends them right back the next day but then he also comes around and asks you why you can't handle such matters in the classroom. Nobody seems to care anymore. It's like hitting your head against a brick wall.

CHARLES   Lane, have you ever considered talking to anyone about this? I mean someone that can help?

LANE   No one other than Lois and now you. I really wouldn't know who to talk to. Who in this school system would want to listen, other than a friend like you?

CHARLES   I guess I was thinking of Dr. Felling, the director of psychological services. He would surely know how to help and it wouldn't cost you anything.

LANE   Not a bad idea, Charles. Thanks a lot! I'll keep it in mind.

It is the first day of classes, and Lane meets his fifth-period American literature class, consisting of 37 students from a variety of ethnic, racial, and socioeconomic backgrounds. After lecturing to them about the organization and purpose of the course, how to study the textbook, and his grading procedures, Lane turns to his expectations for students' conduct.

LANE   Let me just add that this is my seventeenth year of high school teaching, most of them here at Whitmore, and that I'm familiar with all the tricks and excuses that students use to keep from studying. Studying is hard work. But it's your main job as a student, and if you care about a good grade in this class, you'll have to spend time every day studying. You'll find that as you get older the things you'll come to appreciate most in life are those that you have to work the hardest for. *[With annoyance]* You have a question, Ron, isn't it?

RON   Mr. Baxter, do you really believe that stuff? Not only is who you know more important than how hard you work, but you're putting me to sleep.

LANE   *[Angrily]* Another smart guy! Then why are you in this class, if you're so bored and know so much?

RON   Not because I want to be! I can't think of anything more useless than studying American literature. What a bunch of crap!

LANE   *[Controlled]* I've had students like you before, Ron, with big attitude problems. Since you dislike it in here so much I'm going to ask you to leave right now and go to Mr. Profitt's office *[Dean of Boys]*.

RON   *[Getting up]* Gladly. That's sounds a lot more interesting than being here!

It is the end of the first grading period, and three boys meet and talk outside Lane's classroom at the end of the fifth period. Two of the boys, Jeremy and Joe Ed, are in Lane's fifth-period American literature class.

JEREMY   Hey, Carlos, what's happening?

CARLOS   Not much, man. You guys going to class?

JOE ED   Just got out, thank God!

CARLOS   Bad class, huh?

JEREMY   Geez, I guess so. Old man Baxter. What a loser! Boring!

CARLOS   Couldn't be worse than old lady Tyree. She's definitely the worst! Can't stand her, man.

JEREMY   She can't hold a candle to Baxter!

JOE ED   Yeah, I had Tyree last year. Baxter's definitely worse.

CARLOS   Yeah, how?

JOE ED   Boring as crap! Puts you to sleep and jumps down your throat if you breathe too loud! He's such a grump!

JEREMY   He doesn't even try to make things interesting. Acts like he doesn't care whether you get it or not, just as long as you don't cause any trouble. . .

JOE ED   . . .And wake him up! *[All three laugh]*
JEREMY   God, yes! If I was that bored with what I'm doing, I'd quit. *[Bell rings]*

It is four weeks later, and Lane sits in the office of Dr. Lester Felling, director of psychological services.

LANE   Les, I need to talk to someone who can advise me. I figured that if you couldn't help me yourself, you'd know of someone who could.
LES   Of course, Lane. I'm pleased that you thought of me! I have worked with, oh, I'd say half a dozen teachers who felt they were suffering from burnout and trying to decide whether or not to leave teaching.
LANE   I didn't realize you had that kind of background.
LES   Yes. While my doctorate was in school psychology, I did my dissertation on student and teacher stress. The superintendent expects me to have exit interviews with all exiting faculty, so I would have had to have talked to you anyhow.
LANE   *[With surprise]* I didn't realize that!
LES   Yes, the administration is very interested in the reasons for teacher turnover in the school district. After all, good teachers with as much experience as you've had are hard to find, Lane.
LANE   I'm not so sure I'm a good teacher anymore, Les. Things bother me now that didn't used to. I've lost my zest and enthusiasm. Even my wife Lois wonders if I shouldn't move on to something else.
LES   Lane, I'm going to ask you to do something for me before we go any further. Would you please fill out this stress instrument for me? *[Hands instrument to Lane]* As you can see, the instrument is easy to understand, self-scoring, and will give us a profile of the sources of your stress. Just be completely honest. There are no correct answers, just your answers. I'll keep the results in complete confidence. Could we get back together at this same time next week?
LANE   *[Looking at his appointment book]* Yes, that'll be fine.
LES   Great! Bring the completed instrument with you and we'll use it as a starting point for our discussion.
LANE   Sounds good, Les. I feel better already.

The next day, Lane is returning some papers to his fifth-period American literature class.

LANE   *[Angrily]* I just can't believe these papers, folks! I gave you a simple, and I think interesting, assignment: to rewrite the ending of the story by changing the last three paragraphs. I find you can't spell, you can't write paragraphs, you can't make your subjects and verbs agree, and worst of all, you have no original ideas of your own. Every paper, without exception, took an idea from either a recent movie or TV show to rewrite the ending. I don't think there was an original idea in the entire class! *[Pause]* Yes, Teresa.
TERESA   I didn't take my ending from a movie or TV, Mr. Baxter.
LANE   *[Sneeringly]* That's true, Teresa, you took your idea from one of Shakespeare's

plays. That's four hundred years old! *[Class laughs]* I don't think this is funny, people! Your generation is going to be the leaders of tomorrow and I'm not sure you are capable of original thinking. *[Angrily]* Yes, you have a creative comment, Ron? I noticed that you didn't even bother to turn a paper in, as usual.

RON *[Angrily]* Well I don't see where your generation has been so creative in running this country! Look at . . .

LANE *[Interrupting]* Ron, in case you didn't notice, I'm the teacher of this class, not you! When you earn two degrees and a teacher's license, I'll be glad to step aside and let you take over my job. Until then, I'll thank you to . . .

RON *[Angrily, interrupting]* If I couldn't do a better job than you in teaching this class, I'd quit.

LANE *[Waving his arms in anger]* Get out of here, Ron! Now!!!

It is the next week, and Lane sits in Les Felling's office.

LES *[Holding Lane's stress profile in his hands]* As you can see, the instrument measures nine sources of stress as well as giving a total score. Your overall score of 154 is very high, and clearly falls into the high stress category. Of the nine subscales, three of them stand out: student behavior, psychological/emotional symptoms of stress, and stress management techniques.

LANE *[Smiling]* I guess that says I'm stressed out, huh, Les?

LES *[Smiling]* It says more than that, Lane. Look at some of the items. You seem to have a real problem with classroom management.

LANE *[Smiling]* That's true, I guess. I suppose I am a bit hair-triggered these days. I get impatient and angry much more easily than I used to. I guess what bothers me the most is, I haven't always been that way. I used to enjoy relating to the kids, but now. . . .

LES *[Interrupting]* It becomes a vicious circle once it starts. Negative begets more negative.

LANE I guess so. I never really thought of it that way.

LES Lane, would you say you follow a plan as far as classroom management is concerned?

LANE A discipline plan? I started out using behavior modification years ago, but now, well, I guess I really just use a system of increasing punishments. You know, I warn them the first time, lower their grade the second time, maybe change their seating, and so on until finally, I ask them to go to the dean's office as a last resort. I don't know if I have a system or not, anymore! And to tell you the truth I don't have the energy to change things.

LES I see. I guess that helps explain your responses about complaining a lot to others and feeling depressed about your job.

LANE I guess so.

LES Then there's your lack of stress management techniques to cope with the situation.

LANE To tell you the truth, Les, I go home at the end of most schooldays, have a couple of highballs, and talk to Lois. That's all that keeps me sane. *[Pause]* What's happened to the American family, Les? All these working wives and single parents just aren't providing real homes for their children. God only knows what values they're learning at home—if any. Look at all the latchkey children and those that are abused. They just dump them on teachers like me and say, "They're your responsibility, not ours." I'm tired of it, Les!

LES   I hear you, Lane. *[Pause]* Now let me ask you the sixty-four-thousand-dollar question: Do you want to leave teaching, or are you willing to work on yourself and try to salvage your career as a teacher?

LANE   How can I answer that? I don't know! I'm pulled both ways. Is there really anything a stressed-out teacher like me can do to turn things around?

Stress Profile for Teachers[1]

STUDENT BEHAVIOR

    1. I have difficulty controlling my class.
    2. I become impatient/angry when my students do not do what I ask them to do.
    3. Lack of student motivation to learn affects the progress of my students negatively.
    4. My students make my job stressful.

EMPLOYEE/ADMINISTRATOR RELATIONS

    5. I have difficulty in my working relationship with my administrator(s).
    6. My administrator makes demands of me that I cannot meet.
    7. I feel I cannot be myself when I am interacting with my administrator.
    8. I feel my administrator does not approve of the job I do.

TEACHER/TEACHER RELATION

    9. I feel isolated in my job (and its problems).
    10. I feel my fellow teachers think I am not doing a good job.
    11. Disagreements with my fellow teachers are a problem for me.
    12. I get too little support from the teachers with whom I work.

PARTENT/TEACHER RELATIONS

    13. Parents of my students are a source of concern for me.
    14. Parents' disinterest in their children's performance at school concerns me.
    15. I feel my students' parents think I am not doing a satisfactory job of teaching their children.
    16. The home environment of my students concerns me.

TIME MANGEMENT

17. I have too much to do and not enough time to do it.
18. I have to take work home to complete it.
19. I am unable to keep up with correcting papers and other school work.
20. I have difficulty organizing my time in order to complete tasks.

INTERPERSONAL CONFLICTS

21. I put self-imposed demands on myself to meet scheduled deadlines.
22. I think badly of myself for not meeting the demands of my job.
23. I am unable to express my stress to those who place demands on me.
24. Teaching is stressful for me.

PHYSICAL SYMPTOMS OF STRESS

25. With frequency I experience one or more of these symptoms: stomachaches, backaches, elevated blood pressure, stiff necks and shoulders.
26. I find my job tires me out.
27. I am tense by the end of the day.
28. I experience headaches.

PSYCHOLOGICAL/EMOTIONAL SYMPTOMS OF STRESS

29. I find myself complaining to others.
30. I am frustrated and/or feel angry.
31. I worry about my job.
32. I feel depressed about my job.

STRESS MANAGEMENT TECHNIQUES

33. I am unable to use an effective method to manage my stress (such as exercise relaxation techniques, etc.)
34. Stress management techniques would be useful in helping me cope with the demands of my job.
35. I am now using one or more of the following to relieve my stress: alcohol, drugs, yelling, blaming, withdrawing, eating, smoking.
36. I feel powerless to solve my difficulties.

¹ Reprinted from: Wilson, C.F. (1979). *Wilson Stress Profile For Teachers,* San Diego: The Wright Group.

QUESTIONS

1. Evaluate Lane's approach to classroom management. What model or set of beliefs does he seem to employ? What are some alternatives that he might try?

2. Does Lane evidence a high or low sense of teacher efficacy? an internal or external set of teacher attributions? How are such teacher beliefs related to student motivation and achievement?

3. In terms of Maslow's need hierarchy, at what level of needs does Lane seem to be operating? Why do these need deficiencies seem to exist? How does one move toward greater self-actualization in teaching?

4. Would you describe Lane's beliefs about student motivation as intrinsic or extrinsic views? Did Lane have any opportunities to increase student motivation in his class? What are some motivational techniques he might try?

5. What is teacher burnout, and how is it related to teacher stress? What are the common sources of teacher stress, and do they differ by grade level and gender? What are the main sources of teacher stress in Lane's situation?

6. How well might a classroom management model, like teacher effectiveness training, work in Lane's American literature class? How would Lane go about implementing it in his class?

7. How important is administrative support to a teacher like Lane, especially that of the building principal? Would a principal that uses the supporting, coaching, delegating, or directing leadership style work most effectively with Lane at this time? Which would work most effectively with an enthusiastic beginning teacher like Darryl Wilson?

8. What is teacher morale, and how does high or low morale relate to teacher productivity? How would you describe Lane's morale level and why? What can be done to increase teacher morale?

9. What can teacher education programs do to help prepare in-service and pre-service teachers to deal with the common sources of teacher stress? Whose job is it to help teachers suffering from high teacher stress? What role can the school system, colleges of education, and the community play?

10. Should Lane leave or stay in teaching? If he stays in, what changes will he need to make? What can be done to help a teacher cope with severe stress? How effective are relaxation techniques, exercise, attitude-change exercises, and diet changes as helping interventions?

11. What are the most common symptoms of teacher stress? Why are some teachers able to cope with stress while others fail to do so? What is *hardiness*, and how does it relate to a teacher's ability to cope with stress?

12. What is a *teacher mentoring program?* How can such programs help teachers deal with stress?

APPENDIX A

THEORY GUIDE

T he purpose of the theory guide, like the starter questions at the end of each case, is to assist the student in beginning the process of case analysis. Since the authors of this book are specialists in the fields of educational psychology and curriculum and instruction, only theories, models, and sets of principles from those two areas are presented. Specialists in other fields—such as philosophy of education, social foundations, and educational administration—would no doubt suggest different theories and sets of principles as frameworks for analysis.

The theory guide is organized as follows. Content areas, subtopics, and specific theories are presented from the fields of educational psychology and curriculum and instruction. After each are the numbers of the cases that, in our opinion, lend themselves to analysis using the content or theories. Needless to say, the student will need to learn more about the content to see how it applies. The course instructor, the course textbook, and the library are good places to go to learn more about any content presented in the theory guide.

EDUCATIONAL PSYCHOLOGY

1. Developmental Psychology
   a. Middle Childhood 14
   b. Adolescence 23, 25
   c. Child Abuse 22, 24
   d. Drug and Sex Abuse 23, 25
   e. Moral Development 23, 25, 27
   f. Gender Differences 11, 19, 20, 23
2. Learning Theory
   a. Operant Conditioning 1, 3, 5, 8, 11, 14–16, 22, 27
   b. Observational Learning 3–4, 11, 19, 27
3. Cognitive Theory
   a. Information Processing Theory 4, 7, 29
   b. Meaningful Verbal Learning 4
   c. Field Dependence-Independence 19
   d. Bruner's Cognitive Theory 4

Curriculum and Instruction

USING THE CASE METHOD OF TEACHING

he use of the case method of college teaching is increasing, especially in colleges of education. Yet, it seems clear that most college professors still primarily use the traditional lecture–discussion method, and if they are interested in using the case method, aren't sure how to proceed. To make the situation more difficult, there are a variety of ways to use the case method, as well as a number of different types of cases.

Fortunately, practitioners of the case method have begun to share their expertise at national conferences. Also, new how-to books are either on the market or soon will be. For example, Joel Colbert, Kim Trimble, and Peter Desberg of California State, Dominguez Hills (1996) have published a book entitled *A Case for Education: Contemporary Strategies for Using Case Methodology* (Allyn & Bacon) that presents a variety of methods for using cases by different practitioners around the nation. A number of similar books should follow.

Probably the most popular method of using cases is the large-group discussion approach (for example, an entire college class). Leaders of such approaches are very sophisticated in their use of techniques for drawing students out and getting them involved in discussing the various issues involved in the case. However, this approach is often unfocused and nonapplied, and sometimes leaves too many participants out of the discussion. As a result, we have developed a set of procedures for working with students in small groups. It is this set of procedures, which have been in use since 1967, that we will describe in this appendix.

Our case study method, which we call Small-Group Decision-Making (SGDM), is based on certain assumptions. The model used by many, perhaps most, case method instructors is to get the students to: (1) identify the issues in the case; (2) examine the case from multiple perspectives (for example, teacher, principal, parent, child); (3) bring professional knowledge to bear on the case; (4) generate possible solutions to the problem situation; (5) determine the consequences that are likely to result from each solution proposed; (6) choose among the possible solutions and determine how to evaluate the plan proposed.

SGDM makes certain assumptions in relation to this model. First, we assume that students have to learn to analyze a case from one perspective before they begin to examine it in terms of multiple perspectives. Second, we assume that the perspective that pre-service and in-service teachers should begin with is that of the teacher, rather than that of the principal, parent, or student. Learning to view situations from multiple perspectives is a long-term goal, not a beginning exercise.

A third assumption is that teacher education majors should use theories, models, and sets of principles that they are studying in their courses as perspectives for analyzing cases. The goal is one of learning to translate theory into practice. Our fourth assumption is that, as students learn to analyze cases in terms of the course knowledge base, they need to learn the process of defending their analysis by citing appropriate evidence from the case.

Our fifth assumption is that the courses of action that the student decides the teacher in the case should follow to successfully resolve the case should be consistent with the way the student has analyzed the case, reasonable and practical to implement, and described in sufficient operational detail.

The outcomes of SGDM involve the students learning a metacognitive process which we hope will transfer to the real world of teaching. When the teacher later runs into a problem situation that routine responding can't handle, we hope the student will use the case analysis and decision-making processes that have been learned in the case study portion of his or her courses or workshops.

SMALL-GROUP DECISION-MAKING

As has been mentioned, cases are often used with the entire class using large-group discussion procedures. Our approach involves working with students in small groups of three to six members. Some instructors prefer to use only the case study method in teaching a course. We generally use the case method for a portion of the course. Normally, the course content is presented using traditional methods and this is then followed by one or two case studies that involve approximately two weeks of class time each. Students typically work on a case both inside and outside class over a five-week period that involves ten fifty-minute periods of in-class time over a semester, interspersed with regular class meetings. As is true in many areas of education, distributed practice is better than massed practice for doing case studies.

Prior to beginning the first case study, we introduce the students to the process of case analysis through a mini case study that lasts two class periods. In this "mini" session they: (1) begin by stating what's going on in the case in their own words; (2) choose a theory or set of principles that best explains the way they have analyzed the case; (3) cite evidence from the case to support their analysis. They don't generate courses of action for the teacher to follow in dealing with the situation or try to solve the problem in this warm-up exercise. When groups have difficulty getting started, besides the instructor asking appropriate questions, the starter questions at the end of the case and the theory guide are usually helpful. Often all it takes for a group to get started is for the instructor (of an educational psychology class, for example) to ask questions like, "How could you say the same thing in psychological terms?" or "What do you mean when you talk about needs?"

Forming the Groups

How are the small groups of three to six students formed? This can be done in a variety of ways. First, the students can choose with whom they want to work. Second, students can be assigned to groups by means of a table of random numbers. A third approach is to assign them by interest groups. The latter involves giving students three-by-five-inch cards, asking them to skim all the cases, and rank-order the three cases that bother them the most when they think about the job of teaching. Students are then assigned to groups on the basis of their choices. The choice of assignment procedure should be guided by the instructor's objectives and feel for student dispositions and abilities.

Choosing Cases and Theories

Just as the small groups can be assigned in different ways, the case and theory that the group uses can be chosen either by the students or the instructor. The instructor may want all groups to work on the same case or on different cases. Also, the instructor may want the groups to all use the same theory or whatever theory the students feel is most appropriate for the case. For example, if any educational psychology instructor wants the students to learn how to apply the principles of operant conditioning, the instructor will direct the students to use that theory only, either on the same or different cases.

Even if the instructor allows the students to choose the case they wish to work on, it may be wise to limit the number of cases from which they are allowed to select. Some cases lend themselves to an operant analysis, for example, more easily than others. Also, the instructor's evaluation procedure may dictate that only one or a few cases be used by all the groups.

Instructor's Role

Once the small groups are formed, the instructor begins by asking the group members to exchange names, addresses, phone numbers, and schedules (to set up outside-of-class meetings). Since group or committee work is a constant in the life of a teacher, the teacher is usually well qualified to talk about the importance of being an effective group member and strategies for dealing with nonproductive group members.

Once the groups are formed and the case chosen or assigned, each group is asked to select one of its members as group recorder. It is the recorder's job to: (1) keep the instructor informed of when and where of all group meetings are to be held; (2) keep attendance at all official group meetings; (3) be sure that the group paper gets turned in on time and in the proper form; (4) make certain that the group meets with the instructor as needed, and (5) facilitate the collection and turning in of the evaluation form that group members use to evaluate one another's contributions. An example of an evaluation form used by the students will be presented later.

It should be obvious that by appointing a student as group recorder, the instructor does not take over as the leader of each small group and conduct its discussions. Instead, the instructor moves from group to group, sometimes just listening, sometimes answering questions, and at other times asking questions for the group to think about.

The instructor will certainly have to serve as a resource by suggesting books and journal articles the students may need to obtain to learn more about the theory they are using.

From the beginning, the instructor makes clear the evaluation criteria that will be used to evaluate the group product. Sometimes groups subdivide and become separate groups. In other instances, individuals decide to leave a group and do an individual paper. Whatever grade is assigned to a group paper is shared by all the members of the group. Evaluation procedures will be discussed later.

Characteristics of a Good Case Study Paper

When beginning the case study, the instructor may choose to give the students a handout that describes what kind of paper is desired and how it will be evaluated. Following is an example of such a handout for an educational psychology course entitled *Characteristics of a Good Case Study Paper*.

OBJECTIVES

The student will: (1) analyze the case in psychological terms and objectively support the analysis with evidence from the case; (2) present courses of action for the teacher to execute that are consistent with the analysis, feasible to execute, and operationally stated.

1. Begin with an overall statement of the problem in the language of the theory you are using. Cover all the main points and people in the case and use the theory correctly and fully in applying it. This will normally be done in a paragraph or two.
2. Support each main point that you make in your overall statement at the beginning, with evidence from the case. The kind of evidence that you cite will vary according to the theory you use. For example, an operant approach might involve a functional analysis employing only external, observable events. However, be sure that each main point that you have presented in your "big picture" introduction is systematically supported by whatever type of evidence you use.
3. Regardless of the theory used, the support evidence should be presented systematically and objectively. The reader should be able to relate it to the theoretical contentions you are supporting and, in most cases, the evidence should be quoted as it is presented in the case.
4. The "Analysis" and "Decision" parts should be clearly labeled and separated from one another.
5. Each main point you make in the Analysis should be dealt with by one or more courses of action that you recommend in the Decision section. This is a systematic, point-by-point process.
6. Each course of action you recommend in the Decision part should clearly follow from and employ the ideas and language of the theory you used in the Analysis. For example, don't analyze in operant terms and then shift to dealing with self concepts or internal beliefs in the Decision part.

7. Each course of action that you recommend should meet the tests of feasibility and operationality, as presented in the case study book. Feasibility means that a course of action will reasonably work in the context of the case in terms of things like cost, time, and ability. Operationality means that the course of action has been specifically and sufficiently spelled out that the teacher will know exactly what to do and how to do it.

8. The paper should be footnoted and references should be cited at the end on a separate page. In the case of the course text, however, you need only indicate the page number(s) at the end of the text quoted in parenthesis and you do not need to list it in your references. Otherwise, use APA style. The ten-page limitation isn't hard and fast but try to organize your paper so that you can come as close to it as possible. The title page and references do not count as part of the ten pages.

9. Use correct grammar, punctuation and spelling. For example, you should write in paragraphs with topic sentences, subjects and verbs should agree, and words should be spelled correctly. Double-check your typing and get the paper in on time. Remember, one letter grade will be deducted for each day late.

Evaluation

Case study papers, like the one presented in the Introduction to this book, are evaluated in terms of six criteria: (1) accurately and fully applying a theory, model, or set of principles in analyzing the case; (2) supporting the analysis objectively and fully with appropriate evidence cited from the case; (3) choosing courses of action for the teacher in the case to implement that are consistent with the theory used in the analysis; (4) stating the courses of action in an operational form so that specific procedures are spelled out; (5) stating courses of action that are practical, reasonable, and workable in the context of the situation; and (6) organizing the paper into a logical and grammatically correct whole. Following is a summary of these six criteria, presented in a format that can be attached to the paper for feedback purposes.

Case Study Evaluation

I. Application of Theory
_____ a) Theory clearly identified and used correctly
_____ b) Theory fits case
_____ c) Covers all facets of the case

II. Support for Theory
_____ a) Support is cited for all key contentions made
_____ b) Support is objectively cited (quotations, no inferences)

III. Consistency between Analysis and Decision
_____ a) Point-by-point consistency exists
_____ b) Relationship between Analysis and Decision is stated

IV. Feasibility of Solution
_____ a) Courses of action are reasonable and practical for situation described (teacher time, ability, cost)

V. Operationality of Solution
_____ a) Easily replicable (clearly spelled out what should be done and how)

VI. Organization of Paper
_____ a) Two parts clearly labeled (Analysis and Decision)
_____ b) Good, easy-to-follow order of key contentions and courses of action.
_____ c) Typed, 8 1/2-by-11 inch, correct spelling/grammar, approximately ten pages, APA style.
_____ Total points

Before illustrating the use of the six criteria in scoring a paper, a couple of points should be made. While the production of a ten-page paper is the usual group product, the instructor is certainly not limited to that outcome. In some cases, students have acted out the decision they have developed. In one workshop, classroom teachers acted out a case situation while students videotaped the action, and later, the students developed and acted out a decision. The decision was then critiqued by the teachers who did the original acting. The possibilities, given enough time, equipment, and creativity, are many, and certainly not confined to student papers.

Second, groups of undergraduate students are told to focus the decision on the teacher in the case. That is, they are told to generate courses of action for the teacher to execute that follow from the analysis. They are further told that they don't have to concern themselves with presenting their plans to the teacher or motivating the teacher to execute them. They just have to tell the teacher what to do. Of course, the test of any plan is to execute it in the real world and observe the consequences. However, the students won't be able to do that until they are in actual teaching situations.

On the other hand, if an instructor is working with graduate students or in-service teachers, it may be important to learn how to work with the teacher as well as other persons (parents, principal, etc.) in the case. For example, a school psychology major may want to develop consultation strategies, or an educational administration major may want to focus on how to handle the teacher in the case, rather than just develop strategies for the teacher to use. This is, of course, the development of multiple perspectives which was discussed earlier.

Applying the Six Criteria

Let's examine the use of the six evaluative criteria outlined above by applying them to the Analysis and Decision of the *Stay-In Problem* presented in the Introduction of this book. For criterion one, the application of the theory, two theories are used: (1) operant conditioning and (2) self-fulfilling prophecy or teacher expectancy theory. Two theories were used because neither one fully covered all the issues in the case. Of course, the two theories are somewhat incompatible with one another, since one focuses on external behavior and the other on internal perceptions and interpretations of events. Operant conditioning would be difficult to use by itself, since the case is relatively short and a large amount of behavioral data isn't available to do an adequate functional analysis. But what behavioral data is available suits and supports the interpretation that the disruptive male students are emitting attention-getting operants, and attempts at Punishment I by teachers and administrators are actually functioning as positive reinforcers.

While the usual approach to case analysis involves using one theory that explains the events that have occurred, a second theory is brought to bear on the case, to deal with the problem of the expectations regarding the boys' behavior that have developed among the school's faculty. This is an issue that is difficult to put in operant terms, so a second, if somewhat incompatible, theory resulting from the work of Rosenthal and others is used for that purpose. The two theories combined, however loosely, seem to rather fully cover the problems involved. In short, the theories are clearly identified, used correctly, fit the case, and cover the major facets of the case.

Support for Theory

The second criterion is to rather fully and objectively cite evidence from the case to support the application of the theory. Evidence of an external behavioral nature is cited to support the contention that Larry, George, and Jack are speaking without permission, asking off-task questions, and making smart remarks. A sort of functional analysis is attempted, by pointing out that all the behaviors were followed by attempts at Punishment I. The conclusion, then, is that these attempts are actually operating as positive reinforcers. Other evidence of a similar nature is provided in the more objective form of quotes rather than paraphrased statements or summaries.

Quotes are likewise used to support the application of the teacher expectations model. It is made clear that Ray Clark, Ed Irish, and various teachers have developed a set of expectations about the six boys' behavior that a self-fulfilling prophecy cycle culminating in expulsion from school has been set in motion. Overall, each key theoretical contention is supported on a point-by-point basis, and the evidence presented is cited in an objective form. Whether enough evidence has been cited to fully cover the key contentions made is questionable.

Evaluating the Decision

To evaluate the decision part of the paper, the consistency, operationality, and feasibility of each course of action that is recommended for the teacher to take must be examined. Five courses of action are recommended, with four of them following from the operant analysis and the fifth from expectancy theory. Each of the five are clearly related to one of the two theories used in the analysis. Both the language used and the flow of ideas suggest this. So the criterion of consistency is met rather well.

Regarding feasibility, the five courses of action involve: (1) changing teacher expectations; (2) finding out about the boys' interests; (3) changing peer responses to the boys' behavior; (4) cuing and contracting work with the boys; and (5) contacting and involving the parents. The question is, How practical and reasonable is it to expect the teacher, Steve, to carry out each course of action? Changing one's own expectations is difficult. It would be even more difficult to expect a beginning teacher to influence the expectations of the building principal and the dean of boys. The other four courses of action are a bit more feasible, given the threat of expulsion, the idea of meeting with the boys one at a time, beginning with Larry, and finally culminating in a meeting with the entire class. All but the first course of action seem fairly feasible.

Four out of five courses of action somewhat meet the test of operationality; that is, the specifics or how-to that the teacher is to use. How the teacher is to change his own expectations, meet with the boys and the class, and even set up the contingency contract are somewhat minimally explained. One would like more detail in each instance, of course. However, how the teacher is to work with the parents is not made clear. So overall, four of five courses of action minimally meet the test of operationality.

With regard to the sixth criterion, organization and grammar, the paper does rather well. It is well organized, with appropriate headings, and the ideas flow well. Grammar and spelling are also within acceptable limits. So overall, if we were scoring the paper on the basis of a five point score for each of the six criteria (with five being high and one being low), we'd probably give a five for application of Theory, Consistency, and Organization, and we'd give Support for Theory, Feasibility, and Operationality a four for an overall score of 27 out of 30 points. A judgment call, at best, but isn't that true in the case of any type of essay scoring?

Student Group Evaluations

As mentioned earlier, each small group will work somewhat independently of the instructor at times. We usually ask each group member to confidentially evaluate the contributions of the other members of the group and use that information as one measure of course participation. The following instrument may be used for that purpose.

Group # _____

Rate the contributions of each member of your group during the case study by circling the appropriate rating opposite their name. Do *not* rate *yourself*. Also, the *recorder only* in each group should put the number of absences for each group member (including the recorder) from all "official" group meetings in the space provided. Rate each group member's contributions by using the following scale:

O - outstanding
A - above satisfactory
S - satisfactory
B - below satisfactory
U - unsatisfactory

Name (first and last)	Rating (circle one)					(For recorder Only) # Absences
_____	O	A	S	B	U	_____
_____	O	A	S	B	U	_____
_____	O	A	S	B	U	_____
_____	O	A	S	B	U	_____
_____	O	A	S	B	U	_____
_____	O	A	S	B	U	_____

As has already been indicated, a variety of methods has been developed for working with cases in teacher education. SGDM is only one approach, and is certainly not the most common one in use. However, if the instructor's goals include learning how to translate theory learned in the course into practice and helping students learn a decision-making process that will transfer to the real world of teaching, then SGDM should be given serious consideration.

WOMBAT STEW

Marcia K Vaughan

Illustrated by
Pamela Lofts

A Scholastic Press
book
from
Scholastic Australia

For Mum and Dad with love

Scholastic Press
345 Pacific Highway
Lindfield NSW 2070
An imprint of Scholastic Australia Pty Limited (ABN) 11 000 614 577
PO Box 579, Gosford NSW 2250
www.scholastic.com.au

Part of the Scholastic Group
Sydney ● Auckland ● New York ● Toronto ● London ● Mexico City
● New Delhi ● Hong Kong ● Buenos Aires

This edition published in 2002.
Text copyright © Marcia Vaughan, 1984.
Illustrations copyright © Pamela Lofts, 1984.

National Library of Australia Cataloguing-in-Publication entry

　　Vaughan, Marcia K.
　　Wombat stew.

　　ISBN 1 86504 448 2 (pbk)

　　1. Wombats - Juvenile fiction. 2. Dingo - Juvenile fiction.
　　I. Lofts, Pamela. II. Title.

A823.3

Printed in Hong Kong.

10 9 8 7 6 5 4 3 2 1　　　　　　　　　　　2 3 4 5 /0

One day, on the banks of a billabong,
a very clever dingo caught a wombat...

and decided to make . . .

Wombat stew,
Wombat stew,
Gooey, brewy,
Yummy, chewy,
Wombat stew!

Platypus came ambling up the bank.

'Good day, Dingo,' he said,
snapping his bill.
'What is all that water for?'

'I'm brewing up a gooey, chewy stew
with that fat wombat,'
replied Dingo
with a toothy grin.

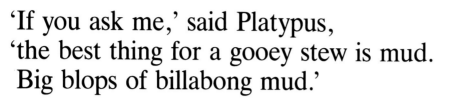

'If you ask me,' said Platypus,
'the best thing for a gooey stew is mud.
 Big blops of billabong mud.'

'Blops of mud?' Dingo laughed.
'What a good idea.
 Righto, in they go!'

So Platypus scooped up big blops of mud
with his tail
and tipped them into the billycan.

Around the bubbling billy,
Dingo danced and sang...

'Wombat stew,
Wombat stew,
Gooey, brewy,
Yummy, chewy,
Wombat stew!'

Waltzing out
from the shade of the ironbarks
came Emu.
She arched her graceful neck
over the brew.

'Oh ho, Dingo,' she fluttered.
'What have we here?'

'Gooey, chewy wombat stew,'
boasted Dingo.

'If only it were a bit more chewy,'
she sighed. 'But don't worry.
A few feathers will set it right.'

'Feathers?' Dingo smiled.
'That would be chewy!
Righto, in they go!'

So into the gooey brew
Emu dropped
her finest feathers.

Around
  and around
the bubbling billy,
Dingo danced and sang...

'Wombat stew,
Wombat stew,
Crunchy, munchy,
For my lunchy,
Wombat stew!'

Old Blue Tongue the Lizard
came sliding off his sun-soaked stone.

'*Sss*illy Dingo,' he hissed.
'There are no flies*ss* in this *sss*tew.
Can't be wombat *sss*tew
without crunchy flies*ss* in it.'
And he stuck out
his bright blue tongue.

'There's a lot to be said for flies,'
agreed Dingo, rubbing his paws together.

'Righto, in they go!'

So Lizard snapped
one hundred flies from the air
with his long tongue
and flipped them into the gooey,
chewy stew.

Around
and around
and around
the bubbling billy,
Dingo danced and sang...

'Wombat stew,
Wombat stew,
Crunchy, munchy,
For my lunchy,
Wombat stew!'

Up through the red dust popped Echidna.

'Wait a bit. Not so fast,' he bristled,
shaking the red dust from his quills.
'Now, I've been listening
to all this advice –
and take it from me,
for a munchy stew
you need slugs and bugs
and creepy crawlies.'

Dingo wagged his tail.
'Why, I should have thought of that.
Righto, in they go!'

So Echidna dug up all sorts of creepy crawlies and dropped them into the gooey, chewy, crunchy stew.

The very clever Dingo stirred and stirred,
all the while singing...

'Wombat stew,
Wombat stew,
Hot and spicy,
Oh so nicey,
Wombat stew!'

Just then the sleepy-eyed Koala
climbed down the scribbly gumtree.

'Look here,' he yawned,
'any bush cook knows
you can't make a spicy stew
without gumnuts.'

'Leave it to a koala to think of gumnuts,'
Dingo laughed and licked his whiskers.

'Righto, in they go!'

And into the gooey, chewy, crunchy,
munchy stew
Koala shook lots and lots of gumnuts.

'Ah ha!' cried Dingo.
'Now my stew is missing only one thing.'

'What's that?' asked the animals.

'That fat wombat!'

'Wait!'

'Stop!'

'Hang on, Dingo!
You can't put that wombat
into the stew yet.'

'Why not?'

'You haven't tasted it.'

'Righto! I'll taste it!'

And that very clever dingo
bent over the billy
and took a great, big slurp of stew.

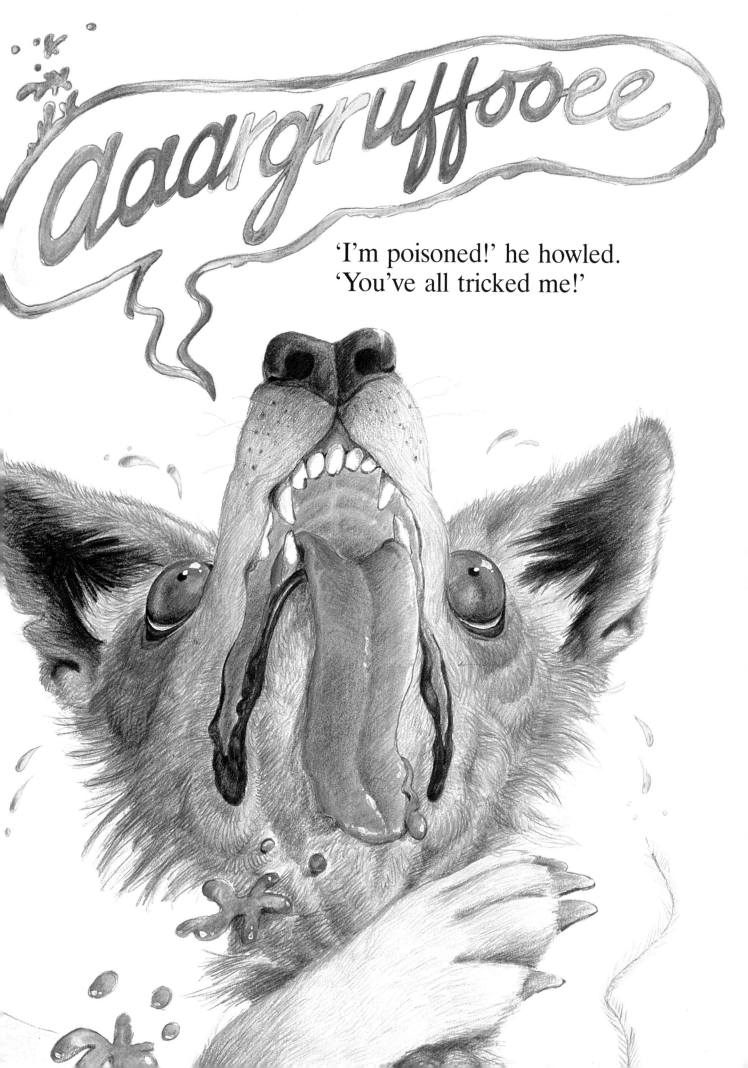

'I'm poisoned!' he howled.
'You've all tricked me!'

And he dashed away
deep into the bush,
never again to sing...

Wom-bat stew, Wom-bat stew,

Goo-ey, brew-y, Yum-my, chew-y, Wom-bat stew!

'Wombat stew,
Wombat stew,
Gooey, brewy,
Yummy, chewy,
Wombat stew!'